Second Dialect Acquisition

What is involved in acquiring a new dialect – for example, when Canadian English speakers move to Australia or African American English-speaking children go to school? How is such learning different from second language acquisition (SLA), and why is it in some ways more difficult? These are some of the questions Jeff Siegel examines in this book, the first to focus specifically on second dialect acquisition (SDA). Siegel surveys a wide range of studies that throw light on SDA. These concern dialects of English as well as those of other languages, including Dutch, German, Greek, Norwegian, Portuguese and Spanish. He also describes the individual and linguistic factors that affect SDA, such as age, social identity and language complexity. The book discusses problems faced by students who have to acquire the standard dialect without any special teaching, and presents some educational approaches that have been successful in promoting SDA in the classroom.

JEFF SIEGEL is Adjunct Professor of Linguistics in the School of Behavioural, Cognitive and Social Sciences at the University of New England, Australia. His recent publications include *The Emergence of Pidgin and Creole Languages* (2008) and *Pidgin Grammar: An Introduction to the Creole Language of Hawai'i* (with K. Sakoda, 2003).

Second Dialect Acquisition

Jeff Siegel

CAMBRIDGE
UNIVERSITY PRESS

CAMBRIDGE UNIVERSITY PRESS
Cambridge, New York, Melbourne, Madrid, Cape Town,
Singapore, São Paulo, Delhi, Mexico City

Cambridge University Press
The Edinburgh Building, Cambridge CB2 8RU, UK

Published in the United States of America by Cambridge University Press, New York

www.cambridge.org
Information on this title: www.cambridge.org/9781107411463

First published 2010
Reprinted 2011
First paperback edition 2012

A catalogue record for this publication is available from the British Library

Library of Congress Cataloguing in Publication Data
Siegel, Jeff.
    Second dialect acquisition / Jeff Siegel.
        p.   cm.
    Includes bibliographical references and index.
    ISBN 978-0-521-51687-7
        1. English language–Variation–English-speaking countries.   2. English
    language–Dialects–English-speaking countries.   3. Languages in
    contact–English-speaking countries.   4. English language–Study
    and teaching.   5. Sociolinguistics.   I. Title.
        PE1074.7.S54 2010
        417'.2–dc22

                                                                2010008740

ISBN 978-0-521-51687-7 Hardback
ISBN 978-1-107-41146-3 Paperback

Contents

Figures

Tables

Acknowledgements

First, I would like to thank my wife, Diana Eades, for her insightful comments and linguistic expertise on Australian English. Second, a big thank you to Vicki Knox for her skilful proofreading and formatting, and to Fiona Sewell for her meticulous copy-editing. For inspiring many of the ideas in this book, I am grateful to my friends in the Bale Group in Hawai'i: Ermile Hargrove, Kent Sakoda and the late Terri Menacker. For other discussion and comments over the years, thanks to Brian Byrne, Carol Chapelle, John Rickford, Walter Seiler and Don Winford. For providing materials, references and other help, I thank Ulrich Ammon, Brett Baker, Carsten Levisen, Inés Anton-Mendes, Javier Caro Reina, Marta Fairclough, Kathy Fischer, Annik Foreman, Mie Hiramoto, Ron Kephart, Matthew Prior, Kathy Rys, Michelle Schouten, Jim Stanford, Mike Terry and Edward Wiruk. Special thanks also go to Duncan Markham and Paul Meier for their enlightening interviews. Finally, I gratefully acknowledge research grants from the University of New England, the Australian Research Council and the (USA) National Science Foundation. Last, but certainly not least, I thank the Freiburg Institute for Advanced Studies for a three-month fellowship which provided the perfect environment for working on this book.

Abbreviations

1st	first
2nd	second
3rd	third
AAE	African American English
AEMP	Academic English Mastery Program
AiA	Americans/Alabamans in Alabama
AmE	American English
AoA	age of acquisition
ASE	American standard English
ASHA	American Speech-Language-Hearing Association
AusE	Australian English
B	Bergen dialect
BesY	Bessarabian Yiddish
BrE	British English
CA	Contrastive Analysis
CALP	cognitive/academic language proficiency
CanE	Canadian English
CAP	Caribbean Academic Program
CAT	Communication Accommodation Theory
CCCC	Conference on College Composition and Communication
CiA	Canadians in Alabama
CiC	Canadians in Canada
CPH	Critical Period Hypothesis
D1	first dialect
D2	second dialect
DIA	Maldegem dialect
ESL	English as a second language
FELIKS	Fostering English Language in Kimberley Schools
FLT	foreign language teaching
fMRI	functional magnetic resonance imaging
GCD	Greek Cypriot dialect
GDR	German Democratic Republic

HC	Hawai'i Creole
HCE	Hawai'i Creole English
IDEA	International Dialects of English Archive
ILEA	Inner London Education Authority
ImAF	Imitative Acquisition and Function Model
IPA	International Phonetic Alphabet
JE	Jamaican English
KEEP	Kamehameha Early Education Program
L1	first language
L2	second language
LCRG	Language Curriculum Research Group
LE	London English
LJ	London Jamaican
LoR	length of residence
M	Maastricht dialect
NAE	North American English
NCTE	National Council of Teachers of English
NEE	Northeastern England English
NEY	Northeastern Yiddish
NIDA	National Institute of Dramatic Art
NZE	New Zealand English
OECD	Organisation for Economic Co-operation and Development
PAM	Perceptual Assimilation Model
PET	positron emission tomography
PNG	Papua New Guinea
RP	Received Pronunciation (standard spoken British English)
S	Stril dialect
SAE	standard American English
SAT	Speech Accommodation Theory
SCE	Singapore Colloquial English
SD	standard Southern (Belgian) Dutch
SDA	second dialect acquisition
SE	Southern (American) English
SEE	Southern England English
SESD	Standard English as a Second Dialect
SLA	second language acquisition
SLM	Speech Learning Model
SMG	standard Modern Greek
StD	standard Dutch (of the Netherlands)
StdE	Singapore Standard English
StGer	standard German
StY	standard Yiddish

TC	Trinidad Creole
TEC	Trinidad English Creole
TESOL	teaching English to speakers of other languages
TOEFL	Test of English as a Foreign Language
TSESD	Teaching Standard English as a Second Dialect
USV	Upper Saxonian Vernacular
VASTA	Voice and Speech Trainers Association

1 Introduction

This book is about learning a new dialect, and how it is different from learning a new language. In this introductory chapter, I start by describing the contexts where this kind of learning occurs and some of the questions the book aims to answer. As I have tried to make the content accessible not just to linguists, I have also included some basic information for readers without a strong background in linguistics. This is about differentiating dialects, describing speech sounds and studying variation in language. The final section presents a brief outline of the book.

1.1 Second language acquisition and second dialect acquisition

The study of second language acquisition (often abbreviated as SLA) examines how people who already speak a first language (L1) subsequently acquire a second or additional language (L2). This book focuses on a special type of SLA – when the relationship between the L1 and the L2 is close enough for them to be considered by their speakers to be varieties of the same language, or different dialects, rather than different languages. In this situation, the term "second dialect acquisition" (SDA) can be used. The study of SDA examines how people who already speak one dialect (D1) acquire a different dialect (D2) of what they or their community perceive to be the same language.

Of course it is notoriously difficult to distinguish language and dialect. One criterion often used is mutual intelligibility: speakers of two different dialects of the same language can understand each other but speakers of two different languages cannot. However, mutual intelligibility itself is not absolute, and depends on factors such as attitudes, beliefs and goodwill (e.g. see Lippi-Green 1994). There is also the well-known situation where Danish and Norwegian are considered separate languages, although they are mutually intelligible to a great extent, whereas Cantonese and Mandarin are considered dialects of Chinese, even though their spoken forms are not mutually intelligible at all.

Another complication is that many people think of a language as the variety that is codified in dictionaries and grammars, and normally used in published expository writing and taught in schools – i.e. the standard variety. And they think of a dialect as a variety that is not codified, not normally used in writing and not taught in the schools – i.e. an unstandardised (or non-standard) variety. Thus, standard English, French, Spanish, Mandarin, etc. are considered languages whereas Cockney, Provençal, Cantonese and African American English are considered dialects. Furthermore, many people think of a language, but not a dialect, as being associated with a particular country. This view is reflected in the well-known saying: "A language is a dialect with an army and navy" (attributed to the Yiddish linguist Max Weinreich). On the other hand, when talking about the different national standard varieties – such as American, British and Australian English – people often refer to these as different dialects of English.

In sociolinguistics, the term "dialect" refers to varieties of the same language that differ from each other in vocabulary, pronunciation and grammar, and that are associated with particular geographic regions or social groups. In this book, I use this definition with the added proviso that the determination of two varieties belonging to the same language depends on the common perception of the speakers of these varieties (as already mentioned), and not on a technical decision made by linguists. That said, however, it is still generally the case that first and second dialects as defined here are more similar to each other than first and second languages, and therefore more mutually intelligible.

This similarity has led to the popular consensus that SDA is easier than SLA. But as Escure (1997: 7) points out, this consensus is "[i]n spite of the paucity of research on dialect acquisition, or perhaps because of it". With regard to the acquisition of standard varieties, she continues (p. 7):

This attitude is obviously reflected in the educational establishment: a standard variety is never taught in a formal, organized manner and, in contrast to foreign language learning, is not supported by any language manual or the "bidialectal" equivalent of bilingual programs.

This is because of the assumption that it is easier for a speaker of African American English, for example, to learn standard American English than to learn French. Escure also observes (1997: 7): "On the other hand, there is apparently no clear opinion concerning the relative learnability of non-standard dialects by standard speakers."

While there actually have been some formal bidialectal programs and some research on dialect acquisition (both described later in this book), Escure's points remain generally true. Very little research has been done on SDA, and what has been done is not widely known. And none of the research has tried to test the widespread assumption that SDA is easier than SLA. This book aims to fill some of the gaps in these areas.

Some other questions considered in this book arise from my own experiences. I was born in the USA (in Chicago) but have lived in Australia for more than twenty years. I'm an Australian citizen, my wife and kids are Australian, I barrack for Australia in the Olympics (even over the USA), and I've developed an Australian outlook and sense of humour (at least I hope so!). Nevertheless, when I'm introduced to someone new, as soon as I open my mouth I get the question "What part of the States are you from?" But when I go back to see my family in Chicago, people tell me I've developed a British accent. So I haven't been able to acquire Australian English but my original way of talking has changed recognisably.[1]

Before coming to Australia, I lived among the South Asian Indian population of Fiji and learned Fiji Hindi (the local dialect of Hindi). When I spoke Fiji Hindi over the phone, people often told me that they couldn't tell I was not a Fiji Indian. Later I went to India, and learned standard Hindi, but when I returned to Fiji, I found it difficult to speak in Fiji Hindi – standard Hindi kept coming out. I also lived in Papua New Guinea (PNG) and learned Tok Pisin, the local dialect of Melanesian Pidgin. Then I lived in Vanuatu and learned Bislama, the dialect of Melanesian Pidgin spoken there. Again, when I went back to PNG, I found it hard to switch back to Tok Pisin. But although I had trouble switching between dialects, I had no problem switching between languages. For example, later at the University of New England in Australia, I had a Fiji Indian friend who had lived in Vanuatu, and when we talked, we both switched easily between English and Fiji Hindi and Bislama.

I also lived for several years in Hawai'i, but never tried to speak the local variety people call "Pidgin" because I got the feeling that it is used only by those born and bred in the islands. While in Hawai'i, I observed that speakers of this local variety often had problems with the standard English used in the schools. The same was true in PNG and Vanuatu, and also with Indigenous people in Australia who speak a variety known as Aboriginal English.

These experiences have raised many interesting questions about the acquisition and retention of dialects as opposed to languages, the ability to switch between dialects, the "ownership" of particular varieties of speech and the formal education of speakers of unstandardised dialects. These questions, among others, are considered in this book.

1.2   Contexts for SDA

SDA is concerned mainly with three broad types of dialects: national, regional and social. A national dialect is a way of speaking a language that is characteristic of a particular country. National dialects include varieties such as Canadian, American and Australian English, European and Brazilian Portuguese, and Moroccan and Egyptian Arabic. Often similar national dialects are combined and given a broader geographic label, such as North American English (covering Canada and the USA).

It must be remembered that national dialects are not homogeneous varieties spoken in the same way by all their speakers. For example, British English covers the varieties spoken in England, Scotland and Wales, some of which are very different from each other. What is important is the particular shared features among the ways a language is spoken in one country that contrast with those from another country. For example, the word *tomato* is pronounced "toe-mah-toe" in British English but "toe-may-toe" in North American English.

However, as already mentioned, many people think of a national dialect as the set of varieties closest to what is considered the "standard". This is actually an abstracted and idealised version of the language as it was originally spoken by the upper middle classes of one dominant region of the country. Varieties close to this standard are believed to be "neutral" or "mainstream" (i.e. not evocative of any minority from a particular geographical area or social group). Thus, such varieties are considered most suitable for public speaking and radio and television broadcasting, and the fact that they are most often heard in these contexts reinforces the view that they are standard. Examples are standard French, Received Pronunciation (or RP) of British English, and standard German (or "High" German). Standard varieties are also often labelled as "general" – e.g. General American English – to distinguish them from varieties which are associated with particular regional or social groups.

In some countries, the spoken standard has become the basis for formal written communication, and further "standardised" by dictionaries, grammars and style guides. This is the case in the USA, the United Kingdom, Australia, Portugal, Brazil and most other countries. In some countries, however, the written standard is based on a variety very different from what is spoken colloquially by most of the population. Such a situation is referred to as "diglossia" (Ferguson 1959) – i.e. strict functional differentiation of two varieties of the same language in different domains. The colloquial variety is learned at home and used in informal contexts such as conversation with family and friends. The standard or literary variety is learned in school and used in formal domains such as expository writing. In such contexts, the majority of the population is bidialectal to some extent in both varieties, and the colloquial dialect is not socially stigmatised. An example is found in Egypt with Egyptian Colloquial Arabic and Classical Arabic (Haeri 2003).

With regard to English, an important subtype of national dialect is what are often called "New Englishes" or "World Englishes" – for example, Singapore English, Indian (South Asian) English, Philippine English, Nigerian English and Fiji English (see, for example, Kirkpatrick 2007; Mesthrie and Bhatt 2008; Schneider 2007). They arose in British or American colonies where English was the language of the education system and learned as a second language by a large proportion of the population. In these countries, new varieties of English emerged, influenced by the indigenous first languages of their speakers. Thus, they are also referred to as "indigenised varieties" of

English, the term I adopt here. Each of these indigenised varieties, still learned mainly as a second language, continues to function as an important lingua franca and educational language after the country's independence (and thus, yet another name for them: "post-colonial varieties"). In some of these countries, a local spoken and written standard has emerged, but in others, one of the more established national standards is used, usually British or American English.

As opposed to a national dialect, a regional dialect is spoken in one particular area of a country. In the USA, regional dialects include Appalachian, New Jersey and Southern English, and in Britain, Cockney, Liverpool English and "Geordie" (Newcastle English). Regional dialects in Norway include those spoken in the Stril and Setesdal regions, and in Germany, in Saxony, Swabia and Bavaria.

In contrast to a regional dialect, a social dialect is a variety of a language spoken by a particular group based on social characteristics other than geography. SDA is most relevant to speakers of social dialects that are based on ethnicity (often called ethnic dialects), such as African American English, Australian Aboriginal English, Native American (or Indian) English and Chicano Spanish. Both regional and social dialects are often stigmatised by speakers of dialects that are closer to the national standards.

As in SLA, the study of SDA can be divided into two broad contexts: naturalistic and educational. Naturalistic SDA refers to learning a new dialect (the D2) without any formal teaching. This most often occurs when people who speak a particular regional dialect migrate to another part of the same country where a different regional dialect is spoken – for example, speakers of various American dialects moving to Philadelphia (Payne 1976, 1980) and speakers of rural Norwegian dialects moving to Bergen (Kerswill 1994). In some cases, the D2 is an unstandardised local regional dialect learned by children who have been brought up speaking a variety close to the standard at home – for example, speakers of standard Belgian Dutch in an East-Flanders village (Rys 2007). In other cases, the D2 is a more prestigious standard dialect learned naturalistically by adult migrants – for example, Brazilian Portuguese as spoken in the capital Brasília learned by rural-dialect-speaking migrants (Bortoni-Ricardo 1985). Naturalistic SDA also occurs when people migrate to another country where a different national dialect is spoken – for example, speakers of Canadian English to England (Chambers 1992; Tagliamonte and Molfenter 2007) and speakers of American English to Australia (Foreman 2003). These examples and others are described in detail in Chapter 2.

One important aspect of SDA in naturalistic contexts that distinguishes it from SLA is that it can be unintentional. Since migrants to a new dialect area can continue to speak in their original dialect (D1) and still be able to communicate, they may not try to learn the dialect of their new home (D2). Nevertheless they may unconsciously "pick up" or acquire some features of the D2 and use them in their speech. This then is the result of "linguistic ambience" (Markham 1997: 50) rather than any intention to acquire the D2, but it is still considered as SDA in this book.

In educational contexts, described in more detail in Chapters 7 and 8, the D2 is learned in formal training. In classroom SDA, the D2 is nearly always the standard dialect – the target language of the education system – and the students are generally children who come to school speaking a dialect markedly different from the standard – a regional or ethnic dialect, or the colloquial variety in a diglossic situation. In dialect coaching and accent modification, the students are normally adults who want to learn how to speak a new dialect for performances in films or the theatre, or who want to change their dialect for some reason, such as improving their job prospects. Instruction is generally one-on-one or in small groups.

In educational contexts, the term "SDA" is also applied to a specific situation involving varieties that are not normally considered to be dialects of the same language. This is where the D1 is an expanded pidgin or creole language and the D2 is the standard form of its lexifier (the language which provided the bulk of its vocabulary) – for example with Hawai'i Creole as the D1 and standard American English as the D2, or Haitian Creole (D1) and standard French (D2). (For definitions of pidgins and creoles, see Siegel 2008.) While most linguists (myself included) would say that such creoles and their lexifiers are separate languages, a large proportion of their speakers view them as different varieties of the same language – the creole often thought to be a degenerate or "broken" version of the standardised form of the lexifier (see Sebba 1993: 47).

Furthermore, there is the factor of the "creole continuum" – a range of different ways of speaking the creole, from what is called the "basilect" (furthest from the lexifier) to the "acrolect" (closest to the lexifier), with intermediate varieties, the "mesolects". This is illustrated below for Jamaican Creole (adopted from Alleyne 1980).

> **acrolect:** *he is eating his dinner.*
> mesolect 1: *(h)im is eating (h)im dinner.*
> mesolect 2: *(h)im eating (h)im dinner.*
> mesolect 3: *im a eat im dinner.*
> **basilect:** *im a nyam im dinner.*

In this example, the acrolect differs from the standard form of the lexifier only in pronunciation, and thus this way of speaking the creole makes it seem more like a different dialect than a different language.

Creole speakers usually control a particular range of the continuum and use varieties more towards the basilectal end with their friends and family and towards the acrolectal end in more formal situations. Variation according to context also occurs in all the types of dialects I have been describing (though not to as great an extent as in creoles). There is not just one way of speaking any dialect; rather, people vary their speech in different situations.

1.3   Dialectal differences

The linguistic differences between dialects of a language can be described under four headings: (1) vocabulary, (2) grammar, (3) pragmatics, and (4) pronunciation. I describe each of these below.

1.3.1   Vocabulary

While different dialects usually share most of their vocabulary (or "lexicon"), they sometimes have completely different lexical items (i.e. words) for the same things. Table 1.1 below shows some examples in American and Australian English (which is closer to British English).

Similarly, the same words can have different meanings in different dialects. Examples in Australian Aboriginal English that differ from both mainstream Australian English and other dialects are *jar* 'to scold', *deadly* 'great, fantastic' and *granny* 'a grandchild as well as grandparent'.

1.3.2   Grammar

Grammatical differences have to do with the way words are formed (morphology) and the way words are put together to make phrases and sentences (syntax).

Morphological differences   In American English, all regular verbs add -*ed* to indicate past tense – for example: *looked, trained, started*. But for some verbs, British and Australian English add -*t* instead of -*ed* – for example: *learnt, spoilt, leapt* and *dreamt* as opposed to *learned, spoiled, leaped* and *dreamed*. In another example, American English has the participle *gotten*, but this is not found in British or Australian English:

> American: *They've gotten a new car.*
> Australian: *They've got a new car.*

African American English has the marker *be* which occurs before verbs, adjectives and adverbs to indicate a habitual state or action. This is not found in other dialects (which instead use adverbs such as *usually* or *always*) – for example (Green 2002: 48):

> African American: *Your phone bill be high ...*
> Other dialects: *Your phone bill is usually high ...*
> African American: *She be telling people she eight.*
> Other dialects: *She's always telling people she's eight.*

Table 1.1 *Examples of American and Australian English lexical items*

American English	Australian English
gas	petrol
trunk (of a car)	boot
hood (of a car)	bonnet
cookie	biscuit
trailer	caravan
sidewalk	footpath
sweater	jumper
candy	lollies
suspenders	braces

Syntactic differences   One syntactic difference has to do with agreement. In Australian English it is common to use the plural form of the verb for a group, whereas in American English the singular form is usually used – for example:

Australian: *The band are getting ready to go on stage.*
American: *The band is getting ready to go on stage.*

In American English, questions with the verb *have* are most commonly formed with *do* but not in Australian English – for example:

American: *Do you have the money?*
Australian: *Have you got the money?*

In some social dialects, the verb 'to be' is often not found where it occurs in other dialects – for instance, *she eight* in the above example of African American English, and the following in Australian Aboriginal English (Kaldor and Malcolm 1991: 74):

Australian Aboriginal: *His name Peter.*
General Australian: *His name is Peter.*

But in some cases, Australian English and other national dialects omit a word where others do not:

Australian: *Her mother is in hospital.*
American: *Her mother is in the hospital.*

1.3.3   Pragmatics

Pragmatics has to do with the ways we use language – the particular words and phrases chosen for a particular purpose. It is closely connected to issues such as politeness. For example, there are many different things you could say to get someone to open a window:

> *Open the window.*
> *Could you open the window?*
> *Please open the window.*
> *Would you mind terribly opening up the window.*
> *Whew, it's hot in here.*

Which words you choose depend on the person you're talking to and how well you know them.

Some pragmatic differences between Australian English and American English also have to do with the choice of words. One example is the use of the word *toilet*. In Australia, it's normal to ask "Where's the toilet?" But in America, this would seem abrupt or rude, and most people would ask "Where's the restroom?" or "Where's the bathroom?" Also, in America, people commonly use terms of address such as *sir* and *ma'am* to people they don't know. But these terms are rare in Australia, and you're more likely to hear what seem like more intimate terms, such as *mate* or even *love* (and American *buddy*, which has suddenly become widely used).

Other kinds of pragmatic differences have to do with interactive styles or modes of discourse. For example, speakers of African American English have several ways of interacting with each other that are not used in other dialects. In one of these, referred to as "call and response", the speaker's statements ("calls") are punctuated by expressions from the listeners ("responses") (Smitherman 1977: 104). These responses often have the function of affirming what the speaker has said or urging the speaker on. Another African American English mode of discourse is "signifying". This is defined by Smitherman (1977: 118) as "the verbal art of insult in which a speaker humorously puts down, talks about, needles – that is, signifies on – the listener". This is often done to make a point, or just for fun.

1.3.4   Pronunciation

When people talk about the differences between national or regional dialects, they most often refer to the different ways of pronouncing words, or what is usually referred to as "accent". This may be in individual words, such as *tomato*, as described earlier. There also may be systematic differences between dialects. For example, in most American dialects, the letter *r* is pronounced wherever it occurs in writing. But in most British dialects, the letter *r* is only pronounced when it is followed by a vowel – so that, for example, *bar* and *bah* are pronounced the same, as are *court* and *caught*. The term "rhotic" refers to sounds represented by the letter *r*. So the dialects in which *r* is always pronounced are referred to as rhotic dialects, and those in which it is not pronounced unless followed by a vowel as non-rhotic (or sometimes "R-less") dialects. Some dialects in America, such as those spoken by some people in Boston and New York City, are non-rhotic as well, just as some dialects in Britain, such as Scottish English, are rhotic.

Pronunciation differences may sometimes occur with other consonants – for example, in British Cockney, the *th* sound (as in *thin*) is sometimes pronounced as *f*, so that *think* is pronounced *fink*. But much more commonly, differences in accent have to do with the pronunciation of vowels. For example, in American English, the *a* sound in words such as *ask*, *pass*, *fast* and *laugh* is pronounced as the *a* in *pat*. But in Australian English, it is pronounced similar to the *a* in *father*. (Vowel sounds are described in detail in Section 1.4 below.)

These differences in pronunciation depend on particular "segments" of sound – vowels, consonants and their combinations. However, other pronunciation differences are not confined to a segment and may extend over more than one segment. These are called "suprasegmental" features. Examples are stress and pitch. Some words in American and Australian English differ according to which syllable is stressed (or accented). For example, in American English, *defence* (or *defense*) can be pronounced *DEE-fence*, whereas in Australia it is *de-FENCE*. Another example is *cliché*: American *cli-SHAY* versus Australian *CLI-shay*.

Pitch has to do with the voice level – e.g. high or low – when speaking. The term "intonation" refers to the pitch pattern over a sentence or utterance. American English and Hawai'i Creole differ in the intonation used for yes–no questions (questions for which the answer is either *yes* or *no*). In most varieties of American English, the pattern is rising, starting with an intermediate pitch and finishing with a high pitch. In Hawai'i Creole, the pattern is falling, starting with high pitch and dropping to low pitch in the final syllable. This is illustrated in the following examples in which the line above the question indicates the intonation pattern:

American English:

Are you the life-guard?

Hawai'i Creole:

Eh, you da life-guard?

Pitch can also be used to indicate the meaning of individual words, in which case it is usually referred to as "tone". There may be two or more words in a language that have the same set of segmental sounds but different lexical meanings – such as a *bank* for money and a *bank* of a river, or *to, too* and *two* – which in speech are differentiated by context. (These are called homonyms.) Some languages regularly use different tones to differentiate the meanings of such words. For example, Thai has five tones, traditionally labelled as: high, middle, low, falling and rising. So, for example, the word *mai* pronounced with a low tone means 'new', with a falling tone 'no' and with a rising tone 'silk'. Tones such as these, that are used to distinguish meaning, are sometimes called "tonemes".

1.3.5   *Differences not covered in this book*

Although pragmatic differences between dialects are very important (and interesting), they have not been examined in detail in studies of SDA. The same is true for dialect differences in body language, proxemics (the distances between people when they interact) and paralinguistic features such as voice quality, loudness and the use of silence. Instead, studies of SDA have focused almost exclusively on the formal linguistic areas of vocabulary, morphosyntax (morphology and syntax) and pronunciation. Consequently, this book has had to adopt a similar focus. Of these three linguistic areas, pronunciation has the most coverage, especially in SDA in naturalistic contexts. The following section presents some background information on this key area.

1.4   Describing speech sounds

In order to describe the pronunciations that differentiate dialects, we need to be able to represent the various speech sounds in some way and to talk about the factors that affect the ways these sounds are produced in the vocal tract. This is especially true for vowels, which often distinguish one dialect from another. These matters are covered in this section, which is aimed specifically at readers unfamiliar with linguistics. (However, such readers should be warned that some of the explanations need to get fairly technical. And linguists might want to skip this section.)

1.4.1   *Representing speech sounds in writing*

The problem with using the conventional alphabet to represent speech sounds is that letters are used inconsistently – for example, the 's' sound is sometimes represented by *s* as in *sent* and sometimes by *c* as in *cent*. The letter *c* can also represent the 'k' sound as in *cat*. With vowels in English, the problem is compounded because we have only five letters *a*, *e*, *i*, *o* and *u*. But there are at least a dozen different vowel sounds that are used to distinguish meaning. As a result, the same letter or letters must be used to represent several different vowel sounds. For example, compare the sound of *u* in the following words: *cut*, *put*, *rule*, and the sound of *ou* in *couch*, *cough*, *soup* and *enough*.

Also, the same letters may be used to represent different sounds in different languages. For example, in German and Dutch the letter *j* represents a sound like the English *y* as in *yell*, so the German word *ja* meaning 'yes' is pronounced as if it were written *ya* in English. And in Fijian, the letter *c* represents the sound usually represented by *th* in English, as in the word *they*, so the Fijian word *caka* meaning 'work' is pronounced something like *thaka*. So there is no consistency between the spelling systems (or "orthographies") of different languages.

Since orthographies are so variable and inconsistent, linguists found that there was a need for a consistent, universally accepted way of representing speech sounds in any language. It was for this reason that the International Phonetic Alphabet (IPA) was developed more than a century ago. Using the symbols of this alphabet, it is possible to represent clearly any sound in any language. In IPA, each symbol represents only one sound. For example, in English, the letter ɡ (or g) can represent two different sounds, as in *girl* and *gem*. But in IPA, the symbol ɡ represents only the sound of *g* as in *girl*. In addition to the twenty-six letters of the English alphabet, IPA uses other symbols, such as ∫ for the 'sh' sound in *ship*, θ for the 'th' sound in *thick* and ð for the 'th' sound in *that*. Some of the IPA symbols for vowels in English are listed below. The example words given in small capital letters (FLEECE, KIT, etc.) are commonly used to identify the sets of words that have particular vowels in dialects of English (see Wells 1982), and are also used in this book for those readers not familiar with IPA symbols.

i	as in the vowel in *beat* and FLEECE
ɪ	as in the vowel in *bit* and KIT
ɛ	as in the vowel in *bet* and DRESS
æ	as in the vowel in *bat* and TRAP
ə	as in the first vowel in *about* and the final vowel in COMMA
ʌ	as in the vowel in *but* and STRUT
u	as in the vowel in *boot* and GOOSE
ʊ	as in the vowel in *put* and FOOT
ɔ	as in the vowel in *draw* and THOUGHT
ɑ	as in the vowel in *father* and PALM

Most of the vowel sounds symbolised by the IPA do not have names. One exception is the vowel ə as in the final vowel of COMMA, which is often referred to as "schwa".

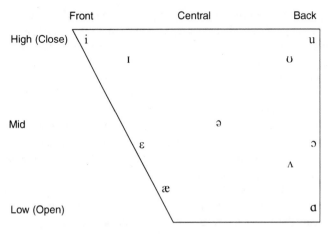

Figure 1.1 Some vowels in dialects of English

1.4.2   Factors affecting production of vowels

The two most important factors affecting how a vowel sound is pronounced have to do with the position of the tongue in the mouth. First is how high or low the tongue is – so there are high, mid and low vowels. Also, the mouth is more closed for the pronunciation of high vowels and more open for the low vowels, so sometimes they are classified as close versus open instead of high versus low. The second factor is how far to the front or the back of the mouth the tongue is – so vowels are classified as front, central or back. Another important factor is whether the lips are rounded or unrounded. Other factors that affect pronunciation are whether the muscles are tense or lax, whether the air flows just out of the mouth or out of the nose as well (as in "nasal" vowels), and whether the length of pronunciation is short or long.

The space in the mouth in which vowels are pronounced is often shown diagrammatically as a quadrilateral, in which vowels are placed according to the dimensions of tongue height (high versus low) and frontness versus backness. This is shown in Figure 1.1.

1.4.3   Phonemes

The particular sounds that are used to distinguish meaning in a language are called "phonemes". So, for example, the different words *beat, bit, bat, but* and *boot* are perceived to have different meanings because of their different vowel phonemes. As mentioned above, there are at least twelve vowel sounds that are used to distinguish meaning in English – i.e. at least twelve vowel phonemes. When describing the sounds of a language, the IPA symbols for phonemes are usually indicated with slanted lines – for example, /u/. Some vowel sounds exist as phonemes in other languages that are not found in English – for example, the rounded high front vowel in French (as in *rue* 'street'), symbolised in IPA as /y/. (Note that the IPA symbol for the 'y' sound in English is /j/. As mentioned above, the letter *j* is used for this sound in many European languages.[2])

While the IPA symbol for a phoneme indicates the general pronunciation of a sound that distinguishes meaning in a language, the exact pronunciation may be slightly different in various dialects, or in different contexts. This is usually shown in square brackets, rather than slanted lines, and often with small additional symbols called "diacritics". For example, the /u/ sound in GOOSE in British English is usually pronounced as a long vowel. This is shown as [uː], with the ":" diacritic indicating length. The /u/ sound in Australian English is produced with the tongue in a central rather than back location in the mouth. This is indicated by the symbol [ʉ].

1.4.4   Mergers and splits

Another way in which dialects differ according to vowels has to do with "mergers" and "splits". These terms usually refer to kinds of historical changes that have taken place in the sound systems of languages or dialects. The fact that such changes have occurred in some varieties and not others has led to dialect differences. For example, in most British dialects (except southwest England), the vowel in *bother* and LOT is a rounded low back vowel, symbolised as /ɒ/. This is distinct from the /ɑ/ in *father* and PALM. However, in most varieties of English in North America, these two vowels are pronounced the same, so that *bomb* and *balm* have identical pronunciations, and *bother* rhymes with *father*. This is known as the "father–bother merger" or the "LOT–PALM merger".

In most English dialects in North America and the British Isles, the vowel of *class* and BATH is the same as that of *bat* and TRAP. But in the dialects of southern England (including the standard RP) and of Australia and New Zealand, they differ from each other. In southern England, for example, the vowel of *bat* and TRAP is [æ] as in other dialects, but that of *class* and BATH is pronounced as *ah* (i.e. [ɑː]), as in PALM. The [ɑː] instead of [æ] pronunciation also occurs in many other words such as *laugh*, *grasp* and *path*. Thus one vowel pronunciation has split into two, each used in a different set of words. This particular case is known as the "TRAP–BATH split".

Some mergers and splits have occurred only in certain linguistic contexts. For example, in my own dialect of Midwestern American English, the words *Mary*, *marry* and *merry* all have the same pronunciation (i.e. *merry*) because the vowels have merged before *r* when it is followed by another vowel. I used to get teased about this when I went to university in New York, where this merger does not exist. Also, later my Australian English-speaking family found it outrageous when we played rhyming games and I'd say that words like *carry* rhymed with *ferry* and *dairy*. (Similarly, I thought it outrageous that they rhymed *bought* and *sport*, since /r/ is not pronounced in Australian English unless it precedes a vowel.)

1.4.5   Diphthongs

In the vowels we have been talking about so far, the tongue position does not change when the vowel is being produced. These are called "pure vowels" or "monophthongs". For example, in the word *met* the vowel is pronounced only as /ɛ/. But in other vowel phonemes, called "diphthongs", the tongue moves from one position to another during production. For example, in *mate* (in North American English) the vowel starts as /e/, a vowel slightly higher than /ɛ/, and ends up as /ɪ/. A diphthong is made up of two elements: the main vowel or "nucleus" and a reduced vowel or "glide". Unlike a full vowel, the glide cannot be stressed or form a separate syllable. So the vowel sound in *mate* or FACE in North American English is /eɪ/, where [e] is the nucleus and [ɪ] is the glide – more specifically, the "off-glide" because it comes after the nucleus. (Some diphthongs, described below, have an "on-glide" which comes before the nucleus.)

Here is a list of some diphthongs in North American English:

eɪ	as in *mate* and FACE
aɪ	as in *might* and PRICE
ɔɪ	as in *boy* and CHOICE
oʊ	as in *code* and GOAT
aʊ	as in *house* and MOUTH[3]

They are shown with regard to tongue position and direction of the glide in Figure 1.2. Note that the first elements of some of these diphthongs – namely [e], [a] and [o] – were not shown in Figure 1.1 because they usually do not occur as monophthongs in English. All these vowel sounds and others from English that we will be looking at in this book are shown together in Figure 1.3.

Several kinds of differences exist between dialects with regard to diphthongs. In the FACE diphthong, the first element (or nucleus) is lower in British English than in North American English, giving /ɛɪ/ as opposed to /eɪ/. Another difference is that the first element of the diphthong in GOAT is more central in British than in North American English – resulting in [əʊ] versus [oʊ]. Another kind of difference is that what is a diphthong in one variety may

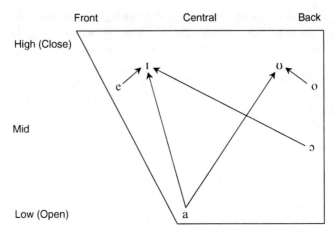

Figure 1.2 Some American English diphthongs

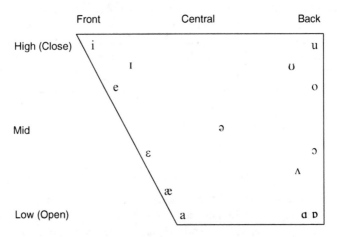

Figure 1.3 Vowel sounds commonly found in dialects of English

be a monophthong in another. For example, in Hawai'i Creole, words like *fake* and *make* are pronounced with a monophthong [e] rather than the diphthong /eɪ/. In contrast, what is pronounced as a monophthong in some dialects may be diphthongised in another. For example, in some varieties of Australian English the vowel /i/ in FLEECE is pronounced with an on-glide as [ᵊiː] or [ˈiː].

SCUSA SAI SE MI PERMETTO,
MA LA MAMMA NON TI HA DETTO
COME USARE IL GABINETTO?
SE TUA MAMMA SI E' SCORDATA
CHE LA GENTE VA EDUCATA,
LA LACUNA VA COLMATA!
NELLA TAZZA, ATTENTAMENTE
LASCIA CIO' CHE AVEVI IN MENTE
MA DI GOCCE IN TERRA NIENTE!
TIRA L'ACQUA PER FAVORE!
IO LO SO CHE NON HAI CUORE
DI LASCIAR CATTIVO ODORE!
SE QUALCOSA HAI DA GETTARE
CHE LA TAZZA PUO' OTTURARE
IL CESTINO DEVI USARE.
QUANDO FUORI SARAI USCITO
LASCIA TUTTO BEN PULITO
SARAI SEMPRE RIVERITO!

Bathroom

Other differences between diphthongs sometimes occur only in specific linguistic contexts. For example, in Canadian English the /aɪ/ diphthong (as in PRICE) is pronounced as [ʌɪ] when it occurs before voiceless consonant sounds such as *f*, *s*, *p* and *t*. (These are sounds in which the vocal cords do not vibrate, as opposed to their voiced counterparts, such as *v*, *z*, *b* and *d*.) For example, in the words *wife*, *price*, *tripe* and *site* the diphthong is pronounced as [ʌɪ] instead of [aɪ]. But in the words *hive*, *prize*, *tribe* and *side* it is pronounced as [aɪ] as in other dialects. Similarly, the /aʊ/ diphthong (as in MOUTH) is generally pronounced as [aʊ] as in other dialects, but as [ʌʊ] before the same voiceless consonant sounds – for example, in the words *house*, *about* and *shout*. (This gives rise to caricatures of Canadians as saying, for example, *I'm going oot and aboot*.) Thus, the nucleus of both diphthongs in this context is [ʌ] (as in STRUT), rather than [a]. (This phenomenon is referred to as "Canadian raising", because [ʌ] is pronounced higher in the mouth than [a].)

Thus in Canadian English, the phoneme /aɪ/ as in PRICE has two different pronunciations: [ʌɪ] before voiceless consonants and [aɪ] elsewhere. These different pronunciations of the same phoneme are called "allophones". Similarly, /aʊ/ as in MOUTH has two allophones: [ʌʊ] before voiceless consonants and [aʊ] elsewhere. Which allophone is used depends on the particular phonological environment the phoneme occurs in. So for the PRICE diphthong, for example, the [ʌɪ] allophone occurs before voiceless consonant sounds and the [aɪ] allophone occurs elsewhere. This determination of the pronunciation of a phoneme by the phonological environment is called "phonological conditioning". This phonological conditioning is part of the knowledge speakers of Canadian English have about their language. Linguists often use the term "rules" to talk about this knowledge. Thus speakers of Canadian English subconsciously know the rule for this phonological conditioning – i.e. /aɪ/ is pronounced as [ʌɪ] before voiceless consonants. Other dialects, such as American English, do not have this rule. Therefore, a speaker of American English would have to learn the rule in order to speak like a Canadian. (The notion of "rules" is discussed further in Chapter 3.)

1.5   Sound changes in SDA

Considering the various ways that dialects differ in terms of sounds, we can now talk about how the sounds (and the sound system) of the D1 would need to be adjusted to match those of the D2. (This assumes that the sounds and sound system of the D1 are the basis for acquiring those of the D2, an assumption examined in Chapter 3.)

Categorical adjustments are those that the D2 learner must make across the board. They may involve either substitution or merging. Categorical substitution needs to occur where a phoneme in the D1 is consistently pronounced in a different way in the D2. So, for example, speakers of North American English who are trying to speak British English would need to learn to substitute [əʊ] for their [oʊ] pronunciation of the diphthong in GOAT. Substitution occurs with one phoneme, and involves a sound not usually used for that phoneme in the D1. In contrast, categorical merging needs to occur when two different phonemes in the D1 are equivalent to only one in the D2, and this one phoneme is usually the same sound as one of the two phonemes in the D1. For example, in order to speak North American English, speakers of British English who distinguish the /ɒ/ vowel in LOT from the /ɑ/ vowel in PALM would need to merge two phonemes into one, replacing /ɒ/ with /ɑ/, so that LOT is pronounced /lɑt/ instead of /lɒt/, and the same for other words, such as *hot*, *bother*, *stop*, *hock*, etc.

While categorical adjustments are those that D2 learners must make in all linguistic contexts (i.e. in all words where the sound occurs), conditioned adjustments apply to those that need to be made only in certain contexts (i.e. only in some words). We've already seen in the discussion of Canadian raising that phonological conditioning refers to cases in which a specific phonological environment, such as the nature of the following consonant, determines the pronunciation of a phoneme. When the D2 has phonological conditioning not found in the D1, D2 learners have to learn the rules that native speakers of the D2 already know for when to make the required adjustments.

Phonologically conditioned merging rules may also have to be learned. For example, speakers of an eastern dialect of American English who want to acquire my Midwestern variety would have to learn to merge the vowels /eɪ/ and /æ/ with /ɛ/ when they occur before /r/, so that *Mary*, *marry* and *merry* have the same pronunciation (/mɛri/).

In "lexical conditioning", whether or not the required adjustment should occur depends on the particular word or lexical item. Rather than being accounted for by a general rule that depends on the phonological environment, the behaviour of the sound in question has to be learned for each lexical item. Splitting is most often lexically conditioned. For example, because of the TRAP–BATH split, speakers of North American English (D1) trying to acquire a southern British English dialect (D2) would have to learn which words with the /æ/ vowel (as in TRAP) in their D1 are pronounced with the /ɑ/ vowel (as in PALM) in the D2 – i.e. words such as *laugh*, *grasp* and *path*.[4] Acquirers of Australian English as a D2 would have to learn a slightly different set of words with /ɑ/ instead of /æ/, because unlike in southern England words such as *dance* are pronounced with /æ/ rather than /ɑ/ (except for some speakers in South Australia).

Lexically conditioned splitting may also involve a new phoneme that is not found in the D1. For example, if speakers of varieties of North American

English with the LOT–PALM merger want to acquire a variety of British English without this merger, they would have to learn a new phoneme /ɒ/ and split what is /ɑ/ in their dialect into /ɒ/ and /ɑ/ in different sets of words. So they would have to learn that words such as *hot, bomb, bother* and *follow* are pronounced with /ɒ/ instead of /ɑ/.

1.6   Research on SDA

Most of the in-depth research on SDA has been on the acquisition of a D2 in naturalistic rather than classroom contexts – the opposite situation from that of research on SLA. In addition, the research has been mostly done by scholars from the fields of sociolinguistics or dialectology, rather than from SLA, and the process of SDA has been viewed mainly as the result of language accommodation (as described in the social psychology literature) rather than as the result of language learning (as described in the SLA literature). These perspectives (discussed in more detail in Chapter 3) have influenced the methodology used to study SDA. This section describes this methodology – again aimed at readers not familiar with it, but still fairly technical by necessity.

1.6.1   Variables and variants

Because of the sociolinguistic and dialectologist perspectives, a major concern of SDA research has been with variability – different degrees of acquisition of different linguistic features by different learners. The particular dialect features that are examined in a study are called linguistic "variables". For example, if we were studying the acquisition of British English (BrE) by speakers of North American English (NAE), one possible variable to examine would be the diphthong in FACE. As we have seen, this is pronounced as [eɪ] in NAE and [ɛɪ] in BrE. Often the variable is given a label which is put in parentheses. For example, this variable could be labelled (ei) or (FACE). Each of the possible pronunciations of a variable is called a "variant". So here [eɪ] and [ɛɪ] would be the variants for the (ei) variable.

In a typical study of naturalistic SDA, we would electronically record the speech of a group of subjects or informants who have moved from North America to Britain. To examine their acquisition with regard to the (ei) variable, we would determine the percentage of their use of the D2 variant – here BrE [ɛɪ] – in the recorded speech of each informant. To do this, we would count the total number of occurrences of the variable in their speech – i.e. in all words such as *face, plate, game, fade, parade, aim, safety, hail,* etc. These occurrences of the variable are called "tokens". For each token, we would determine whether the NAE variant [eɪ] or the BrE variant [ɛɪ] was used. Then we would divide the number of occurrences of the D2 variant [ɛɪ] by the total number of tokens of (ei) and multiply by 100. So, for example, if there were 200 tokens of the (ei) variable in the speech of one informant, and she used NAE [eɪ] 112 times and BrE [ɛɪ] 88 times, the percentage of the BrE variant would be 88 ÷ 200 = .44 × 100, or 44 per cent. This percentage of use of the D2 variant is often interpreted as the percentage of acquisition (see the discussion in Chapter 2).

1.6.2   Types of linguistic variables

The following chapter looks at many studies of naturalistic SDA that examine various variables in the D1 and D2. These variables are divided into five types: lexical, phonetic, phonological, susprasegmental and morphological.

Lexical variables have to do with vocabulary. They are of two types. The first type concerns the use of completely different words to refer to the same thing – for example, North American English *sweater* (an item of clothing) versus Australian English *jumper*, and other items listed in Table 1.1 above. The second type of lexical variable has to do with the differing pronunciations of the same word – for example, the North American versus the British pronunciation of *tomato*, as mentioned above. Here the difference in sounds is only for this item – and not for similar words such as *potato*, which is pronounced similarly in both dialects.

Phonetic and phonological variables are both concerned with meaningful sounds (or phonemes) that consistently differ in pronunciation between the two dialects. Phonetic variables usually concern categorical differences across the board – for example, the (ei) or (FACE) variable just discussed, or the diphthong in GOAT, with the North American English variant [oʊ] versus the British variant [əʊ]. In contrast, phonological variables concern differences that involve phonological or lexical conditioning rules – for example, the diphthong in MOUTH in Canadian raising with the American variant [aʊ] versus the Canadian variant [ʌʊ] but only before voiceless consonants. Often, however, the distinction between phonetic and phonological variables is not clear-cut, and both are grouped under the heading of phonological variables.

Suprasegmental variables, although phonological as well, are treated separately. These concern pitch or tone and intonation – for example, the yes–no question intonation variable described earlier with the American English rising intonation as one variant and the Hawai'i Creole falling intonation as the other variant. This type of variable has been examined in detail in studies of Japanese, Norwegian and Sui (a language spoken in southwest China) – languages in which dialects are distinguished by their use of different pitch patterns for the same word.

Morphological (or morphosyntactic) variables concern the form of grammatical words and prefixes and suffixes on words – for example, the English past tense suffix as in North American English *spoiled* versus British English *spoilt*. Again, this type of variable is not examined very often with regard to dialects of English because they have only a few morphological differences. However, this is not true for dialects of other languages, such as Portuguese, Norwegian and Dutch, as we will see in the following chapter.

1.7   Content and organisation of this book

The remainder of the book is organised into two parts, one dealing with SDA in naturalistic contexts and one with educational contexts. Chapters 2 to 6 are basically a meta-analysis of research concerned with the naturalistic acquisition and use of a second dialect. Chapter 2 outlines seventeen studies relating to attainment in SDA and presents their results with regard to the degree of use of D2 features. It also presents three other studies that focus on dialect shift, and talks about some methodological issues. Chapter 3 discusses some of the outcomes in naturalistic SDA and methods of studying them. Chapters 4 and 5 explore the individual and linguistic factors affecting SDA, and Chapter 6 discusses the special difficulties involved in SDA. In the second part of the book, Chapter 7 talks about SDA in classroom contexts, Chapter 8 describes various educational approaches to SDA and the results of evaluative research, and Chapter 9 accounts for these research results and suggests a more critical approach.[5]

Since this is, as far as I am aware, the first book devoted to second dialect acquisition, I have tried to make it as wide-ranging as possible, covering the many and multi-faceted aspects of the topic that are spread out in the literature from numerous disciplines. Because of this, and the fact that I have written it for a wide audience, some of the topics are not treated with the depth that some readers might expect. However, the many references given will allow readers to explore various topics further.

On the other hand, the numerous summaries of studies presented in Chapters 2 and 8 might be tedious to other readers. However, I felt that presenting information on methodology along with the results would give readers (and future researchers) a clearer picture of the work that has been done on SDA. Those not interested in such details are advised to concentrate more on the other chapters, or to come back to the description of a particular study when it is mentioned in a later chapter.

Finally, as well as presenting and accounting for research findings, I have tried to expose the gaps in the study of SDA with the hope that this will spur on further research.

2   Attainment in naturalistic SDA

This chapter presents summaries of the methodology and results of studies relevant to SDA in naturalistic contexts. The primary aim is to describe how much of the D2 was acquired by individuals and groups of subjects. As in studies of SLA, the particular degree of acquisition is referred to here as the level of attainment. The first section of the chapter deals with the question of how attainment in SDA can be measured. The following two sections outline seventeen studies of SDA, eight done on dialects of English and nine on dialects of other languages. After a summary of the overall results, there are brief descriptions of three other studies that focus on shift from the D1 rather than attainment in the D2. The chapter concludes with a discussion of some methodological issues.

2.1   Measuring attainment in SDA

How can we measure attainment in SDA? Because of the linguistic similarities that usually exist between the D1 and D2, many of the methods used in SLA studies are usually not suitable – for example, grammaticality judgements and measures of fluency and communicative success. This is because D1 speakers normally know the basic grammar of the D2, since it is virtually the same as that of the D1. Furthermore, because of mutual intelligibility, they can usually communicate fluently by using the D1 with D2 speakers. That leaves us with examining observable behaviour – i.e. performance data. More specifically, we need to concentrate on linguistic features that distinguish the D2 from the D1. Thus the focus is on particular linguistic variables – features in which the D1 and D2 have different variants, as described in Chapter 1. Speech containing these variables is elicited through informal interviews and/or by asking subjects to describe pictures or read word lists. The percentage of use of the D2 rather than the D1 variant is then calculated for each variable. This percentage of use is considered to be an indication of the degree of acquisition of the D2 feature. A percentage of more than 90 may be considered to indicate acquisition, a criterion often employed in SLA (Larsen-Freeman and Long 1991: 40).

Of course, some scholars would find various problems with this methodology. First is the assumption that acquisition can be measured by degrees. Some would argue that any changes in linguistic behaviour in the direction of the target variety would be evidence of acquisition. Others would argue that acquisition is equal to knowledge, and either you know something or you don't. So only consistent target-like performance would demonstrate acquisition. Second, even if one accepts that the degree of use reflects the degree of knowledge and therefore the degree of acquisition, inconsistent use of a variant may reflect variation rather than incomplete acquisition – especially when dealing with closely related speech varieties. Third are the problems of scoring and interpreting the performance data – for example: what kind of performance is considered to be "on target"? And what is the minimum number of tokens of a variable needed for a decision to be made? These issues are discussed in Section 2.6 below.

The seventeen studies summarised in the following two sections all provide some data on attainment in SDA in naturalistic contexts. These were actually the only studies I could find that were written in English and that met the following criteria. First, they provide some data on the frequency of use of D2 features by D1 speakers. Second, they focus primarily on acquisition of D2 features and not on loss of D1 features. Third, they clearly distinguish between D1 and D2 variants.[1]

Summarising these studies was a very difficult task because they are extremely varied in their methodology and analysis, and only a handful actually had the goal of describing attainment in SDA. Rather, they were interested in different linguistic or non-linguistic social factors that affect SDA, factors discussed in Chapters 4 and 5. Even then, not all the studies gave information on all the factors relevant to SDA, such as age of acquisition and length of residence. In this chapter, however, we are mainly interested in percentages of use of D2 variants to serve as evidence of the degree of SDA. In the studies surveyed here, this information was not always quantified, and when it was, this quantification was sometimes done with only group scores instead of individual scores, and sometimes only as correlations with linguistic or non-linguistic factors. Therefore, some of the results given here were not explicitly presented in the study under discussion, but rather extrapolated or calculated from other data given in the study.

2.2   Studies on English dialects

2.2.1   *D1 Jamaican English; D2 London English*

One of the first studies relevant to SDA was done by Wells (1973) on the pronunciation of thirty-six adults who were born in Jamaica and later moved to London. The subjects were between the ages of 18 and 42, had arrived in London at ages ranging from 9 to 34, and had lived there for periods ranging from less than a year to 16 years (p. 48). The research was done by tape-recording answers to a standardised questionnaire, and also recording free speech for twenty-four of the subjects.

If we analyse this study in terms of SDA, the first dialect (D1) was Jamaican English and the second dialect (D2) was London English. However, the nature of neither of these "dialects" is clear-cut. Pronunciation in London English ranges from that of what has traditionally been considered as the standard variety of English in England (RP) to that of the Cockney dialect. Nevertheless, there is a great deal of overlap between the two varieties. For example, thirteen out of twenty-one vowels listed by Wells (p. 28) have the same pronunciation in RP and Cockney.

Jamaican English is a continuum of varieties ranging from the basilectal end of the Jamaican Creole continuum to what Wells calls "Jamaican Educated" (1973: 24), now known as "standard Jamaican English" (Irvine 2008). The sound system of basilectal Jamaican Creole is very different from that of London English. For example, the 'th' sounds /θ/ and /ð/ in *thick* and *that* are pronounced as /t/ and /d/ – i.e. /tɪk/ and /dæt/. However, people who have been through the formal education system in Jamaica can switch to standard Jamaican English, which has a sound system much closer to that of London English. For example, it does have the 'th' sounds /θ/ and /ð/.

Because of the similarities between standard Jamaican English and London English, it is difficult to determine whether subjects' use of pronunciations such as /θ/ and /ð/ rather than /t/ and /d/ was the result of education in Jamaica or acquisition after arrival in London. Therefore, we focus on six variables that have different pronunciations in Jamaican English (including standard Jamaican English) and London English. These are described below, using Wells's labels, and the abbreviations JE (Jamaican English) and LE (London English).

(r1) This variable concerned the pronunciation of the vowel and the possible presence of /r/ in words such as *church*, *shirt* and *bird*. In both JE and LE, the *r* is generally not pronounced, but in LE the vowel is a long schwa /ɜː/ (a longer version of the final vowel in COMMA), whereas in JE it is /o/. For example, *shirt* is [ʃɜːt] in LE and most often [ʃot] in JE. However, pronunciation with an /r/ does occur in Jamaica Creole – for example, [bord] 'bird' (p. 96).

(r2) This variable also concerned the pronunciation of the vowel and the possible presence of /r/, but here it is in words such as *beard*, *hoarse* and *pork*. For example, the LE pronunciation of *beard* is [biəd] versus JE [bɪɛd] or [bɛːrd], and the LE pronunciation of *court* is [kɔːt] versus JE [kuɔt] or [koːrt].

Table 2.1 *Percentages of use of London English variants by Jamaican immigrants*

Variable	Percentage of LE variant
(oː)	86
(eː)	83
(r2)	59
(r1)	57
(r5)	43
(eə)	20
Overall average	58

(r5) This variable concerned words that end in /r/, such as *hair, star, four* and *fear*, including when a suffix has been added, as in *stars* and *fourth*. In LE, the /r/ is not pronounced unless it is at the end of the word in connected speech and the following word begins with a vowel (i.e. it is pronounced only as a linking /r/). In JE, however, this /r/ is often pronounced in all contexts.

(eː) This variable concerned the pronunciation of the vowel in words such as FACE, *mate* and *day*. In LE this sound is a diphthong in which the final element is [ɪ] – [ɛɪ] in RP and [æɪ] or [ʌɪ] in Cockney. In JE, this is either a different diphthong [ɪɛ] or a long monophthong [ɛː].

(oː) This variable concerned the pronunciation of the vowel in words such as GOAT, *code* and *nose*. In LE, this is a diphthong – [əu] in RP and [ɐu] or [ʌu] in Cockney.[2] In JE, it is either a different diphthong [uɔ] or a long monophthong [oː].

(eə) The final variable concerned the vowels in pairs of words such as *fear/ fare* and *beer/bear*. In JE, the same vowel occurs in both words – [ɪɛ] or [ɛː], sometimes followed by an /r/ – for example, the Jamaican English pronunciation [bɪɛ] could mean 'beer' or 'bear'. In LE, however, there are two separate vowels [ɪə] and [ɛə] – for example, [bɪə] 'beer' and [bɛə] 'bear'.

For the subjects as a group, results regarding all six variables showed evidence of what Wells called "adaptation towards London speech" (1973: 117), or what we are considering as SDA. For each variable, Wells provided average scores for this adaptation, and later presented them as standardised percentages (p. 117), listed in Table 2.1 from highest to lowest.

It is clear that the subjects made some headway in acquiring the D2. The LE variants of the first two variables were acquired to the greatest extent while the next three to a much lesser extent, and the last one even lesser.

However, on the whole the subjects did not reach 90 per cent for the use for the D2 variant of any of the six variables.

2.2.2   *D1 various American English dialects; D2 Philadelphia dialect*

Another pioneering study on SDA was conducted by Payne (1976, 1980) among families who had moved from various regions of the USA to the Philadelphia suburb of King of Prussia.

Payne studied twenty-four families divided into three groups: (1) those with both children and parents born locally; (2) those with children born locally and parents born non-locally (i.e. in a different dialect region); (3) those with both children and parents born non-locally. She interviewed a total of 108 children and fifty-one adults, and used seventy children and twenty-four adults for her examination of the acquisition of the Philadelphia dialect, concentrating on children whose families had moved to King of Prussia from other locations.[3] Of these thirty-four children, seven had been born locally, and twenty-seven had arrived at ages ranging from 2 to 13. They had lived in King of Prussia from 4 to 16 years. Interviews were modelled on those developed by Labov (e.g. 1966, 1972) to obtain spontaneous speech. There was also a language module in which the researcher elicited attitudes towards the Philadelphia dialect, and had interviewees read word lists, making sure a sufficient number of key words were obtained with the linguistic variables being studied.

Payne examined a total of eight linguistic variables – all phonetic or phonological – based on features considered to be diagnostic of the Philadelphia dialect. Five of these variables had to do with differences in the pronunciation of diphthongs, primarily concerning the nucleus of the diphthong.

(aw) In the Philadelphia dialect, the nucleus [a] of the /aʊ/ diphthong (as in MOUTH) is fronted to [æ] or raised to [ɛ] or [e]. The off-glide [ʊ] is lowered to [ɔ] or [ɒ].

(oy) The nucleus [o] of the /oɪ/ diphthong (as in CHOICE) is raised to [u], so that the Philadelphia variant is [uɪ].

(ay) The nucleus [a] of the /aɪ/ diphthong becomes [ʌ] before voiceless consonants, similar to Canadian raising (or sometimes more fronted [ə]).

(ow) The nucleus [o] of the diphthong /oʊ/ (as in GOAT) is fronted to become the central vowel [ə], except before /l/ (as in GOAL).

(uw) In many dialects of American English, including Philadelphia, the /u/ phoneme (as in GOOSE) is pronounced as a slight diphthong [uʊ] except before /l/, so that *too*, for example, would be pronounced as [tuʊ] whereas *tool* would be [tuːl]. In the Philadelphia dialect in the 1970s, however, the [u] nucleus in this diphthong was becoming fronted, except before /l/.

Table 2.2 *Percentages of acquisition of D2 (Philadelphia) variants for variables involving diphthongs (natural speech)*

Variable Vowel involved	(aw) MOUTH	(oy) CHOICE	(ay) PRICE	(ow) GOAT	(uw) GOOSE
% acquired	40	60	50	68	52
% partially acquired	40	30	44.1	32	48
% not acquired	20	10	5.9	0	0
Number needing to learn the D2 variant	20	20	34	25	25

All five of these features of the Philadelphia dialect were considered by Payne to be phonetic variables, even though at least two of them involve some phonological conditioning.

Payne investigated the use of each variable in detail among only the children whose families came from dialect areas with variants different from the Philadelphia variant for that variable. So for example, fourteen out of thirty-four children were in families who came from dialect areas where the variant for the (aw) variable was the same as that of the Philadelphia dialect. That left twenty who needed to acquire the Philadelphia variant, and the speech of only these twenty was examined with regard to this variable. Payne rated the children according to three categories of learning: (1) "acquired" (using the Philadelphia variant); (2) "partially acquired" (using the Philadelphia variant only part of the time); and (3) "not acquired" (not using the Philadelphia variant at all). Unfortunately, raw scores were not given, so we do not know what the "part of the time" percentages were. The results for natural speech for the first five variables are shown in Table 2.2.[4]

The results show that for four out of the five variables, the Philadelphia (D2) variants were acquired completely by more than half of the children, and not acquired by only small percentages. Even the least acquired D2 variant, for the (aw) variable, was acquired or partially acquired by 80 per cent of the children.

In addition to the variables involving diphthongs, Payne looked at two features of the Philadelphia dialect that involved phonologically conditioned merging. The first, (er), was the merger of the vowels in word pairs such as *ferry/furry* and *merry/Murray*. The second, (ohr), was with the vowels in pairs such as *lure/lore*, *sure/shore* and *moor/more* (1976: 101). In contrast to the first five variables, the majority of children did not acquire the Philadelphia variants for these two variables, as can be seen in Table 2.3.[5]

The variable examined in the most detail by Payne was what is referred to as the "lax short-*a*" versus the "tense short-*a*". In the Philadelphia dialect, as in metropolitan New York, a split has occurred with regard to the phoneme /æ/ as

Table 2.3 *Percentages of acquisition of D2 (Philadelphia) variants for two phonological variables involving mergers (word lists)*

Variable Vowel involved	(er) FERRY/FURRY	(ohr) SURE/SHORE
% acquired	17.6	33.3
% partially acquired	10.3	16.6
% not acquired	72.1	50
Number needing to learn the D2 variant	34	10

in TRAP and *cat*. In some words, such as *bat, pack* and *lap*, it remains as /æ/ (the lax short-*a*). But in others, such as *man, bad* and *ham*, it has become a diphthong [ɛə] (the tense short-*a*), with the nucleus [ɛ] as in DRESS, and the off-glide schwa [ə], as in the last vowel in COMMA. In Philadelphia, this diphthong becomes [eə], with the nucleus raised to [e] or even higher. Minimal pairs of words exist, demonstrating that in the Philadelphia dialect, these two sounds are used to distinguish meaning and therefore may be separate phonemes. For example, in other dialects *can* pronounced /kæn/ could mean either 'be able' or 'metal container', but in Philadelphia *can* pronounced [kæn] means 'be able' but pronounced [keən] it means 'metal container'. Also in other dialects, both *have* and *halve* are pronounced /hæv/, but in the Philadelphia dialect *have* is pronounced [hæv] whereas *halve* is pronounced [heəv]. (This variable is discussed further in Chapter 4, Section 4.3.)

Payne (1976, 1980) divided this feature into two subvariables:

(æ)   The split between the lax short-*a* and the tense short-*a*.
(æh)   The raising of the nucleus in the tense short-*a* so that the diphthong is [eə].

Because of differences between the first dialects of the various families, they had different tasks with regard to acquiring the Philadelphia pattern. However, in terms of overall success, the results with regard to the children's SDA were similar, no matter which dialect area their family came from: they were all unsuccessful in completely acquiring the Philadelphia pattern for short-*a*, although one or two children from different families got close. Interestingly, two whole families of children showed virtually no acquisition of the Philadelphia short-*a* pattern, and in one of these, all the children were born and raised in Philadelphia.

In sum, Payne's research showed that the children, like the adults in Wells's study, acquired some D2 features much better than others. The difference was that, according to Payne, half of the children completely acquired four of the D2 variants.

2.2.3   D1 American English; D2 British English

Shockey (1984) carried out research on four Americans, two male and two female, from the Midwest and California who came as adults to Essex in England. Their length of residence in England ranged from eight to twenty-seven years. Each was recorded for half an hour in casual free conversation with the researcher (herself from the Midwest of the USA). Two subjects were recorded in 1978 and two in 1981.

The researcher observed that the subjects had changed their speech with regard to three features of British English (BrE) that differ from American English (AmE). The first concerned the vowel in words such as LOT, *bother*, *hot, bomb, follow* and *cod*. As mentioned in Chapter 1, in most varieties of English in Britain and Australia, this is pronounced as the low rounded back vowel [ɒ], whereas in most varieties of English in North America, it is pronounced as the low unrounded back vowel [ɑ], the same as the vowel in PALM and *father* (the LOT–PALM merger). All the subjects had changed their pronunciation of the vowel in such words, but to [ɔ] as in THOUGHT, rather than to [ɒ].

The second feature, also mentioned in Chapter 1, is that the first element of the diphthong in GOAT is more central in BrE than in AmE – that is, pronounced [əʊ] versus [oʊ]. The subjects in Shockey's study sometimes used the BrE pronunciation.

The third feature, often called "t/d flapping", was examined in detail. This feature is the result of two processes that occur in normal continuous speech in AmE (and in North American English in general). First, /t/ is voiced – that is, pronounced as /d/ – when it follows a vowel or /r/ and precedes an unstressed vowel. So for example, in AmE, *putting* and *pudding* are pronounced the same in normal speech, as are *hearty* and *hardy*. Second, /d/ is normally pronounced with the tip of the tongue stopping on the ridge above the teeth (the alveolar ridge). But in AmE, this sound is sometimes pronounced with the tip of the tongue just briefly tapping the alveolar ridge or flapping against it, similar to the sound of the /r/ in Spanish words such as *pero* 'but'. This sound is called a tap or flap, and its IPA symbol is [ɾ]. Again, this happens most frequently when the /d/ (or the /t/ that has been changed to a /d/) follows a vowel or /r/ and precedes an unstressed vowel. So for example, the word *atom* is pronounced [ǽɾəm] in AmE but [ǽtʰəm] in BrE, and *bidding* is pronounced [bíɾɪŋ] in AmE but [bídɪŋ] in BrE.[6]

Shockey examined the feature of t/d flapping as two separate variables – one in which the BrE variant would be /t/ and one in which it would be /d/. In each case, the AmE variant would be the flap [ɾ]. She considered only tokens where /t/ and /d/ would be flapped 100 per cent of the time in AmE. She found that the percentage for the BrE variant /t/ ranged between 50 and 83 for the

Table 2.4 *Pronunciation variants studied by Chambers (1992) in southern England*

	Canadian English (CanE)	Southern England English (SEE)
garage	[gəɹɑ́ʤ] or [gəɹɑ́ʒ]	[gáɹɑʤ] or [gáɹəʤ]
half	[hæf]	[hɑf]
banana	[bənǽnə]	[bənɑ́nə]
tomato	[tʰəméɪdo]	[tʰəmáto] or [tʰəmáto]
yogurt	[jóʊgəɹt]	[ˈjóɡɜːt]

four speakers, with an average of approximately 63.8 per cent; the percentage for /d/ ranged from 28 to 42, with an average of approximately 35.5 per cent (1984: 89). The overall average was 49.6 per cent. Therefore, the speakers had suppressed the flapping to some extent so that their pronunciations were closer to those of BrE. Thus, the results showed once again that adults can partially acquire phonological features of a D2, but that they do not use these features consistently.

2.2.4   D1 Canadian English; D2 Southern England English

In probably the best-known study of SDA, Chambers (1988, 1992, 1995) examined the speech of six Canadian youths who moved to Oxfordshire in southern England in 1983 and 1984. In interviews conducted in 1985 – when the youths were at ages 9, 13, 13, 14, 15 and 17 – he elicited lexical and pronunciation variants in their speech, using methods from traditional social dialectology (asking subjects to identify objects pictured on cards). He also interviewed youths from Oxfordshire of equivalent age and gender as a control group.

The study examined the acquisition of both lexical and phonetic/phonological variants, and also focused on the effect of age. The lexical variables consisted of twenty-five items that differ in Canadian English (CanE) and Southern England English (SEE), similar to the differences between American and Australian English listed in Table 1.1 in Chapter 1 – for example: *trunk/ boot* (of a car), *garbage can/dustbin*, *wrench/spanner* and *sweater/jumper*. The pronunciation variants of lexical items comprised the five words listed in Table 2.4 (1992: 677).

The scores for lexical replacement of the Canadian with the English item ranged from 24 per cent to 71.4 per cent, with the youngest speaker having the highest score. The scores for SEE rather than CanE pronunciation of the five lexical items ranged from 0 to 60, with the youngest subject again having the highest percentage and the oldest subject the lowest percentage. For each

Table 2.5 *Percentages of use of D2 (Southern England English) lexical and pronunciation variants*

Subjects by age	9	13X	13Y	14	15	17	Group
% SEE lexical variants	71.4	65	24	64	52	40	52.7
% SEE pronunciation variants	60	20	20	40	20	0	26.7

subject, the score for the use of SEE pronunciation variants was lower than that for lexical variants. (See Table 2.5.)

Chambers then turned to phonological variables. The first of these concerned what he called "T-Voicing". This is a feature of North American English in which, according to Chambers, /t/ becomes pronounced as /d/ following a vowel or /n/, /r/ or /l/ and preceding an unstressed vowel. This is very similar to t/d flapping as described in Shockey's (1984) study and other studies, where the /t/ becomes voiced, but as the flap [ɾ]. Chambers (1992: 683) reported that all the Canadian subjects in the study "made considerable progress in eliminating T-Voicing from their accents". Their scores for absence of T-Voicing – i.e. the SEE feature – ranged from 100 per cent for the youngest speaker to 20 per cent for older speakers, although the 14-year-old scored 90 per cent.

The next variable, which Chambers called Vowel Backing, was concerned with the TRAP–BATH split, described in Chapter 1. This is where words such as BATH, *plant*, *laugh* and *class* have the front vowel /æ/ as in TRAP in North American English but the back vowel /ɑ/ (actually [ɑː]) as in PALM in SEE. The youngest subject used the SEE pronunciation /ɑ/ 100 per cent of the time, but the older two subjects did not use it at all. The score for the 13-year-olds was only 10 per cent, and for the 14-year-old, 20 per cent.

The third phonological variable was what Chambers called the Low Vowel Merger (1992: 687). This concerned the LOT–PALM merger described in Chapter 1 and in relation to Shockey's (1984) study. Recall that /ɒ/ merged with /ɑ/ so that in most varieties of English in North America, *bother* rhymes with *father*, and *bomb* and *balm* are pronounced the same. In Canadian English, a further merger has occurred so that words with the vowel /ɔ/ as in THOUGHT are also pronounced with /ɑ/. As a result, words in the pairs such as *cot/caught*, *Don/dawn* and *tot/taught* have the same pronunciation (with /ɑ/ as in PALM). In SEE, however, the vowel in the first word in each pair is /ɒ/ whereas in the second it is /ɔ/. To speak the SEE dialect, the Canadian subjects had to learn a new phoneme /ɒ/ and reverse both of these mergers to pronounce what was /ɑ/ in their D1 as either /ɒ/ or /ɔ/ in particular words. With regard to 10 word pairs, the 9-year-old and one of the 13-year-olds

Table 2.6 *Summary of the percentages of use of D2 (Southern England English) variants for seven variables*

Subjects by age	9	13X	13Y	14	15	17	Group
% SEE lexical variants	71.4	65	24	64	52	37.5	52.3
% SEE pronunciation variants	60	20	20	40	20	0	26.7
SEE phonological variants:							
% Absence of T-Voicing	100	80	20	90	20	20	55.0
% Presence of Vowel Backing	100	10	10	20	0	0	23.3
% Absence of Low Vowel Merger	90	80	10	0	10	0	31.6
% Presence of R-lessness	10	0	10	30	0	0	8.3
% Intrusive /r/	40	0	0	0	0	0	6.7
SEE phonological variants:							
% average	68	34	10	28	6	4	25.0
Total average	67.3	36.4	13.4	34.9	14.6	8.2	29.1

showed considerable progress, scoring 90 and 80 per cent respectively. The 14- and 17-year-olds made no progress, scoring 0, while the other 13-year-old and the 15-year-old scored 10 per cent.

One of the most salient differences between the dialects is "R-lessness" in SEE (1992: 691). As we saw in Chapter 1 and in the discussion of Jamaican and London English, this means that /r/ is pronounced only when it precedes a vowel – i.e. only when it occurs in a prevocalic position. Thus, words such as *north*, *urban* and *birth* are always 'R-less' and *car*, *fur* and *water* are R-less unless followed in continuous speech by a word beginning with a vowel. In most varieties of North American English, however, /r/ is always pronounced in such words. The Canadian youths made little progress in acquiring R-lessness, with three scoring 0, two scoring only 10 per cent (including the youngest) and one scoring 30 per cent.

The last variable Chambers examined was Intrusive /r/ (1992: 692). This is the result of a rule in which /r/ is inserted at the end of a word ending in a vowel when the following word begins with a vowel – for example, in phrases such as *Cuba/r/ and France*, *sofa/r/ and couch* and *raw/r/ eggs* (p. 692). It can also occur before a suffix starting with a vowel, as in *draw/r/-ing*. This is a variable rule (i.e. one that does not always occur) in SEE, as indicated by differing degrees of its occurrence among the control group, ranging from 100 per cent to only 20 per cent. Also, unlike the other rules considered here, Intrusive /r/ is stigmatised as being non-standard. Of the Canadian youths, only the youngest used this rule, with a score of 40 per cent.

A summary of the results of Chambers' study is given in Table 2.6. The study again demonstrated varying degrees of acquisition of the D2 variants for different variables. The overall level of attainment for most of the youths was not greater than that of the adults in Wells's study, and with regard to T-Voicing, the results were very similar to those obtained by Shockey for t/d flapping (55 per cent and 54 per cent). However, the youngest subject (age 9) clearly outperformed the other youths, and completely acquired two of the D2 features.

2.2.5   D1 Canadian English; D2 Northeastern England English

More recent research on Canadians in England involved much younger subjects. Tagliamonte and Molfenter (2007) studied SDA with the first author's three children, who were all under the age of five when they moved from Canada to northeastern England.[7] Tagliamonte recorded the children's casual conversation nearly every weekend for six years starting in January 1996, six months after their arrival when the children were 2, 4 and 5 years old. The particular variable the authors examined was T-Voicing or t/d flapping, as studied by Shockey (1984) and Chambers (1992) – the Canadian English (CanE) pronunciation of /t/ in the middle of some words as a flap [ɾ].[8] In "standard" British English, this is pronounced as [t]. But in Northeastern England English (NEE) there is an additional variant besides the [t] pronunciation – the glottal stop, symbolised as [ʔ]. This sounds like the break in the flow of speech that occurs between the syllables in the interjection *uh oh*. The glottal stop [ʔ] also occurs in NEE in place of /t/ at the end of words. These variants carry social meaning in England. In the past, the [t] pronunciation was considered typical of careful, upper-class or posh speech and [ʔ] typical of casual, lower-class or rough speech (Tagliamonte and Molfenter 2007: 660). However, this has been changing rapidly and there is increased use of [ʔ] both word-medially (i.e. in place of /t/ in the middle of words) and word-finally (p. 668). Significant variability exists in the use of these variants among NEE dialect speakers themselves – with one study showing [ʔ] rather than [t] occurring approximately 30 per cent of the time word-medially and 70 per cent word-finally (p. 671, Figure 6).

The results of Tagliamonte and Molfenter's study were that all three of the children gradually suppressed the CanE feature of T-Voicing in their speech and acquired the NEE pronunciations, either [t] or [ʔ], while at the same time acquiring the NEE glottal stop variant [ʔ] for final /t/. That is, they gradually increased their use of NEE variants over time, so that after six years in northeastern England, they all sounded as if they came from that region of the country. However, as Tagliamonte and Molfenter pointed out (2007: 671), close scrutiny of the children's speech revealed that they had not fully shifted from their CanE dialect – one of the children using NEE variants approxi-mately 85 per cent of the time, and two 95 per cent.[9] However, the children acquired native-like patterns of variation for the use of the two NEE variants [t] and [ʔ] (p. 672).

Compared to the group performances of older children and adults on a similar variable, the young children in this study had much higher attainment, and two of them acquired the target D2 variants according to the 90 per cent criterion.

2.2.6   D1 North American English; D2 Australian English

One of the most comprehensive works specifically on SDA is Foreman's (2003) investigation of North Americans in Australia. It consisted of a pilot study, the main study (described here) and a subsidiary longitudinal study (described in Chapter 5).

Foreman's main study used two different methodologies – a statistical analysis of the use of six linguistic variables (detailed below) and their correspondence with various non-linguistic factors (described in Chapters 4 and 5), and a qualitative analysis of subjects' experiences and attitudes (described in Chapters 5 and 6). The data for the main study came from recordings made in 1999 of two-part informal interviews with thirty-four residents of Australia (twenty female and fourteen male) who came originally from the USA or Canada at ages ranging from 7 to 46. They had lived in Australia for periods of from less than a year to 46 years. One part of the interview was conducted by the Canadian author, and the other by an Australian woman of approximately the same age (early twenties). Some additional interviews had also been conducted, but were not included in the statistical analysis for various reasons – for example, because it emerged that the subject had lived in other English-speaking countries. However, information from these interviews was included in the qualitative analysis.

Five of the six linguistic variables concerned vowels, which themselves often vary in Australian English. Mitchell and Delbridge (1965) identified three varieties – now generally thought to be points on a continuum. At one end is Cultivated Australian, which is closest to RP, or standard spoken British English. At the opposite end – i.e. furthest from British English – is Broad Australian. In the middle is General Australian. For example, in the Cultivated variety, the diphthong in PRICE is pronounced [aɪ], as in both RP and North American English (NAE), but in the General variety it is [ɑɪ], with the nucleus more back. In the Broad variety it is sometimes [ɒɪ], with the nucleus back and more rounded, so that to an outsider the word *tie* can sound almost like *toy*. These days, however, perhaps less than 10 per cent of Australians would speak the Cultivated variety, and the vowels of Broad and General, which are generally more similar to each other than to Cultivated, are what make the Australian accent distinctive. Therefore, the term Australian English (AusE) generally refers to the Broad and General varieties.

The first of Foreman's variables was "non-prevocalic /r/" (r), which Chambers (1992) called R-lessness. The acquisition of the AusE variant would require eliminating /r/ in environments other than before a vowel – i.e. in non-prevocalic positions.

The other five variables would be classified as phonetic, rather than phonological, as they concern the Australian pronunciation of certain single vowels and diphthongs. The acquisition of the Australian variant would involve simple substitution of AusE for NAE realisations. These variables were the vowels in the following:[10]

(KIT) In NAE, this vowel is pronounced as [ɪ], but in AusE, it is raised slightly, symbolised as [ɪ̝].

(GOAT) As described in Chapter 1, in NAE, this diphthong is [oʊ], beginning with a rounded mid back nucleus [o]. In AusE, it is most commonly [ɑu], [ɒo], [ɐʊ] or [ɐo], beginning with a lower nucleus [ɑ] or [ɒ], and sometimes a lower and more central nucleus [ɐ], and having a higher or lower off-glide [u] or [o].

(FLEECE) In NAE, this is pronounced as a monophthong [i], but in AusE as a diphthong [ᵊiː] or [ᶦiː].

(FACE) In NAE, this is pronounced [eɪ] with a mid front nucleus [e]. In AusE the nucleus is lower [æ] and sometimes more central [ɐ], and the off-glide is sometimes [e] rather than [ɪ], giving the pronunciations [æɪ], [æe] or [ɐɪ].

(PRICE) In NAE, this is pronounced [aɪ]. The AusE pronunciations of [ɑɪ] and [ɒɪ] have already been mentioned. Also, the off-glide is sometimes pronounced as schwa, giving [ɑə].

It should be noted that of these linguistic variables, only the absence of non-prevocalic /r/ is categorical in AusE. In the case of (GOAT), (FLEECE), (FACE) and (PRICE), some speakers in formal situations may shift to Cultivated pronunciations, which are similar to the NAE standard norms. Also, the raised vowel in KIT does not appear to be used consistently by Australians (Foreman 2003: 127).

The results of the main study were that with regard to the six linguistic variables, only twelve of the thirty-four subjects changed their pronunciation to become more like that of the AusE variants. Of the twelve subjects that did acquire some D2 variants, six used AusE-like variants for all six variables, three did so for five out of the six variables, two for three out of six, and one for two out of six. The results for these twelve subjects are shown in Table 2.7, with the initial of the subject in the left-hand column, and the percentage of use of an AusE variant under each variant.[11]

The AusE pronunciation of the FACE diphthong had the greatest percentage of use – 55.7 per cent for one subject, but still only an average of 24.4 per cent

Table 2.7 *Percentages of use of six D2 (Australian English) variants by twelve speakers*

	(r)	(KIT)	(GOAT)	(FLEECE)	(FACE)	(PRICE)	Average
S	1.4	46.4	17.0	14.01	42.9	10.1	22.0
C	20.2	16.8	27.0	8.5	47.0	49.1	28.1
V	5.8	45.8	30.1	8.9	55.7	24.1	28.4
F	5.6	28.3	36.3	10.5	35.0	30.7	24.4
H	0	26.6	4.1	23.8	22.7	13.0	15.0
B	0	0	10.9	2.8	0	0	2.3
L	22.6	24.8	38.9	2.4	25.3	8.2	20.4
J	0.2	14.9	27.6	0	3.8	29.1	12.6
M	7.2	33.0	28.4	7.3	12.9	45.2	22.3
P	0	0	4.7	6.6	25.2	0	6.1
D	0	0.8	1.1	4.7	15.2	5.0	4.5
E	0	0	0	3.0	6.3	20.3	4.9
Average	5.3	19.8	18.8	7.7	24.4	19.6	15.9

for the twelve subjects. (And this would be only 8.6 per cent if all thirty-four subjects were included.) Elimination of the pronunciation of non-prevocalic /r/ (i.e. R-lessness) had the lowest percentage among the twelve speakers.

Foreman looked at some other variables as well, but did not analyse them statistically because of having only a small number of tokens. These variables included the vowels in TRAP and BATH, which are distinguished in AusE as in BrE as a result of the TRAP–BATH split but not in NAE, and the vowels in THOUGHT and LOT, which again are not distinguished in CanE and to some extent in AmE because of the THOUGHT–LOT merger. In both cases, only a few subjects used the distinctions found in AusE, and far from consistently (2003: 158, 162). These results contrasted with those for lexical variables in the pilot study, in which eight out of nine subjects reported the adoption of Australian variants.

Foreman's main study, however, clearly revealed the lowest D2 attainment of all the studies considered so far.

2.2.7   D1 North American English; D2 New Zealand English

Bayard (1995; Starks and Bayard 2002) studied his son's acquisition of New Zealand English (NZE). Although the son was born in New Zealand, he spoke only the North American English (NAE) of his parents as his D1 until he started day-care at approximately age 2 years and 2 months (Bayard 1995: 16; Starks and Bayard 2002: 190).[12] Bayard first tape-recorded his son at home in 1984 at age 6, and then at ages 8, 12, 16 and 20. His Table 1 (1995: 16) indicates that the son used NZE variants for nine out of sixteen vowels, including [ɒ] for LOT, [ʌʊ] for GOAT and [ʉ] for GOOSE. For four other vowels, his pronunciations were closer to NZE than to NAE. He retained NAE pronunciation for only two vowels: [ɪ] for KIT and [æ] for BATH. In the later recordings, Bayard was mainly interested in the use of NZE R-lessness (that absence of non-prevocalic /r/, as in AusE), especially as in the words NEAR, SQUARE, NORTH, START, FIRE, NURSE and LETTER. At age 8, the use of R-less pronunciations in such words was 68.3 per cent. (However, this percentage decreased in later years, as shown in Chapter 5, Section 5.1.1.)

2.2.8   *D1 Southern England English; D2 Australian English*

In a small-scale study in Australia years before Foreman's, Rogers (1981) examined the acquisition of Australian English intonation patterns with twins (a boy and a girl) who had moved from southern England to Australia at the age of seven. This is the only study on SDA of English dialects to examine a suprasegmental variable (see Chapter 1). Rogers recorded the children six times over eight and a half months, and also recorded two Australian children of a similar age. The results were that significant changes towards AusE intonation and speech rate occurred for both English children in "wh" questions (questions with *who, what, where, when, why, how*), in answers to questions and in statements. However, the changes were not progressive and the children often differed in their output.

Trudgill obtained the recordings made by Rogers and analysed the children's acquisition of Australian variants as opposed to Southern England English variants for fifteen phonetic/phonological variables, including the five phonetic variables examined by Foreman (2003) – i.e. the vowels in KIT, GOAT, FLEECE, FACE and PRICE. Trudgill (1981, 1986) observed that after six months both children acquired the Australian variant for nearly all of the variables and sounded very Australian.[13] Both the boy and the girl used the Australian variant consistently for 10 or 11 of the variables, both variants for 2 variables, and the British variant for 2 or 3 variables. However, they followed very different routes of acquisition, and differed in the variables that they had or had not completely acquired. With regard to Foreman's variables, they acquired all AusE variants except the vowel in KIT. Thus, these children differed markedly from the adults in Foreman's study in terms of their attainment in SDA.

2.3   Studies on dialects of languages other than English

2.3.1   *Language: Japanese; D1 Tokyo dialect; D2 Kyoto dialect*

Kobayashi (1981) studied a child whose parents both spoke only the Tokyo dialect of Japanese, but moved to Kyoto, where a different dialect is spoken. The girl acquired the Tokyo dialect as her D1 from her parents (as evidenced by recordings made when she was 2 years 11 months), but some time after age 3, she began to acquire the local Kyoto dialect as her D2. For the study, Kobayashi recorded the child when she was 8 years old, focusing on a suprasegmental variable: pitch accent. This is a complex feature of Japanese that concerns the pitch of a word, which may be in relation to the part of the word that is stressed or accented. Dialects of Japanese are often distinguished by having different pitch accent patterns for the same word, and this is true for the Tokyo and Kyoto dialects. For example, the word that means 'thunder' has this pattern in the Tokyo dialect:

$$\underline{ka \diagup mina' \diagdown ri}$$

but the following in the Kyoto dialect:

$$\overline{ka \ \ mina'} \diagdown ri$$

(The details, too complex to go into here, are discussed by Kobayashi 1981: 7–8.) In a spontaneous dialogue with a peer, recorded and analysed by Kobayashi, the child used the D2 (Kyoto) accent pattern for 170 out of 256 words of different word classes, a percentage of 66.4.[14] This compared to a percentage of 92.4 for another girl of the same age, also recorded by Kobayashi, who was a native speaker of the Kyoto dialect. Kobayashi also mentioned a morphological variable: the copula – 'da in the Tokyo dialect and 'ya in the Kyoto dialect. In the same dialogue, the child of Tokyo parents used the Kyoto variant 30 out of 34 times, or 88.2 per cent.

2.3.2   Language: Brazilian Portuguese; D1 Caipira (rural); D2 standard (urban)

Bortoni-Ricardo (1985) did a very detailed study of SDA among rural migrants in Brazlândia, a satellite city 43 kilometres from Brasília, the capital of Brazil. The D1 was the rural Caipira dialect of Brazilian Portuguese and the D2 was the standard urban dialect. Her fieldwork, conducted in 1980–1, consisted of structured interviews with fifty-three men and sixty-five women, aged 15 to 74. Of these, she focused on two groups. The "anchorage group" were thirty-three adult migrants (sixteen male and seventeen female), all from the Caipira dialect-speaking region, and aged 26 to 71. They had migrated at ages ranging from 18 to 68. The "youth control" group were thirteen children, grandchildren, nephews or nieces of the anchorage group (seven male, six female), aged 15 to 25, who had migrated under the age of 13 (p. 131). The migrants had lived in Brazlândia for periods of from 1 to 35 years.

The researcher examined four linguistic variables, two phonological and two morphological (described below). Each variable had a stigmatised variant associated with the rural areas as opposed to a prestigious variant associated with standard urban Brazilian Portuguese, as spoken by people brought up in the Brasília area. For each variable, Bortoni-Ricardo calculated the percentage of use of the standard variant for each speaker. She presented the results in terms of changes from the rural dialect in the urban environment, and described the rural dialect as becoming diffused. However, these results can also be seen as an indication of the degree of acquisition of the urban dialect by rural dialect speakers.

The first phonological variable concerned the 'l' sound between vowels. Brazilian Portuguese has two 'l' sounds, one similar to English /l/, and another in which the tongue is raised to the palate, which occurs only between vowels. This is called an alveopalatal lateral, and has the IPA symbol [λ]. An example of a word with this sound is *mulher* 'woman', pronounced [muλέr]. In some words in Brazilian Portuguese, what is written as 'l' may be pronounced with the alveopalatal lateral [λ] or as [l] followed by the palatal glide [j] (pronounced as 'y' in English) – so, for example, *família* 'family' is pronounced as [famíλa] or [famílja]. In the rural dialect, however, the 'l' sound, either [λ] or [l], is not pronounced when it occurs between vowels, or it becomes a vowel-like sound itself (in a process called "vocalisation") – in this case [ɪ] or [j]. Thus, *mulher* 'woman' is pronounced as [muʲέr] in the rural dialect, and *família* 'family' is pronounced as [famíʲa] (1985: 176).

The second phonological variable concerned rising diphthongs /ɪa/ and /ɪu/ at the ends of words. The whole diphthong is pronounced in standard urban Portuguese but only the final element is pronounced in the rural dialect. For example, the words *dúzia* 'dozen' and *lábio* 'lip' are pronounced [dúzɪa] and [lábɪu] in the urban standard, but [dúza] and [lábu] in the rural dialect.

The morphological variables both concerned subject–verb agreement – that is, using one form of the verb for particular subjects, and another form for different subjects – for example, in English, *She goes* versus *They go*, and *I am* versus *you are* versus *he is*. In the Caipira dialect of Brazilian Portuguese, the system is reduced and verb endings to distinguish plural subjects are not required for 3rd person ('they') or 1st person ('we'). Rather, just the plain form of the verb is used – for example (Bortoni-Ricardo 1985: 199):

Standard	Caipira	
*Eles **queriam** ir.*	*Eles **queria** ir.*	'They wanted to go.'
*Nós **queríamos** ir.*	*Nós **queria** ir.*	'We wanted to go.'

Thus the two morphological variables concerned subject–verb agreement in 3rd person plural and subject–verb agreement in 1st person plural.

Table 2.8 *Average percentages of use of D2 (standard Brazilian Portuguese) variants by two age groups for four variables*

Variable	Youth group	Adult group
1. Vocalisation of 'l'	81	49
2. Reduction of diphthongs	88	53
3. 3rd person plural agreement	64	27
4. 1st person plural agreement	82	48
Overall average	78.75	44.25

The average percentages of use of the standard variant by each group for each of the four variables are shown in Table 2.8. As in the Australian studies, these results show overall differences in attainment between younger and older D2 learners, but the rates of use of D2 variants for the adult group are much higher in Brazil.

2.3.3   Language: Norwegian; D1 Stril (rural); D2 Bergen (urban)

Kerswill (1994) examined SDA in southwestern Norway among speakers of the rural Stril dialects who had migrated to the city of Bergen, where a different dialect is spoken. Data consisted of tape-recordings of in-depth interviews, conversations and reading of word lists with thirty-nine informants (nineteen male and twenty female), made in 1981 and 1982. The informants were from 24 to 79 years old, and had migrated at ages ranging from 12 to 52. The main aim of this study was actually to account for differences among individual migrants in their acquisition of the Bergen dialect. This aim affected the methodology with regard to the quantification of the variables, and also the presentation of results, which concentrated on correlations with individual characteristics rather than individual scores.

Three types of linguistic features were examined: (1) the overall degree of use of Stril (as opposed to Bergen) lexical and morphological elements, (2) the adaptation of one particular Bergen phonological feature and (3) the production and perception of tonemic contrast. The third of these proved problematic for investigation as a linguistic variable (1994: 101); therefore, only the first two variables are discussed here.

Like English dialects, there are many lexical differences between the Stril (S) and Bergen (B) dialects. First are different lexical items with the same meaning (like *jumper* and *sweater* in English) – for example: S /hotɑ/, B /huskə/ 'remember'. Then there are different pronunciations of what are thought of as the same word (like the different pronunciations of *tomato*) – for example: S /mjɛlk/, B /mɛlk/ 'milk'. However, the extent of

Table 2.9 *Distribution of percentages of use of D2 (Bergen) variants*

Percentage range	Number of informants
0–10	7
11–20	8
21–30	4
31–40	8
41–50	2
51–60	4
61–70	1
71–80	1
81–90	0
91–100	4

morphological variation is much greater than found between English dialects, such as differences in morphological categories. For example, Stril dialects have three genders for nouns, masculine, feminine and neuter, while Bergen has two, common and neuter. There are also differences in the form of function words such as prepositions – e.g. S /jo:/, B /hus/ 'at' – and in the form of grammatical markers such as verbal suffixes – e.g. S /kasta/, B /kastət/ 'threw' (Kerswill 1994: 37).

Kerswill examined the use of twenty-three lexical and morphological variables (1994: 75). But rather than examine each one separately as in the studies described so far, he used a "morpholexical index" – that is, the overall percentage of the use of Stril variants for all the variables combined. The index was calculated for each informant on the basis of an average of 185.5 tokens per informant – with each token being a context where either a Stril or a Bergen variant would be used (p. 79). Since Bergen is a prestigious urban dialect, it could have influenced informants' speech before they moved to Bergen. Therefore, a baseline was determined for each informant on the basis of recordings of people still living in the districts from which most of the Stril immigrants originated, and on the basis of information gathered in the interview (p. 76).

The results were that the morpholexical index scores for the percentage of use of D1 Stril variants among the thirty-nine Stril migrants ranged widely from 98.9 to 0.9 per cent with an average of 64.7. For the use of D2 (Bergen) variants, this is equivalent to a range of 1.1 to 99.1 per cent with an average of 35.3. Table 2.9 shows the distribution of percentages of use of the D2 Bergen variants.[15]

The figures indicate that only ten out of the thirty-nine informants used more than 50 per cent of the D2 morpholexical variants as opposed to their D1 variants.

The phonological variable was labelled "schwa-lowering". It concerned the quality of the schwa vowel /ə/ (as in the final vowel in COMMA) that occurs in unstressed syllables before a pause in words such as *skule* /skʉːlə/ 'school' and *huset* /hʉːsə/ 'the house'. In the Stril dialects, as in most varieties of Norwegian, this vowel has a central, slightly fronted pronunciation, but in Bergen, it is lowered and fronted to [ɛ], [æ] or even [a] (1994: 80) – that is, close in sound to the vowels in DRESS or TRAP. To measure the Stril migrants' adoption of this Bergen feature, Kerswill used a vowel height scale ranging from 0 (for the lowest pronunciation [a]) to 6 (for the highest [e̞][16]) with [ə] assigned the value of 4 (p. 82). The lower the value, the closer to the Bergen dialect.

For words at the end of utterances (final position), the Stril migrants' mean scores for the vowel height scale were 2.1 in the interview data and 2.7 in the conversation data (p. 124). These scores were higher than those of native Bergen residents, but lower than those of Stril non-migrants, indicating that some acquisition in the direction of the D2 variant had occurred. It appeared that the degree of acquisition of schwa-lowering was similar to that of morpholexical features (p. 127).

These results are similar to those of preceding studies, except for the high percentages of use of Bergen morpholexical variants for four informants. This is discussed further in Chapters 4 and 5.

2.3.4   Language: Norwegian; D1 Setesdal (rural); D2 Kristiansand (urban)

In another but smaller-scale study in Norway, Omdal (1994) investigated SDA among twenty-four adults (twelve women and twelve men) who had moved from the rural region of Setesdal to the urban centre of Kristiansand, where a different dialect is spoken. A Kristiansand man and woman together interviewed the twenty-four informants in 1984. They comprised three age groups: 31–9, 42–8 and 56–76. Age of arrival ranged from 16 to 70, and years in Kristiansand from 5 to 51. However, it should be noted that nineteen of the twenty-four speakers had left Setesdal and lived in other areas for periods of from 1 to 35 years before coming to Kristiansand.[17]

To measure the adaptation to (or acquisition of) the Kristiansand dialect, Omdal devised a "language modification index" (1994: 126) based on the percentage of use of the Kristiansand variants for three very frequently occurring linguistic variables: (1) the use of [viː] for the 1st person plural pronoun 'we' instead of Setesdal [meː] or [miː]; (2) not changing the vowel in the present tense of "strong" verbs such as *komme* 'come', as is done in the Setesdal dialect; and (3) use of final /r/ in the indefinite plural of words such as /hestər/ 'horses', instead of Setesdal /hestɑ/.

The results were a mean percentage of use for the non-Setesdal variants of 40.7 for the 1st person pronoun, 55.8 for the verb forms and 47.0 for the final /r/ plurals (p. 129), an overall average of 47.8 per cent. There was a great deal of variation among speakers, however, with scores ranging from 0 to 100 per cent (but some of the percentages were based on only a small number of occurrences of a particular variable in the data). The total language modification index for each speaker ranged from 6.0 to 96.3 per cent. It was found that the younger group had the least modification, while the intermediate group had the most.

These results differ from those of other studies, where the younger speakers have the most modification (i.e. use of D2 variants). The author suggested that this may have been due to the change in the 1960s and 1970s to more positive attitudes towards the use of regional dialects (p. 132).

2.3.5   Language: Swedish; D1 Närpes Finland Swedish; D2 Eskilstuna and standard Swedish

Another study of SDA was carried out in Sweden (Ivars 1994). The thirty-two informants in the investigation (sixteen men and sixteen women) were migrants to the Swedish city of Eskilstuna from the Finnish agricultural district of Närpes. Finland has a large population of Swedish people concentrated in particular areas, and in 1980, approximately 94 per cent of people in the Närpes district spoke Swedish as their first language (p. 204). However, the local dialect used for everyday communication was markedly different from the standard varieties of Swedish used in both Finland and Sweden for more formal communication. Eskilstuna has its own local dialect as well, but because of a large immigrant population, standard Swedish is also used in everyday communication.

The informants all migrated to Sweden at ages ranging from 16 to 49. When interviewed their ages ranged from 28 to 76, and their lengths of stay in the Eskilstuna area were from 3 to 33 years. The interviews were in two parts, conducted by two different interviewers – the first in the Eskilstuna dialect, and the second in the Närpes dialect (Ivars 1994: 208).

The study examined twenty-six linguistic variables – nine phonological and seventeen morphological.[18] Of these, seventeen variables had a variant exclusive to the Närpes dialect as opposed to the Eskilstuna dialect and standard Swedish, eight had a variant exclusive to the Eskilstuna dialect as opposed to the other two varieties, and twenty-two had a variant exclusive to standard Swedish. For each informant, Ivars calculated three indices: the Närpes dialect index, the Eskilstuna index and the standard Swedish index. Each index was the mean percentage of use of the variants for that dialect in the variables that had variants exclusive to that dialect.[19]

Values for the Närpes dialect index ranged from 4 to 93 per cent, for the Eskilstuna index from 0 to 63 per cent, and for the standard Swedish index from 4 to 80 per cent (1994: 210). (Unfortunately, individual scores and group percentages were not given.) Older speakers generally had higher scores on the Närpes dialect index while younger speakers had higher scores on the Eskilstuna index and the standard Swedish index, indicating that they had acquired more of the dialects of their new home in Sweden.

Ivars also calculated the percentage of use of Närpes dialect variants for four morphological variables in the Eskilstuna part of the interview. The range of percentages was from 0 to 99, with an overall average of 21 per cent, which meant that the subjects used D2 variants 79 per cent of the time.[20] This is a higher percentage than found in other studies.

2.3.6   Language: Dutch; D1 standard Dutch; D2 Limburg dialect

Vousten and Bongaerts (1995) reported on a study of SDA conducted in the town of Venray in the Limburg dialect area of the Netherlands (also described by Vousten 1995). The subjects were thirty-eight school students whose families had moved to Venray from other parts of the Netherlands. They had grown up in a home environment in which only standard Dutch was spoken, but had learned the local Limburg dialect to some extent.[21] A "dialect test battery" was administered to the thirty-eight dialect learners and to an equal number of native dialect speakers, who served as a control group (Vousten and Bongaerts 1995: 300). The test measured the subjects' proficiency in phonology, morphology and lexicon. Unfortunately, individual scores and information on age of arrival and length of stay were not given in the article.

The phonological variables focused on were (î): standard Dutch [ɛɪ] versus Limburg [i], and (û): standard Dutch [œy] versus Limburg [u] or [y].[22] For example, the word *pijp* 'pipe' is pronounced [pɛɪp] in standard Dutch versus [pi.p] in the Limburg dialect; *muis* 'mouse' is [mœys] in standard Dutch versus [mu.s] in Limburg; and *beschujt* 'biscuit' [besxœyt] versus [besxyt] (1995: 302). The test included seven lexical items for each of the variables. The results were that the standard Dutch-speaking learners used the Limburg dialect form for (î) an average of 68.4 per cent of the time and one or the other of the forms for (û) 60.6 per cent.[23]

This study also recorded the percentage of use for each variant for native speakers of the D2 (those with the Limburg dialect as their D1). This was because variation existed among the native speakers, as well as among the learners. As the likely consequence of the prestige and widespread use of the standard dialect, some of the native speakers in the control group used the standard Dutch variants instead of Limburg ones – for example, one speaker used the standard Dutch pronunciation ([εɪ] versus Limburg [i]) for the lexical item *strijk* 'ironer'.

Variation also existed when there was more than one possible Limburg variant. For example, *muis* 'mouse' was produced as [mu.s] by 67.6 per cent of the native speakers, and [mys] by 32.4 per cent (p. 302). This meant that for the (û) variable, a learner's pronunciation of either [u] or [y] (as opposed to standard Dutch [œy]) could be considered "on target".

The first morphological variable concerned the form of gender assignment to the indefinite article. In standard Dutch, the article has only one form [ən], but the Limburg dialect uses this form for feminine and neuter nouns but [ənə] for masculine nouns. The learners used this form only 18.0 per cent of the time. But it should be noted that the native Limburg speakers themselves used it only 64.0 per cent of the time (1995: 304).

The next morphological variable had to do with subject–verb agreement. In both standard Dutch and the Limburg dialect, the suffix *-t* is added to the verb stem for 2nd and 3rd person singular. However, in the dialect the vowel of the stem also changes. For verbs with a short vowel, the change is relatively straightforward – for example, for the verb *vallen* 'fall', the verb stem is [vɑl-], and the 3rd singular form is pronounced [vɑlt] in standard Dutch but [vælt] in the Limburg dialect. Learners used the Limburg form an average of 38.3 per cent of the time, but note that native speakers used it only an average of 75.0 per cent.

For verbs with a long vowel, the change is more complicated, especially as the stems have different pronunciations in the two varieties. For example, for the verb *kopen* 'buy', the stem is [kuəp-] in the Limburg dialect and [koːp-] in standard Dutch. In the Limburg Dialect, [kɔpt] is the 2nd person singular form and [kœpt] is the 3rd person, but in standard Dutch, [koːpt] is the form for both. In the tests, both learners and native speakers often used the 2nd person form for 3rd person, and vice versa, and also produced some unique forms, such as [kuəpt], used for both persons. The learners produced the "correct" target form only an average of 29.0 per cent for 2nd person and 26.5 per cent for 3rd person. Note, however, that they used the standard Dutch forms only an average of 25.0 and 27.8 per cent of the time respectively, and that native speakers used the "correct" Limburg forms only 55.7 and 50.0 per cent.

Another morphological variable tested was the formation of plurals. Standard Dutch indicates plural with the addition of a suffix, *-e*, *-en* or *-s* – for example, the word *stok* 'stick' is [stɔk] in the singular and [stɔkə] in the plural. In contrast, for some words in the Limburg dialect, the plural is indicated with a vowel change – so, for example, 'sticks' would be [stœk]. The authors did not give the results for all thirty-seven items tested, so average percentages cannot be calculated. However, the results given for two individual items provide some indication. The learners' average production of the Limburg plural for *stok* 'stick' was only 18.4 per cent and for *muis*

Table 2.10 *Average percentages of use of D2 (Limburg) variants for eight variables*

Variable	D2 learners	D2 natives
(î)	68.4	99.6
(û)	60.6	99.6
Gender on indefinite article	18.0	64.0
Subj–verb agreement – short vowel	38.3	75.0
Subj–verb agreement – long vowel, 2nd person	29.0	55.7
Subj–verb agreement – long vowel, 3rd person	26.5	50.0
Plural marking	17.1	57.9
Diminutives	47.4	83.7
Average	38.2	73.2

'mouse' only 15.8 per cent. Again, native speakers used the "correct" Limburg forms only 60.5 and 55.3 per cent of the time.

The final morphological variable was the diminutive suffix, similar to *-ito/-ita* in Spanish – for example, *perro* 'dog', *perrito* 'little dog, puppy'. In standard Dutch, the diminutive is indicated with the suffix *-je*, so that [stɔkjə] is 'little stick'. However, in the Limburg dialect, it is indicated with a suffix *-ke*, *-ske* or *-tje*, as well as a vowel change in the stem (as with the plural) – for example, [stœkskə] 'little stick'. Again average test results are given for only two items, but they were higher than for the plural: learners used the correct Limburg diminutive form for *stok* 60.5 per cent of the time, and for *muis* 34.2 per cent (an average of 47.4 per cent). The native speakers used "correct" forms more frequently: 94.7 and 72.7 per cent (an average of 83.7 per cent).

The results are summarised in Table 2.10.

2.3.7   Language: Dutch; D1 Southern (Belgian) Dutch; D2 Maldegem dialect

Rys (2007) conducted a large-scale study of SDA in Belgium. Like the study described by Vousten and Bongaerts (1995), Rys's study examined the acquisition of a regional dialect by speakers of standard Dutch. However, in this case the D1 was the southern variety of standard Dutch, referred to as Southern Dutch, Belgian Dutch or Flemish. Also included as the D1 was a more informal variety of Southern Dutch, known as *tussentaal*, literally 'in-between language' (p. 1). The D2 was the local dialect spoken in the village of Maldegem, in the northwest of the province of East-Flanders, about four kilometres south of the border between Belgium and the Netherlands (p. 168). Rys's study differed from others in that the D1 speakers she focused on were not immigrants to the D2 dialect region; rather, they were born in Maldegem but raised speaking either standard Southern Dutch or *tussentaal*. They acquired the Maldegem dialect (D2) to varying extents from their peers when they started school, at approximately age 6.

The study, conducted in 2003 and 2004, was with 164 school students (ninety-one boys and seventy-three girls) in three age groups – sixty-three 9-year-olds, sixty-eight 12-year-olds and thirty-three 15-year-olds. Of these, twenty-one were raised in standard Southern Dutch and 107 in *tussentaal* – together comprising 128 second dialect learners of the Maldegem dialect (D2). There were also thirty-six students raised in the Maldegem dialect – i.e. native D2 speakers – who served as the control group. The interviews with the student informants included informal conversation and the elicitation of 167 words on the basis of picture cards and sentence completion tasks.

One of the main aims of Rys's study was to explore factors affecting the ease of acquisition or learnability of particular features. Therefore, she examined a large number of linguistic features that vary between the D1 and the D2 – a total of thirty-four, too many to describe individually here. D1 variants from standard Southern Dutch or *tussentaal* were labelled SD, and D2 variants from the Maldegem dialect were labelled DIA. Of these variables, twenty-four were phonological and ten lexical. Of the phonological variables, five concerned consonants – e.g. the deletion of /l/ before another consonant in DIA but not in SD – and fifteen concerned vowels – e.g. SD [aː] versus DIA [a] before /ts/ (2007: 228, 232). The lexical variables concerned pronunciation variants between particular lexical items (called "lexical exceptions" by Rys) – e.g. SD [bɑstə] versus DIA [bɔstə] 'fissure'.[24] Note that unlike other studies (e.g. Chambers 1992), Rys's study considered each lexical exception to be a separate variable, rather than grouping them together as instances of one kind of variation.

The results were that the average percentage of use of the D2 lexical variants ranged from 1 to 64, with an average of 27.7 per cent. The average for the D2 phonological variants ranged from 7 to 76 with an average of 45.2 per cent.[25] The results also showed that the control group used the DIA variants from 44 to 97 per cent of the time with an average of 76.2, and that therefore they were still in the process of acquiring their first dialect.[26] Rys concluded (2007: 329): "Our results reveal that the factors that guide second dialect acquisition parallel those that guide the acquisition of a dialect as a first language."

2.3.8   *Language: German/Swiss German; D1 various Swiss German dialects/standard High German; D2 Bernese dialect of Swiss German*

Berthele (2002) conducted a study that examined children's use of the Bernese dialect of Swiss German, as spoken in Fribourg in Switzerland.

Table 2.11 *Percentages of use of D2 (Bernese) variants by seven students*

Student's initial	Percentage of use of Bernese variants
S	93.2
F	92.4
J	87.3
I	86.8
E	80.3
Y	76.6
M	45.7
Average	80.3

In 1996 he interviewed fourteen 9-year-old children in the same class in a primary school. Berthele also observed the children in the classroom and asked them questions in order to determine their patterns of social interaction.

Berthele focused on the use of Bernese variants in eighteen linguistic variables – fourteen concerning vowels (e.g. Bernese lowered vowels), two concerning consonants (e.g. /l/ vocalisation) and two concerning verbal morphology (e.g. diphthongised forms of short verbs) (2002: 333, 343n). (The two consonant variants, as opposed to the others, are not used consistently in the Bernese dialect.) I concentrate on his analysis of the speech of seven students from families who had moved to Fribourg two years earlier from other European countries or other parts of Switzerland. Their D1 upon joining the school was another variety of German – standard High German or the Sense, Basel or Zurich dialect of Swiss German – and they had acquired the Bernese dialect to varying degrees over their two years in the school.

The results showed that all seven of the D2 learners used five of the Bernese vowel variants to a great extent, with percentages of use averaging 98.1 per cent.[27] The other Bernese variants had a greater range of use, with the morphological and consonant variants having the lowest percentages. However, there was a great deal of variation among the seven students, with scores in some cases ranging from 0 to 100 per cent for the same variant. The averages for all the variables combined for each of the seven students are shown in Table 2.11.

It is noteworthy that the averages for the top two students were higher than those of five of the seven students from native Bernese families. Here we see much higher percentages of D2 use than for the children in the Netherlands and Belgium.

2.3.9   Language: Sui; D1 North or South Sandong dialect; D2 South or North Sandong dialect

Stanford (2007, 2008a, 2008b) conducted research among the Sui people of Guizhou Province in southwest China. The Sui language is in a branch of the Tai family, in which Thai and Lao are members. The language is generally thought to have three major dialects, and in each dialect region there are also many different clan dialects. In contrast to some of the other dialects we have looked at, no Sui dialect appears to be more prestigious than another (2007: 20). Like dialects in other parts of the world, they differ from each other in various lexical items and pronunciations of some vowel sounds. However, these dialects also differ in the suprasegmental feature of tone. As described in Chapter 1, tone or pitch is used in some languages to distinguish meaning between words that are otherwise pronounced the same. In the Sui language, every word has a particular tone pattern, and there are at least eight contrasting patterns. The particular tone pattern of a word is indicated by a superscripted number – for example: fa^2 'sheep', fa^3 'cloud' and $lian^3$ 'mosquito', $lian^5$ 'hot pepper' (2007: 74–5). (As the Sui language does not have a writing system, the words are given in IPA.) The dialects differ in the characteristics of some of these tone patterns.

Sui clans have an exogamous marriage system – that is, they must marry a person from outside their own clan. Upon marriage, the wife moves permanently to her husband's village, where a different clan dialect is spoken. Stanford examined the acquisition of the husband's clan dialect by a group of such women.[28] He concentrated on clan dialects in the central Sandong dialect region, specifically what he called the "North" dialect and the "South" dialect (2007: 60). After extensive background research and fieldwork in the period from 1999 to 2004, Stanford recorded a total of forty-four subjects in the North and South clan areas and also in an intermediate "Midlands" area. These included ten women living in the North who had originated in the South, three women living in the South who had originated in the North, and two women in the Midlands who had originated in the South. These fifteen women had lived in their husband's clan dialect area for periods ranging from 9 to 43 years (p. 62). Their ages ranged from 29 to 71. The remaining subjects were men, teenagers and children from the three areas whose recordings served as baseline data with respect to particular dialect features. Other members of the three communities also participated in ethnographic interviews.

In the linguistic interviews, subjects were asked to describe pictures, count, identify objects and actions and provide some free speech (Stanford 2007: 68). Three types of dialect variables (as defined in Chapter 1) were targeted: lexical, phonetic and suprasegmental. The lexical variables were of two types.

The first concerned different words for the same referent – for example: South clan ju^2 versus North clan εj^2 both meaning 'I', and South $qəm^4$ versus North ku^3 'head'. The second type concerned different pronunciations of the same word – for example: South fan^6 versus North $fuən^6$ 'thread' (p. 76). Of special interest were commonly used discourse markers (linguistic expressions inserted in conversation – e.g. in English, the words *well*, *oh* and *you know*). The marker ja^6 is a salient feature of the South dialect, whereas other markers such as tsa^5 are common to both the North and the South.

The two phonetic variables concerned the pronunciation of two diphthongs, designated as (ia) and (ua). In the South dialect, the second element of both diphthongs is [ɑ], so that the pronunciations are [iɑ] and [uɑ]. In the North dialect, the second element is schwa [ə], giving the pronunciations [iə] and [uə] – for example, South/North $mia^1/miə^1$ 'hand' and $lua^5/luə^5$ 'rest' (Stanford 2007: 73).

The suprasegmental variables concerned the pronunciation of two tone patterns, numbers 6 and 1. Pattern 6 has a steady high tone in the South dialect, but a much lower rising tone in the North dialect. Pattern 1 has a low pitch that rises in the South dialect, but a low tone that falls slightly in the North (p. 87). The difference in pattern 6 is striking, but that in pattern 1 is more subtle, and below the level of consciousness for most speakers.

The results of the study showed that overwhelmingly the women did not acquire the clan dialect of their new home, even after living there for nine years or more. Rather, they almost perfectly maintained their original clan dialect. This was true of all lexical, phonetic and suprasegmental variables in both formal and informal speech. The only exception with regard to the lexical and diphthong variants was one woman who spoke a mixed dialect. However, she had an unusual background, having been born in the South clan area but raised by relatives in the North until she was 12 years old. She then moved back to the South, where she stayed for six years until she married and moved back to the North (Stanford 2007: 190). Leaving this speaker aside, and two members of an intermediate midlands clan, there was only one instance of use of a D2 lexical variant out of 566 tokens (0.2 per cent). This apparent lack of acquisition of any lexical features, especially alternative words for particular referents, is especially remarkable in the light of the results of other studies (Chambers 1992; Foreman 2003).

The productions for the two diphthong variables and the two tonal variables were measured acoustically and analysed quantitatively, rather than being categorised as D1 or D2. The analyses are too complex to go into here, but the graphic representations presented by Stanford (2007, 2008a) clearly show that the married women's productions matched those of their original dialect area rather than those of their new home. Again, there was one exception with regard to the tonal variables: one woman from the South lowered the tone in pattern 6 in a way similar to the North dialect. The woman had been married for forty years in the North. This confirmed views expressed by Sui interviewees that while immigrant women do not generally learn the local dialect, in rare cases some long-term residents may acquire some of its features (2007: 188).

2.4   Summary

The overall results of these studies can be seen from two angles: the cup half full and the cup half empty. On the positive side, thirteen out of the seventeen studies reviewed here showed evidence of all the subjects, both adults and children, acquiring at least some linguistic features of the D2. Of the four exceptions the two clearest were Foreman's study in Australia, and Stanford's in China – in which most of the subjects did not use any D2 variants. Thus, both adults and children can acquire features of a second dialect in naturalistic contexts.

On the negative side, those who did acquire D2 features did so to varying degrees, and with different percentages of acquisition for different features. The available average percentages of use of D2 variants are shown in Table 2.12. The last column of the table shows the number of learners who approximated native-like usage for at least some D2 variants. (This was determined either on the basis of the judgement of the author(s) of the study or on the use of the D2 rather than the D1 variant in more than 90 per cent of the tokens of that variable.) The available percentages of acquisition ranged from as low as 0.2 (Stanford in China) to 91.7 (Tagliamonte and Molfenter in England), with a comprehensive average of only 49.6 per cent. Furthermore, in only nine of the seventeen studies did any of the subjects approximate native-like usage for some D2 variants – approximately 63 subjects out of a total number of 486 in all the studies, or approximately 13 per cent. Thus overall, the subjects did not have much success in acquiring a second dialect. Of course, these results are statistically very rough, and do not take into account factors such as age of acquisition and length of residence. (These and other factors are covered in Chapters 4 and 5.)

2.5   Studies of dialect shift

Three additional studies, described below, differ from the seventeen we have just looked at in that they focus on dialect shift or loss. In each of these, subjects had shifted from features of their D1 to use features of one or more other dialects, so SDA must have occurred. Attainment was difficult to determine because it was not always clear which variety or varieties were the target D2.

Table 2.12 *Summary of the results of seventeen SDA studies*

Author	D2	No. of subjects	No. of variables	Average % of use of D2 variants	No. with native-like usage
Wells	London English	36	6	58	0
Payne	Philadelphia English	34	8	–	~17
Shockey	British English	4	2	49.6	0
Chambers	Southern England English	6	7	29.1	1
Tagliamonte and Molfenter	Northeastern England English	3	1	91.7	3
Foreman	Australian English	34	6	5.6	0
Bayard	New Zealand English	1	1	68.3	0[a]
Trudgill	Australian English	2	15	–	2
Kobayashi	Kyoto Japanese	1	1	66.4	0
Bortoni-Ricardo	Standard Brazilian Portuguese	33	4	44.2	0
		13	4	78.8	5
Kerswill	Bergen Norwegian	39	23[b]	35.3[b]	4
Omdal	Kristiansand Norwegian	24	3	47.8	7
Ivars	Eskilstuna Swedish	32	26[c]	~35[c]	0[c]
			4[d]	79[d]	18[d]
Vousten and Bongaerts	Limburg Dutch	38	8	38.2	0
Rys	Maldegem (Belgian) Dutch	164	34	36.4	–
Berthele	Bernese Swiss German	7	18	80.3	6
Stanford	North/South Sui	15	1	0.2[e]	0

Notes: – indicates information not available; ~ indicates approximately.

[a] For R-lessness only.

[b] The morpholexical index only.

[c] Eskilstuna index only.

[d] For lexical variables only.

[e] For four morphological features only.

2.5.1   D1: Upper Saxonia Vernacular (German)

Auer, Barden and Grosskopf (1998) conducted a longitudinal study of dialect shift in Germany. The subjects were fifty-six native speakers of the Upper Saxonian Vernacular (USV), spoken in a part of East Germany – i.e. in the former German Democratic Republic (GDR). Soon after the collapse of the GDR, they settled in West Germany. Each of the subjects, who were aged from 12 to 52 years, was interviewed in standard German (StGer) eight times from 1990 to 1992. A total of twelve variables were examined, concerning nine vowels and three consonants that are distinctive features of the D1 in contrast with StGer. However, it is not clear whether the D2 was StGer or one of the local dialects of the two different regions where the subjects were located. Instead of giving percentages of the use of D2 variants, the study presented percentages of use of D1 variants and of all non-standard dialect variants, which included D1 variants ("strong vernacular" forms) plus other realisations that approximated to but did not match the standard ("weak vernacular" forms).

The overall average use of specifically D1 variants was already low when the study began – 15.1 per cent in the first interview – and it decreased to 9.7 per cent in the eighth interview. Similarly, the use of all non-standard variants decreased from an average of 41.7 per cent to 29.1 per cent.[29] The main purpose of this study, however, was to examine the notion of salience in dialect shift, and this is discussed in Chapter 5.

2.5.2   D1: Ostrobothnia and Savo (Finnish)

Nuolijärvi (1994) studied the abandonment of regional dialect features among people who had migrated to Helsinki as young adults from the Ostrobothnia and Savo areas of Finland in the years 1965 to 1974. Inter-views were conducted in 1982 with forty-eight subjects, twenty-four from each area, each group with twelve men and twelve women. A total of twenty-three linguistic variables were examined – sixteen phonological and seven morphological. Variants were classified as belonging to one of the dialects (D1), to standard (literary) Finnish or to an unmarked colloquial (or Helsinki regional colloquial) variety. However, as one specific variant can belong to several varieties for some variables (p. 156), it is not clear how this classification was made. Nevertheless, the results presented by the author show very low levels of use of D1 features – approximately 6.9 per cent for Ostrobothnia and 4.1 per cent for Savo, i.e. an average of 5.5 per cent.[30] The main purpose of this study, however, was to examine the effect of social factors on the degree of dialect maintenance, as discussed in Chapter 5.

2.5.3   D1: Tôhoku (Japanese)

Hiramoto (in press) described SDA among Japanese immigrants in Hawai'i, where more than 200,000 came as plantation labourers from 1884 to 1924. They originated from four major dialect regions: Chûgoku (western Japanese), Kyûshû, Tôhoku and Okinawa. Chûgoku immigrants were the first to arrive and made up the largest group overall (44.1 per cent). Tôhoku immigrants were the smallest group (8.5 per cent), and typical features of their dialect were highly stigmatised in Hawai'i. Hiramoto examined the speech of fifteen immigrants from the Tôhoku region (six men and nine women) who had come to Hawai'i as young adults in 1899, in 1907 and from 1912 to 1923. The source of data was interviews with the immigrants recorded between 1973 and 1982 by students studying Japanese at the University of Hawai'i.

Hiramoto (in press) looked at seven morphological variables, and classified variants as Tôhoku, Chûgoku or standard Japanese (which became significant in Hawai'i after World War II). Again, classification was sometimes difficult as some variants are characteristic of more than one variety. However, the results show that morphological variants characteristic of only Tôhoku were used approximately 1 per cent of the time, with one exception (approximately 6 per cent). On the other hand, variants characteristic of Chûgoku (and not standard Japanese) were used over 45 per cent of the time. In contrast to morphological variants, phonological features of Tôhoku continued to be used by most of the immigrants – even striking ones such as the pronunciation of /i/ as /u/ after /t/, /s/ or /z/, leading to pronunciations such as [susu] for 'sushi' and [kazu] for /kazi/ 'fire'. This [zu] pronunciation is the origin of the derogatory term for the dialect: *zu-zu ben* '"zu-zu" speech'.

2.6   Some methodological issues

At the beginning of this chapter, I mentioned some methodological problems of scoring and interpreting the performance data. One of the questions was: what is the minimum number of tokens of a variable needed for a decision to be made about acquisition? Although some of the studies cited above are explicit about the number of tokens used, many are not. But it is clear that there is a significant range. For example, Payne (1976) based her conclusions about acquisition on the basis of 3 to 8 tokens of each variable (p. 84), while Rys (2007) had from 128 to 1,028 tokens for each variable (pp. 228–33). These differences must be kept in mind when assessing the validity of the authors' conclusions.

Another crucial factor concerns the linguistic nature of the variables with regard to discreteness. For some variables, the D1 and D2 variants are clearly distinct – for example, when there are different lexical forms for the same referent, such as *jumper* versus *sweater*. In such cases it is easy to determine whether or not the target D2 variant is being used. Similarly, when a phonetic variable involves a consonant – for example, in t/d flapping – the variants are discrete and relatively easy to distinguish from each other. However, when vowels are involved, the variants often have only slight differences in pronunciation mostly due to tongue position – higher or lower in the mouth, or more to the front or the back. These differences are not discrete, but vary along a continuum. For such non-discrete variants, the human ear is often inadequate, and techniques from acoustic phonetics need to be used. For example, a spectrographic analysis of the vowel produced by the subject can be compared to spectrographic analyses of those produced by both D2 speakers and D1 speakers who have not migrated. Such techniques were employed for some variables by Payne (1976), Kerswill (1994), Foreman (2003), Rys (2007) and Stanford (2007).

In cases where the differences between variants are not discrete, the question arises as to how close to the target D2 variant the subject's pronunciation has to be to be counted as an instance of the use of the D2 variant. Again, this was not made clear in most of the studies. And where it was made clear, there were some significant differences in interpretation. For example, Foreman (2003: 123) noted that many of the subjects in her Australian study did not quite hit the target sound, and produced a sound part way between NAE and AusE, or they sometimes "over-shot the target" and produced a slightly exaggerated version of the AusE sound. In her analysis, Foreman treated changes from NAE norms that were in the direction of AusE as tokens of acquisition of an AusE variant. In other words, if the sound could be considered as the result of aiming at an AusE target, it was counted as AusE – for example, if a subject raised the KIT vowel, but it was not exactly the same pronunciation as in AusE. In contrast, Rys (2007) used a different means of interpretation for vowels that were not discrete to transcribers. The acoustic properties of the two variants were precisely measured (in terms of sound wave frequency, calibrated in hertz). An average for the D2 variant was calculated and an acceptable range was determined, allowing for slight deviations above or below the average. In order to be counted as use of the D2 variant, the learner's pronunciation had to fall within this range. Kerswill (1994) took a different approach for his examination of schwa-lowering in Norway, rating speakers' productions along a vowel height continuum rather than deciding whether or not they should be counted as reaching a D2 target.

Consequently, we need to keep in mind the fact that different studies used different criteria for acquisition. Furthermore, we need to explore two other facts revealed by these studies. First, some learners appear to acquire some D2 features but not others. Second, some learners produce linguistic forms that are not found in their D1 but are not in the D2 either. These issues are considered in the following chapter.

3   Acquiring a second dialect

This chapter looks at some of the phenomena involved in acquiring a new dialect and ways of examining them, based on the studies described in Chapter 2 and other research as well. First, I give an explanation for the ways that dialect acquirers are perceived by both D2 and D1 speakers. Then, after talking about imitation, I describe two types of SDA, replacive and additive. In the section that follows I discuss various approaches used to examine SDA.

3.1   Perceptions of dialect acquirers

In Chapter 1, I mentioned my own experience of always being recognised as an American in Australia but being told I have a British accent when I'm in America. Shockey (1984: 87) also commented that her American subjects in England "sounded like Americans to British ears and like British people to Americans". Chambers (1992: 695n) made similar observations:

Dialect acquirers ... invariably discover when they revisit their old homes that their dialect is now perceived as "foreign", yet their neighbors in their new homes also perceive their speech as "non-native". Immigrants, often to their bafflement, come to sound less like the people in the old region without sounding quite like the people in the new region. The old dialect and the new one are not the converse of one another, but poles on a continuum.

The first part of this chapter explains some of the reasons for this "double foreignness".

3.1.1   Factors contributing to non-nativeness in the D2

First, let's look at why dialect acquirers continue to be perceived as "non-native". The most obvious reason was presented in the preceding chapter – the fact that most acquirers do not come close to using D2 variants consistently. But there are other factors as well. One is that acquirers may learn D2 variants for some variables, but continue to use D1 variants for others. We saw this in Foreman's (2003) study with North Americans in Australia: of the twelve subjects who changed their speech in the direction of Australian English, only six did so for all six of the variables that were examined. The others did so only for various combinations of from two to five of the variables. This means that they retained 100 per cent use of their D1 variants for one to four of the variables.

In research in the USA, Bowie (2000) looked at changes that took place in people's dialect when they moved to other dialect areas. Bowie's main subjects were thirteen people (six males and seven females) who had grown up in the Waldorf area of Maryland and moved away as adults (the "Waldorf exiles") (p. 35). Their speech was recorded in interviews conducted between 1997 and 1999, making use of formal language routines (e.g. reading word lists), as well as sociolinguistic interviews to elicit informal speech. They were all in their twenties or early thirties (born between 1965 and 1980), and had spent from 2 to 14 years away from Waldorf, in various places around the United States (and in one case, Canada). The vowels in their speech were compared to those of eleven people who had not left Waldorf ("lifelong Waldorfians") – six males and five females of equivalent ages.

The analysis showed that the exiles maintained most of their Waldorf vowels. For example, /ɪ/ as in KIT and /ɛ/ as in DRESS did not change for speakers who lived in regions where these sounds are pronounced with off-glides, no matter how long they had been away from Waldorf. And the /ʌ/ vowel (as in STRUT), pronounced a bit low and back of centre by lifelong Waldorfians, continued to be pronounced this way by the exiles (Bowie 2000: 60).

However, a few changes did take place, and these led Bowie to use the term "hybridized dialects" (p. iv) to refer to the speech of some of the exiles. This also raises the question of why speakers in new dialect environments change some of their vowels and not others, and whether or not some vowels are easier to change than others. (These questions are considered in Chapter 4 and 5.) Nevertheless, the continued use of D1 features would clearly mark a person as being a non-native speaker of the D2. The use of particular D1 features may also mark a person as being not only non-native but specifically as being from the region where that D1 is spoken. This matter is discussed below.

Furthermore, even if dialect acquirers change all their D1 variants to be more like the D2 and use these D2-like variants consistently, they still may be perceived as non-native. As we also saw in Foreman's (2003) study, subjects often "did not quite hit the target", and not all tokens classified as AusE would have "sounded like archetypal AusE pronunciations to a native AusE speakers' ear" (p. 123). This was because speakers in this study and others produced sounds part way between those of the D1 and D2. For example, Foreman (2003: 122) observed that some of her subjects' realisations of the GOAT diphthong were equidistant between the NAE and the AusE norms. Also, Bayard's (1995) son pronounced the vowel in TRAP as a raised [æ], higher than the vowel in NAE, but lower than the lowered [e] pronunciation of NZE.

Table 3.1 *Intermediate forms produced by learners of the Limburg dialect*

	Limburg dialect	Standard Dutch	Intermediate form
Infinitive	kuəp-	koːp-	
2nd person singular	kɔpt	koːpt	kuəpt
3rd person singular	kœpt	koːpt	kuəpt

A similar phenomenon was reported in the USA, in another study of the acquisition of Philadelphia English. Conn and Horesh (2002) examined two of the variables studied by Payne (1976), (ow) and (æ), with two subjects – a man and a woman, who had moved as young adults from Michigan to Philadelphia and had lived there for approximately twenty years. The researchers performed an acoustic analysis of the production of these variables by these subjects and then compared their productions to those of two groups of speakers of corresponding age, gender and ethnicity – one group being native speakers of the D1 who had stayed in Michigan and the other native speakers of the D2 in Philadelphia. The results showed that both subjects had changed their pronunciation in the direction of the Philadelphia dialect but each only with one of the variables – the man with (ow) and the woman with (æ). However, in both cases the subject had developed a pattern different from the patterns of both the Michigan and Philadelphia dialects. In dialectology, varieties that contain such intermediate, compromise phonetic forms are called "fudged dialects" (Chambers and Trudgill 1980). Here I refer to them as "intermediate forms".

Intermediate forms are not restricted to sounds. For example, Vousten and Bongaerts (1995: 306) reported some compromise morphemes produced by learners of the Limburg dialect in the Netherlands (and by some native speakers as well). Table 3.1 shows such intermediate forms for subject–verb agreement, mentioned in Chapter 2, for the verb *kopen* 'buy'.

Another example comes from Hiramoto's (in press) study of Japanese dialects in Hawai'i. Some speakers produced the intermediate form *dakê* for the conjunction that is *dakara* in the Tôhoku dialect and standard Japanese and *jakê* in the Chûgoku dialect.

Such intermediate forms, found in neither the D1 or the D2, are instances of what Trudgill (1986) called "interdialect". This term is based on "interlanguage" (Selinker 1972), the name for the temporary linguistic system that second language learners develop that is somewhere between the L1 and the L2.

Other examples of interdialect have been labelled "hyperadaptation" by Wells (1973: 30) and "hyperdialectalism" by Trudgill (1986: 66). These are the result of what is called overgeneralisation in SLA, or hypercorrection in sociolinguistics. An example would be if an American trying to speak

Southern England English pronounced *gas* as [gɑːs] rather than its actual SEE pronunciation [gæs], which is the same as in AmE. This would be a consequence of the American having learned about words such as *class* and *pass* being pronounced with /ɑ/ as in PALM in SEE instead of /æ/ as in TRAP as in AmE (the TRAP–BATH split), and then overgeneralising this pronunciation to *gas*.

In the studies reviewed in Chapter 2, there are several reports of such overgeneralisation. One concerned the (eə) variable examined by Wells (1973), relating to the vowels in pairs of words such as *fear/fair* and *beer/ bear*. Recall that in Jamaican English, the same vowel occurs in both words in the pairs: [ɪɛ] or [ɛː], sometimes followed by an /r/, so that the Jamaican English (JE) pronunciation [bɪɛ] could mean 'beer' or 'bear'. In London English (LE) there are two separate vowels [iə] and [ɛə] – for example, [biə] 'beer' and [bɛə] 'bear'. For JE speakers, the biggest task with regard to this variable was changing their pronunciations of the vowel in words such as *fare*, *bear*, *hair* and *air* to [ɛə] to be distinct from that in *fear*, *beer*, *hear* and *ear*. However, some speakers overgeneralised this change to the other word in the pair – for example, pronouncing *beer* as *bear* and *hear* as *hair*.

Tagliamonte and Molfenter (2007) also reported overgeneralisation in their examination of the loss of T-Voicing in the Canadian children in northeastern England. Recall that in CanE, words in pairs such as *putting/pudding* and *writer/rider* are pronounced the same as a result of T-Voicing, and the children had to learn to pronounce the medial *t* as /t/ rather than /d/. In one example, *spider* was pronounced with a /t/ instead of a /d/ (p. 660).

Interdialect forms due to overgeneralisation have also been reported in studies in which the D2 is a lower prestige creole or social dialect – specifically, Jamaican Creole and African American English (AAE). Although these varieties have low prestige in mainstream society, they may have higher prestige within a smaller social group, as a marker of being a member of that group, or as an emblem of rejecting another group (and their speech). This is known as "covert prestige".

Sebba (1993) studied young, second generation Caribbean immigrants in London, the children of the first generation, studied by Wells (1973), who had learned London English (LE) as a D2. While this second generation were native speakers of LE, many of them ironically learned their parents' original variety, Jamaican Creole, as a language of solidarity. This "London Jamaican" was also acquired by young White Londoners. Sebba observed that his subjects did not really speak London Jamaican (LJ) consistently as a D2, but rather added some lexical, phonological or grammatical features from the Creole to their normal LE (p. 48). Different speakers varied in the number of Creole features they used, and for all speakers, the features were used inconsistently along with LE features. Sebba also observed many instances of what he called "misadaptation" (p. 52) – i.e. overgeneralisation creating a form not found in either dialect. An example was the pronunciation of *law* with a final /r/, following the pattern of some words that are pronounced with a final /r/ in Jamaican Creole but not LE, such as *sore* /so:r/ (p. 54).

African American English (AAE) is a clear example of a variety with covert prestige, and also some overt prestige among young people in general, with the popularity of rap and hip hop music (see Chapter 6, Section 6.3.2, for further discussion). Baugh (1992) analysed the speech of Whites attempting to speak AAE and African Americans whose first dialect was standard English but who were trying to learn AAE as a D2. Some examples illustrate the phenomenon of what Baugh called "hypocorrection" – "linguistic over-compensation beyond the nonstandard linguistic target" (p. 317) – for example:

> They **dones** blow them brothers away. (Baugh 1992: 322)

In AAE -*s* can occur with the habitual *be* before a verb as in *He be(s) running*, but not with the completive *done*.[1]

A final type of interdialect results from what is called "simplification" in SLA. This is manifested in reduction of grammatical distinctions or the regularisation of paradigms. An example from Chapter 2 is found in the study of the acquisition of the Limburg dialect by speakers of standard Dutch (Section 2.3.6). Instead of using the separate 2nd and 3rd person forms for certain verbs, some learners used the same form for both.

Thus, as a consequence of incomplete SDA, learners will often use phonological or morphological interdialect forms – intermediate, overgeneralised or simplified. These would sound not quite right to a native speaker of the D2 and clearly identify the user as a non-native.

3.1.2   Foreignness in the D1

Now we turn to the case of dialect acquirers who are then perceived as "foreign" by members of their original dialect community. Evidence of this can be found in an article describing several experiments conducted by Munro, Derwing and Flege (1999). The participants were three groups of ten speakers, each consisting of five males and five females between 20 and 46 years of age. The first group were born and raised in Canada, and living in Edmonton (the CiC group). The second group were Canadians who had taken up residence in Birmingham, Alabama, in the USA, after living in Canada at least up to the age of 18 years (the CiA group). They had lived in the USA for a range of 1 to 23 years, with a mean of 7.7 years (p. 389). The third group were Americans who had grown up and remained in Alabama (the AiA group). The participants were recorded describing in a narrative fashion the events depicted in a cartoon. The speech samples were then digitalised and stored on a disk so that they could be played in random order to listeners.

In one experiment, twenty-seven undergraduate students at the University of Alabama at Birmingham were asked to listen to the speech samples and rate each one on a nine-point scale, ranging from "definitely from Alabama" (1) to "definitely not from Alabama" (9). The results were that the CiA group showed an intermediate distribution of scores with a mean of 5.8 compared to 7.4 for the CiC group and 3.0 for the AiA group. However, there were individual differences within the CiA group, with one Canadian speaker rated as sounding as though he was more definitely from Alabama than two native Alabamans. But on the whole, the Canadian immigrants were rated as sounding more non-Alabaman than Alabaman. Of course, this would be expected following the discussion above.

In another experiment, of more relevance here, a group of twenty-two native Canadian residents in Edmonton were also asked to evaluate each of the speech samples on a nine-point scale, this time ranging from "very Canadian" (1) to "very American" (9) (Munro et al. 1999: 390). The results were similar to those in the other experiment in that the Canadians living in Alabama (CiA) were generally given ratings intermediate between those of the Canadians recorded in Canada (CiC) and the Alabamans (AiA). The mean ratings were 4.0 for the CiA group as opposed to 2.1 for the CiC group and 7.6 for the AiA group. Again, there were individual differences, with one speaker from the CiA group receiving a mean rating of 6.7, higher than that of three speakers from the AiA group. But the important finding here was that on the whole, the Canadians living in America (the CiA group) were rated as more American than the Canadians living in Canada. The authors stated that most speakers in the CiA group had acquired an "intermediate variety" (p. 394).

In Munro et al.'s study, dialect acquirers were recorded in their new dialect area. More surprising, however, is the observation that when acquirers go back to their original dialect area, they are also judged as sounding foreign. The most likely explanation for this is that the acquirers do not switch back to their D1 but use their new hybridised dialects, which include both D1 and D2 features, as well as interdialect features. Thus, for example, if the two subjects in Conn and Horesh's (2002) study described above went from Philadelphia back to Michigan for a visit, they would continue to use their intermediate pronunciations for the (ow) and (æ) variables, and these would sound just as foreign or non-native to the Michiganers as to the Philadelphians. The reasons for this are explored in Secton 3.3.

3.1.3   Linguistic markers and stereotypes

In cases of mixed or intermediate dialects, where speakers have acquired some features of the D2 while retaining some features of the L1, a further question arises regarding the perceptions of their "double foreignness": why do listeners from the D2 dialect area focus on the unacquired D2 features or persisting D1 features, and listeners from the D1 area on the acquired D2 features?

The answer to this question has two parts. First, many people without linguistic training appear to be sensitive to forms of speech that are different from their own. In some cases, they can identify dialect differences fairly accurately. For example, Preston (1996: 320–2) reported on a study concerning varieties of American English recorded in nine different sites on a north–south axis, from Michigan to Alabama. The recordings were played in random order to American respondents (non-linguists) from Michigan and Indiana who were asked to associate each recording with a particular site. The results showed high accuracy in arranging the samples along the north–south dimension, with only one site out of order for each group. Other studies, however, show lower accuracy rates of from 24 to 52 per cent (see the summary in Clopper and Pisoni 2006), but these were for identification of particular dialects rather than recognition of differences.

Second, it appears that many people tend to notice, either unconsciously or consciously, certain linguistic features that are associated with the speech of a particular region or ethnic group. Such features are often called either "markers" or "stereotypes" (Labov 1972: 178–80). A marker may be noticed, but not consciously identified. For example, if an American non-linguist hears someone say *That's an old boat*, and thinks "That guy sounds British", it is probably because of the GOAT diphthong in *old* and *boat*. The [əʊ] rather than [oʊ] pronunciation of this diphthong is a marker of British English, and that is why the speaker sounded British, even though the hearer may not be consciously aware of this particular feature.

In contrast, a stereotype is a feature that people are consciously aware of and one that they may even talk about or mimic. For example, when I went to university at Cornell in upper New York state, the other students, who were mostly from east coast cities, used to tease me about my Midwestern accent. But there was one feature of my dialect that was frequently the target: often referred to as "flat A's". This is the pronunciation of the TRAP vowel /æ/ as the diphthong [ɛə]. Some readers might remember this as the tense short-*a* pronunciation described with regard to Philadelphia English (see Section 2.2.2 above). While the tense short-*a* occurs in some words in east coast dialects (e.g. in New York City as well as Philadelphia), it is only in some words, and never in words such as *fat, tax, cap, have, bath* and *patch*. But in the Chicago dialect (and the dialects of other northern inland American cities around the Great Lakes), all words with /æ/ are pronounced with the tense short-*a* [ɛə], and it is a stereotypical feature of these dialects. Thus the east coast students were well aware of this feature, and often made fun of it, mimicking my pronunciation of words such as *fat* and *tax* as "fe-at" and "te-ax". It seems, however, that I might get the last laugh (or the "le-ast le-aff"), as this feature has been spreading to more and more areas of northern USA (Labov 2001).

For many Australians, non-prevocalic /r/ is a marker of American English, and for some a stereotype. So when I use it in my current speech (which is most of the time, since I have not been able to suppress it), people know straight away that I'm from America. For Americans, the use of the /ɑ/ vowel (as in PALM) in words such as *half* and *bath* is a marker of British English (not Australian English, which most Americans are not that familiar with). But it is not a stereotype. Nevertheless, when I use that vowel in America, people think I've got a bit of a British accent. Along similar lines, Bayard (1995) noted that his son's accent was definitely "American-coloured" to New Zealanders' ears – again most probably because of his use of non-prevocalic /r/ – but his relatives in North America were emphatic that he did not "talk American" (p. 16). Bayard suspected that this was because of his use of NZE vowels in LOT, GOAT and GOOSE, which are markers of dialects other than American English.

Some evidence that people focus on particular linguistic markers or stereotypes when judging a speaker's dialect comes from a third experiment done by Munro *et al.* (1999) on the same three groups of speakers (Canadians in Canada, Canadians in Alabama, and Alabamans in Alabama). This experiment aimed to identify the acoustic differences that listeners used in the first two experiments (described above) to rate speakers as belonging to different dialect groups. One of the features examined was the pronunciation of the /aɪ/ diphthong (as in PRICE). As we have seen many times already, in Canadian English, this diphthong is pronounced as [ʌɪ] before voiceless consonants, in words such as *wife*, *like* and *rifle*, as the result of Canadian raising. In the Southern English of Alabama, this diphthong is often pronounced as a monophthong [a], especially when it occurs at the end of a word such as *I* and *goodbye*, or before a voiced sound, as in *driving* and *highway*. The authors isolated the words *wife*, *like*, *rifle*, *highway*, *driving* and *goodbye* from the recordings of the three groups, and recruited two phonetically trained Canadian listeners to rate sets of words from each group on a scale from "very American" to "very Canadian". The patterns of ratings were "remarkably similar" to those of the two untrained listener groups in the first two experiments (p. 399). This was taken as evidence that the differences in this feature may have been used by the untrained listeners as a basis for their ratings. The authors concluded that "linguistically unsophisticated judges" can "easily recognise different degrees of second dialect acquisition, even when they are presented with short samples ... of speech" (p. 401).

Munro *et al.* (1999: 401) also observed that listeners are "sensitive to partially acquired dialects of native speakers of English, whether the listeners themselves are speakers of the talkers' D1 or D2". However, while this may be true to some extent, it appears that speakers of the D2 are normally more sensitive to the partial acquisition of their dialect than are speakers of the D1. In an example from my own experience, there was a linguist in Australia who I noticed spoke with an accent that was not quite Australian. One day I asked my wife, a native speaker of Australian English, where she thought he was from. She said surprisedly: "He's American. Everyone knows that." (I talk more about this sensitivity to non-nativeness in Chapter 6.)

3.2   Imitation

The use of features of another dialect is not always an indication of acquisition. People will often try to imitate a dialect for various purposes – such as putting on an Irish accent when telling a joke. As an example, Rampton (1995) described British adolescents' use of South Asian English for joking and ridiculing racist attitudes. However, when such imitation occurs, the focus is usually on only the few stereotypical features that the imitator is aware of.

Often the imitation of stereotypes is not accurate either – for example, the way my fellow students at Cornell mimicked the pronunciation of the diphthong [ɛə] in words such as *fat*. Another example concerns the New York City pronunciation of the *ir/er* sound in words such a *bird*, *shirt* and *herd* as the diphthong [əɪ]. Although not very common now, it was once a stereotype of lower-class New York City speech, and often mimicked or imitated in jokes. However, as this phoneme does not occur in most other American dialects, it was most often interpreted as being a similar-sounding existing phoneme, the diphthong /ɔɪ/ as in CHOICE. As a result, there were many jokes about New Yorkers saying "New Joisey" (New Jersey) or "Thoidy-thoid Street" (Thirty-third Street). Of course, this kind of stereotyping is more of a caricature than an accurate imitation.

On the other hand, there is evidence that some people can imitate the production of another dialect so skilfully that they are not perceived as non-native, even by native speakers of that dialect. For example, Markham (1997) conducted an experiment in Sweden in which eight speakers, all with some formal training in phonetics, imitated various regional dialects of Swedish. They did so in two texts, one which they prepared themselves and practised, and another which they were given by Markham and did not practise. These imitations were recorded and mixed together with recordings of similar texts from native speakers of the dialects. The recordings were then judged by eight listeners, all linguists or phoneticians, and including some native speakers of one of the dialects being imitated. They were asked to identify the dialect, and indicate whether they thought it was pure (i.e. without the influence of another dialect) and whether it was natural or an imitation. Three of the speakers produced some imitations that were judged as pure and natural by seven or eight of the listeners, including native speakers (pp. 244–5).[2]

Some actors are also very good at imitating dialects other than their own. Various internet sites and blogs list film and television performers who can produce convincing American or British accents even though they are not native speakers of these dialects. For example, one Press TV Blogger (Davenport 2008) lists Australians Anthony LaPaglia and Rachel Griffiths among "actors who make believable Americans". On another website, the *Boston Globe*'s television critic (Gilbert 2008) gives the British actor Hugh Laurie a grade of A+ for his performances in the series *House*, commenting: "He does East coast acerbic better than real East Coast acerbics." An Australian site (9News 2006) relates the following story about this actor:

Americans probably don't realise just how many TV actors they watch every week are also from Down Under or across the pond. Some sound so genuinely homegrown that people don't even realise the actors are not US born and raised. And even those in the industry can be fooled about this. David Shore, creator of the hit series *House*, has told the story of how, after watching the audition tape of Oxford-born star Hugh Laurie, executive producer Bryan Singer said: "See, this is what I want: an American guy."

Laurie, a household name in Britain since 1980, was not as well known in the US, except to fans of his British series *Blackadder*. The confusion over his nationality was played up during last year's Emmy Award telecast. When Laurie began speaking in his real voice, co-presenter Zach Braff said: "I didn't realise we were doing British accents."

"Well, we're not. I'm British; it's the way I talk," Laurie protested.

Furthermore, unlike many actors who learn to use other dialects with the help of dialect coaches (see Chapter 8), Laurie has reportedly learned American English on his own.

But no matter how good actors are at producing another dialect in a film or television series, they have not actually acquired that dialect. What we see and hear is a performance – that is, imitation of a dialect that they are familiar with rather than linguistic proficiency in this dialect. Thus, Markham (1997: 244–5) pointed out that his three successful speakers produced "almost unanimously convincing imitations of dialects which they had never *acquired*, but which they had been exposed to for at least a few years" (emphasis in original). Because successful imitators have not actually acquired the dialect, they do not use it in their normal speech, as with Hugh Laurie at the Emmy Awards. While imitation may be a first step towards acquisition for some people (as discussed below), actors' aims are normally not to acquire the dialect, but to use it for a performance, and therefore they would have difficulty sustaining use of the dialect outside their performances.[3]

In fact, some actors have difficulty sustaining their dialect imitations even through the duration of their performances. A classic example is Kevin Costner's performance in the film *Robin Hood: Prince of Thieves* (1991).

He starts off with a kind of British English but slips back into American English as the film progresses. Another website (TV Tropes Wiki 2008) lists dozens of other examples from television and films.

There are even more websites and blogs listing performers with dreadful dialect imitations (e.g. BBC News 2003; Nelson 2007). In addition to Kevin Costner, Sean Connery is often listed (e.g. for his role as an Irish cop in *The Untouchables* [1987]). But the prize winner for the worst imitation appears to be Dick Van Dyke for his interpretation of Cockney in *Mary Poppins* (1964). Wikipedia also mentions the whole film *Brassed Off* as "an infamous example of a poor imitation of the Yorkshire dialect and accent".[4] It is clear from these websites that bad imitations of dialects are irritating, especially to native speakers of these dialects.

In my own experience, many years ago I went to a performance in Sydney of American playwright Sam Shepard's work *A Lie of the Mind*, in which the Australian actors attempted to use American English. My Australia-born companions enjoyed the performance, but as a native speaker of American English, I cringed all the way through it. Similarly, many Australians hated Meryl Streep's attempt at Australian English in the film *Evil Angels* (1988) (titled *A Cry in the Dark* outside Australia).[5] I have more to say about negative reactions to imitations of dialects in Chapter 6.

It should be noted, however, that even a perfect imitation is often recognised by native speakers as being "non-native". For example, one of the listeners in Markham's (1997) study judged a reading in the Stockholm dialect to be an imitation because it was "too perfectly" Stockholm (p. 236). A more famous example comes from George Bernard Shaw's play *Pygmalion* (1916), which was adapted into the musical *My Fair Lady*. After Professor Higgins has taught Eliza Doolittle to speak RP (upper-class standard spoken British English), a character who meets her says that she speaks English "too perfectly", and reckons she is Hungarian.

3.3   Replacive versus additive SDA

Later in *Pygmalion*, Eliza says to Higgins: "I have forgotten my own language, and can speak nothing but yours." This statement brings us back to the issue of changes that occur in the acquirer's original dialect. From the discussion in Section 3.1.2 above, it appears that in SDA some acquirers change their original dialect in the direction of the D2, rather than adding an additional dialect to their repertoires. We can call this "replacive" (or "subtractive") SDA. This does not normally happen in SLA; for example, English speakers acquiring French do not change their pronunciation of English in the direction of French. Thus, while my family in the USA have commented that I speak with a bit of a British accent since living in Australia, they have never said anything about me speaking with an Indian accent since living in Fiji and India, where I learned Hindi. The difference is that in SLA, the learner normally maintains the L1 and acquires a new, separate linguistic system, with the possibility of eventual bilingualism. However, in replacive SDA, rather than maintaining the D1 and learning a new separate D2, the D1 is modified so that there is still only one system. So in other words, SDA may lead to dialect change or dialect shift in individuals, rather than to bidialectalism – as shown in the studies done in Germany, Finland and Hawai'i, described in Section 2.5 of the preceding chapter.

Some of the other studies that we have looked at describe SDA in these terms as well. Payne (1976: 104) observed that acquisition of some D2 features required "structural change" – that is, change in the mental lexicon. For example, words that were in separate classes with regard to pronunciation in the acquirers' D1 – such as *lure*, *sure* and *moor* versus *lore*, *shore* and *more* – were now in the same class in their acquired Philadelphia dialect. Bowie (2000) described another example of restructuring with regard to one phonological change that occurred among the Waldorf exiles. In the Waldorf dialect, the diphthong /eɪ/ (as in FACE) is pronounced differently depending on whether it is word-internal (e.g. in *great*) or word-final (e.g. in *play*), where it is pronounced further back. This distinction was lost for individuals who had lived away from Waldorf for more than ten years. Bowie concluded (p. 113) that this pointed to "geographic mobility having a clear effect on the structure of the phonological system". Chambers (1992) discussed SDA in terms of not only acquiring new phonological rules but also "eliminating old rules" from speakers' phonologies (p. 695). However, in the case of the lexicon, he noted (p. 693): "The new lexical items do not eradicate the old ones but can co-exist beside them in the mental lexicon." Thus, some linguistic aspects of the D1 may be restructured, while others are maintained (see below).

Especially with regard to phonology, several researchers see the process of SDA as not acquiring the linguistic features of a new variety, but learning rules to convert the D1 into the D2. Wells (1973: 30–1) called these "adaptation rules", and said that the learner does not approach the D2 as "something to be learnt from scratch", but rather "ADAPTS his existing phonology to fit the new situation" (emphasis in original). For example, a Jamaican learner of London English would learn an adaptation rule that changes the Jamaican English vowel /o/ to London English /ɔː/ in words such as *church*, *shirt* and *bird*. Rys and Bonte (2006: 204) used the term "correspondence rules", following Auer (1993), and assumed that the formation of such rules "is the basic learning strategy of second dialect learners". What is not clear from these viewpoints is whether these rules are used only for switching between the D1 and the D2 or for modifying the D1 to become like the D2.

In addition to the observations that dialect acquirers sound foreign when they return to their original dialect areas, there is other evidence that correspondence rules may lead to modification of the original system rather than to the development of two separate linguistic systems. For example, Tagliamonte and Molfenter (2007: 673) reported that when the children in their study returned to Canada, they did not simply go back to using Canadian English, but retained features of British English. They noted that "the second dialect, once in place, leaves an indelible imprint on the transported individual". Earlier, Labov (1972: 215) noted the difficulty of finding informants who were truly bidialectal in African American English and a standard variety of English:

> We have not encountered any nonstandard speakers who gained good control of a standard language, and still retained control of a nonstandard vernacular ... [A]lthough the speaker may indeed appear to be speaking the vernacular, close examination of his speech shows that his grammar has been heavily influenced by the standard.

The fact that modification rather than retention of the D1 may occur in D2 acquisition explains the difficulty some people have in switching from one dialect to another – for example, the trouble I had with dialects of Hindi and dialects of Melanesian Pidgin (as mentioned in Chapter 1).

This is not to say, however, that SDA is always replacive. In some cases it is clearly additive. For example, in his study in Switzerland (Section 2.3.8 above), Berthele (2002) reported that one of the seven children became bidialectal, acquiring the D2 (the Bernese dialect) like a native speaker but maintaining her D1 (the Zurich dialect) in the family context (p. 335). There are also many reports in the literature of subjects who can code-switch between dialects, even (as opposed to Labov's findings) between non-standard and standard ones – for example, in Norway (Blom and Gumperz 1972), the Netherlands (Giesbers 1989), Italy (Giacalone-Ramat 1995) and Belgium (Vandekerckhove 1998).

Furthermore, in contrast to the results presented by Tagliamonte and Molfenter (2007) and other researchers, at least two other studies have described young children becoming bidialectal – e.g. using their D1 with their parents and the D2 with their peers. The 8-year-old Japanese child in Kobayashi's (1981) study (Section 2.3.1 above) had maintained both her D1 (the Tokyo dialect) and her D2 (the Kyoto dialect).[6] In another study, Dyer (2004) gave an account of her son who was born in the USA but learned her British dialect as his D1, and later acquired American English as his D2. Although he initially mixed the two dialects, by the time he was 5 years old, he could separate them and use them with different people in different contexts.[7] Bayard's study of his son acquiring NZE (Section 2.2.7 above) presented a somewhat different picture – one of semi-bidialectalism. For

pronunciation of the verbal prefix *tse-* from /tsə/ to /tsʊ/. This was unexpected, however, because the suffix is /tsə/ in both BesY and StY, but /tsʊ/ in another regional dialect, Northeastern Yiddish (NEY), which is highly stigmatised. On the other hand, the pronunciations of many of the vowels in this dialect are the same as those of StY, unlike the vowel pronunciations of other dialects such as BesY. Prince argued (1988: 315) that the singer was acquiring StY by accommodating to StY speakers, and that the particular group of StY speakers that she accommodated to were those who had NEY as their D1. This was because with regard to the vowels that the singer was targeting, NEY speakers of StY used standard pronunciations, unlike speakers of other dialects who often used non-standard vowel variants from their D1. However, NEY speakers of StY also sometimes used the non-standard variant of *tse-* from their D1 (i.e. /tsʊ/). This was misinterpreted by the singer as standard and therefore adopted as well.

Trudgill (1986) proposed two kinds of accommodation: short-term (or transitory) and long-term, where repeated short-term accommodations become permanent. According to Trudgill, while speakers normally accommodate to others within their speech community, they can also accommodate to speakers from another community – for example, to those speaking a different regional dialect. Thus, when speakers move to a new dialect area, they may adjust their speech to be more like those around them, and if these accommodations are frequent enough, then they "may become a permanent part of a speaker's accent or dialect, even replacing original features" (p. 40). Trudgill also used the term "dialect acquisition" to refer to this process (p. 16).

Chambers (1992: 675) tried to distinguish between accommodation and acquisition, saying that long-term accommodation appears to be "a sort of basic level of dialect adjustment maintained by the individual in all transactions in the contact area", whereas acquisition is "nonephemeral" (p. 675) and "irrepressible" (p. 676). However, his conclusion was (p. 676): "The distinction between long-term accommodation and dialect acquisition may, with further research, prove to be terminological rather than substantive."

With regard to the results of long-term accommodation and dialect acquisition, I agree there is little distinction. First of all, similar phenomena occur in each. For example, as we have seen, Trudgill's concept of "interdialect" is modelled on "interlanguage" in SLA, and hyperdialectalism and hypercorrection are basically the same as overgeneralisation. Second, many of the findings in the studies described in Chapter 2 that are attributed to long-term accommodation are similar to those in studies of SLA. This is especially true with regard to the effects of both individual factors such as age of acquisition and linguistic factors such as phonological versus morphosyntactic features, both described in detail in Chapter 4.

On the other hand, I do not believe that the terms are equivalent, because long-term accommodation assumes that the social psychological phenomenon of accommodation is the main impetus for the use of features from another dialect. In other words, individual short-term accommodation is always the precursor of long-term accommodation, and if the terms are equivalent, of SDA. However, there are several problems with this assumption.

One of the problems was pointed out by Trudgill himself (1986: 40–1). If accommodation is responsible for dialect acquisition, there must be face-to-face interaction between speakers of the D1 and the D2. However, in some cases, especially concerning acquisition of lexical items and idioms, there is often no evidence of such interaction. And although Prince (1988) argued that the Yiddish singer she studied shifted from her D1 as a result of accommodation in interaction with D2 speakers, she also observed (p. 307) that "a speaker could conceivably undergo dialect shift without ever interacting with a speaker of the target dialect, i.e. without having someone co-present to accommodate to".

Another problem, as Foreman (2003: 27) pointed out, is that the assumption that dialect acquisition is the result of accommodation has been made without testing to see whether speakers involved actually adjust their speech according to the audience involved. In at least two studies, however, there is evidence that speakers do not do so. Chambers (1992: 676) noted that in the interviews for his study, the Canadian youths who had acquired some features of Southern England English did not accommodate to his Canadian English. In Foreman's (2003) study, recall that one part of the interview was conducted by the Canadian author, and the other by an Australian woman of approximately the same age. If accommodation were occurring, one would expect a greater percentage of use of NAE variants with the Canadian interviewer and of AusE variants with the Australian interviewer. However, there was no significant difference, even among those subjects who had acquired some AusE features (p. 231).

A study within the CAT paradigm also throws some doubt on its relevance to SDA. Giles and Smith (1979) recorded a Canadian male reciting eight versions of the same passage. In seven of these he converged towards London English in either one or two of the following dimensions: pronunciation, speech rate and content. These were rated by twenty-eight London English-speaking teachers taking evening classes at a polytechnic school. There were five 9-point rating scales for attributes such as the effectiveness of the communication, the attitude of the speaker towards the audience and how likeable the speaker was. The results were that the ratings were most favourable when there was a combination of convergence in speech rate and content, but when pronunciation convergence was included, the ratings were much lower. These findings appear to contradict the view that accommodation leads to positive reactions in one's interlocutors, and is thus reinforced. (But see further discussion in Chapter 6.)

Auer and Hinskens (2005) present a critique of CAT with regard to its relevance to language change that could also be applied to its relevance to SDA. They point out that while there is evidence of accommodation in extra-linguistic factors such as amount of joking, speech tempo and other prosodic features, very few studies show short-term accommodation of linguistic features.[8] Furthermore, where there is adjustment of linguistic features, it is not in the direction of the observable behaviour of the interlocutors present in the interaction but to a stereotype or abstract model that speakers have of the language of the group they wish to identify with. Speakers adopt certain features (or suppress others) to identify with a certain social group. It is irrelevant whether the present interlocutors belong to the group or not (pp. 337–8).

Another aspect of their critique is more damaging to the notion that SDA results from individual short-term accommodation. It is based on a study by Gilles (1999) of both language change and interpersonal accommodation in the dialects of Luxembourg. It appears that the northern and eastern dialects have been changing to become more like the central dialect spoken in the capital (Luxembourg City). For a community to change to using features of another dialect (D2), individuals in that community must have first acquired these features of that dialect. If acquisition results from accommodation, then we would expect to find evidence of D1 speakers (those who have not yet changed their dialect) accommodating to D2 speakers in the use of these target D2 features or the avoidance of D1 features. This is precisely what Gilles (1999) investigated, concentrating on three phonological variables. He located northern and eastern dialect speakers who still used the old D1 variants, and compared their use of these variants in two conditions: intradia-lectal conversation (with other D1 speakers) and interdialectal conversation (primarily with D2 speakers). If accommodation were occurring, one would expect a much less frequent use of the D1 variants in interdialectal conversa-tion. But on the whole, this is not what occurred. With only a few exceptions, subjects continued to use a significant percentage of D1 variants, or in some cases a higher percentage than in the intradialectal conversation. Thus, this study, as well as others (see Kerswill 2002: 681), did not support either the change-by-accommodation model, or the view that accommodation is respon-sible for acquisition.

Other problems with relying on the CAT to account for SDA lie in the nature of the theory itself. For one thing, many of its claims do not seem to be falsifiable. For example, the theory predicts that in an interaction, a person with less power will converge with (or accommodate to) a person with more power. But the theory also stipulates that this prediction can be overridden by other situational or personal factors. (See also the discussion in Meyerhoff 1998.)

3.4.2   The mechanisms of acquisition

In contrast to the accommodation approach, the acquisitional approach focuses on the processes or mechanisms involved. Although very little has been written specifically about these mechanisms in SDA, it is apparent that most researchers view it as involving both lexical learning and rule learning. Lexical learning entails learning individual words – either new lexical items for the same referents (e.g. *jumper* for *sweater*) or a different pronunciation variant for an existing word, such as the British/Australian versus North American pronunciation of *tomato*. Rule learning entails learning either adaptation/correspondence rules between the D1 and D2 as described above (e.g. BrE [əʊ] versus AmE [oʊ] for the GOAT diphthong), or the phonological and grammatical rules of the D2 that differ from those of the D1 (e.g. that in CanE, the diphthong in MOUTH is pronounced [ʌʊ] before voiceless consonants), or perhaps both kinds of rules.

But having learned a lexical item or a rule of the D2 does not mean that the D2 variant will be used consistently. In other words, linguistic knowledge does not necessarily translate to fluency or accuracy. As has been pointed out for SLA, SDA is a complex skill, like playing tennis or driving a car, and despite having knowledge of what is required, physical performance only improves gradually. The term "automaticity" is used to refer the stage in L2 (or D2) performance when the use of acquired features and the application of rules become automatic and relatively consistent, as with native speakers (Segalowitz 2003).

The distinction is often made between explicit (conscious) knowledge and implicit (unconscious) linguistic competence. According to Paradis (2004), explicit knowledge involves metalinguistic awareness of particular features or rules, while implicit competence involves automatic processing of underlying mental computational procedures (p. 41). These automatic procedures are not the same as the rules described by linguists, and they rely on different neural structures (p. 47).

It is clear from the seventeen studies outlined in Chapter 2 that SDA is gradual, and that a great deal of variability exists in the early stages. Although the D2 acquirers may have learned D2 lexical items and rules (explicit knowledge), automaticity (implicit linguistic competence) is not achieved by the majority, especially with phonological and morphological features. (Some possible reasons for this are discussed in Chapter 4.)

With regard to the mechanisms of SDA, researchers have not distinguished between explicit rules and implicit computational procedures, and have described "rule learning" in general. Thus, in presenting their work, I am unable to make this distinction, even though I believe it is an important one.

Chambers (1992), for example, discussed the acquisition of phonological rules in general. He concluded (pp. 693–5) that such rules develop on the basis of prior acquisition of individual words in which they apply. So for example, a learner of Canadian English would first acquire the Canadian pronunciation in common words such as *house* and *about* in which the MOUTH diphthong is raised from [aʊ] to [ʌʊ]. Once a critical mass of such words is acquired, the rule about using [ʌʊ] before voiceless consonants would emerge, and be applied to rarer words such as *louse* and *pout*. Thus, in the early stages, phonological rules are acquired similarly to pronunciation variants. This can be seen in Chambers' study where group scores for the acquisition of pronunciation variants and for phonological variants are very similar: 26.7 and 25.0 (see Table 2.6 in Chapter 2). Another piece of evidence is that rates of phonological acquisition (measured by use of D2 variants) start off from 0 to 20 per cent, but then jump to 80 per cent or more. Presumably the 20 per cent mark provides the critical mass needed to acquire the phonological rule, which can then be applied to a much larger range of words. Thus, either learners have acquired the rule, in which case they score 80 per cent or more, or they have not acquired it, scoring 20 per cent or less. This results in very few learners in the middle range with scores of over 20 per cent but under 80 per cent. In Chambers' (1992) study, there were five phonological variables and six subjects, giving thirty scores. Only two of these were in the middle range (again, see Table 2.6 in Chapter 2).[9] This is backed up by other studies in which individual scores are given for phonological variables. In Omdal's (1994) study in Norway, only five out of twenty-four subjects had scores in the middle range (30–79 per cent) for the one phonological variable examined. In Berthele's (2002) study in Switzerland, out of 126 scores (seven subjects and eighteen variables), only seventeen were in the middle range.

It may be that scores in the middle range indicate that the learner has still not acquired the rule and is learning each word individually. Some evidence for this is that among the top three acquirers in Berthele's study (those with the three highest overall percentages of acquisition), only two out of fifty-four scores were in the middle range, while among the bottom three, thirteen out of fifty-four were in this range.

On the other hand, Tagliamonte and Molfenter's (2007) study with Canadian children in England showed that acquisition evolved "in fits and starts" but was overall gradual, with scores in the middle range for a sustained period before reaching 80 per cent. This may indicate lexical learning rather than rule learning. And it should be pointed out that not all researchers believe in rule-based models of language acquisition. Another point of view is found in "exemplar-based" models (e.g. Bybee 2001; Pierrehumbert 2003). In such models, languages (or dialects) are learned word by word, rather than by rules, and the properties of each individual word are stored in memory, rather than rules covering the properties of groups of words. Rys (2007) presented the arguments for both rule-based and exemplar-based models, and analysed her substantial findings on SDA in Belgium to see if they would support one or the other. However, the results were not conclusive.

3.4.3   The role of imitation

Earlier in this chapter, we saw that the ability to imitate a dialect is not necessarily evidence of acquisition. Another question, however, is whether or not imitation can lead to acquisition. Studies of first and second language acquisition have largely rejected the behaviourist notion that languages are learned mainly through imitation, because learners produce forms that they have never heard – for example, the intermediate forms and overgeneralisations in SDA described in Section 3.1.1 above. But imitating the target language does provide some learning advantages, especially in developing pronunciation and intonation (Lightbown and Spada 2006: 184).

However, Markham (1997) focuses on imitation as a form of learning and modelling behaviour that is fundamental to acquisition. In his Imitative Acquisition and Function Model (ImAF), he proposes that the imitation that leads to acquisition is triggered by different environmental factors. In the case of different languages, one of these is the need to communicate. But in the case of different dialects, the main factors are accommodation and what Markham terms "linguistic ambience", mentioned in Chapter 1. Accommodation, as we have seen, is socially motivated, arising from an unconscious desire for social approval from one's interlocutors. The linguistic ambience effect "refers to the convergence of speaker characteristics towards the prevailing (ambient) linguistic environment, when no social benefit is overtly sought by or perhaps needed by the speaker" (p. 48). In this case, the imitation is not conditioned by social factors but is "automatic" or "reflexive" (p. 50). Markham gives an example of this occurring when a speaker of British English starts to sound American in an American English environment without any evidence of accommodation (p. 53).

When speakers adapt their speech to the input because of either accommodation or linguistic ambience, rather than trying to impersonate a particular way of speaking for a performance, this leads to the psycholinguistic mechanism of acquisition, defined by Markham as "the mechanism used to establish, elaborate, or revise a system or representation" (p. 50). Once a system or subsystem is acquired, it can be accessed for use in communication.

3.4.4   Mental representation and processing of separate dialects

Assuming that the D2 is acquired as an additional dialect (as in the case of true bidialectalism), rather than replacing the D1, the questions arise as to how the two dialects are represented or stored in the brain, and how they are processed.

Some answers to these questions are found in psycholinguistic studies on bilingualism. The majority of researchers now believe that the two languages of a bilingual person are not organised as a single extended language system (Bialystok 1994). Rather, at least some elements of the L1 and the L2 are stored in separate areas of the brain and processed in different ways. The most popular view of separate representations is the Subset Hypothesis (Paradis 1997: 341–2), in which the L1 and L2 are considered to be subsystems of a larger language system. More specifically, the hypothesis posits that there are two subsets of neural connections, one for each language, which can be activated or suppressed independently. (See also Grosjean 1997 and Poulisse 1997.) This view also seems to apply to lexically similar languages, such as Jamaican Creole and standard English, that are often considered dialects of the same language by their speakers (Davidson and Schwartz 1995).

Two psycholinguistic studies are specifically relevant to SDA. The first dealt with lexical differences between standard Dutch and the Maastricht dialect (spoken in the Limburg dialect region studied by Vousten and Bongaerts 1995; see Section 2.3.6 in Chapter 2 above) – for example: standard Dutch (StD) *ziek* vs. Maastricht (M) *kraank* 'sick', and StD *kopje* vs. M *tas* 'cup'. Woutersen *et al.* (1994) looked into the mental organisation of the lexicon in speakers of these two dialects, using the lexico-semantic model proposed by Levelt (1989, 2001). In this model, each lexical item is associated with a particular concept and each has two parts: the lemma and the lexeme. The lemma contains semantic and syntactic information, including the meaning of the item and the specifications for its use (that is, morphosyntactic and pragmatic information, such as grammatical category and function). It also has information pointing to a particular lexeme. The lexeme contains phonological and morphological information about the actual form of the item. For example, for the concept of "child", there is a lexical item in English with the lemma part having the meaning 'child' and all its semantic associations (human offspring, young age, dependence, etc.) as well as information that it is a noun, singular and countable. The lexeme part has information about the sounds contained in the word, and about the different morphological forms relating to the same concept – e.g. the plural form *children*.

Using a variety of psycholinguistic tests, Woutersen *et al.* found that those they called "non-fluent bilinguals" – i.e. speakers of standard Dutch who had limited familiarity with the Maastricht dialect – appeared to have just one lemma with two associated lexemes, one from the D1 and one from the D2 (see Figure 3.1, adapted from Woutersen *et al.* 1994). For example, they had one lemma for the concept of 'sick' – including its meaning, its grammatical category (adjective) and other grammatical information – and two separate lexemes, one with the form *ziek* and one *kraank*. On the other hand, fluent speakers of both dialects ("fluent bilinguals") had two separate lemmas for a

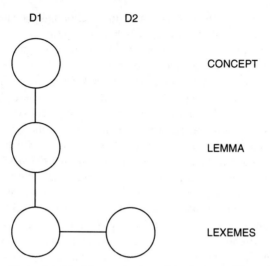

Figure 3.1 Mental organisation of the lexicon of "non-fluent bilinguals"

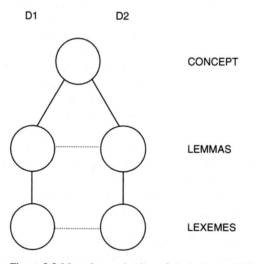

Figure 3.2 Mental organisation of the lexicon of "fluent bilinguals"

concept, one for each variety, and each with an associated lexeme (Figure 3.2, also adapted from Woutersen *et al.* 1994).

In the second study, de Bot (1992) proposed an adapted version of Levelt's (1989) model for monolingual speech production in order to explain bilingual speech production. (See also de Bot 2002.) This model is very complex, and

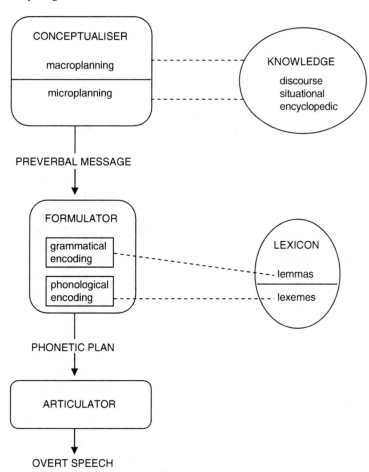

Figure 3.3 Levelt's (1989) model of monolingual speech production (simplified)

only the basics are described here. But it is useful in visualising what is involved in becoming truly bidialectal. Levelt's model consists of four steps and three autonomous information processing components. (See Figure 3.3, based on de Bot 1992: 3, in which boxes represent processing components and ellipses represent knowledge stores.)

The *conceptualiser* conceives the communicative intention and plans the message for speech production. "Macroplanning" consists of selecting the information to express in order to realise the communicative goals. "Microplanning" comprises planning the form of the message – for example, selecting the appropriate speech act and assigning topic and focus. In this planning, the conceptualiser uses knowledge about the immediate environment, the world in general, and what has already been said in the conversation. The output of this component is the "preverbal message".

The *formulator* converts the preverbal message into a speech plan – in other words, it "translates conceptual structures into linguistic structures" (Levelt 1989: 11). Two processes are involved, grammatical encoding and phonological encoding, and use is made of lexical knowledge. A particular entry in the lexicon is activated when there is a match between the semantic information in the preverbal message and the meaning part of a particular lemma. The syntactic part of the lemma then triggers the appropriate syntactic procedures (such as constructing a noun phrase). Finally, the lexeme triggers the appropriate phonological procedures. To put it in another way, the formulator selects the appropriate lexical units and applies the relevant grammatical and phonological computational procedures (as described in Section 3.4.2 above). The combination produces a "phonetic plan" (or inner speech). The next component, the *articulator*, transforms this phonetic plan into overt speech. (There are other more complex aspects to this model, but only these are relevant here.)

In de Bot's (1992) adaptation of Levelt's model to bilingual speech production, there is one lexicon, but with language-specific subsets, and two formulators, one for each language. The knowledge component is not language specific, and neither is the conceptualiser except that microplanning includes the choice of language or language variety. (This model is refined somewhat in de Bot and Schreuder 1993.) However, de Bot pointed out (1992: 9) that the separate components for the two languages (lexical subsets and formulators) are not necessary for all aspects of the languages:

Elements/knowledge of the two languages may be represented and stored separately for each language or in a shared system depending on a number of factors. The most important of these seems to be linguistic distance between the two languages and the level of proficiency in the languages involved.

For closely related varieties, such as dialects of Dutch, there would be more shared linguistic features than for unrelated varieties, such as Dutch and Arabic. Therefore, there would be less need for separate components. Levelt suggested that a single language can have different "registers", by which he meant different subvarieties with "characteristic syntactic, lexical and phonological properties" (1989: 368) – for example, formal varieties and the "baby talk" used to address young children. Since these "registers" do not require separate components, it is assumed that the same would hold for most features of closely related dialects. However, when dialects have many significant differences in phonology, morphology or syntax, then these differences are more like those of separate languages, and therefore separate components

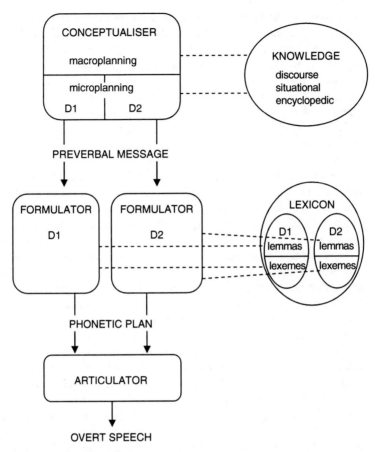

Figure 3.4 De Bot's (1992) model adapted to bidialectal speech

are required. In such circumstances, de Bot's model of fluent bilingual speech (adapted from Levelt's model) can be further adapted to bidialectal speech, as shown in Figure 3.4.

The relevant point here is that in this psycholinguistic model of bidialectalism, there is some separation of the D1 and D2, just as there is with the L1 and L2 in models of bilingualism, so that at least some aspects of the two are stored in different areas and processed in different ways.

The implication is that lack of fluency corresponds to lack of separation. De Bot (1992: 9) noted that a person who knows a few words and phrases in a foreign language will not have developed a separate system for this language. Rather, the new language can initially be treated as an additional "register".

But as more of the language is learned, separate storage and processing components will need to be developed. As Paradis (1994: 414) observed: "The way in which L2 may be processed differently from L1 will depend on the extent of linguistic competence in L2." The same is most probably true for SDA. Some aspects of the D2 can be learned as an additional register, with speakers successfully using the same lexical knowledge and the same processes of grammatical and phonological encoding (i.e. the same formulator) for some aspects of both dialects. However, for complete fluency those aspects that differ markedly from those of the D1 will eventually need to be stored and processed separately.

This is backed up by a study of the naturalistic acquisition of standard German by children who grew up speaking Swiss German (Stern 1988). In role-playing, kindergarten children used single expressions or whole utterances of colloquial standard German (northern German) that they had learned from watching television movies. At the beginning, acquisition was mainly lexical, with children learning the standard German forms for Swiss German words, and the "essential rules of correspondence" between the two dialects (p. 143). This was similar to the development of new linguistic registers with modelling on the first dialect – much like a continuation of L1 acquisition. But later, in some aspects of more complex phonology and in morphology and syntax, it was more like second language acquisition, with initial learning of particular forms followed by rule learning (as evidenced by overgeneralisations). However, this learning took place as the result of the study of written standard German in the school, as children did not receive sufficient input for further acquisition of colloquial standard German from television or other sources (p. 154).[10]

Thus, D2 acquirers may start out by simply learning some new lexemes or pronunciations and use them according to their existing D1 system. However, in some linguistic areas, the D2 may have a different system of lexical correspondences and of grammatical and phonological rules. This is where separate representations (i.e. a separate formulator and subset of the lexicon, according to de Bot's model) must be developed for the D2 if it is to be acquired fully.

3.5   Conclusion

This chapter has answered some of the questions posed in Chapter 1 about the linguistic perceptions of dialect acquirers and the difficulty of switching dialects. It has also provided some understanding of how features of a new dialect may be acquired, and represented in the brain. What it has not done, however, is provide any explanation for the wide variation in the degree of attainment in SDA shown in the studies presented in Chapter 2. This is the task of the following two chapters.

4   Differential attainment: Age effects
and linguistic factors

In addition to examining the extent of D2 learning, most studies of SDA also aim to determine some of the factors that lead to learners differing in their overall attainment, and to some D2 features being acquired more successfully than others. In fact, determining these factors is often the main focus of some SDA studies.

This chapter introduces some of the factors relating to both learners and particular linguistic features, and then concentrates on age of acquisition and two related linguistic factors, linguistic level and complexity of rules. These factors intersect to affect the degree of ultimate attainment. The chapter concludes with a discussion of some possible reasons for these effects.

4.1   Individual and linguistic factors

Why do some subjects in the studies described in Chapter 2 attain native-like usage of D2 variants while others do not use any D2 variants at all? Various non-linguistic factors have been examined to account for such differences in individuals' performance. Some of these factors are connected with intrinsic characteristics of the learners, such as their age. Others have to do with the learning context – age of arrival in the new location or when D2 acquisition began, often called age of acquisition, and length of residence in that location. Another set of factors is associated with the complex notions of motivation to acquire the D2 and attitudes towards it and its speakers. Still others are related to social interaction and identity – the nature of the learner's social networks and the role of the D2 in identity construction.[1] In the SLA literature, these are all referred to as "social factors" (R. Ellis 2008), "affective variables" (Larsen-Freeman and Long 1991) or "individual differences" (Dörnyei and Skehan 2003). Sociolinguistic studies of language variation and change also use the term "social factors", as well as other terms such as "independent variables" (Labov 2001) and "external factors" (Tagliamonte 2006). Other labels are found in the literature on SDA, including "social parameters" (Kerswill 1994) and "speaker-related factors" (Rys 2007). Since in SDA all these factors/variables/parameters concern the characteristics of individuals that affect their individual performance, and so as not to confuse them with linguistic variables, I refer to them here as "individual factors".

The most significant individual factor appears to be age of acquisition, covered in the following section. Other individual factors are described in Chapter 5.

Another question is: why are some D2 features acquired more readily than others by subjects across the board – that is, either faster, by greater numbers of learners or with higher percentages of use? Most studies of SDA have tried to discover the linguistic factors that account for this apparent differential ease of acquisition of various D2 features. (It is interesting that a similar interest in the characteristics of particular target features is not found in studies of SLA.) One of these factors is the type of variable or linguistic level of the feature: lexical, phonological (including phonetic and segmental) or morphological. Another linguistic factor is the complexity of rules of the feature. Both of these factors are discussed in this chapter. Other important linguistic factors, such as salience, are covered in Chapter 5.

4.2   Age of acquisition (AoA) and linguistic level

In the seventeen studies described in detail in Chapter 2, it was clear that age of acquisition (AoA) – sometimes referred to as age of arrival or age of onset – was an important factor in the degree of success in SDA. Those who began acquisition at a younger age, especially 13 years or younger, had the highest averages of percentage of use of D2 variants, and the greatest proportions of individuals who reached native-like usage overall or in particular variables (based on 90 per cent or greater use of the D2 variant or on the judgement of the author(s) of the study). This is shown in Table 4.1, which lists the studies in roughly the order of overall degree of attainment.

The three Canadian children in Tagliamonte and Molfenter's (2007) study in northeastern England (Section 2.2.4 above) were among the youngest acquirers, starting at ages 2 to 4, and they had the highest attainment, two reaching 95 per cent of use of D2 phonetic variants and all three rated as having native speaker-like proficiency. The two British children in Trudgill's (1981) study (Section 2.2.8 above) used the Australian variants for most of the fifteen phonetic/phonological variants examined, and both were also rated as sounding native-like. The AoA for the seven children in Berthele's (2002) study in Switzerland (Section 2.3.8 above) was 7 years, and they reached an average of 80.3 per cent of usage of D2 variants, six of them reaching native-like usage in most of the eighteen variables.

The thirteen Brazilian subjects in Bortoni-Ricardo's (1985) youth group, whose AoA was less than 13 years, had an average use of D2 variants of

Table 4.1 *Studies of SDA listed roughly in order of overall degree of attainment*

Author	D2	AoA (age of acquisition)	LoR (length of residence) in years	Average % of use of D2 variants	No. with native-like usage
Tagliamonte and Molfenter	Northeastern England English	2–4	6	92	3/3
Trudgill	Australian English	7	0.67	–	2/2
Berthele	Bernese Swiss German	7	2	81	6/7
Bortoni-Ricardo (Youth)	Standard Brazilian Portuguese	<13	1–35	79	5/13
Payne	Philadelphia English	0–13	4–16	–	~17/34
Bayard	New Zealand English	2.1	8	68	0/1
Kobayashi	Kyoto Japanese	>3	8	66	0/1
Ivars	Eskilstuna Swedish	16–49	3–33	~35[b] 79[c]	0/32[b] 18/32[c]
Omdal	Kristiansand Norwegian	16–70	5–38	48	7/24
Kerswill	Bergen Norwegian	12–52	2–59	35[a]	4/39
Chambers	Southern England English	7–16	1–2	29	1/6
Wells	London English	9–34	>1–16	58	0/36
Shockey	British English	adult	8–27	50	0/4
Bortoni-Ricardo (Adult)	Standard Brazilian Portuguese	16–68	1–35	44	0/33
Vousten and Bongaerts	Limburg Dutch	–	–	38	0/38
Rys	Maldegem Belgian Dutch	~6	–	36	?/164
Foreman	Australian English	7–46	>1–46	6	0/34
Stanford	North/South Sui	17–28	9–43	0.2[d]	0/15

Notes: – indicates information not available; ~ indicates approximately.

[a] The morpholexical index only.

[b] Eskilstuna index only.

[c] For four morphological features only.

[d] For lexical variables only.

Table 4.2 *Percentages of acquisition of D2 (Philadelphia) phonetic variants according to age of acquisition (natural speech)*

	Variable Vowel involved	(aw) MOUTH	(oy) CHOICE	(ay) PRICE	(ow) GOAT	(uw) GOOSE
AoA 0–4	(n = 17)	60	70	64.7	70	70
AoA 5–9	(n = 14)	40	62.5	50	58.3	66.6
AoA 10–14	(n = 3)	0	0	0	66.6	0

79 per cent, as compared to the adult group, whose AoA was 18 and over, with an average of 44 per cent. (The average percentages of each variant are given in Table 2.8 in Section 2.3.2 above.) Also, five subjects in the youth group reached native-like usage of some variables. However, it is not clear whether this effect was a result of the younger group's greater ability to acquire a second dialect or their greater exposure to the standard dialect in formal education.

Like Bortoni-Ricardo, Payne (1976, 1980) looked specifically at the effect of AoA on the acquisition of D2 variants (Section 2.2.2 above). In contrast to the children who were born in the Philadelphia suburb of King of Prussia or arrived before age 14, most of the parents, who arrived as adults, acquired very little of the Philadelphia dialect. Some who were speakers of New York and Midwestern dialects showed some influence of the Philadelphia variants in the five "phonetic" variables – (aw), (oy), (ay), (ow) and (uw) – but there was no complete acquisition of the kind found with a large proportion of the children. There was no clear evidence of any acquisition among adults of the "phonological" variables – (er), (ohr), (æ) and (æh) (1976: 133). This is relevant to the discussion of the differential effects of different types of pronunciation variables based on complexity, in Section 4.3 below.

For the children, results for acquisition of the D2 variants for the five phonetic variables according to AoA are shown in Table 4.2.[2] Note that Payne divided the children into three age groups: 0–4, 5–9 and 10–14.[3] The AoA of 0 refers to children born in King of Prussia. The percentages indicate the number who acquired the Philadelphia variant out of the total number of children in that age group whose families came from areas with a variant different from the Philadelphia one. So, for example, ten children in the 0–4 age group belonged to families from regions where the dialect differed from that of Philadelphia for the (aw) variable, and six of these ten acquired the Philadelphia variant, making 60 per cent.

It is clear that with the exception of one variable, (ow), the younger the children's age when they arrived in King of Prussia, the more successful they were in acquiring the Philadelphia variant (1976: 119). In fact, the children who were between 10 and 14 when they arrived did not acquire the Phila-delphia variants for four out of five of the variables. From her overall examination of AoA, Payne (1980: 175) concluded that age 8 is the cut-off point for successful acquisition.

Interestingly, all the children in two of the families showed virtually no acquisition of another Philadelphia feature, the short-*a* pattern, and in one of these families, all the children were born and raised in Philadelphia. This led Payne (1980: 174) to the conclusion that unless children's parents are locally born and raised, there is only a slight possibility of acquiring the Philadelphia short-*a* pattern, even if the children are born and raised there. (A possible reason for this is discussed in Section 4.3 below.)

The AoA of the six Canadian youths in Chambers' (1992) study (Section 2.2.4 above) ranged from 7 to 16. (They were interviewed one or two years after their arrival in England.) For lexical replacements, there was a general inverse correlation between the percentage of replacement and the age of the subject (p. 10) – i.e. the younger the subject, the higher the percentage. As mentioned in Chapter 2, the percentages for Southern England English (SEE) rather than Canadian pronunciation of the five lexical items ranged from 0 to 60, again with the youngest subject having the highest percentage and the oldest subject the lowest percentage.

While there was a fairly gradual decline in scores from youngest to oldest for lexical and pronunciation replacements and elimination of T-Voicing, there was a much sharper cut-off between the youngest subject and the others for the other phonological variants: an average of 60 for the youngest, but 22.5 for the first 13-year-old, and then 7.5 for the other 13-year-old, 12.5 for the 14-year-old, 2.5 for the 15-year-old and finally 0 for the 17-year-old. Chambers explained the large difference between the two 13-year-olds as a result of the first one migrating to England at age 11. Thus, like the 9-year-old, who migrated at age 7, he was an "early acquirer" (1992: 688). However, it appeared that a person can be an early acquirer for some features but not others. For example, one of the 13-year-olds was an early acquirer for the absence of the Low Vowel Merger, but not for the other phonological features. It is clear, though, that the early acquirers were always the younger subjects.

With regard to the effect of AoA, Chambers (1992: 689) referred to a pioneering study of SDA in Japan by Sibata (1958). In 1949, Sibata and his colleagues interviewed approximately 500 children who had been sent to Shirakawa City from Tokyo and Yokohama to escape bombing near the end of World War II. They found that the children who arrived before 6 or 7 years of age had adopted the Shirakawa dialect almost perfectly, but those who arrived at the age of 14 or more maintained their D1 completely. On the basis of this and other research, including Payne's (1976, 1980) study, Chambers concluded (p. 689): "A person 7 or under will almost certainly acquire a new dialect perfectly, and a person 14 or over almost certainly will not. In between those ages, people will vary."

Here we have to keep in mind that Payne, Sibata and Chambers were talking about the significant effect of a low AoA on native-like attainment. However, in her study in Belgium (Section 2.3.7 above), Rys (2007) had a slightly different interpretation. Referring to other studies, she noted (p. 40): "There are indications that children who moved to a new dialect region after a certain age do not acquire the target dialect as well as children who have moved at an earlier age." This fact led to her concluding that acquisition becomes "more difficult" after a certain age, and assuming that this meant children's proficiency in a D2 may not continue to increase after this critical age. To see whether or not this was true, Rys examined the use of D2 (Southern Dutch) variants in children of three age groups: 9, 12 and 15 years old. She found that the older the children, the greater their use of D2 features, and therefore concluded that "dialect proficiency continues to increase between the ages of nine and fifteen" (p. 354), with the implication that there is not a significant cut-off point for acquisition, at least up to age 15. However, it must be remembered that the subjects in Rys's study were actually born in the D2 region (p. 40), and thus, although they grew up speaking their parents' dialect, they could have been exposed to the D2 at an early age. More importantly, their acquisition of the D2 began when they started school, which in Belgium is around age 6. Therefore, the children's continuing development in the D2 is not surprising because their AoA was below the cut-off point of age 8 – i.e. in the range of 7 or under.

Of the other studies outlined in Chapter 2, only two appear to contradict the first part of Chambers' conclusion – i.e. that a person with an AoA of seven or under will acquire native-like usage of the D2. The first was that done by Bayard (1995) in New Zealand (Section 2.2.7). Although his son began acquiring NZE at the age of 2 years 2 months, he did not acquire all the NZE vowels and, at age 8, used NZE R-lessness 68.3 per cent of the time when talking to peers – relatively high, but not native-like. And this percentage decreased to only 31.7 when he was 20 years old (see Table 5.5 in the following chapter).

The other possibly contradictory study was the one done by Foreman (2003) in Australia (Section 2.2.6 above), in which she examined and statistically analysed AoA along with seven other non-linguistic factors. One subject, L, arrived in Australia at the age of 7. While she had the highest percentages of use of Australian variants for the (r) (non-prevocalic /r/) and (GOAT) variables, these were only 22.6 per cent and 38.9 per cent respectively, far from being native-like (see Table 2.7 in Chapter 2). For other variables, her percentages were far below those of other subjects with higher AoAs – for example, 2.4 per cent for (FLEECE) compared to the high of 23.8 per cent, and 8.2 per cent for (PRICE) compared to the high of 49.1 per cent. In addition, subject L did not use the AusE vowels at all in TRAP–BATH and THOUGHT–LOT. However, this lack of acquisition may have been the result of special circumstances. Interviews with subject L's mother, recorded in 1988 and 1999, revealed that she was very critical of her daughter's AusE pronunciations, and often corrected her – especially with regard to non-prevocalic /r/. For example, in 1988 she said: "I can't stand the way she says *care* with no *r*, *care* and *dare* and *are*, you know those kind of things and because I think that's just bad English." And in 1999: "I worked very hard when we first got here at not having her uh soften her *r*'s" (Foreman 2003: 255). And in an interview in 1999, subject L expressed similar attitudes towards her own daughter's pronunciations (p. 256). But Foreman noted (p. 258) that other individual factors may also have been at work (see Chapter 5).

On the other hand, in a footnote (p. 237) Foreman discussed subject U, whose AoA was 6 years. She was among the subjects who were interviewed but not included in the statistical analysis because, in her case, she had returned to the USA for one year to go to university when she was in her early twenties. However, her speech was analysed at a later date, and it was found that she used the AusE pronunciation for non-prevocalic /r/ 93.6 per cent of the time, and had very high AusE percentages for three of the other variables: 68.3 per cent for (KIT), 69.2 per cent for (GOAT) and 82.1 per cent for (FACE). In addition, she had acquired the AusE pronunciations of the TRAP–BATH and THOUGHT–LOT vowels. According to Foreman, this subject gave the impression of being a native AusE speaker.

We now turn to the second part of Chambers' conclusion – that a person 14 or over almost certainly will not acquire a D2 perfectly. This is backed up for the most part by the other studies in which subjects with an AoA greater than 13 did not show native-like D2 usage with any of the variables. However, there were three exceptions. The first was the study by Kerswill (1994) in Norway (Section 2.3.3 above). Three of the four subjects who acquired a Bergen-like variety were over the age of 13 when they arrived in Bergen – one 14 and two 16. (The fourth was 12.) One (with an AoA of 16) had a morpholexical index score of 0.9, and the other two had scores of 2.2. These scores indicate use of D2 (Bergen) features rather than D1 (Stril) features 99.1 per cent and 97.8 per cent of the time. These are much higher percentages than we have seen for phonological variables in other studies of second dialect learners with similar ages of arrival.

What is significant here is the linguistic level of the variable involved in the study. The studies referred to so far in this chapter have all concerned mainly phonetic and phonological variables (referred to together as phonological), but Kerswill's morpholexical index was based on lexical and morphological features. Research in SLA has shown that in contrast to phonology, learners can attain native-like morphology and syntax up until at least their mid teens (see Long 2007: 58). Kerswill's successful subjects had AoAs below this cut-off point.

In the two other exceptional studies, native-like D2 usage by subjects over the age of 13 was also with morphological variables. In the first part of Ivars' (1994) study in Sweden (Section 2.3.5 above), which examined a combination of phonological and morphological variables, no subjects recorded native-like D2 usage – i.e. none had an index score of more than 90 per cent of D2 variants. However, in the second part, which examined only morphological variables, eighteen out of the thirty-two subjects did use more than 90 per cent of D2 variants. Of these, fourteen were in the younger age group. Unfortunately, Ivars (1994) did not give figures on AoA, but she noted (pp. 213–14) that the younger individuals were when they arrived in Sweden, the more they had acquired the norms of the D2 (either the Eskilstuna dialect or spoken standard Swedish). And some of these individuals were as young as 16 when they arrived.

The three variables in Omdal's (1994) study in Norway (Section 2.3.4 above) were also morphological. Of the seven out of twenty-four subjects who used D2 variants for one or more of the variables more than 90 per cent of the time, one had an AoA of 16, two of 17, two of 19, one of 22 and one of 25.[4]

These results indicate that the AoA is a significant factor affecting the degree of SDA, but that phonological features and morphological features are affected differently. (Section 4.3 below looks at how different types of phonological features are affected differently as well.) It appears that the optimum AoA for attaining native-like usage of phonological features of the D2 is 7 years or younger, but for morphological features 16 or 17 years or younger. There is still a fair chance for some learners up to the age of 14 to acquire native-like D2 phonological features, and perhaps up to the early twenties for morphological features. But starting acquisition after these cut-off points means that reaching native-like proficiency will be very difficult. The results also indicate that starting acquisition below the age of 8 does not mean that a person will necessarily reach native-like proficiency, as other factors may come into play.

With regard to lexical variables, Chambers (1992) asserted that lexical replacements (i.e. lexical variants) are acquired faster than pronunciation and phonological variants (p. 677). From his data, summarised in Table 2.6 in Chapter 2, this appears to be true if the group average score for lexical replacements (52.3 per cent) is compared to those for pronunciation replacements (26.7 per cent) and phonological variants (25.0 per cent). However, the average score for one of the phonological variants, the absence of T-Voicing

(55.0 per cent), was actually higher than that for lexical replacements. Nevertheless, the findings of other studies back up Chambers' conclusion. For example, in Foreman's (2003) study in Australia, only twelve out of thirty-four subjects used AusE phonological variants, but most of the subjects reported that they had replaced some NAE words with AusE words (p. 170).

So far we have been looking at the effect of AoA on reaching native-like attainment in the D2, and thus concentrating on younger acquirers. However, the studies that deal primarily with subjects who began SDA as adults way past adolescence indicate that some acquisition of phonological, lexical and morphological D2 features can occur even after the cut-off points of 14 and early twenties. The question then is whether AoA still has some affect.

Both Wells (1973) and Shockey (1984) reported no apparent relationship between AoA and degree of acquisition. However, Foreman (2003) reported that a lower AoA generally corresponded to a higher percentage of use of the AusE variant for non-prevocalic /r/, (KIT), and to some extent (PRICE) and (FLEECE), even though those who had the lowest age of arrival did not always have the highest percentages. Kerswill (1994) also suggested that AoA was relevant, with younger arrivals in general adopting Bergen features more extensively than older arrivals in both the morpholexical index and schwa-lowering. As already mentioned, Ivars (1994) stated that AoA was the most significant individual factor in her study: the older the informants were the more they retained the Närpes dialect; the younger they were, the more they acquired the Eskilstuna dialect and standard Swedish. In these studies, however, it is not clear how much the successful attainment of the younger subjects affected the overall correlations.

One final observation about AoA: as noted in Chapter 2, two studies – Foreman (2003) and Stanford (2007) – had subjects who did not use any D2 variants for the variables being investigated. In each case, these subjects were adults when they began SDA. No studies that I am aware of show those who began SDA as children or adolescents not using at least some D2 features. Thus, it appears that those who arrive in a new dialect area before adulthood will almost certainly use some features of that dialect, although not necessarily consistently.

The findings with regard to the relevance of AoA in SDA generally back up those in SLA research. (For overviews, see Ioup 2005; Long 2007: 43–74; Gass and Selinker 2008: 405–16.) It is difficult to attain native-like phonology if acquisition begins after age 7, and likewise with native-like morphology and syntax after the mid teens. With regard to a correlation between AoA and attainment after these cut-off points, however, the SLA literature is not so clear. A study by Johnson and Newport (1989) showed a linear negative correlation between scores on a test of L2 syntax and AoAs ranging from 3 to 15, but no correlation between scores and AoA of 16 or greater. In other words, the lower the AoA the higher the scores up to age 15, but randomly distributed scores for 16 and older. On the other hand, several other studies (e.g. Stevens 1999; Hakuta, Bialystok and Wiley 2003) have shown that the negative correlation between L2 attainment and AoA continues past suggested cut-off points, such as 15 and 20 years. Here too the findings are divided – with Wells (1973) and Shockey (1984) supporting the lack of a relationship between attainment and AoA in adulthood, and Foreman (2003), Kerswill (1994) and Ivars (1994) supporting a continuing relationship.

To summarise what we have seen so far about the combined effect of AoA and linguistic level, the optimal age for acquiring lexical and morphological features of the D2 is the mid teens or younger, while for phonological features it is 7 years or younger, though native-like acquisition is still possible for several years after these ages. Thus, for young adults (i.e. persons aged from approximately their mid teens to their early twenties), acquiring the D2 variants for lexical and morphological variables would generally be easier than for phonological variables.

4.3   Complexity of rules

Another linguistic factor that intersects with AoA and linguistic level is the complexity of rules. This is relevant primarily to phonetic/phonological features. Here the term "rules" refers to either the explicit knowledge or the implicit computational procedures that need to be acquired by the D2 learner (see Section 3.4.2 in Chapter 3 above).

Wells (1973) was the first researcher interested in accounting for varying rates of acquisition of particular phonological features of a D2. In his study of Jamaicans in London, the two variables that had the highest rate of use of D2 variants were (o:), the vowel in words such as GOAT, with 86 per cent, and (e:), in words such as FACE, with 83 per cent (see Section 2.2.1 in Chapter 2 above). In these variables, the change required from the D1, Jamaican English (JE), to the D2, London English (LE), involved what I called (in Chapter 1) categorical substitution – i.e. across-the-board replacement of a sound used in the D1 with the sound used in the D2. This change could be made easily, as there were no differences in distribution or frequency of the sounds. Thus, the differences between the JE and LE variants were only a matter of what Wells called "phonetic realization" (p. 118). Adaptation rules that involve only phonetic realisations appear to be the easiest to acquire in SDA. In contrast, the rules regarding vowels before /r/ are more complex because the learner has to change not only the JE vowel pronunciations but also

Table 4.3 *Average percentages of acquisition of D2 (Philadelphia) variants for seven variables*

Variable/vowel involved	Percentage acquired	Percentage not acquired
(ow) as in GOAT	68	0
(oy) as in CHOICE	60	10
(uw) as in GOOSE	52	0
(ay) as in PRICE	50	5.9
(aw) as in MOUTH	40	20
(ohr) as in SURE/SHORE	33.3	50
(er) as in FERRY/FURRY	17.6	72.1

the distributional patterns regarding the pronunciation of the /r/ sound. As a result, the scores for the three (r) variables were lower (43, 57 and 59 per cent). The scores for the (eə) variable (concerning words such as BEER and BEAR) were even lower (20 per cent) because it involves a phonological split – what is one phoneme in JE has to be changed to two phonemes in LE, and learners have to acquire a contrast between *beer* and *bear*, *fear* and *fare*, *hear* and *hair*, and other similar pairs of words. Wells concluded (p. 118):

The evidence gathered in this survey of the speech of Jamaicans in London thus supports the view that adolescents and adults, faced with a new linguistic environment, can adapt their speech to a certain extent by modifying the phonetic realization of their phonemes; but they do not on the whole succeed in acquiring new phonological oppositions or in altering the distributional restraints on their phonology.

Payne (1976, 1980) also tried to explain the differences in rates of acquisition among the phonetic/phonological variables in her study, shown in Table 4.3. The first five variables in the table are those that she called "phonetic". According to Wells' conclusions as just described, the Philadelphia variants for (aw) and (oy) would have been easiest to acquire since they required only categorical substitution, as opposed to those for (ay), (ow) and (uw) which required phonologically conditioned substitution (see Section 2.2.2 above); yet the variants for (aw) and (oy) do not have the highest rates of acquisition. As a possible explanation, Payne (1976: 94–5) pointed out that similar phonologically conditioned variations occur in many other dialects in similar contexts, such as Canadian raising before voiceless consonants as with (ay), and fronting before /l/, as with (ow) and (uw). These may have made the corresponding Philadelphia variants easier to acquire. Furthermore, acquisition of the Philadelphia variant for (aw) may have been more difficult because its off-glide is a back vowel that is lower than normally found in other dialects

(p. 97). Nevertheless, Payne concluded (p. 99) that the overall success of acquisition of the variants for all five of these variables was that they could be added to the grammar by "simple rule addition". In other words, they could be learned by acquiring straightforward categorical or phonologically conditioned substitution rules.

With regard to the last two variables listed in Table 4.3, which Payne called "phonological", she concluded (1976: 104) that acquisition of the Philadelphia variants was more difficult because it required "structural change", as mentioned in Chapter 3. The mental lexicon had to be reorganised so that words that were in separate classes with regard to pronunciation in the D1 – such as *lure*, *sure* and *moor* versus *lore*, *shore* and *more* – were now in the same class in the D2. In contrast, acquiring the phonetic features – such as a different pronunciation of the vowel /ɔɪ/ in words such as CHOICE in the (oy) variable – did not require any changes in the mental lexicon. Thus, words with the /ɔɪ/ vowel were still distinct from words with other vowels – there was no merger or split.

Recall that the last variable examined by Payne, short-*a* (not listed in Table 4.3), was divided into two subvariables. The first, (æ), involved a split in the phoneme /æ/ as in TRAP – with [æ] (the lax short-*a*) remaining in some words, such as *bat* and *lap*, but a diphthong [ɛə] (the tense short-*a*) occurring in other words, such as *man* and *ham*. In the Philadelphia dialect, the diphthong had become [eə], with the nucleus raised from [ɛ] to [e] or even higher. As opposed to all the other phonetic/phonological variables, no children completely acquired the Philadelphia variant. Again, this could be accounted for by rule complexity.

For a speaker of a dialect without the split in /æ/, the rules for knowing when to use tense short-*a* [eə] instead of lax short-*a* [æ] are extremely complex (see Payne 1976: 37). In general, tense short-*a* [eə] occurs before the five sounds /m/, /n/, /f/, /s/ and /θ/ in words or syllables not followed by another syllable. Lax short-*a* [æ] occurs elsewhere. But there are many exceptions. The adjectives *mad*, *bad* and *glad* are pronounced with the tense short-*a* [eə] even though it is not followed by one of the five sounds just mentioned, and the verbs *ran*, *swam* and *began* and the auxiliaries *am* and *can* have lax short-*a* [æ] even though it occurs before /m/ or /n/. Furthermore, when a suffix such as -*y* or -*ish* is added to a word with tense short-*a* [eə], the sound remains, even though it is followed by another syllable – for example, *classy* [kleəsi] and *mannish* [meənɪʃ]. And when words or proper names with lax short-*a* [æ] are abbreviated or shortened, as in *math*, *Dan* and *exam*, [æ] remains, even though it is now in a one-syllable word preceding one of the five sounds before which tense short-*a* [eə] normally occurs. Thus there is phonological conditioning, lexical conditioning, and even grammatical conditioning. (See Payne 1980: 158–9 for a more detailed description of the patterns.) The lack of acquisition of Philadelphia short-*a* led Payne (1980: 175) to conclude "that children do not freely restructure and/or reorganize their grammars up to the age of 14, but that they do have the ability to add lower level rules".

Chambers (1992: 682) defined simple phonological rules as "automatic processes that admit no exceptions" and complex rules as those having "exceptions or variant forms ... or a new or additional phoneme". And he noted that simple rules are acquired faster than complex ones. Chambers presented T-Voicing as an example of a simple rule even though it does not involve simple categorical substitution, as /d/ replaces /t/ only in particular phonological contexts, such as preceding a vowel in an unstressed syllable. Thus, Chambers agreed with Payne that simple rules (or lower-level rules) can include straightforward phonological conditioning as well as phonetically realised adaptations (Wells 1973). However, the phonological or lexical conditioning rules required for other variables described by Chambers are more complex. For example, for Canadians to acquire the SEE variants for Vowel Backing would involve learning a new phoneme and splitting words with low vowels that have merged in CanE. This is reflected in the group scores of 23.3 per cent for the acquisition of Vowel Backing compared to 55 per cent for the absence of T-Voicing. On the other hand, the score for R-lessness, which appears to involve rules comparable in complexity to those for the absence of T-Voicing, is only 8.3 per cent. (See Table 2.6 in Chapter 2.) Thus, the notion of complexity of rules is far more complex than it appears at first glance.

Chambers (1992: 687) also concluded that the acquisition of complex rules (including new phonemes) "splits the population into early acquirers and late acquirers". Thus, age of acquisition (AoA) has a differential affect on features that involve simple phonological rules and those that involve complex phonological rules. In Section 4.2 above, I referred to Chambers' conclusion that a person with an AoA of 7 years or younger can easily achieve native-like D2 usage, while a person older than 14 cannot. However, this statement applies primarily to D2 pronunciation of variants with complex rules, and not to those with simple rules (p. 689), or, as we have also seen in Section 4.2, to lexical or morphological variants.

Early in Kerswill's (1994) description of his study in Norway (p. 69), he hypothesised that acquiring Bergen (D2) morpholexical features would be easier than acquiring phonological features because in first language acquisition morphology and syntax can be acquired at a later age than phonology. Therefore those who arrived at an older age would be able to acquire Bergen morpholexical features but not phonological rules, especially complex ones such as those involved in schwa-lowering. However, the results showed that to some extent, the vast majority of Stril migrants adopted both morpholexical features and some schwa-lowering, even those who arrived at 17 or older. This seemed to contradict the view that complex phonological rules in a new dialect can be acquired only by younger children (e.g. Payne 1976, 1980). However, Kerswill pointed out (p. 127) that Stril dialects also have a rule in which schwa is fronted at the end of an utterance. Therefore, the migrants already had a complex phonological conditioning rule, and only had to change the realisation of the resulting vowel to a lowered one. Thus, as Chambers (1992: 686) pointed out, "the notion of phonological complexity is relative, not absolute".

Thus we need to revise the conclusion of the preceding section. For young adults, acquiring the D2 variants for lexical and morphological variables would generally be easier than for phonological variables – but only when the D2 variants involve relatively complex phonological rules.

4.4   Discussion of age effects

This section takes a brief look at some of the proposed reasons for the age effects just described – a very contentious area in applied linguistics and psycholinguistics.

4.4.1   Critical period versus sensitive periods

We have seen that there are certain age periods in which different aspects of a D2 appear to be easier to acquire, and native-like attainment more likely. No one really argues with similar findings in SLA. However, a great deal of controversy has surrounded the following question: can acquisition proceed to reach native-like attainment if it begins after these age periods? In other words, is there a critical age period in which language acquisition must begin and after which it will not be possible? Or is there just an age period in which acquisition is relatively easy, after which it gets harder?

The controversy began with Lenneberg's (1967) Critical Period Hypothesis (CPH). This postulated a window of opportunity of from 2 years old to puberty for language acquisition; after this time, normal acquisition cannot occur. It should be remembered that the CPH was framed with regard to first language acquisition, in order to account for phenomena such as feral or abused children who did not get exposed to human language before puberty not being able to fully acquire language later. Nevertheless some scholars have applied the CPH to SLA, saying that it accounts for the lack of native-like L2 acquisition if the AoA is above 13 years. This has led to many studies trying to disprove the CPH with regard to SLA. Some of these have documented adult learners who gained native-like proficiency in an L2 – most notably for our discussion, in naturalistic rather than classroom acquisition (e.g. Ioup *et al.* 1994; Bongaerts, Mennen and van der Slik 2000). Other studies have tried to disprove the CPH by demonstrating a steadily declining curve of L2 attainment from childhood through to adulthood, rather than a sharp decline after the critical cut-off point (e.g. Hakuta *et al.* 2003, mentioned in Section 4.2 above).

However, while the CPH mainly concerned L1 acquisition, Lenneberg (1967: 176) did specifically refer to SLA as follows:

Most individuals of average intelligence are able to learn a second language after the beginning of their second decade, although the incidence of "language-learning-blocks" rapidly increases after puberty. Also, automatic acquisition from mere exposure to a given language seems to disappear, and foreign languages have to be taught and learned through a conscious and labored effort. Foreign accents cannot be overcome easily after puberty. However, a person *can* learn to communicate at the age of forty. (emphasis in original)

Thus, Lenneberg was not really saying there is a critical period for SLA. Rather, his view was an L2 can be acquired after puberty, but it is not as automatic as before puberty, and native-like attainment is difficult – especially in the area of phonology. Therefore, studies that show people continuing to acquire an L2 (or a D2) after puberty do not really refute Lenneberg's views, as he never said there was a critical period for SLA.

With reference to the ideal time frame for SLA (and SDA), Long (1990, 2007) prefers the term "sensitive period", which he defines as "times of heightened responsiveness to certain kinds of environmental stimuli", allowing for gradual increases or decreases in learning ability and some flexibility with regard to age of onset and offset (2007: 44n). And there are differing sensitive periods for different aspects of the L2 and D2: up to 7 years for complex phonological rules, up to 13 for simple phonological rules and suprasegmentals, and up to the mid teens for morphology. Thus, native-like acquisition of these aspects of language during these sensitive periods would not be guaranteed, but would also not be unexpected. However, native-like attainment after these periods would not be expected, but would be possible under exceptional circumstances, such as high motivation, large amounts of L2 input and intensive instruction (Long 2007: 67).[5]

4.4.2   Explanations for age effects

As outlined by Hyltenstam and Abrahamsson (2003), there are three types of explanations for the age effects that are described in the SLA literature and that we have seen for SDA: biological, social/psychological and cognitive. Each of these is briefly described below.

Biological explanations   Lenneberg's CPH was based on the view that as the brain develops, it loses its flexibility or "plasticity", as certain areas of the brain become devoted to particular functions. For example, it is known that the grammar and vocabulary aspects of language are normally associated with the left hemisphere of the brain (at least for those who are right-handed), and the processes involved in seeing and hearing with the right hemisphere. This specialisation of function is referred to as "lateralisation". It was originally thought that lateralisation is complete by puberty. Lenneberg's hypothesis was basically that if the parts of the brain that are normally devoted to language do not become involved in language learning before lateralisation is complete (i.e. by puberty), they will come to be used for some other function, and no longer be available for language. Then how would Lenneberg reconcile this with his view that SLA is still possible after puberty? His answer was as follows (1967: 176):

This does not trouble our basic hypothesis on age limitations because we may assume that the cerebral organization for language learning as such has taken place during childhood, and since natural languages tend to resemble one another in many fundamental aspects ..., the matrix for language skills is present.

However, more recent research has shown many of Lenneberg's views about lateralisation to be incorrect. First of all, for some language functions of the brain, specialisation occurs well before puberty – even before age 5. Second, as shown by studies using PET (positron emission tomography) and fMRI (functional magnetic resonance imaging), many of the language functions are spread out through different areas of the brain rather than being concentrated in particular areas.

Nowadays, biological explanations are more concerned with the brain's neurons. It is thought that learning involves the strengthening of connections between various networks of neurons. The connecting fibres of neurons become covered in a kind of insulation, called "myelin". This allows neural impulses to be transmitted more rapidly, but it also makes further connections more difficult. The process of "myelination" begins before birth and continues at least for another decade on two. Thus, a current view is that brain plasticity decreases as a result of myelination, and therefore learning (including language acquisition) becomes progressively more difficult. This view is discussed by Pulvermüller and Schumann (1994), who also propose that two different systems of cortical connections between neurons account for the different sensitive periods for different linguistic levels – e.g. lexical versus phonological.

Social/psychological explanations   Those who dismiss the biological explanations often cite social conditions or individual factors that differ according to age. (These factors are discussed in Chapter 5.) For example, one claim is that children have a greater integrative orientation and more positive attitudes towards the L2 and its speakers than adults do, and therefore are more motivated to learn the L2. Another claim is that children have not yet developed a strong sense of identity with regard to the L1, which adults have and find hard to give up. Still another is that children receive more simplified input in their interaction with L2 speakers than adults do. However, none of these claims has been backed up by clear evidence, and there are many counter-arguments (see Long 1990; Hyltenstam and Abrahamsson 2003).

With regard to SDA, researchers have generally not tried to explain age effects according to social factors. One example, however, was Kerswill (1994), whose social parameters included perceived pressure on rural Stril speakers to learn the Bergen dialect. He suggested (p. 110): "Stril migrants arriving at a relatively young age (perhaps 16 or 17) are likely to feel a very strong pressure to accommodate their speech in the direction of the Bergen dialect." This could possibly have accounted for the age effect in his study.

Cognitive explanations   There have been some suggestions that the decline in L2 learning ability with age corresponds to an age-related cognitive decline in learning ability in general. However, such a decline does not begin until later in life – and certainly not as early as 7 or 8 years, when the sensitive period for complex phonological rules comes to an end (see Ioup 2005).

A more likely cognitive explanation has to do with speech perception – specifically concerning what are referred to as the "continuous" versus the "categorical" modes. By age 7, children have firmly established the relevant phonetic contrasts that are used to distinguish meaning in their language – in other words they have grouped sounds into different categories or phonemes. This is the categorical mode. On the other hand, younger children attend to tiny differences among speech sounds (e.g. phonologically conditioned variants and social and dialectal differences among speakers). According to Long (2007: 67), this makes them "relatively more flexible and malleable in their search for appropriate phonological targets".

This view is relevant to Flege's Speech Learning Model (e.g. 2003), described in more detail in Chapter 6. According to Flege (2003: 328), the sensitive period for native-like phonological attainment in an L2 is the result of the interference of prior learning, not any loss of brain plasticity. Adults retain the capacity for language acquisition, including the ability to form new phonetic categories (i.e. the mental representations of the characteristics of particular sounds in a language). But the formation of L2 speech categories becomes less likely with increasing age because of the existing categories already established in early childhood. Older children and adult L2 acquirers, who are in the categorical mode, attend only to the perceptual aspects of sounds that signal contrasts between phonemic categories (e.g. /d/ versus /t/ in English). Once categories have become firmly established, learners tend to perceive many new sounds in terms of established categories instead of forming new categories for them.

Other cognitive explanations assume that we are born with inbuilt knowledge of the abstract principles of language that enables us to learn our first language with ease and accounts for the rapidity and universality of first language acquisition. It is posited that this "language acquisition device" is available only to young children, and adults therefore have to rely on general cognitive abilities to acquire an L2 (Bley-Vroman 1989). However, this would not explain the existence of multiple sensitive periods.

4.5   Conclusion

This chapter has shown the significant influence on SDA of one individual factor, age of acquisition, and its interaction with two linguistic factors: type of variable (linguistic level) and rule complexity. With regard to what is the best explanation for age effects on SDA (and SLA), there is still no general agreement. But the interference of prior learning, in either the biological sense or the cognitive sense, seems to have received the most support.

The next chapter looks at some other individual and linguistic factors that affect SDA.

5 Additional individual and linguistic factors

As mentioned in the preceding chapter, in order to account for differential results in D2 attainment, studies of SDA have examined both individual factors relating to learners, and linguistic factors relating to variables. This chapter looks at additional factors in both of these categories.

5.1 Additional individual factors

In addition to age of acquisition (AoA), individual factors studied in SDA include length of residence, social identity, gender, degree of social interaction with D2 speakers, motivation and attitudes, and occupation. These factors and their relationships are described here.

5.1.1 Length of residence (LoR)

One of the most commonly examined factors in studies of naturalistic SDA is length of residence (LoR) – i.e. how long the acquirer has lived in the D2 region. The LoRs, or ranges of LoR among subjects, for each of the seventeen studies examined in Chapter 2 are given in Table 4.1 in the preceding chapter. A quick glance at the first three studies seems to indicate that LoR is not a consistently significant factor, since the children in Tagliamonte and Molfenter's (2007) study reached native-like usage after six years but those in Trudgill's (1981) did so in less than one year, and some in Berthele's (2002) did so in two years whereas others did not. The rest of the figures for LoR are not very helpful because of the wide ranges. But we do find many examples of subjects with long LoRs yet very low percentages of use of D2 variants. For example, two subjects in Kerswill's (1994) study had lived in Bergen for thirty-five and thirty-seven years, yet their use of Bergen morpholexical features was only 12.4 per cent and 15.0 per cent, respectively. Two others, with similar AoAs, lived in Bergen for seventeen years, but had percentages of 39.5 and 42.1.[1] In Omdal's (1994) study, three subjects with LoR in the twenty- to twenty-four-year range had percentages of use of L2 variants of 6.0, 18.0 and 57.0.

Seven studies specifically examined whether there were correlations between individuals' LoR and their use of D2 variants. Of these studies, the following four found no statistically significant correlation between LoR and D2 attainment: Ivars (1994: 214), Omdal (1994),[2] Wells (1973)[3] and Shockey (1984: 90). However, three studies did find that LoR had some effect.

Payne (1976) divided the children in each of the three age groups based on AoA (see Table 4.2 in Chapter 4 above) into two further groups according to LoR in King of Prussia: four to seven years and eight to sixteen years. LoR appeared to be slightly relevant only for the 5–9 AoA group, with those staying for eight to sixteen years acquiring 69 per cent of the total number of variables for the group, and those staying for four to seven years acquiring only 56 per cent (p. 123).

In contrast to Payne's and other studies, Foreman (2003) found an overall positive correlation between LoR and the use of AusE variants for all six of the variables she examined – i.e. the longer the LoR the higher the percentages of AusE pronunciation. This was a statistically significant factor when some of the other possible factors were eliminated – especially AoA. But LoR may have been confounded with AoA, since the subjects were interviewed as adults, and thus those who had arrived at a younger age had longer in the country (p. 208). Kerswill (1994) found intercorrelations between LoR and AoA as well, and therefore included only AoA in his final statistical analysis.

Stanford (2007) also did not find any correlation between LoR and D2 attainment, simply because there was almost no D2 attainment in his study of married Sui women. As noted (Section 2.3.9) in Chapter 2, however, the one exception (with regard to the tonal variables) was a woman had been married for forty years in the North. As also mentioned, interviews revealed that in rare cases some long-term residents may acquire some of the D2 features (p. 188). On the other hand, a long LoR clearly does not necessarily lead to SDA, as seen with two other subjects in Stanford's study with LoRs of thirty-five and forty-three years who did not use any of the D2 features being investigated. In another study, two of Foreman's (2003) subjects had lived in Australia for twenty-five years, but did not use any AusE variants in the six variables examined.

The next question is whether there is a minimum LoR required for SDA. Foreman (2003: 229) reported that all the speakers who acquired some AusE features had lived in Australia for at least five years. With regard to native-like usage of D2 variants, we have seen two different stories. It took the children in Tagliamonte and Molfenter's (2007) study six years to reach native-like usage, but the children in Trudgill's (1981) study only eight months. The difference might be in the complexity of the features that were examined. Tagliamonte and Molfenter looked at the suppression of t/d-flapping as well as the acquisition of the glottal stop variant [ʔ] instead

Table 5.1 *Comparative results over two years for percentages of use of D2 (Southern England English) lexical and pronunciation variants*

	9	13X	13Y	14	15	Group
1985 % SEE lexical variants	71.4	65	24	64	52	52.3
1987 % SEE lexical variants	83	64	64	76	56	72.6
1985 % pronunciation variants	60	20	20	40	20	26.7
1987 % pronunciation variants	60	20	20	60	40	40.0

of [t] at the end of words, while Trudgill looked at the acquisition of fifteen phonetic/phonological D2 variants that involved mainly categorical substitution.

Another question concerns those who have long LoRs but use D2 variants only a small proportion of the time: are they still progressing in their SDA or have they reached a limit of their acquisition? Three longitudinal studies throw some light on this matter. In 1987, two years after his original interviews with the six Canadian youths in England, Chambers (1992, 1995) conducted another set of interviews with five of them. (The eldest had moved back to Canada to go to university.) Chambers looked again at lexical and pronunciation replacements, and recorded the comparative results shown in Table 5.1.

The results show overall gains in both lexical and pronunciation replacements over two years, but they are very modest, except for lexical replacements for one of the 13-year-olds. Chambers (1992: 680) suggested that "dialect acquirers make most of the lexical replacements they will make in the first two years", and from the results in Table 5.1, a similar statement could be made for pronunciation replacements.

The second longitudinal study concerned six of the subjects in Foreman's (2003) main study who had been previously interviewed in 1988 for a study by Clyne (1992). Tape-recorded data from these interviews along with the 1999 interviews of these subjects formed the basis of an additional study (Foreman 2000), which compared the use of the same six AusE variables in 1988 and 1999.

Two of the six subjects, T and J, continued in not changing their pronunciations at all in the direction of AusE, at least with regard to the six linguistic variables. Two other subjects, M and P, increased their percentages of AusE pronunciations for some variables, but decreased them for others. However, these changes were not statistically significant (see Table 5.2).[4]

For a further longitudinal study reported in Foreman (2003), the remaining two subjects, B and L, were again interviewed in 2001, and they also provided earlier recordings of their speech from 1974 and 1981. Thus, data for these

Table 5.2 *Comparative results over eleven years for percentage of use of D2 (Australian English) variants*

	(r)	(KIT)	(GOAT)	(FLEECE)	(FACE)	(PRICE)	Average
M 1988	12.2	25.7	25.6	2.6	6.0	30.8	17.2
M 1999	8.7	31.2	28.8	7.2	14.7	41.6	22.0
P 1988	0	0	4.2	14.7	24.3	0	7.2
P 1999	0	0	4.7	6.6	25.2	0	6.1

Table 5.3 *Longitudinal results for percentages of D2 (Australian English) variants for subject B*

	1974	1981	1988	1999	2001
(r)	0	0	0	0	0
(KIT)	0	0	0	0	0
(GOAT)	0	4.4	10.3	13.9	10.9
(FLEECE)	0	0	0	0	2.8
(FACE)	0	0	0	0	0
(PRICE)	0	0	0	0	0
Average	0	0.7	1.7	2.3	2.3

Table 5.4 *Longitudinal results for percentages of D2 (Australian English) variants for subject L*

	1974	1981	1988	1999	2001
(r)	0	22.2	43.9	25.8	22.8
(KIT)	0	66.6	32.7	33.0	25.1
(GOAT)	0	27.3	44.6	45.1	38.9
(FLEECE)	0	2.2	2.0	0.9	2.4
(FACE)	0	44.1	37.5	45.6	25.9
(PRICE)	0	36.6	18.6	12.5	8.2
Average	0	33.2	29.9	27.1	20.6

two subjects could be analysed from five different interviews over twenty-seven years, starting from approximately six months after their arrival in Australia. The results are given in Tables 5.3 and 5.4.[5] The tables show that it took several years of residence before they began to use any AusE variants, and that there were ups and downs in the percentages of AusE pronunciations of different variables.

Table 5.5 *Bayard's son's percentages of use of R-lessness from 1980 to 1998*

Year	Age	Percentage used talking to peers	Percentage used talking to parents
1980	2	0	0
1986	8	68.3	34.2
1990	12	36.7	19.0
1994	16	41.7	14.9
1998	20	31.7	18.6

The overall results of this longitudinal study also appear to show that migrants who acquired D2 features in their first few years living in the D2 dialect area reached a plateau in the percentage of use of these features, similar to that described by Chambers for lexical variables. Additional years of residence did not lead to substantial increases in their use; rather, there were both modest increases and decreases over the years in the use of different variables. This suggests that the many subjects in other studies with long LoRs may not progress further with more time.

The results also suggest that speakers who do not acquire any D2 pronunciations in the first few years after migrating will not acquire any later, even after many years of residence, as with the two of the six subjects, T and J. The acquisition of at least one feature in the first few years appears to leave open the possibility of later acquisition of other features, as with subject B (Foreman 2003: 204). However, in most cases, if the AusE pronunciation of a variable was not acquired in the first seven years, it was not acquired later.

The third longitudinal study concerned Bayard's son's use of the feature of R-lessness in his D2 (NZE) versus non-prevocalic /r/ in his D1 (AmE). The percentages of use of the D2 variant (R-lessness) since he started acquiring NZE are shown in Table 5.5.[6] This is discussed further below.

Chambers' (1992) and Foreman's (2003) longitudinal studies appear to confirm that what has been called "fossilisation" in the SLA literature also occurs in SDA. (For overviews, see Long 2003; Han and Selinker 2005.) Here I use the term fossilisation to mean the cessation of progress towards to the target variety – the empirically observed phenomenon, not the cognitive process that causes it. In this case the target variety is the D2. Fossilisation in SLA is normally indicated by the continued use of morphosyntactic features that deviate from the norms of the target variety – for example, a lack of past tense marking as in *Yesterday he see the boy*. In SDA, however, fossilisation is indicated mainly by the plateau in the use of acquired features, as described by Chambers and Foreman – i.e. the fact that the percentage of use of acquired D2 variants has stopped increasing even after several more years in the D2 context. Some of the intermediate or interdialect forms (discussed in Chapter 3) that continue to be used after a long LoR may also be evidence of fossilisation, but these have not been studied longitudinally.

Of course, it is appropriate to talk of fossilisation only in learners who have adequate ability, learning opportunities and motivation (Long 2003: 494). In Foreman's longitudinal study, this was especially true for subject L. She arrived in Australia at age 7, and therefore clearly had the potential to reach native-like attainment in AusE. She lived in Australia for 27 years and interacted primarily with Australians. And at least in later interviews, she expressed motivation to speak more like her Australian peers (Foreman 2003: 256). Yet, after reaching a peak of 33.2 per cent of the use of the AusE variants for the six variables studied by Foreman, the percentage gradually decreased rather than increased in the following three recordings, reaching a low of 20.6 per cent in 2001.

Whether or not Bayard's study demonstrates fossilisation is an open question, as his son's use of an acquired feature decreased dramatically between the ages of 8 and 12, and then levelled out. This may indicate a lack of motivation to speak like his New Zealand peers, and may be connected with issues of social identity, discussed in the following subsection.

5.1.2   Social identity and identification with the D2 group

The term "social identity" refers to the part of a person's self-image based on the characteristics and attitudes of the social group or groups which that person belongs to or aspires to belong to. Early inquiry into the role of social identity in SLA again came from the social psychological approach, which considers language to be a salient marker of group membership and thus of social identity. Various theories or models were developed to characterise and quantify social identity on either the group or individual level, and then examine its relationship with other factors, such as motivation and degree of social interaction with L2 speakers, and ultimately with L2 attainment (Pavlenko and Blackledge 2004a: 4).

More recent studies take the view that people have multiple and changing social identities, rather than the unitary static social identity of most social psychological models, and that identity at any particular time depends on the context. However, the characteristics of aspects of a learner's identity are still seen to affect motivation and interaction, and thus ultimate L2 attainment (see Block 2007).

The complex issues of social identity with regard to SDA are discussed in more detail in Chapter 6. Here we will look particularly at the factor of identification with the D2-speaking group.

Underwood (1988) reported on a study undertaken in Texas specifically to look at the relationship between dialect use and identification. He emphasised the distinction between identification with a group, and membership in that group (p. 409) – that is, one can identify with a certain group of people, and therefore aim to speak like that group, without actually being a member of that group. The study concerned the pronunciation of the /aɪ/ diphthong as in PRICE, which in the Texan dialect is pronounced as the monophthong [a], similar to the first vowel in *father*. (This also occurs in other southern American dialects – for example, in Alabama as described in Chapter 3.)

Underwood constructed a six-point Index of Texas Identification, based on answers to a series of questions about attitudes to other Texans, and used this to rate each of 134 subjects. He also recorded each subject reading a one-page passage with sixty-two occurrences of the /aɪ/ diphthong, and then calculated the frequency of the Texan monophthongal variant for each one. As in other studies, the subjects were divided into groups according to age, background (rural, town or city), education, gender, socio-economic class and ethnicity. However, there was no correlation between any particular social group and use of the Texan variant. On the other hand, when the subjects were divided into four groups according to their frequencies of use of the Texan variant, there was a clear relationship to their scores on the Index of Texas Identification – the greater the use of the Texan monophthong, the higher the score on the index. Thus, Underwood concluded (pp. 417–18) that "a speaker's Texas accent, as revealed by the use of the Texas /ai/, is directly related to that person's sense of identity as a Texan".[7]

The degree of identification with the D2-speaking group may be related to fossilisation, as discussed in the preceding section. Of relevance here is an important study by Escure (1997) on SDA in both naturalistic and educational contexts in two very different locations, First, she examined acrolectal varieties of Belize Creole which she assumed were the result of partial acquisition of standard English. Second, she analysed texts of Putonghua (standard Beijing Mandarin Chinese) produced by speakers of other dialects of the language (Wuhan and Suzhou). Escure found that both the acrolects of Belize Creole and the second dialect versions of Putonghua differed from the D1 as well as the "target" D2 (the standard) in some aspects of phonology and morphology. However, they did not differ pragmatically from the D1 in informal discourse structure, using basically the same strategies for marking topics. With regard to persistence of D1 features in production of the D2, Escure observed (p. 275) that the notion of fossilisation "fails to capture the dynamic, innovative, and – at least subconsciously – intentional use of old features to preserve a sociolinguistic identity distinct from the majority (usually dominant) group identity". In other words, people may continue to use features of their D1 rather than those of the D2 not because of factors related to their learning capacity but because of factors related to their social identity – i.e. maintenance of the identity they associate with the D1 or avoidance of the identity they associate with the D2. This is very relevant to SDA in both naturalistic and educational contexts, as discussed in more detail in Chapters 6 and 7.

With regard to the studies of SDA surveyed in Chapter 2, only four looked specifically at the factor of social identity. In Omdal's (1994) study in Norway, informants were asked: "Do you see yourself now as a *setesdøl* (person from Setesdal) or as a *kristiansander*?" (p. 136). Of the twenty-four informants, seventeen identified themselves as being a person from Setesdal (the D1 area), and only two as being from Kristiansand (the D2 area). Five regarded themselves as having a "double identity" (p. 136). Their self-assessment of identity did not correspond to length of time spent away from Setesdal or in Kristiansand, or to the percentage of use of D2 variants.

Foreman (2003) examined the role of national identity as part of the qualitative analysis of interview data in her Australian study. First of all, the question of identity was an important but complicated factor for many of the subjects. Some clearly identified as still being Canadian or American (D1), while others identified as being Australian (D2). But Foreman noted (p. 235) that many were "unsure of their identity or uncomfortable with the topic". (See further discussion in Chapter 6.) One reason for this was that many were not fully committed to staying in Australia and left the door open to return to Canada or the USA. Others who were fully committed to Australia still felt different from those who were born in the country. Still others felt as if they were partly Australian, even though they still considered themselves as Canadian or American. Nevertheless, out of the twelve subjects who acquired some AusE features, eight reported having at least a partly Australian identity, and two claimed not to have any national identity (p. 244). The majority of subjects who did not acquire AusE features maintained only their Canadian or American identity. Of course this could have been a matter of age of arrival as well, since those arriving at a young age and growing up in Australia would be more likely to identify as Australian (p. 244). Nevertheless, an important fact emerged in the interviews with regard to the subjects who were the youngest arrivals. As mentioned above (Chapter 4, Section 4.2), subject U, who arrived at age 6, used a high percentage of AusE features and could pass as a native speaker. Subjects P and C, who arrived at ages 7 and 10, had high percentages for some AusE features, but still sounded like foreigners. One important difference between them was that subject U identified strongly as an Australian while the other two did not (p. 238n).

In Ivars' (1994) study in Sweden, informants were asked whether they considered Närpes (where the D1 is spoken) or Eskilstuna (where the D2 is spoken) to be their home town. The most common answers were those such as "both" or "half and half" (p. 221). This appears relevant to the fact that, as mentioned in Chapter 3, most informants in this study maintained their D1 and added the D2 to their repertoires, so that there was frequent code-switching between the two dialects.

With regard to identity, Ivars noted (1994: 221) that although many of the Finland Swedes came to Sweden with the intention of assimilating, the features of their dialect gave them away as not being local:

They discover quite quickly that they are not immediately accepted as Swedes: time after time they are forced to explain to Swedish friends, neighbors and colleagues how it is that they "speak Swedish so well even though they are from Finland".

They also realised that they have very different backgrounds and ways of thinking from the Swedish Swedes: "You never become Swedish, you know where you have come from" (p. 222). As with the North Americans in Australia who maintained their original identities, and therefore their original dialects, Ivars noted (p. 222): "Finland Swedish identity is most strongly expressed in the preservation of the dialect." But in contrast, the Finland Swedish immigrants appear to have formed a Sweden Swedish identity as well as maintained their original one. Ivars concluded (p. 221) that the immigrants "identify both with their place of birth and their new place of residence", and that "the Eskilstuna and Närpes varieties become the linguistic expression of the double identity they have assumed".

In his study in China, Stanford (2007, 2008a) drew on the information he had gathered on the role of social identity in the local Sui context in order to explain the virtual lack of SDA among married women who moved to a new dialect area. Stanford found out that Sui people identify strongly with their father's clan throughout their lives. Each man, woman and child marks their clan membership and identity linguistically by using features of the dialect associated with their clan. Married women still identify with their father's clan even though they are living with members of their husband's clan, who speak a different dialect. Therefore, the women maintain their original dialect rather than acquiring the dialect of their new home.

Stanford (2007: 40) referred to the model of language use proposed by Le Page and Tabouret-Keller (1985) in their book *Acts of Identity*. According to this model, people project a particular identity by speaking like those they wish to identify with. Stanford concluded that the Sui people perform "acts of clan identity", and when these acts are performed by married women, they "override the norm of dialect acquisition" (p. 40). These linguistic acts of identity thus "promote dialect distinctiveness in the face of long-term contact" (Stanford 2008a: 38).

In summary, in three out of four studies, individual D2 use was affected by the extent to which the person identified with the D2 dialect area or with speakers of that dialect. Thus, social identity would seem to be an individual factor worth examining in future studies of SDA.

5.1.3   Gender

An intricate part of one's social identity is gender. While gender has rarely been considered as a factor affecting variable attainment in studies of SLA, it has frequently been found to be a significant individual factor in sociolinguistic studies of language variation and change. Since many SDA studies have been influenced by sociolinguistic approaches, several have also examined the role of gender. Two of those we have looked at – Wells (1973) and Shockey (1984) – found no statistically significant relationship between gender and D2 attainment. In other words, there was no significant difference between the women's and the men's results. Also, as reported by Rys (2007: 116), Vousten (1995) concluded that gender was not a significant factor in the study in Limburg in the Netherlands (described in Chapter 2 on the basis of the article by Vousten and Bongaerts 1995).

In her Australian study, Foreman (2003) reported that out of the thirty-four subjects (twenty female and fourteen male), the twelve that used some features of AusE were all female. So it would seem that gender was a significant individual factor, suggesting perhaps that women have a better aptitude for SDA. However, as Foreman pointed out (p. 207), all of the subjects with a young age of arrival were female. Also, Foreman interviewed some males for the study who clearly had acquired some AusE features, but they were not among the subjects whose interviews were used for the statistical analysis (for various reasons described above, such as living for a time in another English-speaking country). Therefore, Foreman concluded that the lop-sided results were probably due to chance (p. 207).

In Norway, Kerswill (1994) also found no significant differences between men's and women's index scores for the use of D1 morpholexical variants. However, more detailed statistical analysis showed that these scores were affected by different sets of other individual factors – for example, factors such as age and AoA affecting the women's scores but not the men's. This is a typical finding for gender effects – i.e. that if there is gender differentiation, it is the result of secondary factors, and not any intrinsic differences between females and males.

In Bortoni-Ricardo's (1985) study in Brazil, gender was significant only with regard to the fourth variable, with men using 1st person plural subject–verb agreement much more frequently overall than women. It was also significant with regard to the first variable (concerning the 'l' sound), but only for the youth group, with younger females using the urban variant much more consistently than younger males. (There were also gender differences with regard to social interaction and salience, as described below.)

In her study in Sweden, Ivars (1994) divided her thirty-two informants into four groups according to age at the time of interview and gender: older women, older men, younger women and younger men. Older meant 40 years or over. (Recall, however, that AoA was actually more important than current age.) The younger groups used a higher percentage of D2 variants than the older groups, and the difference was statistically significant. However, the difference between the percentages for the female groups versus the male groups was not significant. On the other hand, Ivars noted that the younger women had the highest percentages of D2 variant use and older women the lowest, with the two men's groups in the middle (p. 213). The younger women's group were also the most consistent in separating features of the D1 and D2, and using each one without mixing in different contexts. The explanation for the gender differences also has to do with occupation and social interaction, as described below in Section 5.1.6.

Two studies, however, did report overall gender differences. In Finland, Nuolijärvi (1994) found that among migrants to Helsinki, men continued to use D1 features more than women, although the percentages were very small for both groups: 6.8 versus 4.0 (p. 159). According to Nuolijärvi (p. 158), these results agreed with those of similar studies (such as Ivars'): "young women readily adopt the manner of speaking of their new environment". However, Nuolijärvi attributed this to women being subject to "more intense social control" than men (p. 158). This is also related to the nature of their occupations (see Section 5.1.6 below).

In Belgium, Rys's (2007) statistical analysis showed that gender had a strong effect on D2 acquisition (p. 275), with boys significantly more successful than girls. Rys suggested (p. 331) that girls who acquire a D2 which is a non-standard dialect (like the Maldegem dialect) are "more reserved with the use of dialect forms" than boys, and that "this may be related to the fact that girls are more sensitive to factors of prestige". The D1, standard Southern (Belgian) Dutch, clearly has more prestige. It is well known that for stable sociolinguistic variables, women do use a higher rate of prestige variants than men (e.g. Labov 2001: 266), but there is no other evidence that this occurs with regard to acquisitional variables. Another factor, suggested by Rys on the basis of other studies on Dutch dialects, is that boys make more efforts than girls to acquire the local dialect, often through seeking wider social interactions with D2 speakers. This brings us to the next individual factor.

5.1.4   Social interaction

It is well accepted that in order to learn a second language, there must be a sufficient amount of social interaction with speakers of that language. The same is assumed to be true for a second dialect. For example, in Hiramoto's

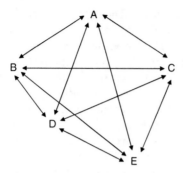

Figure 5.1 A closed (high-density) social network

(in press) study of Japanese immigrants in Hawai'i, Tôhoku dialect speakers who had daily social interaction with speakers of other dialects used D2 morphosyntactic features more frequently than those who did not have such interaction. And in Tagliamonte and Molfenter's (2007) study in England, starting school was an important milestone that resulted in accelerated use of D2 variants. The authors attributed this partially to greater social interaction with D2 speakers (p. 665).

The problem, however, has been finding ways to measure the degree of this interaction. Some studies of SLA in naturalistic contexts have looked mainly at general concepts that determine the amount of contact between learners and L2 speakers – as in Schumann's (1978, 1986) "acculturation model" (see Siegel 2003: 187–8). Others examine the language used in different domains, such as in the home, at work and in social activities. In contrast, some studies of SDA in naturalistic contexts have adopted the concept of social networks, which has also been employed in sociolinguistics (e.g. Milroy 1987).[8]

In sociolinguistics, the term "social network" refers to the patterns of interaction among a group of individuals. Two individuals are considered connected with each other in the network if they regularly communicate with each other. An individual is said to be in a "closed" social network if all of their contacts are also in regular contact with each other, as shown in Figure 5.1. An individual is in an "open" social network when their contacts are not in regular contact with each other, as shown in Figure 5.2.

Closed networks are also described as being of "high density", with open networks as of "low density". When the contacts between individuals are on several different levels – for example, as neighbours, workmates and friends – then the network is called "multiplex". When the contacts are on only one level, it is "uniplex".

With regard to language change, it is claimed that relatively dense multi-plex social networks tend to enforce linguistic norms, and therefore resist

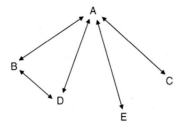

Figure 5.2 An open (low-density) social network

linguistic change. In naturalistic SDA, it would be assumed that dense multiplex networks would initially be with fellow immigrants, and thus promote maintenance of the D1. In contrast, open uniplex networks would be more likely to involve speakers of the D2 – e.g. as either a neighbour or workmate – and therefore promote acquisition of the D2.

Another aspect of social networks is whether or not the network is insulated or integrated. An insulated network among immigrants is restricted to relatives and previous acquaintances from the homeland. In addition, it is often territorially bounded – that is, links are with individuals who live in close proximity to each other. In contrast, in an integrated network contacts are with a wider range of people outside the immigrant community (Bortoni-Ricardo 1985: 116–17). It would be expected that an immigrant in an insulated network would be less likely to interact with speakers of the D2 than one in an integrated network, and therefore that an integrated network would promote SDA.

Bortoni-Ricardo (1985) developed two indices regarding social networks and examined their possible correlations with individual variation in SDA among the adult immigrants in Brazil. The "network integration index" was an indicator of the immigrant's transition from the insulated network that existed before migration, based on relatives and local acquaintances, to a more heterogeneous network, based on people living in the urban environment. Each informant was asked to nominate three people outside the home with whom they talked most frequently, and their individual index score was calculated on the basis of the number of their direct and indirect links (p. 167).

The "urbanisation index" indicated to what degree the members of a migrant's social network were integrated into the urban culture of Brasília. This was determined on the basis of sociolinguistic factors such as occupation, schooling level, degree of exposure to media, spatial mobility, participation in urban events and political awareness (1985: 169).

Bortoni-Ricardo found that a correlation existed between the integration index and frequency of use of the standard urban variant, but only in the first and the third variable (see Chapter 2, Section 2.3.2) and only for men. For the urbanisation index, however, a correlation existed for both men and women in the first variable, and only for men in the third and fourth variable. Bortoni-Ricardo's explanation was that men's integration index scores reflected how heterogeneous their social networks were in the urban environment and thus indicated the degree of exposure to the mainstream urban culture (p. 210). On the other hand, women's integration index scores reflected social networks that were still largely restricted to the home and family. Thus, the degree of exposure and integration into the urban culture was an important determinant of the acquisition of features of the urban dialect, especially when the features were salient, as with the first and fourth feature (see Section 5.2.1 below). The conclusion, however, was that the changes "should not be viewed as an assimilation of the standard urban language but rather as a movement away from the stigmatized Caipira dialect" (1985: 239).

One of the individual factors that Kerswill (1994) examined as possibly affecting individuals' SDA in Norway was the degree of "Strilness" or "Bergenness" of the informant's social network in Bergen (p. 56). A score was given to each informant based on factors such as the frequency of visits to the rural Stril district, the geographic origins of other members of the household, involvement in Stril organisations in Bergen, and the nature of contacts at work and outside work. The higher the score, the more interaction with others from Stril. As expected, higher scores correlated in general with lower percentages of use of Bergen morpholexical variants. However, two of the four informants who attained native-like use of the Bergan variants had higher scores as well. These were the code-switchers (see Chapter 3, Section 3.3) who acquired the Bergen dialect at a relatively early age but still maintained extensive contacts with Stril speakers. The other two, who habitually spoke only the Bergen dialect, had much lower scores, one factor being that they were both married to Bergeners (p. 119).

Foreman (2003) also examined the relationship between social networks and use of AusE variants. A social network score was calculated for each subject based on the number and frequency of contacts with other Canadians or Americans. She also looked at the dialect used at home and at work, and whether or not the subject belonged to a Canadian or American social club. The findings for the main study were that a lower social network score corresponded to higher percentages of use for the GOAT, FLEECE, FACE and PRICE variables, but these correlations were not statistically significant. However, the subjects in Foreman's study differed from those in Bortoni-Ricardo's and Kerswill's studies in that they generally did not maintain close network links with other immigrants (p. 209). AusE, rather than CanE or AmE, as the home dialect also corresponded to greater use of AusE variants. However, the work dialect and social club membership did not show any

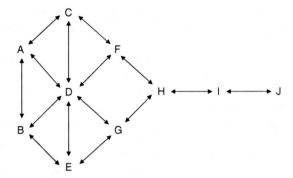

Figure 5.3 Core and periphery of a social network

strong effects because nearly all the subjects worked in AusE-speaking environments and did not belong to social clubs.

Another way that social networks are used in relation to SDA is to see if an individual's position in the network has an effect on their use of the D2. For example, in the network shown in Figure 5.3, individual D has a central position at the core of the network with links to a large number of others, while individual J is at the periphery, with only a single link. At least two SDA studies have examined social networks of children that include both native speakers and acquirers of the D2, focusing on the position of the D2 acquirers in these networks. The assumption was that the more central an acquirer's position is in the network, the greater their interaction with D2 speakers, and therefore the greater the attainment in the D2 (or the higher the percentage of use of D2 variants for the variables under study).

In order to determine whether a child had a central or a peripheral position in the social network of the peer group in King of Prussia (Philadelphia), Payne (1976) extracted information from her interviews with 108 children, including both native D2 speakers and D2 acquirers. For each of the thirty-four children acquiring the D2, she determined the number of times the child referred to their peers during the interview, and the total number of times that child was mentioned by other children in their interviews (p. 265). The implication was that the more a child was mentioned, the more central they would be in the peer group. However, Payne concluded that there was no correlation between position in the social network and attainment in the D2 (pp. 236, 265–8).

On the other hand, using more sophisticated statistical methods, Labov (2001) re-analysed Payne's data on the use of Philadelphia variants and the effects of the individual factors of age, AoA, LoR, and the number of times a child was mentioned by peers, which he said was "the most sensitive index of the density of the speaker's social network" (p. 430). He found that the most significant factor was the number of mentions – and not AoA, as in other studies.

In his study in Switzerland, Berthele (2002) determined individuals' peer group positions on the basis of his observations of classroom interactions and interviews with students. He found that variation of use of D2 variants correlated with the structure of these social networks. The students in a more central position in the peer group used more features of the D2, whereas those in a more peripheral position used fewer features. One student's speech could hardly be distinguished from that of native D2-speaking children (p. 334) and this student was at the centre of the children's social network structure. (This was also the student, mentioned in Section 3.3 above, who became bidialectal, maintaining her D1 in the family context.) In this study, AoA and LoR were the same for all the children, so position in the social network was clearly important.

5.1.5   Motivation and attitudes

One of the most significant factors found to affect attainment in SLA is motivation. This construct, most prominent in social psychological studies of SLA, is usually defined as the inclination to put in effort to achieve a desired goal – in this case, acquisition of the L2. The motivation of subjects is thought to be determined by a combination of several factors, and it is generally measured by using self-report questionnaires. Nearly all social psychological models of SLA distinguish two types of orientation that may affect motivation. "Instrumental orientation" relates to the communicative value of the L2 and the need to learn it for a particular purpose, such as getting a job or fulfilling some educational requirement. "Integrative orientation" relates to the learner's wish to identify with the L2-speaking community (as described in Section 5.1.2 above), and is associated with positive attitudes towards this community and a desire to have more contact with them. The greater the instrumental or integrative orientation and the more positive the attitudes towards the L2-speaking community, the greater the motivation to acquire the L2, and the higher the eventual attainment in it (Gardner 1985; Masgoret and Gardner 2003). However, the concept of motivation has always been surrounded by theoretical controversies, and in the early twenty-first century, a more multi-faceted and dynamic view of motivation in SLA has emerged with input from other fields, such as education, and from other areas of psychology (Dörnyei and Skehan 2003; Dörnyei 2005).

With regard to SDA, it seems the perception may be that there would be little communicative value in acquiring a D2, except for a few lexical items or pronunciations that could lead to misunderstanding. However, instrumental orientation might still be relevant with regard to the acquisition of a standard dialect that is a requirement for employment or education. With regard to naturalistic SDA, however, integrative orientation appears to be more relevant, especially for people who have moved to a new dialect area.

However, very few studies of SDA have examined motivation or attitudes towards the D2 or D2 community as an individual factor. This is somewhat surprising, since it is well known that many people have strong attitudes towards particular dialects (and their speakers) – generally positive attitudes towards standard dialects, such as standard English, and negative attitudes towards unstandardised regional or ethnic dialects, such as Appalachian English and African American English in the USA, and Newcastle English ("Geordie") in Britain. (See, for example, Lippi-Green 1997; and various chapters in Long and Preston 2002.) One reason for some of the studies not considering attitudes may be that they dealt with national dialects – such as Canadian English, Australian English and American English – that nowadays do not usually evoke strong attitudes, positive or negative, from speakers of other dialects. And as mentioned in Chapter 2, the dialects in China studied by Stanford (2007) did not differ from one another in terms of prestige.

Two studies that did examine the effect of attitudes were done in situations where the D1 had lower overt prestige than the D2. Kerswill (1994) included attitudes as one of the social parameters in his Norway study, but these were attitudes towards the D1 (the rural Stril dialect) rather than the D2 (the more prestigious urban Bergen dialect). Attitudes for each informant were quantified on a four-point scale on the basis of statements they made about the Stril dialect and its use, with higher scores indicating more positive attitudes. The implication was that the more positive the attitudes Stril speakers had towards their dialect, the more they would maintain it and continue to use lexical and morphosyntactic features from the D1 (Stril) rather than the D2 (Bergen). This was confirmed in the study by a significant correlation between attitude scores and morpholexical index scores (which indicated the percentage of use of Stril features).

Omdal's (1994) study, also done in Norway, was unique in that one of its main goals was to examine the effect of attitudes on dialect acquisition. These attitudes were of two types: first, attitudes towards the modifications that were occurring in people's speech as the result of rural–urban migration – i.e. attitudes towards SDA itself – and second, attitudes towards both the D1 (the rural Setesdal dialect) and the D2 (the more prestigious urban Kristiansand dialect). Each of the twenty-four informants was asked five specific interview questions to elicit attitudes towards speech modifications. The answers were rated on a five-point scale from negative to positive, and the average score for all five questions calculated. Informants were also asked three questions about the Setesdal and Kristiansand dialects, but only the attitudes towards the Setesdal dialect were quantified, again by giving each informant a score from one to five on each question, and calculating the average. Scores for both types of attitudes were then compared to the language modification index for each informant – i.e. the percentage of use of D2 (Kristiansand) variants. The results were that there was only a weak correlation between positive attitudes towards modification and actual modification towards the D2. And there was hardly any relationship at all, positive or negative, between attitudes towards the Setesdal dialect (D2) and use of its features.

A third study that considered attitudes was done in a situation where the D1 had higher overt prestige than the D2. This was Rys's (2007) research in Belgium with standard Southern (Belgian) Dutch as the D1 and the local Maldegem dialect the D2. Following studies in SLA, she examined the effect of the social psychological construct of motivation and attitude on SDA in Maldegem. To quantify the individual factor of "attitudes/motivation", Rys used a scaled-down version of the Attitude/Motivation Test Battery (Gardner and Smythe 1981; Gardner 1985), as adopted by Vousten (1995).[9] Each informant was asked to agree or disagree with each of fifteen statements about the nature of the two dialects and about speaking them. A point was given for a yes answer to a positive statement about the D2, such as "I think it is important to be able to speak (the local) dialect, because my friends speak it as well." A point was also given for a no answer to a negative statement, such as "I take no trouble to learn (the local) dialect, because everyone understands Standard Dutch" (p. 149). The points for each informant's answers were totalled, with the maximum score of fifteen interpreted as showing the greatest motivation for learning the Maldegem dialect and the most positive attitudes towards it. The results demonstrated that higher scores in the attitudes/motivation test correlated with greater use of D2 dialect features.

In summary, two out of the three studies showed some signficant correlations between attitudes and SDA. One showed that positive attitudes towards the D1 correlate with continued use of D1 rather than D2 variants. The other showed that positive attitudes towards the D2 correlate with the use of D2 rather than D1 variants.

5.1.6   Occupation and interaction of other individual factors

We have seen that various individual factors overlap to some extent (e.g. social identity and motivation) and that it is often the interaction of individual factors that affects SDA rather than any particular factor on its own. One factor that often interacts with others is occupation. For example, as mentioned in the discussion of gender above, in Ivars' (1994) study in Sweden, the younger women had the highest use of D2 variants and the greatest separation of the D1 and D2. Ivars attributed this to occupation, one of the factors that is also usually included in compiling indices of social interaction. Since migrating to Sweden, the majority of the younger women subjects were employed in service occupations that required more language skills than the primarily industrial jobs that the majority of younger men were employed in. Furthermore, before migrating, the younger women had been involved in occupations such as shop assistants and telephone operators that involved using the standard language as well as the local dialect. Thus they had become sensitive to dialect differences and learned how to maintain two distinct dialects and switch between them according to context (p. 217). On the other hand, other characteristics of the younger women's group, such as younger AoAs and higher levels of education, may also have been responsible for their greater D2 attainment and code-switching abilities.

In her study of Japanese immigrants in Hawai'i, Hiramoto (in press) also found that occupation was an important factor but only because of its connection with degree of social interaction. Those in occupations that required frequent interaction with speakers of other dialects (such as salespersons and barbers) were the ones who used more D2 features. Similarly, in Nuolijärvi's (1994) study in Finland, subjects in occupations that involved daily contacts with people they did not know (e.g. bus drivers and waitresses) used D1 features less frequently than those in other occupations (e.g. carpenters and seamstresses). However, Nuolijärvi pointed out (p. 158) that there was still a connection with gender, as women's work in general is more subject to external control than men's.

In Brazil, Bortoni-Ricardo (1985) looked at occupation as well as other individual factors not discussed so far: level of schooling, level of political awareness and level of exposure to the media. This last factor had some significance with regard to two of the variables. However, others on their own were not especially significant, although some were closely related to other factors, such as social networks.

In Norway, Kerswill's (1994) social parameters included occupational status. The effect of this factor was significant: higher occupational status corresponded to greater schwa-lowering. This was surprising, as this is a non-standard feature of the Bergen dialect and occurs less frequently among the higher social classes. However, Kerswill surmised that its use by the Stril migrants may simply be part of "sounding like a Bergener" (p. 126), or a way of signalling orientation away from the Stril rural community and towards the urban one.

5.1.7   Conclusion: individual factors

The most important factors that account for differences in the degree of SDA among different individuals appear to be the age at which they begin to acquire the D2, the degree of social interaction with D2 speakers and perhaps the extent of identification with the D2-speaking community.

5.2   Additional linguistic factors

In addition to linguistic level and complexity of rules (discussed in Chapter 4), factors such as salience and predictability affect the degree of acquisition of particular D2 features. These and other linguistic factors are described here.

5.2.1   *Salience*

The term "salience" refers to the characteristic of being easily noticeable, prominent or conspicuous. But while this notion seems straightforward on the surface, it is surrounded by controversy in studies of dialect change and acquisition.

Trudgill (1986: 11) equated salience with awareness, and stated that "in contact with speakers of other language varieties, speakers modify those features of their own varieties of which they are most aware". With regard to SDA, this seems to say that the awareness must be of the D1 feature, rather than the corresponding target D2 feature. However, Trudgill also talked about salient features being "accommodated to" (p. 16). This implies that the awareness must be of the D2 feature. But awareness would normally result from some sort of contrast – i.e. we notice a feature of our speech because it differs from the way other people talk, or we notice a feature of others' speech because it differs from the way we talk. These alternative features are what we have been calling linguistic variants of a linguistic variable. Indeed, Trudgill also referred to awareness of variables (p. 11). So, it seems that with regard to awareness of features in SDA, Trudgill was referring to either the D1 variant, or the D2 variant or the variable as a whole.

According to Trudgill (1986: 11), awareness or salience is due to one or more of the following factors, each examined individually below: stigmatisation, linguistic change, phonetic distance and phonological contrast.

Stigmatisation   A variant is salient when it is overtly stigmatised by sections of the larger community because it sounds too uneducated or too rural. Another reason may be that it contrasts with a high-status variant that matches the orthography. For example, one reason that "*h*-dropping" (as in *'ouse* versus *house* and *'andle* versus *handle*) is stigmatised is that the word is spelled with *h*. Stigmatised features are often stereotypes that are imitated or mimicked in joking or making fun of that dialect – for example, the flat A's of my Chicago dialect and the former pronunciation of *ir/er* in the New York City dialect (Chapter 3).

In SDA, the prediction would be that a variant in the D2 would be more likely to be acquired when the corresponding variant in the D1 is stigmatised. This was confirmed to some extent in the studies of dialect shift we briefly looked at in Section 2.5 above. For example, Hiramoto's (in press) study of Japanese immigrants in Hawai'i showed that Tôhoku dialect speakers largely abandoned the stigmatised stereotypical morphological features of their dialect and acquired variants from the majority Chûgoku dialect or standard Japanese. However, they still maintained stigmatised phonological features of their L1.

Stigmatised features were mentioned only a few times in the other seventeen studies. One example was in Bortoni-Ricardo's (1985: 175) study in Brazil. She noted that the Caipira D1 'l' vocalisation is very stigmatised, while the other D1 phonological variant, reduction of diphthongs, is not a stereotype, and "many standard language speakers are unaware of its existence" (p. 192). Nevertheless, the percentages of use of the standard D2 variants were higher for the reduction-of-diphthongs variable than for the 'l'-vocalisation variable, for both the youth and adult groups (88 and 53 per cent versus 81 and 49 per cent). In another example, Chambers (1992) demonstrated that a stigmatised feature of the SEE D2, Intrusive /r/, was acquired by the youngest of the CanE D1 youths in his study.

Linguistic change A variant is also supposed to be salient when it is undergoing linguistic change – for example, /æ/ becoming tense short-*a* [ɛə] in northern inland cities of the USA. In his study of Waldorf exiles, mentioned in Chapter 3, Bowie (2000) referred to a recent change that had occurred in the Waldorf dialect. This was that /æ/ (as in TRAP) had become fronted before nasal consonants (e.g. /m/ and /n/), so that, for example, *sand* sounded closer to *send*. This feature was also characteristic of some of the dialect areas in which the exiles were living, and was reflected in the exiles living there who had been away for seven years or less. However, those who had moved away from Waldorf nine or more years earlier, before the change had begun there, showed less fronting, or a tendency towards less fronting (p. 58). Bowie's hypothesis was that "the features that are generally the most susceptible to change in an individual's linguistic system are those which are undergoing a change in the individual's original dialect" (p. 136).

However, Foreman (2003: 271–2) did not find confirmation of this hypothesis in her total Australian data, which included some unquantified variables additional to those described in Chapter 2. Those speakers who did use some AusE variants did so for the vowels in GOAT, GOOSE and FOOT, all of which are affected by recent vowel shifts in AmE and CanE. However, some had acquired these variants in the early 1970s, presumably before the vowel shifts began. Furthermore, subjects were more successful in acquiring the AusE variant for the DRESS vowel, which is not part of any linguistic change in AmE or CanE, than they were for the TRAP vowel, which has been involved in change, becoming tense short-*a*. Foreman concluded (p. 272) that Bowie's hypothesis – and by extension, Trudgill's factor of linguistic change – may be relevant only when there is "a phonological match between the D1 and the D2".

Payne (1976: 97) had the opposite view of the effect of linguistic change. She suggested that a possible factor responsible for the relatively lower rate of acquisition of the Philadelphia variants of the (aw) and (ay) variables was that these variants were actually the result of changes in progress in the Philadelphia dialect. As a consequence of this, she concluded, these features were not so salient to speakers.

Phonetic distance   According to Trudgill (1986: 11), a variant is salient when it is phonetically "radically different" from the corresponding variant of that variable. For example, in the R-lessness variable, one variant is the presence of a sound (non-prevocalic /r/) and one is its absence. Thus, there is no similarity between the variants. This kind of variable would be more salient than one in which the two variants are similar – as with the KIT variable for AusE and NAE, where the AusE variant is only slightly raised compared to the NAE variant. However, the results of the studies do not back up the relevance of this factor. For example, in Foreman's (2003) study in Australia, the use of AusE variants for vowels phonetically close to those of NAE, such as for the KIT vowel, was much greater than the use of the AusE variant for non-prevocalic /r/.

Phonological contrast   A variable is purportedly salient if it is involved with distinguishing meaning. Trudgill (1986: 11) gave the example of words such as *huge*, *cue*, *view* and *tune* in which the vowel can be pronounced as either [ʉː] or [jʉː] in the Norwich dialect. When the second variant is used, it distinguishes the meaning between words in pairs such as *Hugh/who, dew/do* and *feud/food*. This factor would be relevant to mergers and splits. For example, in the LOT–PALM merger, the distinction between /ɒ/ and /ɑ/ was lost, so that words such as *bomb* and *balm* are both pronounced the same (with /ɑ/). In Chambers' (1992) study, this concerns the variable that he called Low Vowel Merger. This variable would be salient because the SEE variant distinguishes /ɒ/ and /ɑ/, and therefore words such as *bomb* and *balm*. T-Voicing could also be considered a merger, and thus a loss of a phonological contrast, with words in pairs such as *latter/ladder* and *writing/riding* pronounced the same.

In Payne's Philadelphia study, two variables involved merging, and thus phonological contrast: (er), concerning word pairs such as FERRY/FURRY, and (ohr), concerning pairs such as SURE/SHORE. Thus, by Trudgill's criteria, these variables should have been salient. However, as shown in Section 2.2.2 above, their rates of acquisition were much lower than those for the five phonetic variables in the study that were presumably not so salient.

In summary, while Trudgill's four factors may make a feature salient, this salience does not appear to have any straightforward affect on the degree to which a D1 variant is abandoned or a D2 variant acquired. Furthermore, although Trudgill hypothesised that if a D2 feature is salient, it should be easily "accommodated to" (i.e. acquired to some extent), this clearly is not true in some cases. Trudgill's explanation (1986: 16) was that salience is not the whole story; there are some intervening factors that can "delay, inhibit or even prevent accommodation". For example, although non-prevocalic /r/ is a salient feature of American English, it is not used by speakers of British English in America. This was attributed to a phonotactic constraint in the phonology of British English that prevents /r/ from occurring anywhere except before a vowel. In another example, the BrE pronunciation of /ɒ/ in words such as *hot* and *cod* was not changed to the /ɑ/ of AmE. This was attributed to the avoidance of "homonymic clash". In other words, if the pronunciation of *hot* and *cod*, for example, were changed to the AmE /hɑt/ and /kɑd/, they would have virtually the same pronunciation as the words *heart* and *card* in BrE, and thus create new homonyms (words with the same pronunciation but different meanings). In yet another example, the AmE pronunciation of the vowel in *dance*, *last* and *class* as /æ/ rather than /ɑ/ was not immediately adopted by southern BrE speakers in the USA. The explanation here was that the vowel /æ/ is "*too* salient an American feature" and "it sounds, and feels, *too American*. The stereotype is too strong" (p. 18, emphasis in original).

Several researchers (e.g. Hinskens 1996; Kerswill 1994; Kerswill and Williams 2002: 88–91) have criticised Trudgill's notion of salience as being ad hoc and circular. The most obvious example of this is the use of the same notion of salience to account for both the adoption and non-adoption of a D2 feature. For example, British pop singers are described as using the AmE /æ/ pronunciation in words such as *dance* because it is a salient feature of AmE, for both the singers and other British people (Trudgill 1986: 13). But then, as just mentioned, some British people are described as not using the same AmE pronunciation because it is too salient (p. 18).

Auer *et al.* (1998) also described various criteria for determining the salience of a variant in "long-term dialect accommodation". These were based on criteria proposed by the Russian dialectologist Schirmunski (e.g. 1930), as well as some of those proposed more recently by Trudgill (1986) and other linguists, such as Hinskens (1996). These criteria were divided into two groups. Objective criteria are those that can be determined by linguistic analysis of a particular feature – i.e. they are language-internal. Subjective criteria are those resulting from an analysis of speakers' perceptions and use of the feature in question – i.e. they are extra-linguistic. The objective criteria were as follows (p. 167):

> articulatory distance
> areal distribution
> phonemicity
> continuous versus dichotomous
> lexicalisation

The first criterion, articulatory distance, is the same as Trudgill's phonetic distance, and phonemicity the same as his phonological contrast. The areal distribution criterion predicts that dialect features used only in a restricted area will be more salient and therefore given up in dialect contact. Continuous features are those that can have intermediate forms – for example, the GOAT diphthong which is [oʊ] in NAE and [ɑu] (or other variants) in AusE, but can sometimes be pronounced [ʌu] by acquirers of AusE. Dichotomous features, on the other hand, have two distinct variants – for example, either the presence or absence of non-prevocalic /r/. Dichotomous features are said to be more salient. Lexicalisation, a term with many meanings in linguistics, here refers to the type of conditioning involved in the rules for the use of a particular sound. Recall that in straightforward phonological conditioning, rules can be applied to a sound across the board, no matter what word it occurs in. In contrast, in lexical conditioning, whether or not the rule can be applied depends on the particular word the sound occurs in. Thus, the rule is said to be lexicalised. As we have seen in the discussion of complexity in Section 4.3 above, rules that involve lexical conditioning (or lexicalisation) are more complex than those that involve straightforward phonological conditioning. Here variants that depend on complex lexicalised rules are said to be more salient than those that depend on simple phonological rules.

The subjective criteria for determining the salience of a variant were as follows (Auer *et al.* 1998: 167):

> perceptual distance
> usage in code-alternation
> representation in lay dialect writing
> stereotyping/mimicking
> comprehensibility

Perceptual distance refers to speakers' perceptions of phonetic distance. Again, distant variants are considered more salient. Use of a dialect feature when switching to or speaking in another dialect, or in writing (especially when it requires changes in the usual orthography), is also an indication of the salience of that feature. Stereotyping is basically the same as Trudgill's stigmatisation. And features that impede comprehension between speakers of different dialects are also judged to be salient.

Unlike Trudgill (1986), Auer *et al.* (1998: 168) proposed a useful distinction between dialect acquisition and dialect shift (or loss), and the effect of salience of features in each. As explained earlier, while studies of dialect acquisition focus on which features of a new dialect (D2) are adopted by speakers, studies of dialect shift focus on which features of the original dialect (D1) are given up. Salience according to different criteria may have differential effects depending on whether we are considering dialect acquisition or dialect shift. For example, as the authors pointed out (p. 168), features involving complex lexicalised rules are salient, and thus such features of the D1 are likely to be given up early in language shift. But as we have seen in Section 4.3 above, the same kinds of features when they occur in the D2 are very difficult to acquire. Similarly, if a feature is stigmatised or stereotyped in the D1, it is likely to be abandoned, but if such a feature occurs in the D2, it is not likely to be adopted.

In order to assess their criteria for salience, Auer *et al.* (1998) used data from their study of dialect shift in Germany (summarised in Section 2.5.1 above), which examined replacement of Upper Saxonian Vernacular (USV) features with standard German (StGer). Three objective criteria were examined in the analysis: phonemicity (where merging was involved – i.e. a phonemic opposition in StGer was neutralised in USV); continuous versus dichotomous structure; and lexicalisation (here, exclusive lexicalisation, when a certain variable occurs only in certain lexical items). Three subjective criteria were also examined: code-alternation (actually shifting between informal interview style and reading aloud style); representation in writing; and stereotyping/mimicking. Auer *et al.* (1998: 170) concluded that the articulatory (or phonemic) distance criterion was impossible to examine because "there is no phonetically satisfactory method to measure phonetic difference *across* variables" (emphasis in original). The same held true for perceptual distance. Areal distribution could not be examined because all the features under investigation are found throughout the Upper Saxonia area. No data were available for comprehensibility.

Although a stated aim of the analysis was to see if salience was a good predictor of dialect loss and acquisition (1998: 164), it actually focused on whether or not the salience of each of the twelve variables correlated with the degree of attrition in its use over a two-year period. This attrition was calculated in three ways. First, it was based on the percentage of use of the USV (D1) variant over time. Second, and only for continuous rather than dichotomous variables, it was based on the percentage of use of both the USV variant and any intermediate forms – in other words, on the total percentage of use of non-standard forms. Third, and again only for continuous variables, it was based on the percentage of use of only intermediate forms. As mentioned in Section 2.5.1 above, the actual D1 variants were referred to as strong USV forms, and the intermediate forms as weak USV forms.

The D1 variants of two variables, (AI) and (AU), were clearly the most salient, fulfilling all six objective and subjective criteria, while two others, (O:) and (U:) were the least salient, fulfilling none of the criteria.[10] When considering the use of only strong USV forms, there was no attrition for (AI) and relatively little (20 per cent) for (AU). On the other hand, attrition was moderately high (49 per cent) for (O:) and high (74 per cent) for (U:) (1998: 179). Thus, on this basis, the degree of attrition clearly did not correspond to the degree of salience. On the other hand, when considering the use of only weak USV forms (i.e. intermediate forms), there was a strong correlation between degree of attrition and degree of salience (p. 182). But since none of these variables involved phonemicity (as represented by merging) or was dichotomous or was lexicalised, no objective linguistic criteria – i.e. only subjective criteria – were relevant.

Kerswill and Williams (2002) examined salience on the basis of the results of dialect contact in three cities in Britain. Like Auer *et al.* (1998), they found that extra-linguistic factors were crucial in determining salience. These include "cognitive, pragmatic, interactional, social psychological and socio-demographic factors" (2002: 105). However, the authors concluded that at least one language-internal factor appears to be necessary for a feature to be salient. With regard to Trudgill's (1986) factors, they pointed out (p. 90) that stigmatisation is actually sociolinguistic, and a sign of salience rather than an explanation for it. And the linguistic change factor is circular, if salience is being used to account for aspects of language change, such as acquisition. But the authors included Trudgill's factors of great phonetic distance and the presence of phonological contrast among the possible language-internal explanations for salience.

Another language-internal explanation that Kerswill and Williams referred to was perceptual prominence (2002: 84). This is mainly concerned with morphological variants. For example, a grammatical marker, such as an affix for tense or agreement, is more noticeable (i.e. salient) if it is a separate, stressed syllable. In her Brazil study, Bortoni-Ricardo (1985) concluded that this kind of salience was important with regard to the standard D2 variants for the morphological variables. For example, the third person singular–plural opposition for some tenses of some verbs involves a small vowel change in an unstressed ending (in the spoken, not written, language) – e.g. the present tense singular *come* /kɔ́mi/ 'eat' versus the plural *comen* /kɔ́mĩ/, in which the final unstressed vowel becomes nasalised. Compare this to the preterite (past) tense singular *falou* /fálou/ 'talked' versus the plural *falaram* /fálaru/, in which the final ending is stressed and there is a significant vowel change as well as an additional ending (1985: 203). As would be predicted, standard subject–verb agreement was more frequent with verbs that have a more salient (or noticeable) change in the verb ending. Thus, this is one case where it seems possible to establish salience on the basis of linguistic-internal factors alone, and this salience appears to be a determinant of the degree of use of a D2 feature.

But in general, salience is determined by an extremely complex set of linguistic and non-linguistic factors. Hinskens, Auer and Kerswill (2005: 45) conclude (with regard to dialect convergence and divergence):

> In the end it may not be possible, even in principle, to predict levels of salience. It may also be impossible to determine whether a given level of salience, once established, leads to the adoption or the non-adoption of a feature.

However, with regard to SDA it appears that some degree of salience is a necessary but not sufficient condition for a D2 feature to be acquired (see Auer *et al.* 1998: 167). In other words, in order to be acquired, a D2 feature must be salient enough to be noticed by a D1 speaker, but this salience does not mean that the feature will necessarily be acquired.

This view is supported by research in SLA. If learners are going to develop a new mental representation for the L2, they must have exposure to input from the L2. But exposure alone is not enough. As pointed out by Rod Ellis (1994), input can be converted to implicit knowledge (or the cognitive skills necessary to use language) only when three processes occur: (1) noticing, (2) comparing and (3) integrating. The first process is crucial here. According to Schmidt's "noticing hypothesis" (1990, 1993, 2001), a target language (L2) form will not be acquired unless it is noticed by the learner, and awareness through attention is necessary for noticing. And as we have seen, awareness is closely associated with salience.

That awareness or salience is not a sufficient condition for D2 acquisition has been shown in several of the studies described in Chapter 2. For example, Stanford's (2007) study in China showed that overwhelmingly the Sui women did not acquire the clan dialect of their new home, even after living there for nine years or more. This was true of all lexical, phonetic and suprasegmental variables in both formal and informal speech, and regardless of the salience of the features. Thus, even though tone pattern 6 was salient (as opposed to tone pattern 1, which was below the level of consciousness), it was not acquired at all.

5.2.2   Predictability

As part of her study in Belgium, Rys (2007) proposed that the learnability (i.e. the ease of learning) of particular dialect features depends on

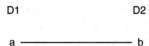

Figure 5.4 A one-to-one relationship between D1 and D2 variants

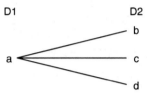

Figure 5.5 A one-to-many relationship between D1 and D2 variants

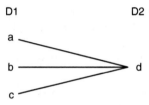

Figure 5.6 A many-to-one relationship between D1 and D2 variants

"predictability" – the degree to which a learner can predict the D2 form on the basis of the D1. Predictability is determined by a number of interrelated factors, which she operationalised individually for her study. Some of these factors are related to rule complexity and salience, as discussed above. The factors are outlined below.

Number of competing variants   It was hypothesised that when there is a one-to-one relationship between D1 and D2 variants, as shown in Figure 5.4, learnability of the D2 variant will be easiest.

But when there is a one-to-many (or many-to-one) relationship, learnability is more difficult. This is when there is more than one possible variant in the D2 corresponding to a single variant in the D1 (Figure 5.5), or when two or more variants in the D1 correspond to one variant in the D2 (Figure 5.6).

Note that the case in Figure 5.5 corresponds to what we have been calling splitting and the case in Figure 5.6 to merging.

For each of the thirty-four variables used in Rys's study, the number of competing variants was determined in both the D1, standard Southern

(Belgian) Dutch (SD), and the D2, the Maldegem dialect (DIA). SD values ranged from 1 to 5 and DIA from 1 to 6.

Incidence (or type frequency) This factor refers to the lexical distribution of the variable – i.e. in how many different lexical items it occurs – for example, the number of different words in which SD [aː] before /ts/ corresponds to DIA [ɑ] (e.g. DIA [kɑtsn̩] and SD [kaːtsən] 'to bounce'). The incidence for each variable except the productive ones (see below) was determined on the basis of two vocabulary lists for Belgian Dutch, with words removed that would not occur in the Maldegem dialect (p. 139). The hypothesis was that the higher the incidence, the greater the learnability.

Frequency of usage (or token frequency) This refers to the number of times a variable is actually used in speech – e.g. the total number of occurrences of words in which SD [aː] corresponds to DIA [ɑ] before /ts/ in a particular corpus of speech. The frequency of usage assigned to each variable, again except the productive ones, was determined from the Corpus of Spoken Dutch, which contains approximately seven million words (Rys 2007: 143). Material was selected from the informants speaking dialects most closely related to Maldegem, and the frequency of each of the 167 words on the word list was calculated. The frequency of usage figure for each variable was based on the average of the frequencies for the words containing the feature. The hypothesis was, again, that the higher the frequency of usage, the greater the learnability.

Conditioning environment The prediction here was that if the environment for phonological conditioning of the target D2 feature is clear (e.g. occurring before a particular sound, such as /ts/), it will be easier to acquire. If the feature is lexically conditioned, rather than phonologically conditioned, it will be more difficult to acquire.

Productivity Productive features are those that would apply to new words, such as loanwords, as well as to already existing words. For example, in DIA /l/ is deleted and the preceding vowel lengthened before a consonant. This feature occurs in loanwords and proper names from English – for example, [bodibiːdɪŋ] 'body-building' and [æːvis] 'Elvis'. Productive D2 features are hypothesised as being more learnable than non-productive features.

Geographical distribution The hypothesis was that dialect features found only in a small geographic area would be more salient and therefore acquired better than those found over wider geographic areas and thus less noticeable. Each feature was assigned a figure from 1 to 24 based on the extent of its geographical distribution.

Results   The results of Rys's analysis (2007: 227–73) showed that all the hypotheses were borne out, except one. The D2 features acquired best were those that had fewer competing variants in the D1, higher incidence and frequency of use, clear conditioning environments, productivity and smaller geographic distribution. Surprisingly, however, the number of competing variants in the D2 did not have a significant effect, contradicting the findings concerning splitting in other studies (p. 311). On the other hand, this factor appeared to be significant in interactions with others, such as conditioning environment, productivity and average frequency (2007: 329). Rys also explored interactions between other factors, but these are too complicated to go into here.

5.2.3   Other linguistic factors

Several other linguistic factors have been proposed to account for different rates of acquisition of D2 variants. These are described briefly here.

Comprehensibility   Comprehensibility was a factor mentioned by Auer *et al.* (1998). Speakers are likely to use a D2 feature when use of a D1 feature impedes comprehension among D2 speakers. Trudgill (1986) gave a few examples concerning changes he made to his British English in America. One was his use of non-prevocalic /r/ in *Barb* so that it wouldn't be confused with the American pronunciation of *Bob* (p. 15). Another was his use of the intervocalic flap for /t/, in order to avoid misunderstanding of the type that occurred when he said his first name, *Peter*, and the hearer thought he wanted a *pizza* (p. 23). Trudgill (pp. 22–3) also referred to Shockey's (1984) study of Americans in England (Section 2.2.3 above) in which subjects repressed AmE flapping of /t/ much more than /d/ (63.8 per cent use of BrE /t/ versus 35.5 of BrE /d/). His explanation was that because the flap is much closer to BrE /d/ than to /t/, unflapping /t/ is more important for comprehensibility of words such as *putting* (versus *pudding*) and *latter* (versus *ladder*).

In my own experience, I quickly acquired the AusE (and BrE) pronunciation of *can't* as /kɑnt/ (with the PALM vowel). This was because my AmE pronunciation /kænt/ (with the TRAP vowel) was confused with the AusE pronunciation of *can*, which is /kæn/ (with the TRAP vowel) when it is emphasised in a sentence. Comprehension was especially difficult in a sentence where the verb started with a /t/ – e.g. *I can't talk to you now*, which using the AmE pronunciation would sound to an Australian like *I **can** talk to you now*.

New rules versus old rules   Chambers (1992) asserted that the elimination of old rules occurs more easily than the acquisition of new ones, pointing out (p. 695): "The process of dialect acquisition involves not only coming to sound more like the people in the new region but also coming to sound less like the people in the old region." This can be seen in the group average scores in Table 2.6 (Chapter 2). The absence of T-Voicing and of the Low Vowel Merger, instances of eliminating old rules (according to Chambers), have higher scores (55 and 31.6 per cent) than the presence of Vowel Backing, R-lessness and Intrusive /r/ (23.3, 8.3 and 6.7 per cent), instances of acquiring new rules. However, in some cases, Chambers' distinction is somewhat fuzzy. For example, the absence of the old Low Vowel Merger, which Chambers counts as elimination of old rules, requires the acquisition of a new phoneme /ɒ/, as well as learning which words affected by the merger have this vowel and which ones have /ɑ/.

Literacy and orthography   Chambers (1992) also posited that orthographically distinct variants are acquired faster than orthographically obscure ones (p. 697). His explanation for the very low percentage of use of the SEE feature of R-lessness by the Canadian youths was that words such as *four, forty* and *summer* are spelled with 'r', but the 'r' is not pronounced in SEE – and thus the variant is orthographically obscure. In contrast, with regard to T-Voicing, although word pairs such as *putting/pudding* and *hearty/hardy* are pronounced the same in CanE, they have different spellings, and thus are orthographically distinct. So it is easier to learn that in SEE what is spelled with 't' is pronounced as /t/ rather than /d/. Of course, as Chambers pointed out (p. 697), a crucial factor is that for this principle to apply, the second dialect acquirers must be literate. As already mentioned, in their study with Canadian children in northeastern England, Tagliamonte and Molfenter (2007) also reported that starting school was an important sociocultural milestone that resulted in accelerated use of NEE variants for T-Voicing (including use of /t/ instead of /d/ or a flap). They also attributed this to the acquisition of literacy, as well as to greater social interaction with NEE speakers (pp. 664–5).

Bortoni-Ricardo's (1985) study in Brazil may provide some support as well. For both phonological variables, the D2 variants (lack of vocalisation of the alveopalatal lateral [λ] and full pronunciation of the diphthongs /ɪa/ and /ɪu/) had high percentages of use, especially in the youth group, who attended school. Both of these are orthographically distinct – the lateral [λ] represented by *lh* as in *mulher* 'woman' and the diphthongs by *ia* and *io* as in *dúzia* 'dozen' and *lábio* 'lip'. However, the lateral [λ] also occurs without the *lh* spelling, when *l* is followed by *ia* or *io* as in *família* 'family' and *Basílio* (a man's name). This inconsistency may account for the higher scores for

Table 5.6 *Word types and percentages of D2*
(Australian English) variants

Word type	Percentage
Noun	30.4
Verb	24.5
Utterance modifier	19.9
Adjective	11.5
Pronoun	7.4
Preposition	3.1
Adverb	2.1
Qualifier	1.2

use of the diphthongs than for use of the lateral (see Bortoni-Ricardo 1985: 179–80).

Word class   On the basis of her study of dialect shift towards standard Yiddish (see Section 3.4.1 above), Prince (1987) hypothesised that target D2 variants would be used more frequently in open-class words (e.g. nouns, verbs and adjectives) than in closed-class words (e.g. pronouns, prepositions and determiners such as *the*, *this*, *that*). The reason is that more attention is paid to open-class words. This hypothesis appeared to be confirmed by the data for some variables in the study.

Similarly, Foreman (2003) found in her Australian study that low frequency words with greater semantic content, such as nouns and verbs (i.e. open-class) had a higher percentage of AusE pronunciation than high frequency words with grammatical functions, such as pronouns and prepositions (i.e. closed-class). However, what she called "utterance modifiers" also had a relatively high percentage. These include discourse markers, sentence particles or hedges, such as *you know*, *well*, *I suppose*, *like*, *sort of*; interjections, such as *oh*, *yes*; focus particles, such as *still*, *anyway*; and conjunctions, such as *and*, *but*. The percentages for each word type are given in Table 5.6.[11]

Foreman noted (2003: 175) that the term "utterance modifiers" is used by Matras (1998), who pointed out that these kinds of words are commonly vulnerable to code-switching – i.e. when bilinguals alternate between languages, or use words from one language they know when speaking the other. There are many possible explanations for this phenomenon in studies of bilingualism and SLA (see Foreman 2003: 184–6).

Foreman also mentioned two other linguistic factors that may be relevant. First, the AusE pronunciation of single vowels and diphthongs was more likely when they occurred at the end of words with one syllable – for example, *say, day, go, no*. Second, the AusE pronunciation was more likely in stressed syllables or stressed words of one syllable (p. 174). This may seem to support the role of salience; however, the opposite was true for non-prevocalic /r/.

5.2.4   Conclusion: linguistic factors

The most important linguistic factors that account for differences in the degree of acquisition or use among D2 variants appear to be the linguistic level of the variable (lexical, phonological, morphological) and rule complexity (also referred to as conditioning environment), as discussed in both Chapter 4 and this chapter. Other, less straightforward, influential linguistic factors are the degree of salience (as determined by perceptual prominence) and frequency (both type and token). However, in order to be acquired, a variant must be salient enough to be noticed.

6   The difficulty of SDA

As mentioned in Chapter 1, the popular consensus appears to be that SDA is easier or "less traumatic" than SLA (Escure 1997: 7). This is because of the small linguistic distance between the D1 and the D2 compared to that between the L1 and L2. However, some scholars have the opposite point of view – that SDA is more difficult than SLA – and for the same reason – i.e. the small distance between the D1 and D2. For example, Haugen (1964: 125) wrote: "Bidialectalism may actually be harder to acquire than bilingualism. All scholars have agreed that it is harder to keep two similar languages apart than two very different ones." And Wolfram and Schilling-Estes (1998: 287) noted: "In some ways, it may be easier to work with language systems that are drastically different, since the temptation to merge overlapping structures and ignore relatively minor differences is not as great."

Rather than get into an argument about whether SDA is more difficult than SLA overall, this chapter presents some of the particular aspects of SDA that are especially difficult compared to SLA. Of course, because of the age effects described in Chapter 4, these difficulties do not pertain to children 7 years and younger, and are relevant mainly to older children, adolescents and adults. While I still restrict the discussion to naturalistic contexts, some of the observations are also relevant to educational contexts, as described in later chapters. In the first section below, I describe some of the relevant differences between research in SDA and SLA, and the goals and tasks of learners in each. Then I go on to explore the ramifications of the small distance between the D1 and the D2. The next section goes into the sociolinguistic factors that make SDA different from SLA. This is followed by an illustration of how the difficulty of acquiring a second dialect may be relevant to contact-induced language change.

6.1   SDA versus SLA

Comparing SDA and SLA is not an easy or straightforward task for several reasons. First of all, while it would be illustrative to compare the levels of attainment reached in the SDA studies described in Chapter 2 to those of similar studies in SLA, it is hard to find similar naturalistic studies of SLA. It is even harder to find SLA studies that give percentages of acquisition of particular L2 features – especially phonological features, which are emphasised in SDA studies. Nevertheless, we can compare overall success in other ways.

The fairly recent SLA studies that do deal with the acquisition of phonology in naturalistic contexts give native speakers' evaluations of subjects with regard to their perceived nativeness, rather than performance data. For example, Bongaerts *et al.* (2000), mentioned in Section 4.4.1 of Chapter 4 above, studied thirty well-educated L2 speakers of Dutch with various L2 backgrounds who had settled in the Netherlands between the ages of 11 and 34 and learned Dutch naturalistically. Recordings of their speech, randomly mixed with recordings of the speech of ten native speakers, were rated for foreign accent by twenty-one judges, all native speakers of Dutch with tertiary education, and eleven of them teachers of Dutch as an L2 (the experienced judges). They were asked to rate each speaker using a Dutch version of a scale ranging "from 1 (very strong accent: definitely non-native) to 5 (no foreign accent at all: definitely native)" (p. 301). The results were that two of the subjects, with AoA of 14 and 21, passed as native speakers. Two other subjects were also considered native-like according to the ratings of only the experienced judges (Bongaerts *et al.* 2000: 305). If we compare these results to those of the SDA studies, we do not see any examples of similar success in reaching native-like performance in the D2. None of the subjects with an AoA over 13 years was reported as being native-like or reached consistent native-like usage (90 per cent or more) of the D2 variants of the phonetic/phonological variables examined.

As another comparison, we can look at the acquisition rates concerning one variable in both SLA and SDA. Beebe (1980) studied nine adult L1 speakers of Thai who were living in New York and were acquiring American English as an L2. One subject was 40 years old but the rest ranged in age from 25 to 33. The data came from recorded conversation and word list reading in interviews. The variable examined was the use of /r/ in initial and final position in AmE. The 'r' sound in Thai is a trill, similar to that in Spanish, and thus different from English. Furthermore, the 'r' sound in Thai does not occur in final position – which is non-prevocalic – and in this way Thai is similar to non-rhotic (i.e. R-less) dialects of English, such as British and Australian English. In Beebe's study, the average of the percentages of use of the correct L2 form of /r/ in final position for the nine subjects was 35 per cent for conversations and 72 per cent for word lists (p. 437). Compare these results to the relative lack of acquisition of non-prevocalic /r/ among speakers of British English in America. For example, Trudgill (1986: 15) observed that "the vast majority of English English speakers in the USA do not acquire this feature until they have been in America for a considerable period (say ten years), if at all". Also, the percentages for the opposite side of the coin, the use of R-lessness by North Americans in England and Australia, were much lower – 8.3 per cent in Chambers (1992) and 6.7 in Foreman (2003).[1]

Nevertheless, conclusions about the relative difficulty of SDA and SLA cannot be made on the basis of overall attainment because the two differ in their starting points and ultimate goals for attainment. For example, one could say that SDA must be harder than SLA because in no SLA studies would you find large numbers of learners not acquiring any phonological features of the L2 as in some studies of SDA – e.g. Foreman (2003) in Australia and Stanford (2007) in China. But at the same time, one could say that SDA must be easier than SLA because at the end of all the studies learners can communicate effectively in the D2 in any context, even after as little as two years of acquisition.

These examples may seem a bit silly, but they illustrate the important point that with regard to linguistic knowledge, the starting points for SDA and SLA are very different. L2 learners typically have no linguistic knowledge of the L2 when they begin SLA. But D2 learners know most of the lexicon, phonology, morphology and syntax of the D2 when they start SDA, and just have to learn the relatively few aspects of the D2 that differ from the D1. This is illustrated in Figure 6.1. In each case, the line represents the total knowledge of the language or dialect. Point x represents the starting point for the learner, and point z the point at which a mature native speaker would be. Thus the knowledge needed to be acquired to reach native speaker proficiency in each case is represented by the distance from x to z. It is clear that much more knowledge needs to be acquired for SLA than for SDA. $D2^b$ represents a dialect that is more distant from the D1 than $D2^a$ (in other words, it has more lexical, phonological, morphological or syntactic differences). But even for SDA with dialects that are more different from one another, the required learning is not as great as for SLA.

On the other hand, Figure 6.1 also illustrates that it is relatively easier to make perceptible progress in SLA. Learners who get halfway from point x to point z in SLA would cover a much greater distance along the line than those who get halfway to point z in SDA. Thus, for learners judging their own progress, SDA may appear to be more difficult.

Furthermore, there is a difference in the overall nature of the knowledge that needs to be acquired in SLA and SDA. It appears that in terms of the amount of knowledge that needs to be acquired, and the characteristics of this knowledge, starting D2 learners are at a stage of acquisition similar to that of advanced L2 learners (Long 2007). This is illustrated in Figure 6.2, where point y represents the stage of acquisition reached by an advanced learner, and x the initial stage for a beginning D2 acquirer. Another way of looking at

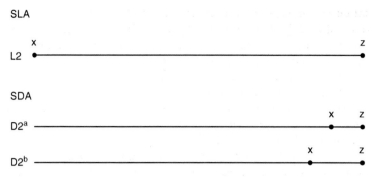

Figure 6.1 Different starting points for SLA and SDA

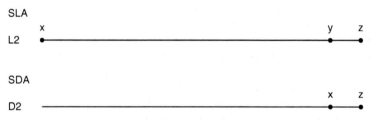

Figure 6.2 Similar stages of acquisition for advanced learners in SLA and beginners in SDA

this is that the advanced L2 learner's proficiency in the L2 is similar to the beginning D2 acquirer's proficiency in the D2. Thus, for both types of learners, the distance between their current state of knowledge and that of a mature native speaker (y to z and x to z in Figure 6.2) is similarly small. This point is relevant to the following section on language distance.

There is also a similarity in the amount of knowledge the learners have to acquire, and perhaps in the particular aspects of this knowledge as well. The difficulty for advanced learners in bridging this last small gap is well known, and often they can proceed no further and remain as "near native speakers" (Han and Selinker 2005). While this may occur at all linguistic levels (lexical, morphological, etc.), it is most common in phonology. Thus, a person may be fluent in an L2, but still retain some non-native production of certain sounds – i.e. a foreign accent. For SLA, this is the rule more than the exception, and it is common to hear comments like "Tobias speaks English with a German accent." With regard to SDA, however, the gap between x and z may be almost exclusively phonological – for example, between national dialects such as American English and Australian English. And in such cases, while incomplete acquisition is common, it would seem odd to say: "Jane speaks Australian English with an American accent." This would generally not be true when a standard dialect is the D2. For example, there's nothing odd about saying: "Anna speaks standard German with a Bavarian accent" or "Clinton speaks (American) English with a Southern accent." But in cases where the D1 and the D2 are equal in status or prestige, or the D1 is higher in this regard than the D2, then SDA seems to be a matter of all or nothing, and in such cases, the goal for ultimate attainment would be higher than that for SLA, and thus more difficult to achieve.

The reasons for learning a D2 versus learning an L2 may also differ. In SLA, the reasons may be communication, utilisation and integration, or various combinations of these. For example, a learner may want to acquire enough of the L2 to be able to communicate when travelling in the country where the language is spoken. Learners who live in this country, however, may want to acquire enough of the language to get a job and interact with L2 speakers (utilisation). And those that plan to stay there may want to acquire enough to sound as though they are part of the community (integration). If the reason for learning is not integration, then the end result the learner is aiming for does not have to be native speaker-like proficiency. For example, with the increasing importance of the use of English as an international language, the focus is generally only on intelligible communication and utilisation. In SDA, on the other hand, communication is usually not perceived to be an issue, because the D1 and the D2 are generally mutually intelligible. Utilisation may be important in some contexts, especially when the D2 is the standard variety. But the most important reason for SDA, especially in naturalistic contexts involving migration, appears to be integration – the desire to be a part of the new community and be viewed as a local, or at least someone who is not "straight off the boat". Thus, again, the ultimate goals for D2 acquirers are often higher than those for L2 learners.

Closely connected to the goals of acquisition is motivation, as discussed in Section 5.1.5 above. A person who ends up in a new country where a different language is spoken will usually acquire some of the L2 for basic communication, even if they have no instrumental or integrative motivation. But, as just mentioned, a person who ends up in a new dialect area may not perceive any communicative reason to acquire the D2, and if they have no instrumental or integrative motivation, they may acquire very little of it, if any.

6.2   Distance between the D1 and D2

As referred to above, some scholars have attributed the difficulty of acquiring a second dialect to the small linguistic distance between the D1 and the D2 – i.e. to their similarity. Referring to standard and non-standard vernacular dialects, for example, Wolfram and Schilling-Estes (1998: 287) pointed out:

When two systems are highly similar, with minor differences, it is sometimes difficult to keep the systems apart. In such cases of widescale overlap, more careful attention to the small differences is required – especially if one language has already been thoroughly habituated ... Naturally, dialectologists tend to emphasize differences rather than similarities between dialects, but in reality, standard and vernacular dialects show only minor differences, and these differences may be difficult for the learner to sort out.

Long (2007: 122) made similar observations about advanced L2 learners who continue to make errors in particular areas: "Mere exposure, even when input is mostly comprehensible, is not enough. It is logically impossible, moreover, to 'unlearn' L1 options in the absence of evidence in the input about their impossibility in the L2." This is especially true "if the L2 structures are perceptually nonsalient and/or communicatively redundant".

These views are supported by the noticing hypothesis from SLA, referred to in Section 5.2.1 above: a feature from the target language (L2 or D2) will not be acquired unless it is noticed by the learner. Because of similarities or overlap between the D1 and D2, dialect acquirers often do not notice the small differences that do exist, and therefore do not acquire them. Such features are even less likely to be noticed when they are not salient, and thus less likely to be acquired.

6.2.1   Transfer

The implication of the above statements by Wolfram and Schilling-Estes and by Long is that if the differences between the D1/L1 and D2/L2 are not noticed, the learner will continue to use the D1/L1 features when speaking the D2/L2, and thus produce non-native forms, or "errors". In the field of SLA, this is usually referred to as language "transfer", particularly negative transfer.[2] Weinreich (1953) was one of the first scholars to present examples of different types of negative transfer in phonology (which he called "interference"). Although he was referring to the results of language contact between languages, his classifications have been applied to SLA, and could equally be applied to SDA. Thus, for illustration I give three of Weinreich's categories with examples from the dialects we have been looking at.

> *Sound substitution:* The learner uses the nearest equivalent in the D1 for a D2 sound – for example, an American living in England continuing to pronounce the GOAT diphthong with AmE [oʊ] rather than BrE [əʊ].
> *Phonological processes:* The learner uses phonological conditioning rules from the D1 when speaking the D2 – for example, a Canadian

living in the USA continuing to pronounce the MOUTH diphthong as [ʌʊ] before voiceless consonants (Canadian raising) and [aʊ] elsewhere instead of [aʊ] in all contexts, as in AmE.

Underdifferentiation: The learner does not distinguish between two sounds that are distinguished in the D2 – for example, an American living in England continuing to use the /ɑ/ sound (as in PALM) for words such as LOT and *cod*, even though these words are pronounced with /ɒ/ in BrE.

In the 1950s, it was thought that most learner errors were the result of this kind of transfer. It was also thought that by comparing the features of the L1 and the L2, one could predict the kinds of errors learners would make on the basis of the linguistic differences between the languages. This was called Contrastive Analysis (CA) (e.g. Lado 1957). However, it soon became apparent that not all learner errors are the result of transfer, and that linguistic differences between the L1 and the L2 do not necessarily lead to errors. In the 1970s, a "moderate version" of CA emerged, which claimed that features of the L1 and L2 that are similar cause more difficulty than those that are dissimilar (see Major 2001: 34). Nevertheless, SLA research in the 1970s (e.g. Dulay and Burt 1973) showed that transfer accounted for only a small proportion of non-target forms in interlanguage, and that there were natural sequences of morphological and syntactic development that were unconnected with the L1. As a result of these findings and others, SLA research began to concentrate instead on the role of universal processes of language acquisition.

But transfer made a comeback in the 1980s and 1990s, and a large amount of research resumed in this area, much of it examining the factors that promote or inhibit transfer. One of these factors was found to be language distance – the degree of typological similarity or difference between the L1 and the L2. When corresponding features are similar, transfer is more likely (e.g. Kellerman 1977; Wode 1978). For example, a study of Swedish–Finnish bilinguals learning English (Ringbom 1978) demonstrated greater lexical transfer from Swedish (typologically more similar to English) than from Finnish (typologically more distant from English). With regard to phonology, Wode (1981: 237) suggested that "reliance on the L1 [i.e. transfer] can take place only between equivalent elements, i.e. between items which meet crucial similarity requirements". Otherwise, learners will follow normal developmental sequences, similar to those found in first language acquisition.

These findings are very relevant to SDA, where the D1 and D2 are, by definition, typologically very similar. Thus, a high level of transfer would be expected in SDA, and indeed, there is some evidence for this. Young-Scholten (1985) studied errors made in standard German by Swabian dialect-speaking children in grades 1 and 2. She found that 87 per cent of phonological errors and 73 per cent of morphological errors were due to transfer, rather than developmental sequences. She attributed these high percentages to the similarity between the two varieties.

Another factor is also relevant to the likelihood of transfer in SDA. Kellerman (1977) noted that actual linguistic distance may not be as important as the set of speakers' perceptions about the distance – what he called "psychotypology". In other words, transfer from L1 to L2 is more likely if the languages are perceived as similar. Since dialects are again, by definition, considered by speakers to be varieties of the same language, the perceived similarity would be very high, leading to the prediction of more transfer in SDA than in SLA. In other words, both actual and perceived similarity between the D1 and the D2 would lead to greater continued use of D1 forms in SDA than of L1 forms in SLA.

6.2.2   Superficial similarity in sounds

The role of phonological similarity between varieties is crucial to Flege's Speech Learning Model (SLM) (e.g. Flege 1987, 1995, 2003), mentioned in Section 4.4.2 above. According to this model, a learner can establish a new separate phonetic category for an L2 sound if it is different enough from the nearest L1 sound for the learner to be able to perceive some phonetic differences between the two. But if the learner does not perceive any difference between the sounds, they will treat the new L2 sound as if it were the nearest L1 sound. This is called "equivalence classification". This equivalence classification blocks the formation of a new phonetic category, and the learner perceives and produces the L2 sound as if it were the L1 sound.

As an example of equivalence classification, after I first came to Australia, I found that when I spelled my surname on the telephone, the person on the other end often heard the second letter as "A" instead of "I". In AusE, the PRICE diphthong in the name for the letter "I" is pronounced as [ɑɪ] or [ɒɪ], with the nucleus a low back vowel [ɑ] or [ɒ]. But in my AmE, the pronunciation was [aɪ], with the nucleus [a] a low front vowel (see Figure 1.3). The AusE FACE diphthong (as in the name of the letter A) is most commonly pronounced as [æɪ], with the nucleus a low front vowel [æ]. Although [a] is slightly lower than [æ], it is much closer to it than to [ɑ] or [ɒ]. Thus, the AmE pronunciation of [aɪ] for "I" was perceived as its closest AusE equivalent [æɪ], written as "A".

I also found that listeners had trouble understanding my AmE pronunciation of the letter "E" – the FLEECE vowel. This is because in AmE it is pronounced as a monophthong [iː], but in AusE as a diphthong [ᵊiː] or [ˈiː]. As a result of the miscommunication involving both vowels, I started to use a very exaggerated stereotypical AusE pronunciation when spelling my name over the telephone – i.e. something like *ess, oiy, uh-ee, juh-ee, uh-ee, ell.*

This was always to the great amusement of my AusE-speaking wife and kids. But I got my turn to laugh when we moved to the USA for a few years. When my wife tried to spell her surname, Eades, over the phone, there was similar miscommunication. First, her pronunciation of "E" was perceived as "A". This was because her AusE pronunciation of "E" as the diphthong [ᵊiː] appeared closer to the AmE diphthong [eɪ] in "A", than to the AmE monophthong [iː] in "E". Second, her pronunciation of "A" was perceived as "I". This was because her AusE pronunciation of "A" as [æɪ] appeared closer to the AmE pronunciation of the PRICE diphthong [aɪ] in "I" than to the FACE diphthong [eɪ] in "A". So her spelling over the phone was something like: *eeee, eh-ee, deee, eeee, ess*. Of course, these misperceptions were of single sounds out of the context of words, and would not occur so frequently in normal speech.

According to Flege (2003: 328), "the SLM predicts that the greater is the perceived phonetic dissimilarity of an L2 speech sound from the closest L1 sound, the more likely it is that a new category will be created for the L2 sound". And the creation of a new separate phonetic category is necessary for acquisition. For example, a study of adult English-speaking learners of French showed that eventually they were more successful in acquiring native-like pronunciation with the French /y/ vowel (the rounded [i] sound in words such as *rue* 'street' or *tu* 'you [familiar]') than they were with the French /u/ vowel (as in *route* 'route, road' or *vous* 'you [plural, formal]') (Flege 1987: 48). This is because the /y/ vowel is very different from any English vowel, but the /u/ vowel in French is very similar to /u/ in English, but pronounced with a slightly higher tongue position.

If this model is valid, then it has significant ramifications for SDA. Since sounds in the D2 are usually very similar to corresponding sounds in the D1, it will be difficult for learners to perceive the differences. Therefore, they will not create a new phonetic category for the D2 sound, and will not acquire it, but rather continue to use the similar L1 sound.[3]

The degree of similarity between varieties is also important to Best's Perceptual Assimilation Model (PAM) (e.g. Best 1995; Best and Tyler 2007). However, this model differs from SLM in several ways. First of all, while SLM aims to account for the perception and production of speech by L2 learners, PAM focuses on speech perception by naïve, monolingual non-native listeners. Nevertheless, PAM has relevance to SLA because beginning adult learners (especially in naturalistic contexts) are often naïve monolingual listeners. Second, and more importantly, as implied in the preceding discussion, the SLM view is that speakers and listeners have the language-specific characteristics of speech sounds specified in mental representations referred to as phonetic categories. In contrast, the PAM view is that such mental representations do not exist; rather, speakers/listeners are tuned into particular "articulatory gestures" that are used in the production of the sound. These gestures include, for example, tongue positioning, degree of constriction in the vocal tract, and location and timing of this constriction. In the PAM model, the term "phonological category" refers to the particular articulatory gestures and their relationships that are used to distinguish meaning – i.e. what we have been calling phonemes. Listeners are attuned to these in their language. In contrast, "phonetic category" refers to gestural relationships that listeners may not be attuned to, but that signal allophones or differing realisations of a particular phonological category in another dialect (Best and Tyler 2007: 25).

According to PAM, on hearing a non-native speech sound, naïve listeners (or beginning learners) may "assimilate" it into the existing system with regard to the native phoneme that is closest in articulation (i.e. in articulatory gestures). If they perceive the sound as a possible exemplar of the closest phoneme, then they assimilate it into that category – i.e. it is "categorised". If not, then it is "uncategorised", and a new category can be created. This is analogous to SLM's equivalence classification. But PAM differs in that learners can still become perceptually attuned to phonetic distinctions within a single phonological category, and "the listener should be able to maintain the L1 and L2 phones as separate phonetic realizations of the one phonological category" (Best and Tyler 2007: 26). This is especially relevant to SDA, where the phonological categories of the D1 and D2 are for the most part the same, but the phonetic realisations differ in different dialects. For example, AmE and AusE have a single phoneme for the vowel in GOOSE, but its realisation in AmE is [u] and in AusE a more centralised [ʉ]. However, for dialect learners to maintain separate D1 and D2 realisations, they have to be able to discriminate between the phones (i.e. sounds) in the two dialects, and to do so they must be perceptually attuned to such distinctions. This may not occur without some guided attention, which of course does not occur in naturalistic SDA.

6.2.3   Superficial similarity in morphology and syntax

Because dialects are so closely related, the D1 and the D2 may use the same form for a grammatical marker, but the form may have different functions or meanings in the two dialects. For example, according to the grammatical rules of African American English (AAE), *be* occurs before verbs, adjectives and adverbs to indicate a habitual state or action (as shown in Section 1.3.2 above). This can be misinterpreted by speakers of other dialects that do not have this rule, as shown in the following example from Smitherman (2000: 25):

SCENE: *First grade classroom, Detroit*
TEACHER: Where is Mary?
STUDENT: She not here.
TEACHER: (exasperatedly): She is *never* here!
STUDENT: Yeah, she be here.
TEACHER: Where? You just said she wasn't here.

When the student said *she be here*, the intended meaning was "she is habitually here" (but just not today). But the teacher, who did not know this rule of AAE, interpreted it according to the rules of standard American English.

This is similar to what Spears (1982) calls "camouflaged forms". If AAE was being acquired as a D2 by a speaker of standard AmE, for example, the function of *be* would be hard to see, or camouflaged, because it could be interpreted as having the function of the same form in the D1. In this example, the difference between the D2 and D1 would not be too difficult to notice because of context and the likelihood that misunderstanding would occur at some point and need to be sorted out. However, another example given by Spears is more subtle. This is the AAE semi-auxiliary *come*, which expresses indignation on the part of the speaker (p. 855), as in:

We sitting there talking, and he come hitting on me for some money. (p. 854)

In this sentence, *he* is included in the referent of *we*, and *hitting on me for some money* means 'asking me to borrow some money'. This is a camouflaged form because in most contexts it could be interpreted as being a motion verb, as in other dialects – for example:

A neighbor came asking to borrow a cup of sugar. (p. 853).

Such camouflaged forms may be difficult to notice in a D2, and therefore difficult to acquire.

6.2.4   *Superficial similarity in lexicon*

It would seem that a D2 would be much easier to learn than an L2 because nearly all the vocabulary is the same. This is true on one level, but as in SLA, there are "false friends" – words and expressions that have the same form but different meanings in the two varieties – e.g. the word *gift*, which means 'poison' in German. And there are many more false friends between dialects than there are between languages. Some of these are familiar to most people. For example, if an American says "I'm rooting for Brazil in the World Cup", an Australian will know that the AusE meaning of *rooting* (i.e. 'having sexual intercourse') does not apply. Others may cause some initial confusion, but they are quickly sorted out, as shown by a couple of examples from my own experiences. Soon after coming to Australia, I was in a big department store and asked a salesperson where I could find bed sheets. The answer I got was:

"In Manchester". I didn't know then that in AusE, *manchester* refers to sheets, towels, etc. and to the section of the store that sells them. And one night a few years earlier, when I was a young teacher in New Zealand, I was saying good-night to a fellow teacher (female), who lived in the flat next door, and she said: "Knock me up in the morning, would you?" I quickly realised that in that context *knock me up* couldn't have the American meaning of 'get me pregnant', but it took a few moments to figure out the New Zealand/British/ Australian meaning: 'knock on my door to summon me'.

Wikipedia lists over 600 words that have different meanings in British and American English.[4] While most of these are fairly obvious, there are some differences that are extremely subtle, and would be difficult to notice. A good example is the word *quite*. In AmE, this always means 'totally' or 'to the fullest extent or degree', whereas in BrE, it can also mean 'fairly' or 'to a certain extent'. This is especially true if *quite* is used before gradable adjectives such as *good*, *intelligent* and *clever*. So, if someone says a movie is "quite good", a speaker of BrE (or NZE or AusE) would most probably interpret this as 'fairly good' (e.g. 6 out of 10), whereas a speaker of AmE would interpret it as 'very good' (e.g. 8 or 9 out of 10). Most speakers of these dialects are not aware of these different meanings. Janet Holmes (1995) pointed out how the difference led to her colleagues at a New Zealand university misinterpreting some comments in American letters of recommendation for job applicants. For example, "X's scientific training is quite strong" was almost certainly meant as 'very strong' but interpreted as 'fairly strong'. Despite having lived in Australia for many years and being married to an Australian, I was never aware of this difference, and neither was my wife, until it was pointed out to us a few years ago.[5] (Now I understand why my wife said I was "quite good-looking".)

Such subtle dialectal differences in meaning can lead to more serious cases of misinterpretation. Eades (2007) described the case of an Australian Aboriginal man who was charged with murder after he stabbed his drunk and out-of-control brother. In his police interview, the accused referred to his brother's violent behaviour with statements such as "that's the way he carries on when he's drunk" and "he carries on silly like that". The police officers appear to have interpreted the expression *carrying on silly* in terms of the general AusE meaning – something like 'acting foolish or stupid'. But in Aboriginal English, *silly* is often used to mean "insane, out of one's mind", or "wild or violent as a result of being drunk" (Arthur 1996: 110). This is clearly what the accused was talking about, as his answers in other parts of the police interview should have made obvious – i.e. his brother "smashing up things", and causing serious injury to people, such as fracturing the accused's spine on one such occasion. Eades wrote a linguistic report on this matter for the defence which resulted in the prosecutor dropping the charge of murder and replacing it with the lesser charge of manslaughter. This case reveals the difficulty of noticing some of the differences in the meaning of words between dialects, and therefore the difficulty of completely acquiring the lexicon of a new dialect.

6.3   Sociolinguistic factors

Other factors that may make SDA difficult are sociolinguistic (or social psychological). In many cases, particular dialects are more bound up with people's social identities than languages are, and thus the use of a particular dialect may be seen as one of the main distinguishing characteristics of belonging to a social group. This is especially true for some ethnic dialects, such as African American English, which, for example, Rickford and Rickford (2000: 222) characterise as an important "symbol of identity" for African Americans.

Because of sensitivity to issues associated with identity, when people try to speak in a dialect that is not their own (a D2), they often get negative reactions from speakers of the D2, and sometimes from other speakers of the D1 as well. Such reactions may be a consequence of any of three factors, discussed below: misinterpretation of the speaker's motives, folk views about identity, and feelings about ownership of a dialect. This sensitivity and the resultant negative reactions are not normally found in SLA.

6.3.1   Misinterpretation of motives

Negative reactions to outsiders trying to speak one's dialect may result from two kinds of misinterpretation. The first kind occurs in contexts where the D2 is an unstandardised variety and has a history of denigration and stigmatisation by speakers of other dialects, especially speakers of varieties close to the standard. Creole languages often fall into this category. For example, Hawai'i Creole has a history of being labelled with negative terms such as "lazy", "ungrammatical", "sloppy", "slothful" and "ugly", and in the 1930s and 1940s, it was even considered a speech defect (Da Pidgin Coup 1999: 6–8). In 1962, a major local newspaper compared it to the language of animals in an editorial entitled "Why not just grunt?" (*Honolulu Star-Bulletin*, 13 February 1962). Such extreme statements are now getting harder to find, but the language is still commonly referred to as "bad English" or "broken English". In recent years, most speakers of Hawai'i Creole have learned standard English in formal education and have become bilingual (or bidialectal, as the term is being used here). If such speakers are addressed in Hawai'i Creole by a standard English speaker, this might be interpreted as an indication that the speaker thinks they are uneducated and do not know standard English. Similarly, with regard to Jamaican Creole, Lawton (1964: 18) observed: "Bilingual Jamaicans are offended by outsiders speaking Creole to them." Along the same lines, Winer (1985) described the special difficulties of learning Trinidad English Creole (TEC) in Trinidad. She wrote (p. 47): "Many Trinidadians found it difficult to believe that I actually wanted to learn TEC, or even tried to discourage me." She explained one reason as follows (pp. 47–8): "People sometimes resented my trying to learn something they themselves were trying to avoid, or took my speaking TEC as implying that they could not understand English."

In another situation, a colleague of mine from Denmark, Carsten Levisen, related his experiences as a speaker of standard Danish living for a year on Bornholm Island, where strong regional dialects of Danish are still spoken. He reported that the people objected to his speaking their local dialect and said it was silly to be learning it. (The only contexts in which he could get away with using it involved humour.) In contrast, there was a young Norwegian woman also living there who didn't know standard Danish, and no one objected to her speaking the dialect.

Another way that D2 speakers may misinterpret the intentions of dialect acquirers has to do with stereotyping, as described in Sections 3.1.3 and 5.2.1 above. The first D2 features that an acquirer may begin to use are often the most noticeable ones, and as we have seen, these also may be the features that are stereotyped. And often because of incomplete acquisition, the acquirer's productions of these features may sound like caricatures. Thus, speakers of the D2 may think that acquirers are mimicking their dialect and making fun of it, and D2 speakers often have strong negative reactions to such imitations. For example, in Markham's (1997) imitation experiment in Sweden, described in Section 3.2 above, two reactions of one judge to a caricatured imitation of his Stockholm dialect were "repulsive" and "cocky at its worst" (p. 236). Poor imitations of dialects can provoke negative reactions from their speakers, even in written form. For example, in a review of a book set in the American South, Smith (2001) commented that "attempts by authors to portray 'Southern-speak' usually come off as irritating, even insulting".

In my own experience, one day a few years ago, my wife suddenly asked me: "What happened to your vowels?" When I asked for some clarification, she said that I had changed my vowel in *mate*. I replied defensively that maybe I had adjusted it towards the Australian English pronunciation. But she thought that people might think I was "taking the piss".[6] I'm still not sure exactly what aspect of my vowel she was referring to, but it may be that my FACE diphthong had changed slightly to sound to her like the PRICE diphthong /aɪ/, which is the stereotype for the AusE pronunciation of the FACE diphthong with a lower onset – e.g. [æɪ]. Thus, the caricatured pronunciation of AusE *mate* would be the same as *might* in other dialects, and in fact, speakers of other dialects often hear the AusE [æɪ] as /aɪ/. For example, an Australian colleague, Brett Baker, reported that when he lived in the USA, many people thought his surname was Biker. There are lots of jokes about this – for example, the one about the Japanese tourist in Sydney who ended up in hospital overnight. She burst into tears when the nurse came to see her the next morning and said: "You're going today" – which because of AusE she heard as "You're going to die." At any rate, I tried to go back to my old AmE pronunciation so that I wouldn't upset anyone.

I have heard many second language speakers of AusE using a pronunciation of the FACE diphthong very close to the stereotype, but this does not seem to evoke negative reactions. However, it seems clear that in Foreman's (2003) study, many of the subjects were aware of Australians' sensitivity to speakers of another English dialect using features of AusE that might be interpreted as exaggerated or stereotyped. Thus, Foreman concluded (p. 242): "The subjects may be less likely to experiment with AusE pronunciation when they are not sure of the probable meanings that would be associated with its use, and when it might result in an unintended negative meaning."

6.3.2   Folk views about identity

While social scientists have shown the existence of multiple social identities in a single individual, many people believe that there is only one "true self" and therefore, they can have only one true identity. Turner and Gordon (1981: 39) describe the self as "a subjective construct in the individual's experience, rather than an objectively locatable entity or dynamism". In other words, individuals develop conceptions of themselves that do not necessarily conform to the view of others or correspond to their typical behaviour.

In addition, as Mason-Schrock (1996: 177) points out, the "true self" is "an artifact of a folk theory" and "a powerful fiction". According to Lakoff and Johnson's Folk Theory of Essences (1999: 363), people commonly have the following belief: "Every entity has an 'essence' or 'nature', that is, a collection of properties that makes it the kind of thing it is and is the causal source of its natural behavior." This view applies to people as well (p. 306): "Each person has a moral essence that determines his or her moral behavior. That moral essence is called someone's 'character'." A person's basic character, or "essential self", is thought to be formed by the time they reach adulthood.[7]

Gecas and Burke (1995: 49) discuss the notion of consistency in the construction of the self, referring to Lecky's (1961) argument "that individuals seek to maintain a coherent view of themselves in order to function effectively in the world". They also observe (pp. 51–2): "People work hard to verify and maintain the self-concepts or identities that they already hold, and do not easily change them." This is related to the "unity principle": individuals need to maintain the unity and consistency of their conceptual system (Epstein 1981).

The true or essential self is often opposed to the "spurious self" (Turner and Gordon 1981: 40). Thus, the true self is seen as the authentic self and any behaviour that contradicts it as inauthentic. According to Erickson (1995: 121) authenticity is conceptualised "in terms of a commitment to self-values", and "one's sense of relative authenticity can be regarded as the extent to which one fulfils the expectations or commitments one has for self" (p. 131). Turner and Gordon's (1981: 57) observation is: "Subjects who are driven by a quest for achievement or realization of a value discover themselves doing things they don't want to do and presenting a contrived front to their associates, which makes them feel inauthentic."

The preceding discussion points to a view of the self, identity and authenticity that an individual "imagines" (Weedon 1987: 31). This is in stark contrast to the view of sociolinguists in which the self and identity are contingent on changing contexts and social relationships, and in which authenticity is not an issue. However, individuals' own views, whether or not they are based on folk theories, can have a powerful influence on their actions.

The folk view of the true or authentic self goes back at least to Shakespeare's time, as expressed by Polonius in *Hamlet*: "This above all: to thine own self be true." Nowadays it can be seen on various websites devoted to personal advice and self-improvement – for example, on www.myauthenticself.com and Dr Phil's advice site:[8]

The authentic self is the you that can be found at your absolute core. It is the part of you not defined by your job, function or role. It is the composite of all your skills, talents and wisdom. It is all of the things that are uniquely yours and need expression, rather than what you believe you are supposed to be and do.

Many people apply the folk view of the authentic self to the behaviour of others as well as themselves. Expressions such as "putting on airs", "hiding behind a mask", "Who does she think she is?", "faking it" and "putting on a false face" all refer negatively to someone who is not behaving according to what people see as their true nature.

These folk theories are very relevant to attitudes to SDA. Many people believe that the way they talk is an intrinsic part of their authentic self and to change it would be spurious or inauthentic. If there is no communicative reason to change one's way of talking, doing so may also be interpreted by others as being false or affected – or at least not being true to oneself. In other words, the expectation that many people have for themselves and for others is that people should maintain their original way of speaking – i.e. their own first dialects. This is not usually the case for SLA, where another language must be learned in order to communicate.

   This view is expressed in a discussion on the internet.[9] On 17 July 2006 one blogger wrote:

We consider it normal to learn and speak another language, but strange and dishonest to employ a different dialect or regional pronunciation. I've always wondered why this is the case, since it would certainly be easier to learn a new accent than an entirely new language, and it might come in handy for preventing misunderstandings. But if you try it, you'd be accused of "faking" or "affecting" an accent.

Another replied:

I think this goes to show that people consider accent to be a part of one's identity, and if they deviate from that, then they're seen as not being true to theirselves, not "keepin' it real". We know the reasons why someone would speak another language, but for what reason would someone want to speak another accent/dialect if they are already understood in their native accent/dialect?

The novelist Zadie Smith (2009: 41) expressed a similar view, specifically with regard to Britain:

Voice adaptation is still the original British sin ... If you go (metaphorically speaking) down the British class scale, you've gone from Cockney to "mockney", and can expect a public tar and feathering; to go the other way is to perform an unforgivable act of class betrayal. Voices are meant to be unchanging and singular. There's no quicker way to insult an expat Scotsman in London than to tell him he's lost his accent. We feel that our voices are who we are, and that to have more than one, or to use different versions of a voice for different occasions, represents, at best, a Janus-faced duplicity, and at worst, the loss of our very souls.

Another example is from the USA. As mentioned in Section 3.1.1 above, because of the popularity of rap and hip hop music and the covert prestige of Black culture and language, many White Americans use features of African American English in their speech – an example of crossing (Rampton 1995). But as Sweetland (2002: 519) has noted, this is "seen by white and black peers as inappropriate or inauthentic", and speakers are often disapproved of and called "sellouts" by other Whites or "wannabes" by both Blacks and Whites (Cutler 1999: 439; Sweetland 2002: 518).

   If we turn to the studies of SDA described in Chapter 2, we can find some good examples of lack of acquisition of the D2 because of such views. As shown in Stanford's (2007, 2008a) study in China, the expectations of the Sui community are that people identify with their original clan; therefore, married women are expected to continue speaking their original dialect even though they now live among their husband's clan. As Stanford (2007: 274) pointed out: "Sui people have very strong motivation to maintain their group membership since ridicule and admonition are the consequences of linguistically straying from one's original clan loyalty." For example, one woman described what would happen if a woman from the South came to the North and spoke like people from the North clan: "[E]veryone would laugh. She'd feel embarrassed. She wouldn't speak that way any more" (Stanford 2008a: 38).

Similar to the situation with African American English, but concerning national rather than ethnic boundaries, Foreman (2003: 241) reported that when her North American subjects in Australia were talking about themselves or other people changing their accent or dialect, they used words like "fake", "pretentious", "phony" and "fraud". She noted (p. 242) that "they may fear that others will negatively interpret their acquisition of a D2 and label them as 'fakes'". For example, one subject commented that when he tried to use typically Australian expressions, "people just sorta laugh at you and ... I feel phony" (p. 239). Foreman (p. 241) noted that "there is a feeling among these people that to modify one's accent is indicative of some kind of inauthenticity and a lack of loyalty". Her conclusion was that "the sentiment seems to be that changing one's accent is an attempt to belong somewhere one does not really belong or to be someone (an Australian) that one is truly not; thus it is fake" (p. 241). This view is reflected in the title of her dissertation: "Pretending to be someone you're not: A study of second dialect acquisition in Australia".

That such negative reactions appear to be a consequence more of SDA than of SLA was pointed out by Foreman (2003: 244–5):

There do not appear to be similar sorts of reactions to bilingualism reported in the literature ...; that is to say, if someone learns to speak Spanish, their friends and family will probably not accuse them of 'trying to be/appear/pretend to be Spanish', of being pretentious or fake.

Of course, such reactions are not always the case for SDA, as we saw in Section 5.1.2 above with the immigrants in Sweden who maintained their Finland Swedish identity but acquired a Swedish Swedish identity as well, and became bidialectal. However, in the SLA literature, it appears to be more common for individuals to be willing to change the nature of their identity, or acquire a new one, through the acquisition of another language (e.g. Kinginger 2004). In fact, a recent SLA theory, Dörnyei's (2005, 2009) "L2 Motivational Self System", refers to a different, more flexible view of the self from the psychological literature: the "ideal self". This is used as a basis for reconceptualising the notion of motivation in SLA (Section 5.1.5 above). According to the theory, L2 learners are motivated by their vision of the attributes they would ideally like to possess – not restricted by a perceived need to remain true to their existing attributes.

6.3.3   Ownership

Closely related to authenticity is the notion of ownership of a dialect and its significance in constructing a particular identity. This is again especially significant for varieties that are stigmatised by members of the wider community. For example in Hawai'i, speaking Hawai'i Creole, commonly referred to as "Pidgin", is an important aspect of projecting local identity despite (or perhaps because of) its history of denigration (Section 6.3.1 above). In ethnic terms, being local in Hawai'i usually means being an indigenous Hawaiian or a descendant of the indentured plantation workers who came from China, Portugal, Japan, the Philippines, Korea, Puerto Rico and many other countries. This is contrasted with being a *haole*, the Hawaiian word used to refer to White Americans (Eades *et al.* 2006). Locals generally speak Pidgin; *haoles* do not. The ownership of Pidgin by locals can be seen in the report of a survey on language attitudes in Hawai'i (Leong 2000: 20):

Seventeen out of twenty-three participants acknowledge HCE [= Hawai'i Creole English – i.e. Pidgin] as being a special language unique to Hawai'i, belonging to the locals; they also found that an advantage of speaking HCE is that it lets one bond with other locals. Maka [one of the participants] said "Pidgin is an integral part of the local culture. We all need to belong and in Hawai'i, Pidgin is the glue that binds us together."

Thus a *haole* trying to speak Pidgin when they obviously don't know the language is usually interpreted by locals as not only demeaning, but also presumptuous. It is as though the person is trying to claim ownership of something that belongs to someone else; they have no right to do so. On the other hand, a *haole* who grew up in Hawai'i and already speaks Pidgin like a local, and who uses Pidgin in daily interactions, can be seen to have ownership of the language, because the way they speak identifies them as a local.

Similarly, Sweetland (2002: 518) reported negative reactions to Whites trying to speak African American English, but being "idiosyncratic and unsystematic" in their use of superficial stereotypical linguistic features of the language. In another example, Jacobs-Huey (1997) described a study she carried out in which she recorded three middle-class male subjects speaking AAE. One was a White postgraduate student who was interested in hip hop and identified with adolescent urban African American culture. The other two were African Americans, both recent college graduates. Ninety-two people listened to excerpts of the recordings and made judgements about the speakers' ethnicity, class background and personality. These "judges" included forty-five African Americans, thirty-three Anglo Americans, eight Latinos and six Asian Americans (p. 356). On the basis of his speech, the White subject was classified as being African American by 92 per cent of the judges, even though most of these also thought he had over-performed to some extent (pp. 357–8). When judges (especially African Americans) found out that he was White and from a middle-class background, many were "extremely critical of him" (p. 363). As Hill (1999: 554) points out, this kind of language crossing is "often seen by source populations as theft, as th. illegitimate use of a resource" – i.e. "genuine appropriation".

Such crossing, however, can be contrasted with the everyday use of African American English by a 23-year-old White woman, who has been character-ised as "sounding black" (Sweetland 2002: 520), and whose use of the dialect "is accepted and reinforced by her black peers" (p. 525). This woman was born and raised in the "ghetto" and continues to live there and work and socialise with African Americans. Thus, "she is able to lay claim to an ethnically-marked dialect" (p. 516) because she is seen as a member of the community partially identified by speaking that dialect. The fact that she speaks like other members of the community makes this possible even though she is of a different ethnicity.

Thus, it appears that in some cases where speaking a particular dialect is important in signalling membership of a particular social group, the right to speak that dialect belongs only to those who are members of this group. And speaking that dialect fluently and naturally is one factor that allows a claim to group membership. Imitations of the dialect or even genuine attempts at learning it indicate that one is not a member of the group and therefore may evoke negative reactions. This may be true for a wide range of dialects, not just stigmatised ones. For example, the study by Giles and Smith (1979) mentioned in Section 3.4.1 above showed that British participants did not react favourably to a Canadian speaker shifting his pronunciation towards British English. The authors' explanation was as follows (p. 62):

The addition of pronunciation shifts could have been perceived as patronizing or ingratiating. Alternatively, or in combination, pronunciation shifts plus the other convergences may have been perceived as threatening ... English listeners may have felt that they were losing their cultural distinctiveness as the Canadian adopted perhaps the most distinguishing attributes of their group identity – a "British" accent.

Speaking Australian English is an even more significant part of an Australian identity. The *National Policy on Languages* (Lo Bianco 1987: 72) stated: "Australian English is a dynamic but vital expression of the distinctiveness of Australian culture and an element of national identity." More recently, Moore (2008: 206) asserted that speaking Australian English "is by far the most important marker of Australian identity". It was clear in Foreman's (2003) study that this role of the national dialect in projecting an Australian identity was a key factor in Australians' reactions to North Americans – not accepting them as Australians because they did not speak Australian English, and reacting negatively when they did try to speak it. According to Foreman (p. 234), some subjects noted that they felt they were Australian but Australians didn't feel the same because they talked differently. One subject observed (p. 239) that his accent was probably giving a false message that "if Canada

h Australia I'd fight with the Canadians". Therefore, he
tried to adjust his speech towards Australian English.
ralians reacting negatively to speakers of another dialect
lian English, other North Americans did not even try. For
..mented (p. 240): "I don't even attempt it cause I know I'll be
..y detected." Thus, Foreman surmised (p. 233): "Keeping the
..nt and language identity of the native country was less problematic than
trying to approximate a language identity that they might never be able to fully
appropriate as their own."

6.4   Relevance to contact-induced language change

The difficulty of acquiring a second dialect is relevant to both new dialect
formation and language change in general, as discussed below.

6.4.1   New dialects

When speakers of several dialects of the same language migrate to a new
region, a process of language change may occur that involves dialect mixing,
levelling and simplification. This process is called "koineisation", and the
end result is often a mixed new dialect or "immigrant koine" (Siegel 1985;
Trudgill 1986; Kerswill 2002; Kerswill and Trudgill 2005).[10] Examples are Fiji
Hindi (mentioned in Chapter 1), and the dialects spoken in the newly established towns of Høyanger in Norway and Milton Keynes in England. Various
national dialects of English – such as those spoken in Australia, New Zealand
and South Africa – are also thought to be the result of koineisation.[11]

Besides a mixture of dialect features, these new dialects often have other
features that appear to be the result of speakers trying to learn other dialects in
the contact situation – i.e. interdialect forms, as described in Section 3.1.1
above. For example, Fiji Hindi has the intermediate form *tumār* for the 2nd
person pronoun, derived from *tohār* and *tumhārā* in the contributing dialects.
In addition, there is simplification: instead of using separate forms of the verb
for 1st and 2nd person as in the contributing dialects, Fiji Hindi uses the same
form for both (Siegel 2001). In fact, it may be that the simplification found in
most new dialects is a consequence of incomplete SDA.

6.4.2   Language change

The particular difficulties adults have in fully acquiring a second dialect,
especially its phonology, are relevant to theories of language change in
general. In a recent article, Labov (2007) distinguishes between linguistic
change (primarily sound change) resulting from transmission within a speech

community and linguistic change resulting from diffusion across communities. Transmission is defined as the "unbroken sequence of native language acquisition by children" (p. 346). Linguistic change resulting from transmission occurs in tiny increments, often over several generations, and involves the preservation of abstract linguistic structure. Diffusion is the spread of a linguistic feature from one speech community to another as a result of language contact (i.e. contact between speakers of different languages or dialects).

Change resulting from diffusion can be more substantial and occur more rapidly, but the abstract linguistic structure of the original feature is not maintained. Labov's hypothesis is that the difference between the two types of change can be attributed to two different kinds of language learning – one involving children and one involving adults. Children are the learners in transmission, and they have the ability to replicate the form and structure of their parents' language faithfully. In contrast, language contact is primarily between adults, and therefore they are the learners in diffusion. But, as Labov points out (p. 349): "adults do not learn and reproduce linguistic forms, rules, and constraints with the accuracy and speed that children display".

Most of the changes by diffusion described by Labov concern features of dialects – for example, the short-*a* pattern that we looked at in the Philadelphia dialect. Thus, the study of SDA is very relevant to Labov's hypothesis.

Recall from Section 4.3 above that in the short-*a* pattern, the phoneme /æ/ has split so that in some words it is a diphthong [ɛə] or [eə] (the tense short-*a*) while in others it remains [æ] (the lax short-*a*) – for example, *ham* [hɛəm] versus *bat* [bæt]. A similar short-*a* pattern is found in the New York City dialect, but it has some differences from that of Philadelphia. For example, words that end in voiceless fricatives such as *sh* /ʃ/ (as in *mash*) or in some voiced consonants such as /b/ (as in *crab*) have the tense short-*a* [ɛə] in New York City but the lax short-*a* [æ] in Philadelphia.

Labov (2007) describes how the New York City short-*a* pattern diffused to four other locations: New Jersey, Albany, Cincinnati and New Orleans. However, in each case, the diffused pattern is "not a faithful copy" (p. 360) because some of the complex aspects of the pattern were "not perfectly transmitted" (p. 368). For example, in New York City, /æ/ occurs as tense short-*a* [ɛə] before /n/ as in *plan* [plɛən]. But there is a constraint that keeps it as [æ] in open syllables (those not ending in a consonant) although it occurs before /n/ in the following syllable, as in *planet* [plænɛt]. In the Albany short-*a* pattern, however, this constraint has been lost (p. 360), so that *planet* is pronounced [plɛənɛt].

Labov attributes this incomplete transmission of the full pattern to adult language learning (or in this case, dialect learning), and concludes that in diffusion in general, adults "acquire the new variants of the originating community in a somewhat diluted form" (p. 380). This is what we have seen with phonological variables in many of the studies of SDA described in earlier chapters, such as the one done by Payne (1976, 1980), which Labov refers to. Children can hit the target and produce D2 features with native-like ability, but adults often fall short of the target or go beyond it, producing intermediate forms, or learning only some of the rules for complex phonological features.

Thus, while existing studies of SDA appear to support Labov's hypothesis, further research on SDA in naturalistic contexts is needed. As Labov notes (2007: 383), "it would be helpful to know more about the limitations on children's ability to learn new dialects and on adults' inability to learn them".

7   SDA in classroom contexts

We now move on to look at SDA in educational contexts. This differs from SDA in naturalistic contexts in several ways. Most significantly, the learners are normally students enrolled in a course or an educational institution who want to, or are required to, learn a new dialect for a specific purpose – usually for progressing in the formal education system or for working in a particular profession.

Chapter 1 mentioned that there are two different types of educational contexts for SDA. One normally involves individual or small-group tutoring in dialect coaching or accent modification training. In both kinds of tutoring, the learners are generally adults who have chosen to be involved in SDA, and the emphasis is on phonological features of the D2. Teaching approaches for dialect coaching and accent modification training are discussed in Chapter 8.

The other, and much more common, type of educational context for SDA is in the classroom. In most cases, the learners are initially children who come to school speaking a regional or ethnic dialect, a colloquial variety, or a pidgin or creole as their D1 – what we refer to here as unstandardised dialects or vernaculars.[1] These students need to acquire as a D2 the standard dialect that is used in the formal education system. Adolescents and young adults who speak unstandardised dialects continue with SDA in secondary and tertiary formal education. In this context the lexical and morphosyntactic features of the D2 needed for reading and formal writing are more important than phonological features. Thus, when we refer, for example, to the acquisition of standard American English (SAE) in classroom contexts the emphasis is on grammar and vocabulary.

As pointed out in Chapter 1, however, it is rare for educational institutions to provide special programs or teaching approaches to help students acquire the standard dialect as their D2. For example, children are taught how to read and write in the standard as if they already know it, and in some contexts, alongside children who do already know it. This chapter begins with a description of the educational situations for different kinds of D2 learners and some of the problems caused by the lack of consideration of their special needs. This is followed by an account of additional obstacles faced by unstandardised dialect-speaking students. The next section outlines a few studies that have been done on SDA in the classroom context. The last section critically examines some of the arguments against having educational programs specifically for D2 learners. The following chapter looks at some of the special approaches and teaching programs that do exist for D2 learners.

7.1   D2 learners in the classroom

Five different groups of learners involved in classroom SDA can be distinguished on the basis of the nature of their D1, as described in Chapter 1: regional dialects, colloquial varieties (in diglossia situations), ethnic dialects, indigenised varieties and creoles. Descriptions of the educational conditions for each group are summarised in the following subsections.

7.1.1   Speakers of regional dialects

Many scholars have written about the situation regarding speakers of various regional dialects in Europe learning the standard dialect of their country. In Germany, for example, Wegera (1983) described problems in the acquisition of standard German (StGer) by children speaking linguistically divergent dialects. Children from the Swabian dialect area in particular (in the southwest of the country) have been studied by several linguists. Fishman and Lueders-Salmon (1972) reported that the majority of Swabian children learn StGer well because their D1 is accepted in the classroom as the starting point for SDA. However, Ammon (1977, 1989a) painted a very different picture, focusing on those who do not acquire StGer so well. He pointed out that children who come to school speaking only the local Swabian dialect are disadvantaged in comparison to those who already have some knowledge of StGer. This was backed up by research comparing the results of school achievement tests for three groups of fourth graders from fourteen different schools, seven urban and seven rural. The groups were broad dialect speakers (those using the most dialect features in their informal speech), moderate dialect speakers (those who used a majority of standard features, but still had at least a regional accent) and standard speakers.

The results were that in spelling, the broad dialect speakers made significantly more errors than the other groups. In writing, the two groups of regional dialect speakers made more errors overall than the standard speakers, and the difference in transfer errors was statistically significant. The broad dialect speakers also wrote shorter compositions with fewer word types than the other groups. In reading aloud, broad dialect speakers made the most errors, and read the most slowly (although the differences were not statistically significant). In oral class participation, the broad dialect speakers were the weakest in terms of frequency and length of utterances, with the differences between the broad and moderate groups statistically significant. Finally, broad dialect speakers had lower marks in all subjects, including mathematics.[2]

In interviews with 106 primary school teachers from the region, Ammon found that 9.4 per cent claimed there were no problems faced by dialect speakers, and 28.3 per cent said there were only small difficulties. According to Ammon (1989a: 134), teachers often expressed the view that "the pupils who were intelligent had few if any difficulties as the result of their dialect". He surmised that "there is a danger that those teachers who gave opinions of this kind will assume that dialect speakers who have educational difficulties are less intelligent, rather than that they have dialect-related problems", and thus teachers may not try to help them overcome these problems. Furthermore, Ammon discovered that most of the teachers had little linguistic knowledge of the regional dialects, and 62.3 per cent reported that they had not heard anything about dialect and educational problems during their teacher training (p. 134). A more recent article by Davies (2000) confirmed the existence of this state of affairs.

Ammon (1977: 62) concluded that "it cannot be doubted any longer that there really are serious problems for dialect speakers". This conclusion was backed up in Rosenberg's (1989) summary of eleven other studies on dialect and schooling done in other areas of Germany in the 1970s and 1980s. His synopsis of one of the wide-ranging studies was (p. 70): "Teaching ratings of pupil performance as well as actual test results showed that dialect speakers, irrespective of social class background, are clearly disadvantaged."

In the Netherlands, Stijnen and Vallen (1989) reported on the initial findings of a large-scale research project on education in the town of Kerkrade. The D1 there is a variety of the Limburg dialect (referred to in Section 2.3.6 above) and the D2 is standard Dutch. A battery of tests was given to 360 students ranging from 4 to 12 years of age to compare the educational achievement of Limburg dialect speakers and standard dialect speakers. The findings were predictably that Limburg dialect-speaking preschool and primary school students had greater problems with oral and written production in the D2, mainly because of errors caused by transfer and code-switching into the D1. However, these differences between the two groups were not found in later years of schooling, nor were there differences in other subjects. Teachers' assessments, however, did not match these test results. Limburg dialect-speaking children were rated less favourably than standard-speaking children in both their fluency in Dutch and their expected level of achievement at school. In addition, Limburg dialect speakers received lower marks than standard speakers for some subjects (e.g. language and reading in later years of school), and a higher percentage of dialect speakers than standard speakers were not allowed to proceed to the next grade (p. 149).

In Sweden, Österberg (1961) did research with children who spoke the dialect of the northern Piteå district as their D1 and who learned standard Swedish as their D2. He related the difficulties in communication and resultant social and emotional problems that children such as these face when they do not know the language or dialect of the school, and there are no special programs to teach it to them. (The author developed an experimental program to teach initial literacy in the D1 to children from this region, described in Chapter 8.)

In Britain, Cheshire (1982) recounted the common belief that children who speak regional dialects do not experience any serious difficulties at school (p. 53). However, using data from her study in Reading, which examined the language of eight children (four boys and four girls) between ages 11 and 14, she demonstrated that this is not true – these children do have significant problems. For example, the Reading dialect uses *was* for all persons and numbers – e.g. *We was in bed ...* (p. 55). Although children in school adjusted their speech and writing to some extent, the non-standard D1 use of *was* in D2 writing was still 60.0 per cent for the boys and 19.4 per cent for the girls (p. 56). Teachers were not aware that these were D1 features and saw them as mistakes indicative of careless work (p. 57). However, they did not consistently correct all these errors, often for fear of discouraging the students. Furthermore, as students were frequently confused about what forms they should use in writing, they often made "real" mistakes – producing forms that are not used in either the D1 or the D2. Many of these were due to hypercorrection or overgeneralisation, as described in Section 3.1.1 above. For example, in the children's D1 initial *h* is often omitted in words such as *has* and *hill*. Sometimes, students inserted it inappropriately, as in *Debra ... ran has fast as she could* (p. 62). (See also Williams 1989.)

Cheshire and Edwards (1998) described how students can be alienated from school when their spoken language is corrected for no apparent communicative reason. For example, they quoted one student (p. 199) as saying: "I feel very angry because I know what I am saying and so does the teacher." However, other students simply ignore correction – for example (p. 200): "I am not really bothered: I know what I mean and so do they." For others, the reason for correction is either not clear or misunderstood – for example (p. 199): "When I say *I saw something* they (the teachers) say to say *seen* but my parents say the opposite. That confuses me." Cheshire and Edwards concluded (p. 199) that "correcting pupils' speech is a waste of time and is likely to lead to confusion about the linguistic relationship between features of standard and non-standard English".

7.1.2   Speakers of colloquial varieties in diglossia settings

Recall that in diglossia settings, the D1 is the colloquial variety used in informal contexts throughout the community, while the D2 is learned in school and used for formal domains such as expository writing (Section 1.2 above). A classic case of diglossia occurs in Arabic-speaking countries where the local colloquial dialect is the D1 and Classical Arabic (or Modern Standard Arabic) is the D2. In a discussion paper on Arabic diglossia and education, prepared for the World Bank, Maamouri (1998: 41) described a situation that could apply to many classroom SDA contexts:

Pupils entering school have to "unlearn" or even suppress most of their linguistic habits while they try to acquire a new set of "rigid" rules. The burden of internalizing these new habits is not helped or reinforced by classroom practices focused on the exclusive use of the "official" language of instruction. A clash seems to occur … between two conflictual practices. On the one hand, teachers deliberately try to neglect and undermine the actual speech habits of the pupils. On the other, the same teachers find themselves often obliged to use the colloquial to communicate with their learners.

Maamouri said that this occurs across Arabic-speaking regions, and "leads to serious pedagogical problems and even to feelings of linguistic insecurity in formal school communication among high numbers of young Arab learners" (1998: 41). As an example of the educational problems in the Arab world, he referred to an assessment achievement in the Arabic language done on fourth graders in Jordan. The average percentage of correct answers was only 54.2, and Jordan has one of the highest levels of literacy and educational standards in the Arab region (p. 15). Maamouri's recommendation was that initial literacy should be taught in colloquial Arabic – i.e. the D1 (p. 62).

Ibrahim (1983) and Alrabaa (1986) also pointed to problems of students in acquiring literacy in Classical Arabic, and attributed this to the great linguistic distance between it and the colloquial varieties. Saiegh-Haddad (2003) did a study with sixty-five kindergarten and grade 1 children in northern Israel whose D1 is the Northern Palestinian variety of colloquial Arabic, examining phonemes and syllable structure that differ between this D1 and the Classical Arabic D2. On the basis of the results, she concluded that the linguistic distance between colloquial and Classical Arabic "interferes with the acquisition of basic reading processes" in Classical Arabic (p. 445).

Diglossia also exists in Cyprus with the Greek Cypriot dialect (GCD) as the D1 and standard Modern Greek (SMG) as the D2. A survey of 133 primary school teachers in fourteen Cypriot schools examined issues concerning use of GCD by students and its effect on educational attainment (Pavlou and Papapavlou 2004; Papapavlou and Pavlou 2007a). A large majority of the respondents acknowledged that students experience difficulties expressing themselves in SMG and that they feel discouraged when repeatedly corrected when they use GCD in the classroom. Papapavlou and Pavlou (2007a: 108) observed that the students' educational attainment is "not up-to-standard because they are evaluated, by teachers and by the educational system itself, according to the linguistic standards of SMG and not GCD".

The responses of sixty-seven Greek Cypriot university students to another survey (Papapavlou 2007) reflected their personal experiences in their early years of education. In answer to a question on the likely positive effects of bidialectal education, the respondents agreed overwhelmingly that it would have the following benefits: first, children would feel more comfortable by being able to express themselves orally; second, they would be less confused in choosing "appropriate" words between GCD and SMG vocabulary; and third, they would feel less embarrassed about their own linguistic abilities (p. 205).

Another context of diglossia occurs on the other side of the world – in Brunei, where Brunei Malay is the D1 and Bahasa Melayu (standard Malay) is the D2, although this is further complicated by the widespread teaching and use of English as an L2. The situation, as reported by James (1996), is similar to that in Arab countries in that while both teachers and students are supposed to use the standard D2 in school, they often have to resort to the D1 in order to communicate. James (p. 252) suggested a model in which children are free to express themselves in their home language – i.e. Brunei Malay – which would be treated with respect instead of being denigrated.

7.1.3   Speakers of ethnic dialects

The educational underachievement of African American children in the USA is well known. Statistics continually show African Americans lagging behind Whites in levels of reading, writing, mathematics and other school subjects – the so-called "achievement gap". Figures from the 2007 National Assessment of Education Progress, shown in Table 7.1, demonstrate that much higher percentages of Black students (predominantly African American) are below the basic achievement level compared to Whites (and to Asian Americans/ Pacific Islanders as well).[3] For example, 45 per cent of Blacks in grade 8 scored below the basic achievement level in reading compared to 16 per cent of Whites.[4]

Of course, these poor results among Blacks are a consequence of a complex combination of many factors, including poverty and some of the social and attitudinal obstacles described in Section 7.2 below (see Craig and Washington 2006: 83–93). However, there is general agreement that part of the problem stems from the need for African American English-speaking children to acquire

Table 7.1 *Percentages of students below basic achievement level, National Assessment of Educational Progress, 2007*

	White	Black	Hispanic	Asian Am./ Pacific Is.	Amer. Indian
Reading grade 4	22	54	50	23	51
Reading grade 8	16	45	42	20	44
Writing grade 8	8	19	20	8	21
Writing grade 12	14	31	29	14	30
Mathematics grade 4	9	36	30	9	30
Mathematics grade 8	18	53	45	17	47

standard American English (SAE) in order to succeed in the formal education system. This has been confirmed to some extent by recent research. A study of seventy-five AAE-speaking grade 2 students by Terry *et al.* (forthcoming) revealed that morphosyntactic features of AAE that contrast with SAE have significant negative effects on performance in mathematical reasoning tests. Research by Charity, Scarborough and Griffin (2004) showed that for 217 African American children from kindergarten to grade 2, greater familiarity with "School English" (i.e. SAE) corresponded to higher achievement in reading, as measured by standardised tests. Craig and Washington (2004) found that students who reduced their AAE in school and shifted to SAE performed six times better on standardised reading tests than those who maintained their AAE and did not shift. Shifting to (or acquiring) SAE also led to significant positive results in tests on vocabulary development.

Yet AAE-speaking children are generally not treated as learners who need to acquire SAE in school. Rather, like regional D1-speaking students, they are treated as careless or lazy speakers of standard English, and many are sent to special education classes (van Keulen, Weddington and DeBose 1998). As in other settings, children may be constantly corrected by teachers, leading the children to withdraw into silence or rebel against the education system. Smitherman (1977: 217–18) presented a classic example of this. Although it has been given in other publications (e.g. Green 2002: 232), it is too illustrative not to repeat here:

STUDENT (EXCITEDLY): Miz Jones, you remember that show you tole us bout? Well, me and my momma'nem –
TEACHER (INTERRUPTING WITH A "WARM" SMILE): Bernadette, start again, I'm sorry, but I can't understand you.
STUDENT (CONFUSED): Well, it was that show, me and my momma –

TEACHER (INTERRUPTING AGAIN):   Sorry, I still can't understand you.
(Student, now silent, even more confused than ever, looks at floor,
says nothing.)
TEACHER: Now, Bernadette, first of all, it's *Mrs* Jones, not *Miz* Jones. And you
know it was an *exhibit*, not a show. Now, haven't I explained to the class over
and over again that you always put yourself last when you are talking about
a group of people and yourself doing something? So, therefore, you should
say what?
STUDENT: My momma and me – t
TEACHER (EXASPERATED):   No! My mother and I. Now start again, this time right.
STUDENT: Aw, that's okay. It wasn't nothin.

As Winford (2003: 34) observed, "Everyone knows that the methods currently used to teach reading, writing and language arts to African American
children are an abysmal failure".[5]

Another ethnic dialect in North America is American Indian English (Leap
1993) – a range of varieties of English spoken as a D1 by various groups of
Native Americans. Writing about the situation in Canada, Heit and Blair
(1993: 115–16) noted: "A great deal of damage has been done to Indian and
Metis students who have been misdiagnosed as having language or learning
problems due to differences in their spoken English that have been misunderstood by educators." They observed that constant correction by teachers is
interpreted by students as a rejection of their language and culture, and is
partially responsible for students retreating into silence in the classroom and
for high attrition rates. Epstein and Xu (2003: 6) stated that English-speaking
Aboriginal (i.e. Indian) students are "disadvantaged at school compared with
non-Aboriginal students" because there is little emphasis on their need to
learn standard Canadian English as a second dialect. Therefore, the authors
recommended a bidialectal approach – i.e. using both the D1 and D2 in the
classroom. The situation with American Indians in the USA is not clear, but
Table 7.1 shows large percentages below the basic level for academic achievement, comparable to those of African Americans. Since most American
Indians are now native speakers of a variety of English, these figures may
also indicate that SDA is a problem.

In Australia, there is also a large educational gap between non-Indigenous
and Indigenous (Aboriginal and Torres Strait Islander) people (Malcolm and
Königsberg 2007). Australia participates in international tests of the OECD
Program for International Student Assessment, which report results for Indigenous and non-Indigenous students. In 2006, the proportion of Indigenous
15-year-old secondary students who reached the benchmark (level 3 or above)
for mathematics literacy was 32.4 per cent, compared to 67.5 per cent of non-
Indigenous students. There were similar results for reading literacy: 33.5
compared to 66.5 per cent.[6] As in the USA, there are many factors responsible

for this gap, such as poverty and racism. However, since speakers of Aboriginal English comprise nearly 80 per cent of the Indigenous population, the problem of having to learn the educational standard variety as a D2 again appears to be significant (Partington and Galloway 2007: 251).

Malcolm (1982) reported on a survey of standard AusE-speaking teachers and Aboriginal English-speaking students about communication problems in the classroom in Western Australia. Teachers referred to the common problem of Aboriginal children being sometimes uncommunicative and withdrawn in the classroom and at other times unrestrained and disruptive. Aboriginal people, on the other hand, referred to "being lost for words in the White context of the school and genuinely afraid – afraid of the teacher's censure, afraid of ridicule from their mates, and afraid of being wrong" (p. 166). Malcolm continued (p. 166):

It was a common complaint that the teachers had employed "big words" and talked "above the heads" of the Aboriginal pupils. They often felt that the teachers were unaware of the problems they were having with [standard] English.

Malcolm (1982) also presented some actual examples of classroom communication breakdown caused by the teacher's frequently "standardising" the children's utterances, as well as by linguistic, paralinguistic and pragmatic differences between the D1 of Aboriginal students and the D2 of non-Aboriginal teachers. More recent work has concentrated on differences in interactional styles and cultural schemas (e.g. Malcolm 2007; Malcolm and Sharifian 2005; Sharifian 2005).

A somewhat different situation regarding ethnic dialect speakers is found in what are called "heritage language learning" settings. In the USA, there are millions of speakers of varieties of Spanish associated with particular ethnic groups such as Chicanos and Puerto Ricans. Many members of these groups choose to study standard Spanish as a D2 in school. In the past, as reported by Valdés (1981: 7), such students "were being placed in beginning Spanish classes for non-speakers to help them 'unlearn' their 'bad' habits and begin anew as foreign speakers". But such policies led to obvious problems in that these students, compared to others, already knew quite a bit of the target language. Later, "bilingual tracks" were established for such students, so that they did not inhibit the true L2 learners (or contaminate them with non-standard features) (Valdés 1995: 300). Nowadays, such students are referred to as "heritage language learners", and many colleges and universities offer a track of courses in Spanish for Native Speakers or Spanish for Heritage Learners (Fairclough 2005: 57). Heritage language education exists for speakers of other languages as well, such as Chinese and Japanese (see chapters in Brinton, Kagan and Baukus (2008). However, as most has been written about Spanish, that is the focus here.

The situation of Spanish heritage language courses differs from that of other cases of SDA in that the primary language of some heritage language learners is not the D1 but English, and they may not be fluent in the D1, or in some cases they may understand it but not speak it. However, even when the D1 is the mother tongue and primary language, as in other classroom SDA situations, there are accounts of learners of standard Spanish as an L2 eventually surpassing learners of standard Spanish as a D2, especially in literacy skills (Fairclough 2005: 63) – the precise skills in the standard that they need to acquire the most.

7.1.4   Speakers of indigenised varieties

Settings where indigenised varieties of English are spoken are multilingual, with the variety used as a lingua franca. For most of the population, English is learned in school as a second or additional language. SDA is relevant when the standard selected as the educational language is not based on the national variety – for example, in Fiji, where British English rather than Fiji English is the target. Since in such situations the target variety and norms are those of native speakers from an external country, Kirkpatrick (2007: 184) calls this an "exonormative native speaker model", and points out some of its disadvantages. Students, for example, are forced to learn a variety most of them will not need to use unless they travel to another country, and one that differs from what they hear in everyday contexts. If they already know the local indigenised variety to some extent, they face problems similar to those of speakers of regional, colloquial and ethnic dialects, as just described. Similarly, teachers who are not native speakers of the external variety find it difficult to teach. At the same time, however, they feel compelled to adopt the monolingual teaching methodology associated with this model, which does not allow the L1 (or in this case, the D1) in the classroom.

Another indigenised variety context in which SDA is relevant is when the commonly spoken colloquial variety is very different from the local educational standard – as in diglossic situations in other countries. This is the case in Singapore, where children who speak Singapore Colloquial English have to acquire Singapore Standard English in school (Gupta 1991). However, the success rate for D2 acquisition in Singapore is much higher than that in other SDA situations. In 2007, for example, the pass rate in English in the Primary School Leaving Examination was 97.6 percent.[7] Gupta (1991: 144) pointed out that children, especially from middle-class families, learn Singapore Standard English rapidly because it is used widely in their community for formal functions, and it is not seen as a variety belonging to another social group. However, since this is also true for other diglossic contexts, it may be that the comparative linguistic closeness of the two varieties in Singapore is a more important factor. Still another factor may be teaching methods which, as described by Gupta (1994), do not involve constant correction of students (see Section 8.4 in the following chapter).

Classroom SDA is also relevant to speakers of indigenised varieties of English who have migrated to another English-speaking country. In these contexts, some problems are again caused by the differences between the variety used in the education system and the students' D1, and by teachers' lack of awareness that the problems are caused by these differences. For example, Govardhan (2006) showed how the rhetorical style of written Indian (South Asian) English leads to Indian students' writing in America being judged as non-linear, wordy and full of clichés. However, instructors do not help students understand the differences between the writing styles of the two varieties. And Tayao (2006) described how speakers of Philippine English in the USA face difficulties in their comprehension of both spoken and written American English.

7.1.5   Speakers of creoles

In nearly all countries or territories where creole languages are spoken, the standard form of the lexifier, and the language of the former or continuing colonial power, is the educational language that must be learned and used by all students in the formal education system. So for example, children speaking Guadeloupe Creole, lexified by French, learn standard French, and those speaking Guinea-Bissau Kriyol, lexified by Portuguese, learn standard Portuguese. With regard to the former British colonies in the Caribbean where creoles are spoken – such as Jamaica, Guyana, Trinidad and Tobago, and Grenada – Craig (1971: 375) noted that they are, "in a way, trapped within their Standard English traditions", in that they have adopted English as the official language of government and education. Therefore, a goal of the education system is proficiency in standard English. But because of various difficulties for creole-speaking students, this goal has largely not been met. Over the years, the success rates in the Caribbean-wide examinations in English have been very low (Le Page 1968; Craig 1971, 2001; McCourtie 1998). In the 2007 results for the English-A exam for the Caribbean Secondary Education Certificate, only 43 per cent attained passes at levels I to III in the January sitting, and 49 per cent in the May/June sitting (Caribbean Examinations Council 2007: 8, 11).

Craig (1983) outlined various sociolinguistic reasons for the lack of success in SDA in creole settings in the Caribbean (and in other settings as well), such as learners' negative attitudes towards standard English and its speakers, and the lack of relevance of the D2 to the social needs of most of the students. But in most of his work, Craig put the blame mainly on the various teaching methodologies that have been used, criticising especially what he later referred to as the "English-as-the-mother-tongue tradition" (2001: 66). In this monolingual tradition, students are considered to be merely poor speakers of the standard language, rather than language learners, and this has led to many other problems, as discussed below. Craig (1967, 1977) believed that students' home language should be utilised in at least the first few years of formal education and that "the teacher has to accept the natural speech of the child without the inhibiting practice of intermittent 'correction'" (1967: 134).

Educational problems of creole-speaking students are compounded when they migrate to countries where teachers and fellow students are not familiar with their language. The problems facing immigrants from the Caribbean in British schools received a great deal of attention in the 1970s and 1980s (e.g. Edwards 1979; Richmond 1986). In the 1990s, the focus shifted to North America. As pointed out by Winer (2006: 109–10), Caribbean Creole-speaking children in North America continue to be dealt with in one of three ways: mainstreaming, special education, or ESL (English as a second language) programs. In mainstreaming, they are put in classes along with other students who already know the varieties close to the standard. Coelho (1988: 144) described the situation in Canada when this occurs:

Divergence from Standard English usage by Caribbean students is usually not regarded with the same tolerance as errors made by students who are learning English as a Second Language, because Caribbean students are generally not regarded as language learners. They are regarded as English speakers who are careless with the language.

In the USA, Pratt-Johnson (1993) and Winer (1993) reported that teachers' lack of familiarity with Caribbean creoles and culture has led to difficulties in communication in the classroom, and to creole-speaking children being put in special education, remedial or even speech therapy classes (as with AAE-speaking children). This sends an unwarranted negative message to both children and parents.

Educators who recognise the legitimacy of creole-speaking students' language often place them in ESL programs along with speakers of Japanese, Russian, etc. But this causes other problems. First of all, creole speakers usually see themselves as speakers of English (Nero 1997, 2001), and as Winer (2006: 110) noted: "They are astonished and resentful at being treated in this fashion." Second, beginning and intermediate ESL classes are not really appropriate because creole speakers have a large vocabulary and a good receptive knowledge of English compared to other learners. Third, many creole-speaking students are eventually outperformed, especially in formal writing, by other ESL students who started out with much less English. This is frequently due to a lack of recognition of how certain standard English structures differ from those of the creole, and the persistence of negative transfer (Calchar 2004; Winer 2006). De Kleine (2006, 2009) described similar problems with immigrants from West Africa (Ghana, Liberia, Nigeria and Sierra Leone) who speak expanded pidgins and creoles (or in some cases, indigenised varieties). She also presented extensive examples of negative transfer in their writing.

7.2 Obstacles faced by D2 learners in educational contexts

The preceding section has shown that students in all five D1 groups (except for heritage language learners and some speakers of indigenised varieties) are generally disadvantaged in at least three ways. First, they have to learn how to read and write in a variety of a language that they do not already know (the D2), and learn content in subjects such as mathematics in that variety as well. Second, since they are not considered to be language learners, they are not given any special instruction to help them learn the D2 (except for creole-speaking immigrants in ESL programs, which are not suitable anyway). Third, they may become frustrated by constant correction and not being able to express themselves in the variety they do know, their D1, which is usually denigrated in and/or not considered appropriate for the classroom. Regional and ethnic dialect speakers in mainstream programs and immigrants speaking indigenised varieties and creoles are faced with the additional disadvantage of having to compete with classmates who already know the D2. However, there are other obstacles that students must overcome if they are to acquire the standard variety of the education system. These are described here.

7.2.1   Negative attitudes of teachers

As mentioned in the preceding section, teachers in some SDA contexts often do not know about their students' D1. Therefore, they cannot distinguish errors caused by systematic differences between the D1 and the D2 from those caused by carelessness. This can lead teachers to form opinions about students' general abilities on the basis of their dialect. In Britain, for example, Cheshire (1982: 63) observed that "teachers who see the use of dialect forms as 'mistakes of grammar' may unwittingly form a low opinion of the dialect-speaking pupils' competence", and that "teachers often use language as a cue for their assessment of pupils". These negative assessments lead to lower expectations about overall student performance. Similar views have been expressed by writers referring to several SDA settings, and are backed up by experimental research. For example, in a study in the USA by Cecil (1988), fifty-two teachers were randomly assigned to listen to a tape-recording of either five children speaking AAE or five children speaking SAE. They were then asked to rate the speakers' intelligence, their chance for successful academic achievement and their predicted reading ability. The results were that the SAE speakers were rated significantly higher than the AAE speakers in all three categories. (See also studies by Granger *et al.* 1977, and Cross, DeVaney and Jones 2001).

Furthermore, as Cheshire (1982: 63) pointed out, "it has also been found that teachers' expectations have a significant effect on the scholastic performance of their pupils". Many studies in the USA have shown that teachers, both African American and White, have lower expectations for AAE-speaking students than for standard-speaking students, and that this leads to lower results (e.g. Ogbu, 1978: 133–5; Fairchild and Edwards-Evans 1990: 78–80; Irvine 1990: 43–61). This situation is often referred to as "self-fulfilling prophecy" (Rist 1970). In this case, teachers judge students as being unintelligent on the basis of their D1, and then treat them accordingly. This message is internalised by the students, who perform according to the teachers' expectations. In the end, the teachers' predictions are fulfilled, but this is largely a consequence of the teachers' behaviour, not of the students' shortcomings. (See Tauber's 1997 facetiously titled *Self-Fulfilling Prophecy: A Practical Guide to Its Use in Education*, and the original research by Rosenthal and Jacobson 1968.) With regard to creole-speaking immigrants in Britain, Edwards (1979: 97–8) described how attitudes based on ignorance about the students' D1 can lead to a vicious circle of linguistic prejudice: teachers mistake language problems of creole-speaking children for stupidity, then stereotype, and eventually lower expectations, leading to lower student performance and thus reinforcing the stereotype.

In addition to internalising teachers' negative attitudes about their academic ability, students may also adopt teachers' beliefs about their D1 – that it is an incorrect form of the standard, rather than a legitimate variety with its own linguistic rules (e.g. Fischer 1992a: 100). We have already seen that constant correction of the D1 makes some students retreat into silence, and denigration has the same effect. The result is that some children develop a negative self-image because of the rejection of their language, and by association, their culture, while others respond by rejecting the formal education system itself.

These detrimental effects of teachers' negative attitudes have been described in other classroom settings as well – for example, with children speaking American Indian English (Heit and Blair 1993) and with heritage learners of Spanish (Martínez 2003; Parodi 2008; Valdés *et al.* 2008).

7.2.2   *Peer pressure and identity*

The marginalisation of D1 language and culture in the education system and in other institutions is one factor that has led to the development of an oppositional social identity (see e.g. Ogbu 1978). This is when an individual or group define themselves according to how they are different to another group (or "outgroup"), usually a dominant group. Therefore, it is unacceptable to adopt characteristics of this outgroup. As a result, use of the D2 – the standard variety that typifies the outgroup – is often stigmatised within the D1 community, and students who use it are ridiculed or even ostracised by their peers. In Britain, Cheshire and Trudgill (1989: 100) noted that the use of non-standard linguistic features actually increases in adolescence, and quoted a student from Birmingham: "You always try to be the same as everyone else. You don't sort of want to be made fun of . . . sort of posher than everyone else. Then you get sort of picked on."

With reference to Pidgin (Hawai'i Creole), Tamura (1996: 439–40) quoted an intermediate school student: "If we speak good English [i.e. standard English], our friends usually say, 'Oh you're trying to be *hybolic* [acting superior by using big words] yeah?!'" And referring to her survey about attitudes to Pidgin, Leong (2000: 25) reported: "Several people said they find that at times using Pidgin is necessary so they won't be seen as someone who is *high makamaka* [a person who tries to act high and mighty]."

In Australia, Hudson (1983: 16) told the story of an Aboriginal woman: "She recounted an experience where she was speaking to a white woman using [standard] English and her friends nearby were laughing at her, making fun of her for speaking 'high' English, a sign of snobbery."

Regarding AAE, Kareem Abdul-Jabbar related in his autobiography (Abdul-Jabbar and Knobles 1983) how he had learned standard English at home but when he transferred to an all-Black school, he "became a target" among his classmates: "I spoke correctly and was called a punk. I had to learn a new language simply to be able to deal with the threats" (quoted in Fordham and Ogbu 1986: 177). Fordham (1998: 209) noted: "Black people who choose discourses that mimic those of Whites *while in predominantly Black contexts* may be marginalized by their communities" (emphasis in original). (See also Wolfram and Schilling-Estes 1998: 287.)

The key issue here again appears to be social identity. Fordham (1999: 275) asserted: "Language is central to the maintenance of group identity within African American communities." Thus, if students do not reject the language of the dominant White culture – i.e. standard English – "they are accused by their peers of 'acting White'" (p. 277). In a survey of ninth and eleventh graders at a predominantly African American high school, a large majority (79 and 72 per cent respectively) identified speaking standard English as an example of "acting White" (Fordham 1999: 279). Similarly, in Hawai'i Roberts (2004: 342) quoted students who described their friends making fun of them when they used "good English" rather than Pidgin, and calling them "haoles" ('Whites') or using racialised taunts such as "black haoles" and "sunburned haoles".

It appears that what is operating here, in conjunction with the oppositional aspect of identity, is the belief that there is only one true self (as described in Chapter 6), and that this should be reflected in language use. This is illustrated in a quotation from a speaker of an unstandardised British dialect (Cheshire and Edwards 1998: 203): "I enjoy speaking the way I do as I think it's me." In the case of African Americans, Fordham (1998: 211) referred to the notion of "the essential Black Self". In another work (Fordham 1999: 284), she described the views of one student, Maggie, with regard to her mother "talking White" – i.e. using standard English: "Maggie views her mother's speech practices as fraudulent – 'She's trying to be someone she's not' – and deceptive – 'You can't tell whether she's White or Black'." This appeared to reflect a lack of acceptance of bidialectalism. Thus, like the learners in naturalistic contexts described in Chapter 6, students in classroom SDA contexts may feel they have to make a choice between the language of their own community (the D1) and the language of the dominant community to which they don't really belong (the D2).

7.2.3   Lack of awareness of differences

As we have seen in the first part of this book, SDA involves learning the features of the D2 that differ from those of the D1. Second dialect learners in classroom SDA contexts are normally expected to learn these features of the D2 – the standard dialect – without any special instruction. As several researchers have pointed out, however, students often do not recognise these differences, and they may not even realise that there is a different variety of language that they are supposed to learn. For example, Cheshire (1982) pointed out:

Children may not even be aware of the existence of the variety of English that linguists label "standard English". They may simply recognise that school teachers and news-readers, for example, do not speak in quite the same way as their family and friends.

Evidence that speakers of AAE have trouble recognising differences between their D1 and standard English comes from a study by Geiger and Greenberg (1976). The subjects were thirty African American children from an inner-city public school in Washington, DC. They comprised three age groups of ten each: 6 years, 8 years and 10 years. A tape-recording was made of an African American bidialectal speaker reciting ten pairs of sentences that were identical except for items of vocabulary that distinguish AAE from SAE. The subjects were trained to point to a photograph of a well-known Black television personality when they heard a sentence that sounded like "TV talk, the kind of talk you hear on television, at the movies and that Mr B (the principal) uses", and to point to a photo of Black children in the school's playground

Table 7.2 *Percentages of accurate responses for three age groups in differentiating five morphosyntactic features of African American English and Standard American English*

Feature	6 years	8 years	10 years	Total
3rd person singular marking	38	46	60	48
Copula in the progressive	36	54	64	51
Habitual *be*	52	56	60	56
Possessive marking	42	24	40	36
Negation	42	52	40	44
Average	42	46	53	47

when they heard "everyday talk, the kind of talk you hear on the playground, at home and in the cafeteria" (p. 29).

For the actual test, the subjects were asked to follow the same procedure, but this time with a recording made of the same speaker reciting ten different pairs of sentences, each identical except for morphosyntactic features that distinguish AAE from SAE. Five different features were included, as illustrated with the examples below from the study, where N indicates "non-standard" (i.e. AAE) and S "standard" (i.e. SAE) (p. 32):

1. 3rd person singular marking: N: *He have a bike.*
   S: *He has a bike.*

2. Copula in the progressive: N: *She playing in the street.*
   S: *She's playing in the street.*

3. Habitual *be*: N: *My uncle Jack be working all the time.*
   S: *My uncle Jack is working all the time.*

4. Possessive marking: N: *He ate that boy lunch.*
   S: *He ate that boy's lunch.*

5. Negation: N: *They never do nothing.*
   S: *They never do anything.*

The percentages of accurate responses for each feature (as opposed to inaccurate or uncertain responses) are shown in Table 7.2.[8] The figures demonstrate that on the average, the subjects could differentiate the D1 (AAE) from the D2 (SAE) less than half of the time. On the whole, the older group was more successful than the younger groups, but not consistently, and with never more than a 64 per cent accuracy rate. Also, some features were more difficult to distinguish than others – for example, possessive marking versus the copula in the progressive, for which the difference in average rates was statistically significant (p. 31).

Regarding creole settings, Craig (1966, 1971) proposed that standard English features are divided into four classes with respect to creole speakers:

A those actively known (used spontaneously in informal speech)
B those known but used only under stress (in formal situations – but not habitual)
C those known passively (could be understood according to context, but not produced)
D those not yet known

Because of classes A, B and C, many creole speakers are under the illusion that they already know the standard, and this affects motivation in the classroom. This has also been pointed out by Fischer (1992a) and Nero (1997) with regard to Caribbean immigrants in the USA. Also, because the target patterns of classes C and D above are often very closely linked to those of classes A and B, "the learner often fails to perceive the new target element in the teaching situation" (Craig 1966: 58). This view has been reiterated by Simmons-McDonald (2001: 40), who observed that "learners (and in some cases teachers) have difficulty in determining the differences in some grammatical structures of the varieties". Similarly in the Netherlands, van den Hoogen and Kuijper (1989: 223) observed that speakers of regional dialects of Dutch learning standard Dutch often cannot detect "errors" in their speech caused by linguistic differences between the varieties. And as we have seen in Section 5.2.1 above, if a linguistic feature is not perceived or noticed, it will not be learned.

Craig (1983) suggested that the four classes of features and the failure to perceive differences also apply to teaching situations involving AAE as the D1. Valdés (1995: 312) demonstrated that this view applies to situations involving heritage learners of Spanish as well. However, she added another class of features: those that are used exclusively in the D1 and that are highly stigmatised by D2 speakers. Valdés observed that these features are sometimes used by learners in attempting to speak the standard dialect under the mistaken assumption that they belong to class A or B.

Craig also pointed out (e.g. 1988) that in foreign or second language learning situations where English is the target, English does not form part of learners' native language repertoires and therefore remains separate and distinct. But in classroom SDA situations in creole settings (and in the other settings as well), there is an "area of interaction" between the learner's familiar speech and standard English. Because of this interaction, as well as the close links between known and target features, separating the two varieties is often a problem, as indicated in Section 7.1 above.

7.3   Studies of SDA in classroom contexts

Valdés (1997: 23) drew attention to the fact that "few theories exist on how standard dialects are acquired by speakers of non-prestige varieties". This is because, as mentioned earlier, very little research has been done specifically

Table 7.3 *Percentages of use of non-standard features across three grades*

	% grade 3	% grade 5	% grade 7
Presence of (habitual) *be*	24	02	00
Subject–verb disagreement	90	41	28
Possession absence	86	54	47
Copula absence	91	80	74
Multiple negation	97	88	92
	$n = 40$	$n = 40$	$n = 34$

on how SDA occurs in classroom contexts. This section describes the few relevant studies that I have been able to find.[9]

7.3.1   D1 African American English; D2 standard American English (primary level)

Isaacs (1996) investigated the persistence of the use of non-standard dialect features of English among 114 children (57 African American and 57 White) in grades 3, 5 and 7 in four North Carolina schools. The non-standard features, similar to those examined in the study by Geiger and Greenberg (1976) described above, were as follows, using labels for the features and examples found in the study (p. 441):

Presence of (habitual) *be*	*Thomas be playing hard all the time.*
Subject–verb disagreement	*They was the last ones to go home.*
Possession absence	*I saw Sharon brother at the mall.*
Copula absence	*She going to the circus.*
Multiple negation	*He don't have no money for gas.*

The first four features are typical of AAE, while the last one is commonly found in both AAE and other unstandardised varieties of English.

To obtain the data, the study used the Sentence Production Task of the Test of Dialect Dominance (Wiener, Lewnau and Erway 1983), which was administered to the subjects while in the school. This test uses pictures and prompts to elicit production of the five variables that have the non-standard variants listed above (p. 437). The percentages of use of these variants are shown for each grade level in Table 7.3 (Isaacs 1996: 438).

The results were that the overall use of non-standard variants decreased significantly from grade 3 to grade 7.[10] However, as can be seen in Table 7.3, while the use of some features (the presence of habitual *be* and subject–verb disagreement) decreased dramatically, others decreased to a lesser extent and one (multiple negation) actually increased from grade 5 to grade 7.

Interestingly, there was no significant difference overall between African American and White students in their use of the non-standard variants, though African Americans used absence of possession and absence of copula significantly more than Whites in grade 3 (Isaacs 1996: 438). So in this situation, the AAE-speaking students may not have been as disadvantaged as in others where their classmates speak the standard.

In the concluding discussion of the study (1996: 438), Isaacs highlighted the finding that the gap between the production of the non-standard and standard dialect narrows as the students progress through school. But if we stand back and look at the results from the point of view of SDA, we get a different picture. After seven years of formal education in the D2 (SAE), the continued use in the school environment of four out of five D1 features ranged from 28 to 92 per cent of the time. To put it in another way, the use of the D2 variant for four out of five of the variables examined ranged from 8 to 72 per cent, significantly below the 90 per cent level that indicates acquisition.

The reasons for this could possibly be found in another part of the study, which is relevant to the lack of awareness of differences described above. To see whether the children could discriminate between non-standard and standard dialect, Isaacs constructed a dialect discrimination task similar to that used in Geiger and Greenberg's (1976) study. This consisted of twenty sentences involving the five variables described above, some with the standard variant and some with the non-standard variant. The sentences were recorded in a random order, and the students were asked to judge whether each one was "school talk" or "not school talk" (1996: 436). The average percentages of correct responses were 56 in grade 3, 65 in grade 5 and 80 in grade 7. Again, the results seem positive, showing a significant increase in discrimination. But from the SDA angle, after five years of formal education, students could not distinguish between D1 and D2 features 35 per cent of the time, and two years later, still 20 per cent.

Of course, there may be another reason for the results. In studies involving speakers of minority ethnic dialects, percentages of use of D2 variants are often not accurate indicators of acquisition, since students may not want to use the standard, for reasons described in Section 7.2.2 above. As Delpit (1990: 251) observed, children often have the ability to speak standard English, but choose "to identify with their community rather than with the school".

7.3.2   D1 African American English; D2 standard American English (tertiary level)

A very different type of research was done by Price (1993): a qualitative study focusing on the individual and contextual factors affecting high attainment in SDA in formal education. The author was a teacher of English and speech for over thirty years. He did the study at a college where he taught 200 to 250 African American students each year, and worked with 300 to 400 in a language laboratory. The vast majority came from urban areas, had gone to predominantly African American high schools, spoke AAE as their D1, and had only AAE-speaking peers (p. 94). Out of all these students, only a very small minority had successfully acquired SAE as a D2 and were bidialectal. The subjects in this study were four of these students (three male, one female).

The subjects all had similar backgrounds – growing up in single-parent households in urban ghettos, living in public housing, and being able to attend college only with financial assistance (1993: 236). In addition to this disadvantage, earlier in their education they had to face the obstacles to SDA described above, such as people saying they "talk White" (p. 114). Price's aim was to discover the factors that contributed to the students' success in SDA and enabled them to overcome the obstacles. The main data for the study came from in-depth interviews conducted in 1988. Each student was asked fifty-six questions at random exploring various influences on their education and their awareness of dialect difference.

Price (1993) uncovered eight "positive factors" shared by all four of the students (p. 241). First was thorough instruction in grammar in a very prescriptive way, and a clear indication of what was "right" (i.e. standard) and what was "wrong" (i.e. non-standard). Second was a nurturing influence from family members, teachers, counsellors and, in one case, the basketball coach. Third and fourth were a background of reading good literature and the enjoyment of reading. Fifth was creativity – for example, all four wrote poetry. Sixth was an awareness of the differences between AAE and SAE (p. 253). Seventh was the motivation to learn SAE for a particular career – what we referred to earlier as instrumental orientation. And the last factor was extensive writing experience. It should also be noted that three out of four of the subjects had positive attitudes towards AAE and used it in their interactions with other African Americans.

It is clear that these students were special cases (and young adults, not children) who were highly motivated, creative and lucky enough to have had exposure to literature at a young age and support at home or in school. But it is noteworthy that two of the eight factors had to do with clearly differentiating the D1 and the D2.

7.3.3   D1 unstandardised varieties of Spanish; D2 standard Spanish

Fairclough (2005) conducted a very detailed and theoretically informed study of SDA in the classroom context. It was done in a heritage language setting with standard Spanish as the D2, and again with young adults, not children. This differs from other settings in that the D2 learners do not have to face the obstacle of learning initial literacy in the D2 because they have already acquired it (in this case, in English). In addition, since they already know a great deal of the target language (in this case, Spanish), they have an advantage over their fellow students who are learning it from scratch as a second language.

Fairclough's subjects were two groups of university students studying Spanish at a university in Houston, Texas. The first group were 141 heritage learners, bilingual in English and an unstandardised dialect of Spanish and learning standard Spanish as a D2 (the H^{er} group). The second group were 142 traditional L2 learners of Spanish as a second language (the T^{rad} group) (2005: 76). Each group consisted of students enrolled in courses at five different levels of proficiency. In the first two levels, the groups were in different courses – the H^{er} group in Spanish for Native Speakers courses and the T^{rad} group in intermediate courses for L2 learners. In the three higher levels, the students were in the same courses. There was also a smaller-scale longitudinal study of three heritage learners.

One of the overall aims of the study was to compare the SDA of the H^{er} group with the SLA of the T^{rad} group, in both attainment and the learning processes. Another aim was to determine whether the acquisition of the D2 for the H^{er} group was replacive or additive (see Section 3.3 in Chapter 3 above). An additional aim was to examine the pedagogical implications of the findings.

The study focused on one particular linguistic variable that has different variants in the D1 and D2 – the form of the verb used in hypothetical sentences – for example, in English:

> If it rains tomorrow, I'll stay home.
> If it had rained yesterday, I would've stayed home.

The first sentence is sometimes referred to as [−PAST] hypothetical (or conditional), and the second as [+PAST] hypothetical (or conditional), or "counterfactual". With regard to Spanish, speakers of an unstandardised D1 often use tenses that are different from those of the D2. For example, in the first part of the first [−PAST] sentence above, *if it rains*, speakers of standard Spanish would use the conditional form of the verb, but D1 speakers would often use the imperfective subjunctive, infinitive, present, future or other forms (Fairclough 2005: 47). In the first part of the second [+PAST] sentence, *if it had rained*, the verb *hubiera* – the pluperfect subjective form of *haber* 'to have' – would be used in standard Spanish, but the verb *fuera* – the imperfective subjunctive form of *ser* 'to be' – would often be used in the D1. Fairclough (p. 76) gave the following examples:

> D2: *Si **hubiera** sido mi fiesta, yo no habría invitado a Jorge.*
> D1: *Si **fuera** sido mi fiesta, yo no habría invitado a Jorge.*
>   'If it had been my party, I wouldn't have invited Jorge.'

Table 7.4 *Average percentages of target L2/D2 (standard Spanish) hypothetical forms in the cloze-type test*

	Level 1	Level 2	Level 3	Level 4	Level 5
T^{rad} group	0.0	15.2	12.0	16.2	35.2
H^{er} group	46.0	51.4	54.2	56.0	62.5

Table 7.5 *Average percentages of target L2/D2 hypothetical (standard Spanish) forms in the oral data*

	Level 1	Level 2
T^{rad} group	0	47
H^{er} group	61	69

In order to collect written data, students were asked to write four short paragraphs in Spanish, to do a cloze-type test (inserting appropriate verbs in blanks in a written passage) and to do an acceptability judgement task. For oral data, students participated in 15-minute semi-structured interviews with peers. For the longitudinal study, the three heritage learners were interviewed when they were at the intermediate level and then later at the advanced level.

With regard to attainment, the results for percentage of use of target D2/L2 forms are shown in Tables 7.4 and 7.5.[11] The H^{er} group produced statistically significant higher percentages of target L2/D2 forms than the T^{rad} group, both before and after instruction. However, the degree of improvement was much greater for the T^{rad} group from Level 1 to Level 2 in both sources of data, and from Level 4 to Level 5 in the cloze-like test. This is, of course, because they started from scratch, and it underlines one of the differences between SLA and SDA described for naturalistic contexts in Section 6.1 above.

Fairclough (2005: 124) partially attributed the relatively slow rate of progress of the H^{er} group to interference (i.e. negative transfer) from the D1. This occurred with the H^{er} group because of the similarity between the D1 and D2, but not with the T^{rad} group because of the greater differences between the L1 and L2, as discussed in Section 6.2.1 above. As an example, Fairclough (p. 124) mentioned the H^{er} group's use of the D1 imperfective indicative form *podia* 'would be', instead of the D2 form *podría*. In contrast, none of the T^{rad} group used the L1 form *would be* in place of *podría*.

With regard to the processes of acquisition, Fairclough (2005: 125, 129) noted that the T^{rad} group used a greater variety of verb forms, while the H^{er} group generally used either the target D2 forms or forms from their D1.

But they also used some simple forms in place of the required target compound forms – for example, the conditional *adaptaría* instead of the pluperfect subjunctive + past participle *hubiara adaptado* (p. 113). Another difference concerned "backsliding" (Selinker 1972) – a decrease in target-like performance. This occurred with the T^{rad} group between Levels 2 and 3 in the cloze-like test, but not with the H^{er} group (see Table 7.4). As in SLA and naturalistic SDA, some overgeneralisation occurred. One example given by Fairclough (p. 113) was the use of simple forms such as *adaptaría* (just mentioned above), which are acceptable in [–PAST] hypothetical sentences, being overgeneralised to [+PAST] hypothetical sentences, where the compound is required.[12] Another process evident in the data that is also found in SLA is avoidance – paraphrasing or circumlocution to compensate for gaps in linguistic knowledge (p. 104). This occurred more often with the H^{er} group than with the T^{rad} group. Finally, both groups produced higher percentages of target L2/D2 forms in tasks where more attention is paid to form – i.e. in paragraph writing versus interviews – an effect reported as well in the SLA literature.

Turning now to the question of replacive versus additive SDA in the H^{er} group, on the basis of oral data and the small-scale longitudinal study, Fairclough (2005: 131) concluded that overall the instruction did not result in the D1 forms being replaced with D2 forms. Rather, some D2 forms were acquired to fill in the gaps where needed in the D1, leaving the existing D1 forms unaffected. According to Fairclough (p. 131): "This may well be evidence of strengthening of the local dialect rather than failure to acquire new constructions." She suggested that this may have been a consequence of "the emotional value" of the D1 and its "role as an ethnic identifier" (see Section 5.1.2 above). However, on the basis of the acceptability judgement task, it was clear that there was a great deal of uncertainty about which forms were acceptable in the D2. And the longitudinal study showed a great deal of free variation between some D1 and D2 forms. Advanced students used standard forms in their repertoires that they already knew or that they learned in the classroom, but they were not distinguishing standard D2 constructions from unstandardised D1 ones (a problem we have seen before in classroom SDA). Fairclough (p. 131) concluded that "these heritage learners do not seem to differentiate their Spanish as two separate systems". She described this as an "additive process" in that learners added D2 forms to their existing D1 systems; however, it is clearly not additive in the sense described in Section 3.3 above, in which a new system, the D2, is added while the old system, the D1, remains intact.

Now we turn to the pedagogical implications of the study for SDA. For the H^{er} group, the formal instruction in hypothetical constructions was effective in enabling students to acquire the forms to fill in the gaps in the D1, but it did not result in acceptable use of the D2. Fairclough (2005: 132) concluded:

"One can argue, therefore, that explicit grammatical instruction alone is insufficient for SDA." She continued:

[I]t could be assumed that heritage learners lack the sociolinguistic knowledge and metalinguistic awareness necessary to separate standard from dialect. Therefore, in order to develop separate systems, instruction also has to promote language awareness.

Fairclough suggested that a "contrastive approach" would be beneficial (2005: 134), that validation of the students' D1 is very important (p. 135) and that giving students an understanding of the social significance of different dialects should be the first step (p. 136). Programs that include this type of instruction are described in the following chapter.

7.3.4   D1 Caribbean creoles; D2 standard American English

Calchar (2004, 2005) conducted two research studies to compare patterns of acquisition in SDA and SLA of tense and aspect marking on verbs.[13] In both studies, the participants were speakers of English-lexified creoles from the Caribbean who had been living in Florida for two years or less. In the 2004 study, there were forty-three grade 9 and 10 students who had been placed in ESL writing programs in a Florida public school. In the 2005 study, the participants were forty-eight students enrolled in basic writing programs in two community colleges in south Florida. In both studies, students were classified according to their place on the creole continuum (Section 1.2 in Chapter 1 above) – basilectal (furthest from standard English) to acrolectal (closest to standard English), with mesolectal in between. As most participants clustered around the mesolectal range of the continuum, the classifications were basilectal-mesolectal, mesolectal and mesolectal-acrolectal. Students in the 2005 study were also divided into four groups or cohorts according to their level of proficiency in the use of English past tense forms.[14]

   In the field of SLA, the "aspect hypothesis" (Andersen and Shirai 1994) predicts that L2 learners acquire English verbal morphology (such as *-ing* and *-ed*) in a predictable way. Verbs are divided into four categories depending on their inherent meaning. "Achievements" are verbs that indicate an instantaneous action or a clear end point, such as *arrive, recognise* and *die*. "Accomplishments" have some duration, but again a clear end point – such as *make (a diagram), build (a boat)* and *calculate (an answer)*. "Activities" have duration as well, but no specific end point – such as *dance, read* and *sing*. Last, "statives" are verbs that indicate states, without involving effort or action – for example, *want, love* and *know*. According to the aspect hypothesis, L2 learners first use the past tense marker *-ed* on the verbs that can be classified as achievements or accomplishments. Later they use it on verbs classified as activities, and finally on statives. Similarly, the use of the progressive marker -*ing* is acquired in a specific order – but in this case, first with activities, then accomplishments, and finally achievements and statives.

The explanation for these patterns is that learners perceive a connection between the meaning of the tense or aspect marker and the inherent meaning of a particular verb category. The past tense marker -*ed* indicates that the action or event occurred in the past and has therefore ended. This is first associated with the categories of verbs that have a clear end point – i.e. achievements and accomplishments. On the other hand, the progressive marker -*ing* indicates a continuing action or event, and is first associated with the categories of verbs with duration – i.e. activities (with no end point) and then accomplishments. Thus, the hypothesis predicts that in interlanguage data from L2 learners, the use of past tense marking and progressive marking will be concentrated in particular categories of verbs rather than spread evenly over all categories. This prediction has been supported by many studies of the SLA of tense and aspect markers on verbs in English and in many other languages as well. (For references, see Bardovi-Harlig 1999.)[15]

Data for Calchar's studies were collected by showing two silent films on separate occasions and then asking the students to retell the story of each film in writing. The verbs in the two writing samples for each subject were categorised. The use of past tense marking with each category was calculated in both studies, and progressive marking calculated as well in the 2004 study.

In both studies the results of the most proficient group of students (those in the mesolectal-acrolectal range, and cohorts 3 and 4) conformed to the predictions of the aspect hypothesis for ESL learners. However the results for the least proficient groups did not conform, with the use of past tense marking (and progressive marking in the 2004 study) being evenly spread across all four verbal categories. Calchar (2004: 161, 2005: 322) attributed these results to two factors: the linguistic features of the students' creole D1, and the characteristics of the creole continuum. First, the overlapping vocabulary of English-lexified creoles and standard English often obscures distinctions between the two varieties, and disguises existing grammatical differences, as discussed above in Section 7.2.3. Second, these creoles have a large number of verbal markers, especially for aspect, that differ in fundamental ways from those of standard English. Third, there is a great deal of variability in the creole continuum, as well as code-switching between creole and standard English. Therefore, it is difficult for students to identify clearly the meaning and functions of the standard English tense and aspect markers, as opposed to the creole ones, and to associate them with particular categories of verbs, even though students may already know the meanings of the verbs because of the vocabulary overlap.

Calchar (2004: 163) concluded that these students "have difficulties building a separate mental representation for standard English because of the blurred boundaries between standard and creole-English and their habit of constantly shifting back and forth between these varieties". She observed that such difficulties do not occur for the usual ESL students. Therefore, creole-speaking students do not fit into either mainstream or ESL programs that reflect the usual dichotomy between native and non-native speakers of English. Thus, Calchar (2005: 324) stressed the need for "a specialized curriculum that addresses the specific writing needs of English-based creole speakers, who are neither native nor non-native speakers of English". Such a curriculum would help learners perceive the differences between the D1 and the D2.

7.4   Arguments against SDA programs

In the light of the problems and obstacles outlined above in Sections 7.1 and 7.2, and the studies outlined in Section 7.3, many linguists and educators believe that there should be special educational programs to help students acquire the D2 in formal education. These programs should validate the D1 and use it as the starting point for learning the D2 – for example, by contrasting the functions and features of the two dialects. In other words, instead of ignoring the language known by the students, schools should follow the common educational principle of moving from the known to the unknown in the curriculum. With regard to AAE, this was recognised thirty years ago in the 1979 "Black English trial". Judge C. W. Joiner, in his judgement in the case, directed the Ann Arbor Michigan school district to "identify children speaking 'Black English'... as a home or community language and to use that knowledge in teaching such students how to read standard English".[16] Yet in general AAE continues to be excluded from the educational process, and further proposals for including it have been subject to ridicule and public outcry, as was seen following the Oakland School Board's 1996 resolution to use Ebonics (AAE) in the classroom. (For discussions of the Ebonics debate, see articles in *Black Scholar* [Vol 27, 1997]; Baugh 2000; Rickford 1999, 2002; Rickford and Rickford 2000.)

The following subsections take a critical look at some of the arguments against the need for special programs for SDA and for the exclusion of AAE and other unstandardised dialects from the classroom.

7.4.1   Similarity

We start back at the beginning with the view that because differences between the D1 and D2 are so small, SDA is relatively easy. In arguing against the use of AAE (and by implication other first dialects) as a bridge to learning standard English, McWhorter (1998: 209) asserted that "we see hundreds of cases around the world where schoolchildren sail over just this type of narrow dialect gap". As examples, he said it is no problem for children speaking Canadian French to learn standard French and similarly for rural Southern White children in the USA to learn SAE. However, in contrast to these examples (for which no evidence was given), we have just seen in the first two sections of this chapter some of the problems and obstacles faced by students who speak unstandardised dialects when they are expected to learn the standard with no special instruction.

McWhorter also argued that compared to other dialects – such as Swabian (German) and Scottish English – AAE is a lot more similar to the respective standard variety. He questioned why, if speakers of these dialects do not need special programs to help them learn the standard, speakers of AAE should. Leaving aside the issue of whether or not Swabian speakers need special programs (see Section 7.1.1 above), many scholars would disagree about how typologically close AAE and standard English really are. For example, Palacas (2001: 344) submitted that "an unbridgeable chasm separates the grammatical systems of these two languages". He also noted (p. 349): "The difficulty for student and teacher is not in a confusion that comes from the fact that the two language varieties are very similar, but a confusion from the fact that they are so very different yet *seem* so very similar" (emphasis in original). This view is backed up in a study in which AAE-speaking pre-college and first-year college students were given the Test of English as a Foreign Language (TOEFL) (Pandey 2000). Their first-time performance was similar to that of low-level students of English as a second/foreign language.

7.4.2   Immersion

McWhorter (1998: 242) also argued that "people learn speech varieties best by immersion", and he pointed to successful language learning by English speakers in French immersion programs in Canada and by immigrants in English-medium schools in the USA. However, there are several problems with this argument. First of all, the L2 immersion programs in Canada are actually bilingual programs. Teachers are bilingual and the content in the L2 is modified to make it more understandable to students. After the first few grades, there is a strong emphasis on development of the L1 and instruction is in both languages (see García 1997). This certainly does not happen for students speaking AAE or other unstandardised dialects. Furthermore, it has been found that genuine L2 immersion programs are effective only for learners from dominant, majority-language groups, whose L1 is valued and supported both at home and by society in general (Auerbach 1995: 25). Again, this is clearly not the case for the D1 in classroom SDA contexts – the D1 may be valued and supported at home, but as we have seen, it is usually maligned by wider society.

With regard to immigrants, the vast majority of so-called immersion programs are really submersion or "sink or swim" programs, where "linguistic differences are not overtly recognised in the curriculum" (García 1997: 411). Research has shown that such programs have negative effects on many children (e.g. Cummins 1988: 161). Of course, it is this type of program that is generally the rule for learners of a standard D2, and again, as we have seen in Section 7.1 above, such immersion (really submersion) simply does not work for a large proportion of children in the different classroom SDA settings.

7.4.3   Legitimacy and appropriateness

A half century of work in sociolinguistics has demonstrated that unstandard-ised dialects are legitimate, rule-governed varieties of language. But this view has clearly not filtered down to the general public, and as Mackey (1978: 7) pointed out: "Only before God and linguists are all languages equal." This is very evident whenever there is a call for making use of a vernacular dialect in the formal education system, as with the Ebonics proposal. More recently, there was a proposal in 2005 to include AAE in the curriculum for children in the San Bernardino City Unified School District in California (Lemus 2005). One opinion piece (Hutaff 2005) stated with reference to AAE that "rambling incoherently and showing adverse reactions to proper grammar, spelling and pronunciation isn't a language, it's an abomination".

Another opinion piece (Jones 2001), this time in response to a proposal to use Jamaican Creole in Jamaican classrooms, included the following:

I draw a line when anyone suggests that this disfigurement of speech be officially recognised as a tool of communication in our institutions of formal education ... It is a facile tool of communication used amongst persons in a given locality. However, to the rest of the world it is little more than punctuated mumbo jumbo that defies analysis and parsing ... What is Jamaican Patois? It is essentially broken English, not an original language as some would like to believe.

In Hawai'i, Pidgin (Hawai'i Creole) is also still commonly referred to as a corrupt form of English, as indicated by this extract from a letter to the editor of a local newspaper: "It's broken English. And when something is broken, you fix it" (*Honolulu Star-Bulletin*, 12 October 1999). Another letter stated: "For the benefit of Hawai'i children, pidgin should become a thing of the past ... There are some things that deserve to die" *(Honolulu Advertiser*, 4 September 2002). And some people still make statements such as the following: "pidgin is not a language, it's a sign of a stupid [person] that is lazy, and it rubs off on others" (from a *Honolulu Advertiser* blog, 31 March 2008).

Even some people who accept the legitimacy of unstandardised varieties still believe that they have no place in the classroom. For example, Hargrove and Sakoda (1999: 60–1) quoted part of a letter to a local Hawai'i newspaper from a grade 4 teacher:

Don't criticize me as being ignorant or having a lack of understanding for the "beauty" of pidgin. Yet, pidgin has a right to exist – at home, on the playground, in original pieces of literature where pidgin is the chosen style of writing, and in Frank DeLima's [a local comedian] show, but not in my classroom on a daily basis.

It is clear from these quotations that many people get quite stirred up by proposals to use the D1 in the formal education system. In countries where such proposals have been carried out, there has been a great deal of controversy among parents, teachers and national leaders of both an educational and a political nature – as described, for example, by Schnepel (2005) with regard to the French-lexified creole in Guadeloupe.

Some of these views appear to be the result of two existing ideologies with regard to language (see Siegel 2006b). An ideology, as defined here, is a way of looking at things (or a system of beliefs) that is prevalent in a particular society. The views or beliefs it holds are considered to be basic common sense, even though they are not necessarily based on fact. And the views and beliefs often benefit the interests of a particular powerful segment of society.

Most relevant is the "standard language ideology" (Lippi-Green 1997; Silverstein 1996; Winford 2003; Wolfram 1998a). This is the pervasive belief in the superiority of the abstracted and idealised form of language based on the spoken language of the upper middle classes – i.e. the standard dialect. Part of this ideology is the "doctrine of appropriateness" (Fairclough 1992b) – the position that because of its superiority, the standard dialect is the only variety appropriate for use in the education system and other formal contexts. The perpetuation of beliefs about the superiority of the standard and the inferiority of other varieties is maintained by mainstream institutions such as the media and the education system.

The media's role in denigrating and stigmatising unstandardised varieties in the past can easily be seen. Hawai'i Creole's history of being denigrated in the media as being "sloppy" and "slothful" has already been described in Section 6.3.1 above. During the Ebonics debate, journalists applied a variety of negative labels to AAE, such as "mutant English", "fractured English", "mumbo jumbo", "slanguage" and "linguistic nightmare" (Rickford and Rickford 2000: 195). In the recent controversy regarding the San Bernardino schools (mentioned above), one opinion piece (Hutaff 2005) similarly maligned AAE in the Ebonics initiative: "Its legitimization by Oakland was and is a shameful attempt to convert illiteracy into a cultural and social asset. Trust me – there is nothing cultural about being a dumbass."

The education system also promotes the standard language ideology. Students who speak unstandardised dialects are taught that the standard is superior in both structure and importance (e.g. for getting a good job). At the same time their own dialects are shown to be inferior if not by denigration, then by being excluded from the educational process. The belief that unstandardised dialects are inferior and therefore inappropriate for use in formal contexts is the major reason for the current educational practice of keeping them out of the curriculum, and this practice helps to perpetuate the belief that these varieties are inferior.

Furthermore, a large number of people who speak unstandardised dialects accept this ideology, even though it disadvantages them. This is the "hegemony of 'The Standard'" (Silverstein 1996: 286). Following, Gramsci (1971[1948]), the concept of hegemony is seen as the exercise of control on the basis of wide-ranging consent or agreement – "the dominated become accomplices in their own domination" (Corson 2001: 18). As Corson (1991: 235) pointed out, "in their language usages the non-dominant adhere to the linguistic norms created by dominant groups while not recognising that they are being 'voluntarily coerced'".

A closely related hegemonic ideology that is responsible for not allowing unstandardised dialects any role in the education system is the "monoglot ideology" (Silverstein 1996; Wiley and Lukes 1996; Blommaert 2005: 253). This ideology, especially prevalent in English-speaking countries, sees monolingualism as the normal condition – and monolingualism in standard English, of course, as the ideal. It is this ideology that is at least partially behind the general practice of keeping other languages and dialects out of the classroom, as in the teaching methodology of the exonormative native speaker model described above (Section 7.1.4) in the context of indigenised varieties. Bilingualism or bidialectalism is seen as being divisive (as argued in the English-only movement in the USA) as well as an impediment to education and communication. This view is reflected in another example from Hawai'i. In reaction to perceived falling academic standards, the chairman of the State Board of Education was reported as saying the following (*Honolulu Advertiser*, 29 September 1999):

If your thinking is not in standard English, it's hard for you to write in standard English. If you speak pidgin, you think pidgin, you write pidgin ... We ought to have classrooms where standard English is the norm.

Part of this ideology is the belief that a person can have only one language or culture – or this case, one dialect – and that if they are exposed to more than one, they must choose between them. As we have seen, many unstandardised dialects have their own covert prestige and are an important part of their speakers' social identity. But because of the monoglot ideology, many speakers feel that to learn and use another variety, such as the standard, they would have to give up their original group identity. This ties into folk views about the true or authentic self, described in Section 6.3.2 above. Because of these views and the monoglot ideology, many people do not realise that it is common to have complex identities, and that this may involve the knowledge and use of more than one language variety – in other words, that they can become bilingual or bidialectal and still maintain their original vernacular identity.

7.4.4   Concerns for students

Another argument is that the use in formal education of an unstandardised variety, whether legitimate or not, will be detrimental to students. This argument is based on three different concerns: ghettoisation, waste of time and interference.

Ghettoisation   The first concern is that using unstandardised varieties in special SDA programs will further disadvantage already disadvantaged D1-speaking students by not giving them an education equal to that of other students. The term "ghettoisation" in this context is related to the belief that the use of language varieties other than the standard is a major factor that keeps groups disadvantaged – and in some cases confines them to living in urban ghettos (Snow 1990). For example, in Australia Shnukal (1992: 4) noted that in the Torres Strait, many people were "reluctant to accept the use of creole as a formal medium of instruction in their schools, seeing it as a method of depriving them of instruction in the kind of English that white people use, and thus condemning them to permanent under-class status". With regard to the proposal to use AAE in San Bernadino, mentioned above, a spokesperson for an African American group, Project 21, referred to the plan as "a disservice to the black community that will severely limit our children's skills in the job market" (Hunter 2005). And in Jamaica, Jones (2001) wrote:

There are those believing that we discriminate if we do not cater to children more fluent in patois [Jamaican Creole] than in standard English. They think that in order to teach, it is necessary to go down to the dim levels of the unlettered rather than urge them up the stairs leading to sunlight and the stars. I disagree with this and think that such advocacy can lead to charges of obscurantism and a subconscious desire to perpetuate the darkness in which some people find themselves.

These concerns arise partially from a misconception that the students' D1 will be the medium of instruction and the subject of study instead of standard English. For example, when the Oakland School Board proposed to make use of Ebonics (AAE) in the classroom to help improve the educational perform-ance of African American students, many people thought that teachers would be teaching Ebonics itself rather than standard English – as Rickford and Rickford (2000: 172) jokingly put it: "helping students therefore to master 'I be goin', you be goin', he/she/it be goin', and so on". This impression was reinforced by newspaper headlines such as "Oakland Schools OK Teaching of Black English" (Rickford and Rickford 2000: 189). This was clearly not the case, and as is shown in the following chapter, the objective of all special SDA teaching programs has been for the students to acquire the standard dialect. While some use the D1 as a vehicle for acquiring literacy, none has been involved in "teaching" the D1.

Another part of the concern is that in schools where there are both unstandardised and standard dialect-speaking students, students in special SDA programs will be isolated, and not get the chance to interact with students who do speak varieties closer to the standard. However, as shown in the following chapter, most special programs do not separate D1- and D2-speaking students.

Waste of time   The next concern, closely related to the first, is that paying attention to the D1 will take away valuable time that could be devoted to learning the standard D2 – i.e. that SDA programs would be a "waste of time". At first glance, this may seem to be plain common sense. If an important goal of formal education is to become proficient in the standard dialect, then it seems logical that as much time as possible should be spent on learning it. Any time taken away from this – that is, time devoted to the D1 – would appear, then, to be time wasted. For example, with regard to the Caribbean, Elsasser and Irvine (1987: 137) said that one of the reasons for the lack of use of the local creole for writing activities in the classroom is the belief that "time devoted to writing in Creole detracts from students' ability to learn to write [standard] English".

But behind this view are at least two underlying assumptions, both problematic. The first is that the greater the amount of instruction time spent in learning a new language variety (L2 or D2), the greater the achievement will be in this variety – the "time-on-task hypothesis" (Cummins 1993, 2001). The second assumption with regard to SDA is that the time used on the D1 in the classroom would have absolutely no benefits for learning the D2, but rather would have a negative effect – the "no benefits" hypothesis.

In the USA, the waste-of-time concern has been reinforced by inaccurate media reports about children in bilingual programs not doing well in SAE. However, these reports are based on short-term studies that test students' progress during or soon after bilingual programs. The results of rigorous research conducted on the long-term effect of bilingual education are generally not reported. For example, comprehensive studies by Ramirez (1992) and Thomas and Collier (2002) followed students' progress up through grades 5–6 and beyond. They showed that time taken away from the study of English and devoted to students' home language does not detract in the long term from students' achievement in English. These results clearly refute the time-on-task hypothesis. Furthermore, after the initial few years of education, students who have studied in their mother tongue perform better in English (and mathematics) than comparable students who have studied only in English. This means that use of the mother tongue must provide some advantage as well, thus refuting the no-benefits hypothesis.

One might argue that the situation with regard to unstandardised dialects and creoles is different from that of the bilingual programs, which use totally distinct languages. However, research described in the following chapter demonstrates similar results.

Interference   The third concern is that the D1 will get in the way of or interfere with students' acquisition of the standard. As we have seen in Chapter 6 above, interference is another term for negative transfer – the inappropriate use of features of the D1 when speaking or writing the D2 – in this context, the standard dialect. There are many reports showing that fear of interference has kept dialects, expanded pidgins and creoles out of the classroom. For example, with regard to the Caribbean, Elsasser and Irvine (1987: 137) observed that one of the reasons for the lack of teaching literacy in the local creole is the assumption that "students' limited writing ability is due to linguistic interference". Similarly, Winer (1990: 241) noted that "both educators and the public are concerned over the extent to which acceptance of the vernacular might negatively affect students' competence in standard English".

With regard to Bislama, the dialect of Melanesian Pidgin spoken in Vanuatu, Thomas (1990: 245) referred to deliberations at the 1981 Vanuatu Language Planning Conference: "One of the most common fears concerning the introduction of Bislama as a language of education is that, owing to lexical similarities, negative transfer occurs when pupils subsequently learn English." This point of view was also expressed by Charpentier (1997) in a book on vernacular literacy. He described hostility towards the idea of teaching in Bislama because of the danger of learners confusing Bislama and English (p. 236):

The combination of English and Pidgin (or source language X and lexically X-based pidgin) seems to lead to a social, psychological, and pedagogical blockage, seriously compromising any passage to literacy. The children in particular cannot seem to figure out the respective roles and characteristics of the two codes.

From research described in Sections 6.2.1, 7.1.1 and 7.3.4 above (e.g. Young-Scholten 1985; Ammon 1989a; Fairclough 2005; Calchar 2004, 2005; de Kleine 2006, 2009), it is clear that such interference does occur in classroom SDA. In another example, Winer (1989) reported that in Trinidad, interference from the local creole accounted wholly or partially for 65 per cent of students' "errors" in standard English.[17] Also as shown earlier, the more similar varieties are, the more likely it is that learners will have trouble separating them and that inteference will occur. Of course, unstandardised dialects and creoles are similar to the standard variety, at least superficially, especially in their lexicons. So, as Lin pointed out (1965: 8): "The interference between two closely related dialects – such as a nonstandard dialect and standard English – is far greater than between two completely different languages." Therefore, the fear of the D1 interfering with the acquisition of the standard may appear to be justified.

However, all the research showing interference from the D1 in the acquisition of the standard D2 has been done in conventional monolingual D2 contexts where the D1 does not have a role in the classroom. There is absolutely no evidence that using the D1 in the classroom will exacerbate the problem of interference, which is what this concern is all about. Thus, we need to examine studies of programs where the D1 has actually been used to see if this had a detrimental effect on students' achievement in the standard and in general education as well. This is done in the following chapter, where we will see that in fact using the D1 in the classroom has positive rather than negative effects.

8   Educational approaches for SDA

This chapter is concerned with the educational approaches and programs that have been used specifically for the purpose of assisting the acquisition or use of another dialect. The characteristics of each of these are described, as well as any evaluative research that is available.

The chapter starts off with depicting two types of dialect teaching that normally do not occur in the classroom: dialect coaching and accent modification. As mentioned in Chapter 7, students in such programs are usually adults who are interested in acquiring the phonological features of another dialect for professional purposes. The remaining sections deal with classroom approaches for younger students who are required to learn the standard dialect in the formal education system. Some historical background is first presented about approaches and methodologies used in the 1960s and 1970s. Then, three types of current approaches are described: instrumental, accommodation and awareness.[1]

8.1   Dialect coaching and accent modification

8.1.1   Dialect coaching

In Chapter 3, I talked a bit about actors' imitations of dialects, and mentioned that most actors who perform in dialects other than their own have used a dialect coach. There are dozens of websites on the internet for dialect coaches (or voice coaches) – often with lists of films, plays and other productions that they have worked on. Two well-known examples are Victoria Mielewska in Australia and Paul Meier in the USA. There is also an association of dialect coaches and related professionals: the Voice and Speech Trainers Association (VASTA), which has a newsletter, accessible over the internet (www.vasta.org).

Educational institutions that offer courses or workshops on learning dialects for acting are also prominent on the internet. For example, the National Institute of Dramatic Art (NIDA) in Australia offers a Graduate Diploma and Masters degree in Dramatic Art/Voice Studies, both of which include courses on learning to perform in various dialects.

In addition, many books are available for actors who want to learn to produce other dialects, or, perhaps more accurately, accents (since they generally cover only phonological features) – for example, *Accents: A Manual for Actors* (Blumenfeld 2002). Nearly all these books include exercises, texts, and an accompanying cassette or nowadays a CD. Most of them use the International Phonetic Alphabet (IPA) to indicate pronunciations. In the acting world, the terms "dialect" and "accent" both include foreign accent as well. For example, *Actor's Encyclopedia of Dialect* (Molin 1984) covers 136 dialects, which include English as spoken by speakers of Spanish, German, Russian, French, Hungarian and many other languages, as well as what we have been calling dialects – for example: British English, Australian English, Irish English, Cockney and Indian English. Interestingly, the book also covers social and regional varieties of some national dialects – such as British English as spoken by an Oxford graduate, a London executive, a London shopkeeper, and speakers from Sussex and Norfolk. Some books, however, are far more specialised – e.g. *Speaking American: The Australian Actor's Guide to an American Accent* (Shapiro 2000).

There is a view, however, that the dialects presented in such books and taught in courses are really theatrical stereotypes. For example, Meier (1999) wrote in the VASTA Newsletter that "what passes for authenticity in the theater is a convention". In order to try to provide more authentic models of dialects for actors to use, Meier created the International Dialects of English Archive (IDEA) in 1997. This is a free, online library of primary source recordings for the performing arts. The downloadable recordings cover a multitude of dialects and accents recorded by a wide range of speakers. It also contains text files giving the speaker's biographical details, and in most cases some transcription.[2]

8.1.2 Accent modification

As also mentioned in Chapter 3, actors are mainly trying to learn how to imitate a particular dialect for the purpose of performance; therefore, those making use of the dialect coaches, courses and books just described are normally not aiming for dialect acquisition as we have been defining it. However, people enrolled in a closely related type of training generally do have the aim of dialect acquisition. This kind of training – called "accent modification" or "accent reduction" – has become very popular. In fact, the *US News & World Report* (11 December 2008) listed "accent reduction specialist" as one of the "best-kept-secret careers" for 2009. Here students (or clients) want to change their dialect or acquire an additional dialect – mainly in terms of pronunciation or accent. Others, who are second language speakers, want to get rid of their foreign accent. Here I talk mainly about those who want their speech to sound like that of another dialect of English.

Many of the individuals and educational organisations that offer dialect coaching and courses for actors provide accent modification training as well. However, there are many others (also found on the internet) whose main business is accent modification. Since speaking a particular dialect is clearly not a speech disorder, it may be surprising that speech pathologists are among the professionals offering dialect modification training – for example, at the Auburn University Department of Communication Disorders in the USA. Such institutions are often careful to refer to a report by the American Speech-Language-Hearing Association (ASHA) that made the following statement (ASHA Multicultural Issues Board 2002):

[N]o dialectal variety of American English is a disorder or a pathological form of speech or language. Each dialect is adequate as a functional and effective variety of American English. Each serves a communicative function as well as a social-solidarity function. Each dialect maintains the communication network and the social construct of the community of speakers who use it. Furthermore, each is a symbolic representation of the geographic, historical, social, and cultural background of its speakers.

The report was also written to provide "guidance to the professionals in the field of speech-language-pathology regarding the provision of services to speakers of various American English dialects who wish to acquire proficiency in a dialect other than their own". It noted that these are "elective services", in addition to the traditional role of providing clinical services to individuals with communication disorders. The accent modification done by speech pathologists is clearly aimed at additive rather than replace acquisition, as indicated by the guidelines (ASHA Multicultural Issues Board 2002):

[T]he role of the speech-language pathologist is to assist in the acquisition of the desired competency in the second dialect without jeopardizing the integrity of the individual's first dialect. The approach of the elective service must be functional and must emphasize the appropriateness of the first and second dialects for different contexts.

On the other hand, many of the private agencies emphasise accent reduction rather than modification and promote the view described in Chapter 1 that a dialect or accent is a non-standard or non-local way of speaking, and something to be avoided. This view is reflected in some of the published resources available, such as *Lose Your Accent in 28 Days* (Ravin 2004) and *Accent Reduction Made Easy* (Wellborn 2003) (with CDs so you can "learn in your car").

Why do people want to modify or reduce their accents? One reason, as we have seen in earlier chapters, is to fit in better in their adopted country. For example, Duncan Markham, head of Ear & Speak Linguistic Consultancy in Australia, told me in an interview (29 September 2005) that his clients have included Americans who said they didn't want to "stick out" so much in

Australia. Ear & Speak also offered a kind of dialect refresher course for Australians. The description (which backs up some of my comments on identity in Chapters 5 and 6) was advertised on the website as follows:

Sometimes Australians who go overseas for a while come back with a mixed accent, and they find that this makes people react strangely. If it's a problem, we can help you get rid of some of the more conspicuous "foreign" sounds, or if you really want, we can work with you to sound 100% Australian again.[3]

People may also want to be able to speak a different social dialect. One report described a trend in England to do the opposite of what Eliza did in *Pygmalion*. Speakers of RP (standard spoken British English, associated with the upper classes) are undergoing accent reduction training to get rid of their "posh" accents and learn Estuary English, the popular speech of southeast England based on London English (*Spectator*, 26 January 2002).

But the most common reasons for accent modification are practical ones connected with business and employment. One important area concerns the "call centre" industry in countries such as India and the Philippines. Since the 1990s, many companies in the USA, Britain and Australia have been out-sourcing telephone services such as customer inquiries to these countries, where different indigenised varieties (i.e. Indian English and Philippine English) are spoken. To improve communication with customers, many call centres require that their employees undergo training to replace some of the more noticeable features of their variety with features of American or British English (see Mesthrie and Bhatt 2008: 216–18). Many websites advertise accent modification/reduction courses with specific reference to call centre employment. One site, "Outsource to India", has links to 171 different companies that provide such training.[4]

Most often, however, people want to change their dialect to be more like the standard or general dialect of the country where they live. For example, the ASHA report noted (ASHA Multicultural Issues Board 2002):

Given that SAE is the linguistic variety used by the government, the mass media, business, education, science, and the arts in the United States, speakers of other varieties of American English may find it advantageous to be able to speak SAE.

In business, for example, speaking a dialect different from the general standard can be a great disadvantage. Cukor-Avila (2000) and Markley (2000) reported on a study of the effect of dialect on hiring practices. The two researchers recorded ten males, each from a different part of the USA, reading the same passage of text. The men were from Texas, Georgia, Louisiana, Alabama, North Carolina, Minnesota, California, Boston, Chicago and New Jersey, and each spoke the local dialect of his place of origin. The speakers were all White and their ages could not be detected through their voices. A CD with the recordings was sent to fifty-six human resource executives responsible for hiring new employees in large companies or institutions. They were asked to rate various personal characteristics of each of the speakers on the basis of their speech, and to put each one into one of four job categories. The speakers from Louisiana, Georgia and New Jersey – who had recognisable accents – were rated the most negatively and put in the lower-level job categories. Those from California and Minnesota – who had the least identifiable accents – were rated the most positively and put in higher-level job categories.

8.1.3   Teaching methodology

As an example of teaching methods used in both dialect coaching and accent modification, we will look at the work of the well-known practitioner Paul Meier, mentioned above. He told me in an interview (21 September 2005) that the only way to learn another dialect is by imitation. The methodology he uses is exemplified in his booklet *The Standard British English Dialect (Received Pronunciation)* (Meier 2004). In the introduction (p. 2), Meier states: "Learning an accent or dialect is essentially an exercise in mimicry." His "Seven-Step Method" attempts to aid the learner's own natural ability to mimic or imitate. Step One introduces the "signature sounds" of the dialect. For example, for British English these sounds include some of the variants examined in the studies described in Chapter 2: use of /t/ rather than T-Voicing or flapping; the BATH lexical set in which words like *past, ask, laugh* and *can't* are pronounced with the /ɑ/ vowel as in PALM rather than the /æ/ vowel as in TRAP; and R-lessness (the absence of non-prevocalic /r/). These sounds are presented on the accompanying CD and represented in writing by IPA.

Step Two describes additional features of the dialect – for example, stressed syllables different from other dialects in words such as *defence* and *cliché*, as mentioned in Section 1.3.4. Step Three covers special aspects of rhythm, intonation and tone. Step Four gives the signature sounds in sentence context – for example, for the three features mentioned above (p. 10):

> *A lot of better writers print a lot of little words.*
> *He laughed as he danced to the bath past his aunt in pyjamas.*
> *The first early bird murdered thirty turning worms.*

In Step Five, students listen to real-life speakers on IDEA, the International Dialects of English Archive, referred to above, with commentary to guide their listening. Step Six consists of coordination exercises – texts with several signature sounds in close proximity. The texts are written out with the number of the signature sound (from Step One) beneath each example in the text, and the complete IPA transcription below. Finally, Step Seven provides recordings of two monologues from a play or film requiring the dialect. The text is also given, with the signature sound numbers and IPA transcriptions as in Step Six. Each of these steps, except Five, requires the learner to imitate the pronunciations of the target dialect.

The success of dialect teaching for acting has not been formally evaluated. The only evidence we have is the performance of trained actors and testimonials by those who have used dialect coaching services. For example, one generally agreed-upon successful outcome was the use of Australian English in the film *Holy Smoke* (1999) by Kate Winslet, who was coached by Victoria Mielewska, mentioned above (Raynor 2007). Many testimonials can be found on the internet, such as the following from the film director Ang Lee about Paul Meier:

> Paul worked for us on *Ride With The Devil* as dialect and dialogue coach, developing dialect tapes for all seventy speaking roles, coaching all the actors, and was invaluable in developing a cohesive vocal and dialect design for the US region that was the setting for the film. We had numbers of non-American actors in the film ... all of whom needed Southern or Plains dialects. Under Paul's expert coaching they blended marvelously with the American members of the cast ... Many critics praised the film for capturing the romanticism of the era through language, and Paul's contribution through speech, voice and dialect was crucial.[5]

With regard to accent modification or reduction, it is difficult to find any information that evaluates the success of such training in terms of SDA. There are hundreds of testimonials for various practitioners and companies on the internet, but these are almost exclusively for foreign accent reduction. In one study, Weil, Fitch and Wolfe (2000) examined the pronunciation of four subjects who had "successfully completed an accent reduction program initiated by a university speech and hearing clinic" (p. 152). Their D1 was Southern English (SE) and the D2 was standard American English (SAE). They were all telephone operators whose employer (a telecommunications company) requested that they do the program. Two diphthongs were examined: /aɪ/ as in PRICE and /ɔɪ/ as in CHOICE. Subjects were asked to read a passage and a word list that contained words with these diphthongs under two conditions: as they would speak to family and friends (the SE condition) and as they would speak to customers on the telephone (the SAE condition). The analysis showed a distinct difference in the length of the diphthongs in the two conditions, especially for /aɪ/, both being shorter in the SE condition. We have seen in Sections 3.1.3 and 5.1.2 that the /aɪ/ diphthong tends to be pronounced as a monophthong /a/ in SE, but there is some controversy about whether it is longer or shorter than in SAE (p. 152). Unfortunately, the authors of this article did not give any base data from speakers of SE who did not do the accent modification program or from SAE speakers, so we do not know if the subjects' D1 pronunciation had changed or how closely they approximated the D2 pronunciation.

In my interview with Duncan Markham, director of Ear & Speak Linguistic Consultancy, I asked about the success of accent modification programs with his American clients in Australia, as mentioned above. He said that the best results were with one client who was able to modify his accent so that he no longer "stuck out" as an American. Although most people still realised he wasn't Australian, many now thought he was Irish! Perhaps this indicates the difficulty of acquiring another dialect for everyday use as opposed to learning one for performance.

Thus, with regard to SDA, accent modification appears to be successful in helping speakers to avoid some of the more noticeable phonological features of their original dialect. But it is not so successful in promoting complete acquisition of corresponding features in another dialect.

8.2   Classroom programs: Historical background

8.2.1   Teaching standard English as a second dialect

After sociolinguistic research in the 1960s demonstrated that regional and social dialects and pidgins and creoles are legitimate rule-governed varieties of language, the first special teaching programs for speakers of these varieties began to appear. The aim was to teach the standard dialect while affirming the legitimacy of the first dialect and promoting additive bidialectalism.

Stewart (1964) used the term "quasi-foreign language" situation to refer to the learning of standard English by speakers of English-based pidgins and creoles and "radically non-standard" dialects of English, such as AAE. Although learners have native or near-native command of some aspects of the standard dialect, such as vocabulary, there are other areas, especially in morphosyntax, where the learners' D1 differs markedly from that of the standard D2. According to Stewart, these cases warranted the use of foreign language teaching (FLT) procedures. This idea was soon embraced by the growing field of teaching English to speakers of other languages (TESOL) and came to be known as Standard English as a Second Dialect (SESD) (e.g. Alatis 1973). For at least a decade, these L2 teaching methods were advocated for teaching SESD to speakers of AAE in the USA and to speakers of English-lexified creoles in the Caribbean and Hawai'i. Following the audiolingual approach popular at that time, the emphasis was on habit formation and oral fluency, with teaching focused on particular grammatical structures. Contrastive Analysis (CA) of the D1 and D2 was done to determine which structures should be taught, and pattern practice and drills were used to get students to practise these structures.[6]

Later, however, the problems of the uncritical use of L2 teaching methods for students speaking unstandardised dialects began to be pointed out by many scholars, such as Politzer (1973). First was the problem of the ineffectiveness of the teaching methods themselves. The SESD approaches were implicitly based on the premise that SDA and SLA are similar processes.

However, as Shuy (1969: 83) noted, the assumption that FLT or TESOL techniques are valid for learning a second dialect was without any solid proof. Di Pietro (1973: 38–9) also warned that teachers should be wary of using such techniques in teaching SESD, and that much more research was needed to test their applicability. (And as we have seen with recent research described in Section 7.3.4 above, there are significant differences between patterns of acquisition in SDA and SLA.)

The other problems had to do with significant differences between the SDA and SLA situations (as also described in Chapter 7). In SLA, two different autonomonous linguistic systems are easily recognised. The learners' L1 often has its own dictionaries and grammars, just like the L2. But in SDA, because the learners' D1 is unstandardised and because of its similarities to the standard, it is not recognised as a separate variety of language. This leads to both teachers and students thinking that there is only one legitimate language involved, and that the learners' dialect is just "sloppy speech" (Johnson 1974: 154). Furthermore, in classroom contexts, the D1, unlike the L1, is almost always socially stigmatised by dominant social groups, even though it has its own covert prestige as a part of its speakers' social identity. Also, as we have seen, students may fear that learning the D2 means abandoning their dialect and thus risking being ostracised from their social group. Finally, because of the fears of ghettoisation mentioned in Section 7.4.4, there were some strong reactions to the notions of teaching SESD and bidialectalism (e.g. Sledd 1969, 1972), portraying them as yet another attempt to institutionalise inequities, as reported by Di Pietro (1973: 38).

Some research was done in the 1960s and 1970s on the effectiveness of the L2 teaching methods in teaching the D2, using either a pre-test/post-test or an experimental design or both, and measuring the acquisition of particular targeted D2 structures. Some modestly successful results were reported – for example, by Lin (1965) and Hagerman (1970) for speakers of AAE; Ching (1963), Crowley (1968) and Peterson, Chuck and Coladarci (1969) for Hawai'i Creole; and Craig (1967) for Jamaican Creole. On the other hand, Torrey (1972) reported only very limited positive results. Thus, as behaviourist views of language acquisition were abandoned in the 1970s, so were most of the associated teaching methods, for both SDA and SLA. Publications on SESD and bidialectalism also became as rare as behaviourists. At the same time, SLA began to emerge as a distinct field of research, but with only a few notable exceptions (e.g. Edwards and Giles 1984; Sato 1989; Politzer 1993), second language researchers were not concerned with the acquisition of dialects.

8.2.2   Dialect readers

Wolfram and Fasold (1969: 144) observed that if the goal of SESD was really additive bidialectalism, then the value of the students' first dialect would be affirmed by using it in the educational process – especially in reading materials. Stewart (1969) also advocated using reading materials written in the students' dialect, pointing to the educational advantages of being able to learn to read in one's mother tongue and then transferring these skills to the target language. Since that time, the notion of "dialect readers" has been extremely controversial, with both educational and sociolinguistic arguments for and against. Goodman (1969), Venezky and Chapman (1973) and others proposed that using standard dialect reading materials should not cause problems with reading acquisition if children are allowed to read as they speak. On the other hand, an early study by Leaverton (1973) found that the reading performance of African American students improved when they used texts in AAE as well as SAE.[7]

A reading program for AAE-speaking students using dialect readers was published in 1977, the *Bridge* series (Simpkins, Holt and Simpkins 1977). A preliminary version of the program was tested over a four-month period in 1975 in five areas of the USA with 540 students from grades 7 to 12 (Simpkins and Simpkins 1981). The experimental group (417 students in 21 classes), who used the dialect readers, showed significantly higher gains in the Iowa Test of Basic Skills in reading comprehension in SAE than the control group (123 students in 6 classes), who were doing conventional remedial reading activities. Results from a questionnaire completed by teachers indicated that students found the *Bridge* program to be very enjoyable and easy to work through independently. Teachers reported fewer discipline problems in the classroom, and higher motivation among the students, even among the low achievers. Two earlier studies had also demonstrated increased motivation and enjoyment of reading among students using reading materials in AAE (Simpkins 2002: 173–8). The program was published in 1977 on the basis of these positive results; however, the publishers stopped promoting it in reaction to strong objections from parents and teachers, again for reasons discussed in Chapter 7 above.

Nevertheless, the potential benefits of dialect readers continued to be discussed, not only for AAE (Labov 1995; Rickford and Rickford 1995) but also for Chicano and Puerto Rican Spanish (Bixler-Márquez 1988). More recently, Green (2002) and Simpkins (2002) returned to the idea of using dialect readers in AAE, this time recognising the complicated issues of community acceptance of such materials.

8.2.3   The Language Curriculum Research Group

In 1974, the Conference on College Composition and Communication (CCCC) in the USA passed the "Students' Right to Their Own Language" resolution (Smitherman 2000: 376–7):

We affirm the students' right to their own patterns and varieties of language – the dialects of their nurture or whatever dialects in which they find their own identity and style. Language scholars long ago denied that the myth of a standard American dialect has any validity. The claim that any one dialect is unacceptable amounts to an attempt of one social group to exert its dominance over another ... A nation proud of its diverse heritage and its cultural and racial variety will preserve its heritage of dialects. We affirm strongly that teachers must have the experiences and training that will enable them to respect diversity and uphold the right of students to their own language.

The same year, a similar statement was passed by the National Council of Teachers of English (NCTE).[8]

Following on from these statements, the Language Curriculum Research Group (LCRG), based at Brooklyn College and the Borough of Manhattan Community College, developed a unique SESD course for speakers of AAE that was way ahead of its time (e.g. see Reed 1973). The methodology and philosophy of this course have recently been revisited by Wible (2006). Students in the course were taught not only to examine differences between AAE and SAE, but also to study AAE as a legitimate area of inquiry in the classroom. They explored the origins and development of AAE, read examples of its use by African American writers, conducted ethnographic research on its use in their own communities, and wrote essays about their own experiences with AAE and people's attitudes towards it (Wible 2006: 447). Students were given the freedom to write using their own voice, and taught the skills to change their drafts into SAE when required by the education system or prospective employers. But the examination of both the D1 and D2 went deeper than just the surface features (p. 451), encompassing the students' own cultural practices and world views as well as those of White society.

The LCRG also created a teachers' manual that provided guidance for teaching the course and raised awareness about issues concerning AAE and the results of conventional teaching practices. Teachers were encouraged to learn from their students about AAE and its role in the community. In fact, they were told that the students, rather than the curriculum materials in the course, should be their primary sources of information (Wible 2006: 456). The LCRG also ran workshops and tutorials for teachers and teacher trainees, and arranged collaborative learning sessions with AAE-speaking students.

The LCRG course was written up as a manuscript for a textbook, and was submitted to several commercial publishers and sent to reviewers. However, at that time, the "back to basics" movement began to sweep across the USA. Statistics appeared to show that literacy levels were declining, and use of AAE in the classroom was considered as a sign that standards were slipping. As Wible (2006: 460) noted, to many critics "pedagogies like the LCRG's represented academic permissiveness in the name of improving minority students' self-esteem". So instead of viewing the course as an alternative way of improving standards where traditional methods (such as drilling) had failed, educators, parents and politicians saw it as permissive and insisted on going back to the traditional methods. Consequently, the course and teachers' manual were never published. Nevertheless, various aspects of the course have been incorporated into the modern approaches described below, and have inspired some of the further steps presented in Chapter 9.

8.3   Instrumental approach

Now we turn to more recent classroom approaches. The instrumental approach uses the students' D1 as a medium of instruction to teach initial literacy and sometimes content subjects such as mathematics, science and health. Instrumental SDA programs are similar to transitional bilingual programs in that the children's home language (D1) is initially used while they are learning the language of the educational system (D2). Such an approach is most suitable in situations where the D1 is clearly distinguished from the D2 and where all students in the classroom are speakers of the D1. To date, such programs have been implemented only for speakers of expanded pidgin and creole languages – for example, in Haiti, Australia, Papua New Guinea and Guinea-Bissau.

In Haiti, a presidential decree issued in 1979 allowed the use of Haitian Creole (French-lexified) in schools along with French, and in 1982 the Ministry of Education issued its own decree reorganising the education system so that the creole became the medium of instruction and an object of study in primary school. However, the government did not attempt to implement this education reform until 1989 (Howe 1993: 294). Haitian Creole was made an official language along with French in the 1987 constitution, and it is now used in primary education throughout the country.

In Australia, a bilingual program with Northern Territory Kriol (an English-lexified creole) and English began at Barunga School in 1977. It was among other bilingual programs involving Aboriginal languages run by the Northern Territory Department of Education. Kriol was used for teaching reading and writing from grade 1 until English was introduced in grade 4 or 5. After then, Kriol was restricted to subjects about cultural heritage (see Siegel 1993). Also in Australia, the Home Languages Project began in 1995 at Injinoo School in north Queensland. In this project, preschool and grade 1 children have been taught to read and write in their home language, a variety of Torres Strait Creole (Turner 1997).

A thorough evaluation of the bilingual program at Barunga was made by Murtagh (1982). The purpose of his study was "to find out whether or not a bilingual program which uses Creole and English as languages of instruction facilitates the learning of both Standard English and Creole" (p. 15). Murtagh compared several measures of oral language proficiency in Kriol and English of students in the first three grades at two different schools: the Kriol/English bilingual school at Barunga and an English-only school at

Beswick Reserve, where the children were also Kriol speakers. The overall results were that students at the bilingual school scored significantly better than those at the monolingual school, especially in grade 3. Despite such results, this bilingual program, along with others, was terminated by the Northern Territory government at the end of 1998.

In Papua New Guinea, a total reform of the nation-wide education system began in the 1990s. This changed the six years of primary schooling in the medium of English to three years of elementary school followed by six years of primary school. The language of instruction and initial literacy in elementary school is chosen by the community; English is introduced in the second or third year of elementary school and becomes the medium of instruction in primary school. Although exact figures are not available, many communities, especially in urban areas, have chosen Tok Pisin, the local dialect of Melanesian Pidgin, for their schools (Ray 1996). In one rural area of the country, in the Sepik Province, there are at least twenty-six elementary schools using Tok Pisin (Wiruk 2000).

Before the reform began, there was a community-run preschool program in the Ambunti district of the Sepik Province that taught initial literacy and numeracy to children through the medium of Tok Pisin before they began formal education in the standard English-medium primary schools. This was called the Tok Pisin Prep-School Program. From 1989 to 1995 I conducted an evaluation of the program, mainly to investigate the validity of claims that use of the D1 in the classroom would be detrimental to students' later acquisition of the D2 in primary school because of interference (i.e. negative transfer). The evaluation (Siegel 1992a, 1997) involved interviews with primary school teachers, village committee members and parents about the program and the progress in formal education of the students who had completed it. Formal comparative research was also carried out in the primary school at the district centre (St Joseph's Community School) with three cohorts of students, based on the year they started primary school (1988, 1989 and 1990). It involved comparing the educational achievement, based on term test results, of those who had gone through the prep-school program and those who had not. These tests are normally held at the end of each of the four terms in the school year, and are in three subject areas: English, mathematics and "general subjects" (health, social science, etc.). Results were examined in upper as well as lower grades for each cohort.

The interviews revealed overwhelming satisfaction with the program. This could also be seen in the rapid growth of the program: it started in 1985 with 2 schools and 150 students and by 1996 it had expanded to 45 schools and 1,245 students (Wiruk 1996). With regard to the acquisition of English, the teachers reported that there were no special problems of interference. In fact, the students who had learned initial literacy in Tok Pisin were said to learn standard English more easily than the other students. The statistical analysis of the data on academic achievement showed that children who had been involved in the prep-school program scored significantly higher in term tests than those who had not been involved. These results included English, where those who learned initial literacy in Tok Pisin actually scored higher, not lower, than those students who learned literacy only in standard English. Furthermore, on the basis of the test scores, the prep-school children showed significantly higher academic achievement in English across time (i.e. in upper grades as well). This study clearly refuted arguments that using the D1 in formal education would exacerbate interference and adversely affect students' acquisition of the D2.

In Guinea-Bissau (Africa), the language of education is standard Portuguese, but the vast majority of the population speak Crioulo (or Guinea-Bissau Kriyol), a Portuguese-lexified creole. Children come to school without a knowledge of the language of instruction, and most teachers also have difficulty with this language. In 1986, the Ministry of Education started an experimental program which included using Crioulo to teach literacy and content subjects in the first two years of primary education, followed by transition to standard Portuguese. Benson (1994, 2004) conducted a detailed evaluation of the program during the 1992/3 school year on the basis of sociolinguistic surveys, interviews (with parents, teachers and education officials), classroom observations and assessments of student performance.

Performance of students involved in the program was measured in Crioulo, Portuguese, mathematics and creativity, and compared to that of students involved in other programs. This performance was measured in schools in three communities – in grades 1 and 2 in the first, grades 1 to 3 in the second and grades 1 to 4 in the third. The results, however, showed that except for a predictably better performance in Crioulo, there was no statistically significant difference between students involved in the program and those not involved. The program could possibly have been more effective if the 1992/3 school year had not been curtailed by a high level of political unrest and strikes by teachers (who were not receiving their salaries). The results in grades 3 and 4 may have been due to the fact that the transition to the D2 (standard Portuguese) occurred after only two years of schooling in the D1, a shorter period than the three to five years usually recommended for bilingual programs.

Nevertheless, the evaluation demonstrated various advantages of the program. First, the learning of literacy in Crioulo and its use in teaching topics such as health and agriculture enabled students to understand their lessons. Second, more students spoke in class, and there was less reliance on rote learning. It was clear that education in the D1 did not hurt the students, as they performed as well as if not better than those in other programs. Taking into account the positive results, Benson concluded that the "waste of time" argument was not borne out by any of the assessment results.

Two other instrumental programs have more recently begun in the Caribbean region. In Jamaica, a Bilingual Education Project was approved by the government and implemented in 2004 in two pilot schools (Devonish and Carpenter 2007). The project involves full and equal use of Jamaican Creole alongside standard Jamaican English in all aspects of formal education in grades 1 to 4. And in the San Andrés Islands (Colombia), an experimental "trilingual" program was started in 1999, using the local creole (referred to as "Islander English"), standard English and Spanish (Morren 2001).[9] The creole is used as the medium of education in the two pre-primary years of school and grade 1. Oral English is introduced in grade 1, and oral Spanish (the official and national language) in grade 2. English is used for reading and writing and to teach some subjects from grade 2. Spanish is similarly used from grade 3. By grade 4 all subjects are taught in English or Spanish. Morren (2004) presented the preliminary results of an Islander English diagnostic reading inventory administered to children after they completed grade 1. These indicated that the program had been successful in teaching the various skills needed to become a successful reader.

Three experimental studies have examined the instrumental use of the D1 in reading materials to teach literacy. In the first two studies, these materials were used to teach initial literacy, unlike the dialect readers described above, which were used with older students. The first study was carried out in Sweden by Österberg (1961) with speakers of the dialect spoken in the Piteå district, mentioned in Section 7.1.1. Approximately 350 students were involved in the study, divided into two groups of equal size. In the first year of the research, methods and texts for teaching in the D1 (the Piteå dialect) were developed and teachers were trained to use them. In the second year, one of the groups, the experimental group, was taught for ten weeks to read in the D1. This was followed by twenty-five weeks of reading instruction in the D2 (standard Swedish), which included an initial four weeks of transition from the D1 to the D2. The control group followed the normal practice of being taught to read entirely in the D2 (standard Swedish) for the thirty-five week period. Österberg reported (p. 135) that "the dialect method showed itself superior both when it was a question of reading quickly and of rapidly assimilating matter" and that the same was true for "reading and reading-comprehension". He also observed (p. 136) that in no case was the control group superior in test results, even when the standard was the test language for both groups. This was despite the fact that the control group had thirty-five weeks of instruction in the standard while the experimental group had only twenty-five weeks.

In Norway, Bull (1990) conducted similar research with students speaking regional dialects in three different areas: Tromsø in the north, Stranda on the west coast and Stavanger on the southwest coast. More than 200 students were taught to read and write in their D1 during most of their first year in school in 1981/2. Towards the end of the school year, teachers gradually started to use one of the two standard varieties of Norwegian (Bokmål or Nynorsk). They were very explicit in their teaching, explaining why they used a particular variety, and they did not correct the students' writing. Rather, they encouraged the students to pay attention to and analyse their own writing. In spring 1982, an experimental group of seven classes of these students (approximately 130) were assessed with standardised tests of reading in the standard. A control group of four classes who did not learn to read in the D1 (about half the size of the experimental group) were also tested. On the basis of the test results, Bull concluded (p. 78) that "the vernacular children read significantly faster and better than the control subjects". She also observed (p. 78): "It seems as if particularly the less bright children benefit from this kind of teaching. They made superior progress during the year compared with the poor readers in the control group."

Bull (1990: 82) noted that her research was originally published in Norway in 1985, and that the revised national curriculum, completed in 1987, included the principle of teaching to read and write in the D1 as a possible methodology. However, it was not widely adopted, despite the positive results it produced. She concluded (p. 82):

Popular opinions and prejudices about written languages as "real" languages, opposed to vernaculars or spoken dialects, which are considered perverted versions of the written language, are still dominant among teachers and parents.

In the Caribbean, Kephart (1992) examined the effects of teaching literacy through the English-lexified creole spoken in Carriacou to a small group of 12-year-old students who had failed to learn to read standard English competently. Reading materials were based on stories and anecdotes contributed by the students, and represented with a phonemic orthography. The students were tested at regular intervals in standard English during the project and these results were compared with those of a control group who did not use reading materials in the creole. At the end of the project the experimental group's test scores improved overall more than those of the control group, but the differences were not statistically significant. However, using reading materials in the creole clearly did not confuse the students or impair their reading in standard English, as predicted by some educators. And it had the positive effects of promoting enthusiasm and enjoyment of reading in the students.

8.4   Accommodation approach

In the accommodation approach (Wiley 1996: 127), also referred to as the integrative approach (Roberts 1994), the D1 is not a medium of instruction or subject of study, but it is accepted to some extent in the classroom. This may occur in several different ways. In the early years of school, students may be free to use their home varieties of language, without correction, for speaking. In addition, teachers may utilise their students' own interactional patterns and stories for teaching the standard. At the higher levels, literature and music from students' communities may be accommodated into the curriculum. Unlike in the instrumental approach, speakers of unstandardised dialects involved in the accommodation approach can be in a mainstream classroom alongside other students who speak varieties closer to the standard.

With regard to regional dialects, van den Hoogen and Kuijper (1989) evaluated aspects of the research project carried out in Kerkrade in the Netherlands (referred to in Section 7.1.1), which took place from 1973 to 1982. In this project, the researchers encouraged the use of the local Limburg dialect of Dutch in the classroom by both teachers and students (who were from 5 to 12 years old and in grades 1 to 4). An analysis of recordings of classroom observations showed that the use of the D1 in the classroom increased the rate of participation of dialect-speaking children as well as the mean length of their utterances.

With regard to AAE, many articles and dissertations have been written that support accommodation in the classroom. In one of the earliest examples, Piestrup (1973) examined the effectiveness of six different teaching styles among teachers of 200 mostly AAE-speaking first graders. The most successful teachers (in terms of the students' reading scores) were those who used both SAE and AAE with the children, and encouraged them to talk by listening to what they had to say, not how they said it. The least successful teachers were those who constantly interrupted students to correct their pronunciations or grammar. Cullinan, Jagger and Strickland (1974) evaluated a literature-based oral language program that involved full acceptance of children's natural language (AAE) in the classroom. The levels of the students ranged from kindergarten to grade 3. The experimental groups in each grade, who were involved in the program, showed greater gains in control over SAE than the control groups, who were not involved, with statistically significant differences for the kindergarten groups. Campbell (1994) reported on a program in an inner-city senior high school that allowed freedom of expression in either the students' D1 or the D2 (SAE), and included some discussion of language variation. The results were increased self-esteem among the students and increased use of SAE.

In a more recent study, Bohn (2003) described an African American grade 1 teacher's effective teaching techniques in her multi-ethnic classroom (60 per cent African American, 30 per cent Anglo American and 10 per cent Mexican American). While modelling SAE pronunciation and grammar, she intentionally employed typical discourse modes of AAE (see Section 1.3.3 above). These included the use of rhythm and repetition to get attention, call and response exchanges and frequent playfulness and teasing (see Smitherman 1977). The teacher also sometimes switched into AAE, and did not correct her students when they used it themselves. These techniques were successfully adopted by other teachers who had some familiarity with African American culture.

As an alternative to dialect readers, the University of Pennsylvania, with the support of the Netter Center, developed reading materials called *The Reading Road* (Labov and Baker 2006), which are available on the internet, along with a guide for teachers, *Spotlight on Reading* (Labov 2006). The style and content of the materials are tailored to the interests and concerns of children in schools in low-income areas, and aimed at dealing with the special decoding problems of African Americans, Latinos and other minority groups whose D1 differs from the D2 used in the classroom. In addition to teaching children phonemic awareness (the ability to recognise individual sounds in words), the materials focus attention on the most problematic areas where there are mismatches between students' D1 pronunciation and spelling in the D2 – for example, in words such as *find*, *desk* and *kept*, in which the final consonant is not pronounced in AAE. Teachers are advised to let students pronounce such words as they would in their D1 when they are reading. According to the website:

The program has been used successfully with African American, Latino and White children in the 2nd to 5th grade who were one-to-two years behind in reading grade level. It has been particularly successful with discouraged and alienated readers.

Various accommodation programs have existed in Australia for speakers of Aboriginal English. They were often referred to as the Teaching Standard English as a Second Dialect (TSESD) approach (Kaldor, Eagleson and Malcolm 1982; Malcolm 1992), even though they had little in common with the American SESD approaches of the 1970s. The Australian approach, which was adopted in many schools, emphasised recognising and understanding the linguistic and pragmatic features of the students' dialect, avoiding correction of students' speech, using group activities appropriate to Aboriginal culture and using children's own stories. Kaldor *et al.* (1982: 213) noted that while materials written in the dialect, such as dialect readers, would be educationally desirable, they would be unacceptable to parents and would prove divisive in racially mixed schools.

One of the best-known accommodation programs for SDA was in Hawai'i. The Kamehameha Early Education Program (KEEP) was started in the 1970s for ethnic Hawaiian children, mostly speakers of Hawai'i Creole (HC). In teaching reading, the program made use of discourse modes and participation structures similar to those in a speech event found in HC called *talk-story*. At least a dozen studies (e.g. Speidel 1987) showed increased reading achievement and development of spoken SAE as a result of using these HC patterns of interaction in the classroom. (See Boggs 1985 for a detailed description of the program and other references to evaluative research on it.)

Day (1989) described an experimental program involving HC-speaking children from kindergarten up to grade 4. In this program, teachers were first made aware of the history of creole languages and the logic of vernaculars such as HC. The teachers accepted HC as a valid linguistic variety, and did not react negatively to students using it in class. The study showed a significant increase over time in the scores of the students involved in the program on standardised tests of abilities in both HC and SAE. Rynkofs (1993) presented an ethnographic study of one teacher's program of writing workshops for HC-speaking students in grade 2. The children were allowed to speak and write in any variety, and early versions of their work included many HC features. But through a process of modelling and recasting in the workshops, rather than correction, the students became more proficient in written SAE (see also Rynkofs 2008).

Concerning speakers of indigenised varieties, Gupta (1994) described a teaching situation where both students and teachers used the D1 in the classroom in the early stages of SDA. The D1 was Singapore Colloquial English (SCE) and the D2 Singapore Standard English (StdE). Gupta's description was based on her observations in the nursery classes of a kindergarten where she participated as a teacher's aide in 1991. There were 384 children 3 to 4 years old in sixteen nursery classes, each class having two teachers. About half the students came to school already knowing SCE (pp. 160–2). Gupta noted that although the teachers knew StdE, they often used SCE in the classroom, despite this being deplored by the educational authorities. She observed (pp. 163–4):

Far from being detrimental to the development of English, the use of SCE by teachers in certain circumstances may actually facilitate the learning of StdE because the teachers tailor the use of English to the level of understanding of the children, rather than bewildering them by the sudden introduction of a variety that few of them have been much exposed to before beginning school.

Instead of correcting students, the teachers modelled various expressions in StdE, and gradually moved from using SCE to using StdE. By the end of the school year, students used and understood enough StdE for teaching to be done primarily in this variety.

In the English-speaking Caribbean, accommodation has involved increased acceptance of creole languages in schools, mainly in literature and creative writing. Winer (1990) reported that in Trinidad and Tobago, the Ministry of Education's 1975 syllabus called for the recognition of "the vernacular", i.e. Trinidad Creole (TC), "as a real language and as a legitimate vehicle for oral and written expression" (p. 245). Educators were asked to accept the students' spoken and written "dialect" in school work and examinations. Although there were initially adverse reactions to this syllabus in the community, Winer concluded (p. 245):

This attitude no longer generally holds ... TC has a measure of officially sanctioned and even required educational use, and is widely available in written form ... Although few would advocate the use of TC as the primary educational medium, even in primary education, there is a widely recognized need, from teachers and community, for its use in education as complementary, additive, and transitional to standard English.

Still in the Caribbean, Christie (2003: 46) reported that according to the recent Reform of Secondary Education in Jamaica, "students should be allowed to express themselves freely, employing whatever variety makes them comfortable in the classroom and outside". However, it is questionable whether accommodation has actually gone this far in most classroom contexts.

Accommodation is also one possible component of the awareness approach, described in the following section.

8.5   Awareness approach

In the awareness approach for SDA (Hudson 1984; Siegel 1993, 1999b), the students' D1 is seen as a resource that can be used for learning the standard D2 and for education in general, rather than as an impediment. It has some similarities to "language awareness", popular in Britain in the 1980s and 1990s (e.g. Hawkins 1984; James and Garrett 1991), and a great deal in common with "dialect awareness" in the USA (Adger 1994; Wolfram 1998b, 1999, 2009), although the approach described here is more focused on dialect acquisition. Like the accommodation approach, it can be used in classrooms where students have a variety of linguistic backgrounds.

Teaching programs using the awareness approach have at least two of the following three components. In the accommodation component, students' D1 is accepted in the classroom in various ways, as described in the preceding section. In the sociolinguistic component, students learn about variation in language and the many different varieties that exist, such as types of dialects and creoles. They also find out about the socio-historical processes that lead to the acceptance of a particular variety as the standard. As students are studying the world around them, this component of the approach is sometimes more like social studies than language arts. In the contrastive component, students learn about the rule-governed nature and linguistic characteristics of their own varieties and see how they differ from those of the varieties of other students and from the standard. This is sometimes called contrastive analysis (Rickford 1999, 2002; Wolfram and Schilling-Estes 1998), but it should not be confused with the CA of the 1950s and 1960s, described in Section 6.2.1 above.

In the remainder of this section, I talk first about awareness materials for teachers, and then about some of the pioneering awareness programs. Following, I describe awareness programs with various D1s that have been evaluated in some way, as well as some experimental studies.

8.5.1   *Resources for teachers and curricula*

The first step in implementing an awareness approach is educating the teachers themselves. Many useful materials have been written for teachers. Some are about teaching students who speak unstandardised dialects in general (e.g. Wolfram and Christian 1989, and the works on dialect awareness, mentioned above). Others are focused on specific locations, such as North Carolina (Reaser and Wolfram 2007),[10] or on particular groups of D2 learners, such as speakers of Caribbean creoles in Canada (Coelho 1988, 1991) and in the Caribbean itself (Craig 1999). (See Siegel 1999b for other references.)[11]

A comprehensive resource for primary school teachers in Australia is Fostering English Language in Kimberley Schools (FELIKS), a professional development course. It was developed with the aim of training educators about Kriol and Aboriginal English so that they can more effectively teach speakers of these varieties. The FELIKS course starts by showing participants that Kriol is a valid language and Aboriginal English is a valid dialect of English; they are not "poor English". It goes on to illustrate some of the systematic semantic, phonological and grammatical differences between each of these varieties and standard AusE, and the potential for miscommunication when these differences are not understood. Participants also learn about some basic sociolinguistic terms such as pidgin, creole and speech continuum. The course emphasises the importance of students having control of both standard AusE and Kriol or Aboriginal English. Teachers come to understand that each of these varieties can be used appropriately in different contexts, and that children need to be able to switch between them if they want to participate in both Aboriginal and non-Aboriginal Australian society.

FELIKS has been published as a kit (Catholic Education Office 1994) which contains all the material needed for running a two-day (seven-session) course. It includes a manual for presenters, audio- and videotapes, overhead transparencies, participants' booklets and handouts for group activities and games. A resource book for teachers based on the FELIKS materials has also been published (Berry and Hudson 1997).

Education departments in a number of Australian states have developed similar programs and packages (including recordings and texts) for teachers of Aboriginal English-speaking children. For example, the Aboriginal Curriculum Unit of the New South Wales Board of Studies (1995) published the *Aboriginal Literacy Resource Kit*. It includes a booklet that informs teachers about the origins of Aboriginal English, its role in Aboriginal identity, some of the features of its grammar, phonology and vocabulary, and significant aspects of Aboriginal communicative style. An important part of the preparation of this kit was the input from Aboriginal teachers and education department officials, all speakers of Aboriginal English, as well as the circulation of a near-final draft to all regional Aboriginal Education Consultative Groups in the state. A similar package, *Deadly Eh, Cuz!* (McKenry 1996), was developed in the state of Victoria. And the Western Australia Department of Education (2002) produced *Ways of Being, Ways of Talk*.

An organisation that promotes awareness for SDA for speakers of Pidgin (Hawai'i Creole) has been in existence since 1998. Its name is "Da Pidgin Coup" (all puns intended). In 1999, members wrote a position paper for educators and the general public titled "Pidgin and education". It presented information about the complex relationship between Hawai'i Creole (HC) and SAE, and about the equally complex issues surrounding the use of HC in education. The paper can be seen on the web at www.hawaii.edu/sls/pidgin.html. Some members of Da Pidgin Coup, especially Kent Sakoda, Ermile Hargrove and Terri Menacker, have run awareness workshops for teachers at various venues, including teachers' conferences. One part of the workshop is a demonstration of how HC is rule-governed, and in some areas, more complex than SAE.

This demonstration is often done with HC negatives. Positive sentences are presented, and the teachers who are HC speakers are asked how to make them negative, and whether or not alternative constructions "sound OK". Two columns of examples follow in the writing system that has been developed specifically for HC. In the first column are positive sentences and in the second column the same sentences put into the negative. Also included are some sentences beginning with an asterisk, indicating that the sentence sounds strange, or that it is not the usual way of saying something. In other words, the asterisk indicates that the sentence is ungrammatical in HC, just as saying "*I are eating" is ungrammatical in SAE.

Da kaet it fish.	*Da kaet **no** it fish.*
'The cat eats fish.'	'The cat doesn't eat fish.'
Da gaiz wrking.	*Da gaiz **nat** wrking.*
'The guys are working.'	**Da gaiz **no** wrking.*
	'The guys aren't working.'
Dei ste lisining.	*Dei **no** ste lisining.*
'They're listening.'	**Dei **nat** ste lisining.*
	'They aren't listening.'
Mai sista wan bas jraiva.	*Mai sista **nat** wan bas jraiva.*
'My sister is a bus driver.'	'My sister isn't a bus driver.'
Ai kaen du twenti pushap.	*Ai **no** kaen du twenti pushap.*
'I can do twenty pushups.'	'I can't do twenty pushups.'
Da baga braun.	*Da baga **nat** braun.*
'The guy is brown.'	'The guy isn't brown.'

Kaerol haeftu wrk.	*Kaerol **no** haeftu wrk.*
'Carol has to work.'	'Carol doesn't have to work.'
Yu sapostu du daet.	*Yu **nat** sapostu du daet.*
'You're supposed to do that.'	'You're not supposed to do that.'
Ai wen si om.	*Ai **neva** si om.*
'I saw it.'	**Ai **no** wen si om.*
	'I didn't see it.'
Get kaukau in da haus.	***Nomo** kaukau in da haus.*
'There's food in the house.'	**No get kaukau in da haus.*
	'There isn't food in the house.'
Nau wi get ka.	*Nau wi **nomo** ka.*
'Now we have a car.'	**Nau wi **no** get ka.*
	'Now we don't have a car.'

On the basis of examples such as these, teachers come up with rules for making negative sentences in HC, such as the following:

> ***Nat*** is used: (1) before the predicate in sentences without a verb; (2) before the *-ing* form of the verb when it's not preceded by *ste*, and (3) before the modal *sapostu*;
> ***No*** is used (1) before the plain, unmarked verb; (2) before the modals *kaen*, *gata* and *haeftu*; (3) before the progressive marker *ste*;
> ***Neva*** is used before the verb to indicate both negative and past tense simultaneously;
> ***Nomo*** is used as a negative existential to mean 'there isn't' or as a negative possessive to mean 'don't/doesn't have'.

The teachers are usually surprised to discover these rules (and HC-speaking teachers often thrilled), especially when comparisons are made with the much simpler rules in English, where *not* (or its contracted form *n't*) is the only sentential negative marker.

These workshops have two functions: informing teachers about the nature of HC (and other unstandardised language varieties) as well as providing them with a model for awareness activities in their own classrooms.

8.5.2 Some pioneering awareness programs

The Hawai'i English Program, which ran from 1968 to 1983, used the awareness approach in several ways. First, it had some exercises comparing features of HC to SAE. Second, it included some stories written in HC and children were sometimes given the choice to read either these or others in SAE. Third, there was a unit on dialects that looked at dialect diversity outside Hawai'i, as well as containing activities described by Rogers (1996: 233) as follows:

These activities encourage elementary school students to view HCE [Hawai'i Creole English] as a complete and legitimate language form, to undertake some simplified linguistic analyses of HCE, and to witness dialectal flexibility in local role models.

However, because of negative attitudes towards the use of unstandardised varieties such as HC in formal education, as described in Chapter 7 above, these components of the program were not widely covered by teachers (Eades *et al.* 2006: 158).

Another early educational program that used the awareness approach for SDA was the Afro-Caribbean Language and Literacy Project in Further and Adult Education, aimed primarily at Caribbean creole-speaking immigrants in Britain. It was established by the Language and Literacy Unit of the Inner London Education Authority (ILEA) in 1984, and culminated in the publishing of a book of language materials for teachers and students: *Language and Power* (ILEA Afro-Caribbean Language and Literacy Project in Further and Adult Education 1990). The proposed program, as described in the book, actually goes beyond most other awareness programs in emphasising the students' own expertise (see Chapter 9 below), as can be seen in this extract (p. v):

The book is based on the belief that a key part of the language curriculum for all students should be an outline of the social and political factors which helped to determine the development of Standard English. It is also necessary to make available to both students and teachers as much information as possible about languages in general and about the history and development of Caribbean Creole languages in particular. This includes an understanding of their grammatical structure, pronunciation patterns, vocabulary and idiom. The students themselves can contribute a great deal of this information, and their confidence will grow when their expertise in this area is acknowledged. Students' own knowledge and understanding of different languages and language varieties are an invaluable resource for language teaching. It is in this context that progress on the language issue in the multilingual classroom can be achieved, not just for students of Afro-Caribbean origin, but for students of all races and backgrounds.

The state of Western Australia has also supported development of a large-scale awareness program – the "Two-way English" program for Indigenous students who speak Aboriginal English. The program has the following goals (Malcolm 1995: 13–14):

(1) To help teachers better to understand Aboriginal English and to see, through it, distinctively Indigenous ways of approaching experience and knowledge.
(2) To help teachers, through the principle of two-way education, to develop the capacity to provide learning experiences which exploit Indigenous ways of organising and expressing knowledge while also promoting the appropriate use of standard English as a second dialect by Indigenous learners.

The program has several books for helping teachers (e.g. Malcolm *et al.* 1999) as well as a resource kit, *Deadly Ways to Learn* (Cahill 2000).

8.5.3   D1 Greek Cypriot dialect; D2 standard Modern Greek

The diglossia situation in Cyprus with the Greek Cypriot dialect (GCD) and standard Modern Greek (SMG) was referred to in Section 7.1.2 above. Yiakoumetti (2006) described an evaluation of an experimental awareness program conducted in Cyprus in 2000/1, involving final year primary school students. The program used a specially written textbook that valued the D1 and D2 equally and contained contrastive activities concerning both varieties. An experimental group (ninety-two students) was taught one period a day (45 minutes) for three months using the textbook. (Teachers of these students had previously received training for the program.) The control group (ninety students) was taught using the conventional textbook, which dealt only with the D2. For the evaluation, both groups were given one oral and two written tests (one in language essay writing and one in geography essay writing). These were administered four times: (1) prior to the experimental program, (2) midway through it, (3) at the end of the program and (4) three months later. The tests measured the degree of "dialectal interference" (p. 303) – i.e. the use of inappropriate D1 features when speaking or writing in the D2.

The results in the oral evaluation were that the experimental group showed statistically significant improvement – i.e. reduction in dialectal interference – between the first and second tests, and between the second and third tests. (There was no significant change after three months in the fourth test.) Significant improvement occurred in all four linguistic categories examined: phonology, morphology, syntax and lexicon. The control group showed no significant improvement (i.e. reduction of interference). In both written evaluations, the experimental group's results were similar to those of the oral evaluation – i.e. a significant decrease in interference.[12] In contrast, the control group had a statistically significant increase in interference after the first test in both written evaluations, and this was maintained thereafter with no significant improvement.

8.5.4   D1 African American English; D2 standard American English

Several studies from the 1980s and early 1990s report on successful use of various components of the awareness approach in teaching African Americans. Taylor (1989) used contrastive techniques with an experimental group of AAE-speaking university students to make them aware of differences between their speech and the standard. She used conventional English teaching methods with a control group. After 11 weeks, Taylor examined the use of non-standard features in the standard English writing of both groups. The results were a decrease of 59 per cent in the experimental group compared to an increase of 8.5 per cent in the control group.

Hoover (1991) described a program with AAE-speaking teacher trainees where they discussed the rule-governed nature of AAE and looked at African American patterns of interaction and writing genres. At the end of the program, 200 African American students scored above mainstream (White) students in a writing proficiency test.

Schierloh (1991) reported on an adult education program that respected the students' spoken language and used a contrastive approach to examine unstandardised dialects and SAE. In the 1988/9 school year, twenty students were given a pre-test on transforming examples of student writing with non-standard features into the standard. The average score on the pre-test was 37 per cent, but in the post-test at the end of the program it was 67 per cent. Furthermore, in contrast to the usual high drop-out rate, 71 per cent of the students in the program re-enrolled in the following school year.

In Georgia, the DeKalb County school system's Bidialectal Communication Program (Harris-Wright 1987, 1999) includes a contrastive component which is careful not to devalue students' D1. Figures presented in Rickford (2002: 37–8) showed that from 1995 to 1997, students involved in the program made positive gains of from 6.7 to 12.8 per cent each year in reading composite scores (based on pre-tests and post-tests). In contrast, students in control groups, who were not involved in the program and used only SAE in the classroom, made a gain of 5.2 per cent in one year but losses in two other years.

In California, the Los Angeles Unified School District has the Academic English Mastery Program (AEMP), formerly known as the Linguistic Affirmation Program (Hollie 2001; LeMoine 2001). In this program, teachers have been trained to develop knowledge and understanding of unstandardised vernaculars and the students who use them, and then integrate this knowledge into instruction in SAE and other subjects. The handbook for this program, *English for Your Success* (Los Angeles Unified School District and LeMoine 1999), also outlines activities for contrasting AAE and SAE.

A comprehensive evaluation of the AEMP was conducted in the 1998/9 school year (Maddahian and Sandamela 2000). The evaluation again had a pre-test/post-test design, here using the Language Assessment Writing Test. Results showed "a statistically significant and educationally meaningful difference between experimental and control groups", with the AEMP program participants outperforming those who did not participate in the program (p. vii). The researchers concluded that the AEMP is "an effective program in improving academic use of English language for speakers of non-mainstream English language" (p. vii) and recommended that the program be continued and expanded.

Two experimental studies have also been carried out. Fogel and Ehri (2000) compared the effectiveness of three instructional treatments in improving the SAE writing of groups of AAE-speaking grade 3 and 4 students, targeting six syntactic features which differ in the two varieties. They found that the most effective treatment was instruction which included guided practice in translating sentences from AAE into SAE and then providing corrective feedback. This is one technique sometimes used in the contrastive component of awareness programs.

Finally, Pandey (2000) studied the effectiveness of a six-week experimental program using what she called "the contrastive analytic approach" to teaching SAE as a second dialect. This approach had both the contrastive and the sociolinguistic components of an awareness program. The subjects were a group of AAE-speaking pre-college and first year college students, who were raised in the inner city and were basically monodialectal. These students were initially tested with the Test of English as a Foreign Language (TOEFL), as mentioned in Section 7.4.1 above. Pandey found that the approach led to more relaxed attitudes towards learning, increased bidialectal awareness and marked improvement in performance on subsequent TOEFL tests.[13]

8.5.5   D1 Hawai'i Creole; D2 standard American English

Hawai'i's Project Holopono, which took place from 1984 to 1988, was a program involving approximately 300 students of limited English proficiency in grades 4 to 6 in eight schools. Half of these students were Hawai'i Creole (HC) speakers. The program included some awareness activities, such as studying literature containing HC and contrasting features of the creole and SAE. The evaluation of the final year of the project showed an increase in oral proficiency in SAE among 84 per cent of the students (Actouka and Lai 1989).

Another Hawai'i program, Project Akamai, ran from 1989 to 1993. It involved more than 600 HC speakers in grades 9 and 10 in eleven schools. It also included the use of literature in HC and some contrastive activities. An evaluation of the final year of the project reported increases of between 35 and 40 per cent on tests of SAE use and oral language skills (Afaga and Lai 1994).

8.5.6   D1 Caribbean English Creoles; D2 standard English

In the Caribbean, Elsasser and Irvine (1987) described an experimental program integrating the study of the local Creole and standard English in a college writing program in the US Virgin Islands. They reported that the program did not interfere with the learning of the standard, and it led to increased interest in language in general, and to a greater "understanding of the role of grammatical conventions, standardized spelling, and the rhetorical possibilities of both languages" (p. 143).

Decker (2000) gave an account of an experimental study carried out over 13 weeks in a grade 3 classroom in Belize. Four grammatical areas were identified which differ in Belize Kriol and standard English: plural marking on nouns, past time reference, present time reference and subject–verb agreement. The teacher discussed with the students, in Kriol, how these features function in Kriol, and students were asked to write in Kriol using these features. The teacher then moved on to describe, again in Kriol, how the corresponding features function in standard English, and then gradually switched to discussing this with the students in English. Students were then engaged in various story-telling, writing and translation activities using these features in both languages. Although there were some methodological problems with the study, the results on the basis of a pre-test and post-test were that the students involved showed statistically significant improvement in performance in these areas of standard English.

In the USA, the Caribbean Academic Program (CAP) at Evanston Township High School near Chicago is an awareness program for Creole-speaking high school students who have migrated to the area from the Caribbean. Both SAE and various Caribbean English Creoles are used in the classroom for speaking, reading and writing, and issues concerning these languages and SAE are discussed (Fischer 1992a; Menacker 1998). A study was done on the progress of the students involved in the program. In the 1991/2 school year, 73 per cent of the 51 CAP students were placed in the lowest of the four levels (or tracks) in the school based on academic ability; none of them was in the two highest levels. But after one year in the program, only 7 per cent remained in the lowest level; 81 per cent had moved up at least one level; 24 per cent had moved up two or more levels; 26 per cent were in the two highest levels (Fischer 1992b).

8.6   Conclusion

In summary, while dialect coaching has been successful in helping actors to perform in dialects other than their own, accent modification has faced a more difficult task in helping adult learners to change their pronunciation to that of another dialect in everyday speech. With regard to classroom SDA, the evaluations of instrumental, accommodation and awareness approaches demonstrated that the use of the students' D1 in the classroom had none of the detrimental effects predicted by educators and parents. On the contrary, the approaches in general led to higher scores in tests measuring reading, writing or oral skills in the standard D2 and in some cases to increases in overall academic achievement. Other benefits included greater interest and motivation, and higher rates of participation. Some of the reasons for these results are discussed in the following chapter.

9 Explaining the results and taking further steps

Chapter 7 described some of the negative outcomes of both mainstream and ESL approaches in the formal education of speakers of unstandardised dialects. Chapter 8 showed little evidence of success in actual D2 acquisition in accent modification programs and the failure of SESD classroom approaches in the 1970s. However, much more positive outcomes were described for dialect coaching for performance and for instrumental, accommodation and awareness approaches in the classroom. This chapter explores some of the reasons for these results, both negative and positive. In doing so, it refers back to some of the factors that affect naturalistic SDA, as presented in Chapters 3 to 6. The chapter moves on to a discussion of further steps that can be taken to promote SDA in classroom contexts, followed by a short conclusion with some suggestions for further research.

9.1 Unsuccessful outcomes

9.1.1 Accent modification

As we saw in Sections 3.2 and 7.1 above, while actors can learn to produce other dialects for performance, it is much more difficult to acquire another dialect to the extent that it can be maintained in everyday use. The difference is that production for performance requires only explicit knowledge or conscious awareness of some of the features of the D2, and the ability to imitate them accurately. Actual acquisition of the D2, however, requires not only this explicit knowledge but also implicit competence, or the set of computational procedures needed to produce the D2 features automatically and consistently, as well as accurately. This competence is what is affected by age of acquisition.

We have seen in Chapter 4 that there are sensitive periods for L2 and D2 acquisition in different linguistic levels. With regard to acquiring the complex phonological procedures involved in the pronunciation of another dialect, the optimum age of acquisition is up to 7 years. There will be variable success up to age 13, but for 14 and over, it will be very difficult. As the learners in accent modification programs are adults, it is not surprising that reports of successful results for D2 acquisition in such programs are difficult to come by.

9.1.2   *Mainstream and ESL approaches*

With regard to classroom contexts, some people might be tempted to argue that the difficulties in acquiring the standard D2, as described in Section 7.1 above, are also a consequence of sensitive periods for acquisition. However, this argument can easily be refuted. First of all, if we assume that SDA starts when children enter the formal education system, then the age of acquisition begins before the age of 7 years. Second, the target features of the standard D2 are generally lexical and morphosyntactic rather than phonological. As described in Chapter 4, the optimal age for acquiring these features is the mid teens or younger. Therefore, most school students would still be in the optimal range.

Better explanations for the lack of success of mainstream and ESL approaches for D2 learners were discussed in Chapter 7 – e.g. difficulty in distinguishing D1 and D2 features, negative attitudes of both teachers and students, and lack of motivation and participation by students. The following section describes how dealing with these and other problems accounts for the positive results of the teaching approaches tailored for D2 learners.

9.2   Positive results

As shown by the evaluations described in the preceding chapter, special approaches for promoting SDA in classroom contexts are successful in achieving higher scores in tests measuring oral, reading and writing skills in the standard D2, and in some cases in leading to improvements in students' motivation and overall academic achievement. Here I present several possible explanations for these results.

9.2.1   *Ability to separate varieties and notice differences*

Sections 6.2 and 7.2.3 above discussed how the similarities between the D1 and the D2 may make it difficult for learners to separate the two varieties, and all four studies in Section 7.3 described the importance of being able to distinguish between features of the D1 and the standard. This ability was clearly promoted by both the instrumental and awareness approaches, and this is one of the most important reasons for their successful outcomes.

In the study of the Kriol/standard Australian English bilingual instrumental program in Australia described in Section 8.3 above, Murtagh (1982: 30) attributed the higher language proficiency of the bilingual program students to their "progressively greater success at separating the two languages", as a consequence of "the two languages being taught as separate entities in the classroom". Of course, here we are treating Kriol and standard AusE as two dialects, and as discussed in Section 3.4.4, a prerequisite for additive bidialectalism is the development of separate mental representations of the D1 and D2.

Using the D1 in educational programs also makes learners aware of differences between it and the standard that they may not otherwise notice. In other words, as the result of such programs, certain D2 features become salient to the learner, and as pointed out in Section 5.2.1, this salience is a necessary condition for acquisition. As we have seen with regard to naturalistic acquisition, Schmidt's noticing hypothesis (1990, 1993, 2001) stipulates that an L2 or D2 form will not be acquired unless it is noticed by the learner. This may occur in instrumental programs as a result of the juxtaposition of the two varieties or in the contrastive component of the awareness approach.

With regard to making D2 features salient, the awareness approach in particular often uses methods that are analogous to ones advocated in the SLA literature, and this may also account for some of the positive results. First there is "consciousness raising" (Sharwood Smith 1991), later referred to as "input enhancement" (Sharwood Smith 1993), where attention is drawn to particular grammatical features of the target but students are not expected to produce or practise them. Second is the "focus on form" teaching method (e.g. see Doughty and Williams 1998; Doughty 2001).[1] According to Long (2007: 122–3):

Focus on form ... involves briefly drawing students' attention to problematic linguistic targets, when certain conditions are met, in context, in an otherwise communicatively oriented lesson. It can help learners "notice" items in the input (in the sense of Schmidt 2001 and elsewhere) that otherwise may escape them, as well as mismatches between the input and deviant forms in their output, especially when there is no resulting communication breakdown that might serve the purpose.

An important difference from the SLA method is that in the awareness approach in SDA the shifts in focused attention are not normally triggered by students' comprehension or production problems. Rather, they are part of a classroom activity on language and dialect diversity.

A major difference between awareness approaches in SDA and form-focused approaches in SLA is in the role of contrastive activities. While such activities have been all but abandoned in SLA methodology, they are being promoted in SDA. As we have seen, teachers help students to examine linguistic features of their own D1 and then to compare these with features of other varieties, including the standard. James (1996: 255) called this activity "interfacing" and described it as follows:

It involves juxtaposing or confronting D1 and D2 and helping the learner to notice the differences between them, sometimes subtle and sometimes gross. It is a modern development of contrastive analysis ... which is now done by the learner himself rather than by the teacher.

This is most useful in SDA situations where the D1 and D2 are similar enough for the differences that do exist not to affect communication. But it is interesting to note that the value of what James (1992) referred to as "contrastive consciousness raising" is also being recognised for the advanced stages of SLA, as described in Section 6.1 above, where the differences between learners' interlanguage and the target language are also so small that they cause no communicative difficulty (see Swain 1998).

Finally, the use of the D1 in educational programs also has a positive effect regarding interference. As indicated in Sections 6.2.1 and 7.4.4, because of the similarities between the D1 and D2, negative transfer or interference is more likely to occur in SDA than in SLA. And as we have seen, several studies involving SDA have produced evidence of interference from the D1 in formal writing in the D2 (e.g. Fairclough 2005; de Kleine 2006, 2009). According to Politzer (1993: 53), errors caused by interference are "not likely to disappear without specific instructional effort and without being called to the learner's attention". A similar statement is found in the study of errors made by Swabian dialect-speaking children learning standard German, referred to in Section 6.2.1 (Young-Scholten 1985: 11): "[T]hose errors due to interference from a crucially similar first language will tend to persist if the learner's attention is not drawn to these errors." Thus, Winer (1989: 170) suggested that "an overtly contrastive method" of comparing Caribbean Creole with standard English would help deal with interference. And in the experimental awareness program in Cyprus (Section 8.5.3), Yiakoumetti (2006) attributed the significant reduction of interference to drawing students' attention to the subtle differences between the D1 and D2 that cause it. She concluded (p. 307): "Students' greater awareness of what constitutes dialectal interference may have simply assisted their efforts to reduce it." Thus, the use of the D1 in the educational process did not exacerbate the problem of interference, as predicted by some critics, but rather diminished it.

9.2.2   Easier acquisition of literacy and academic skills

A well-known principle in education is that it is easier for children to acquire literacy in a variety of language that is familiar to them. Also widely recognised is that literacy skills can be transferred from one language to another

(Cummins 1981; Snow 1990; Thomas and Collier 2002). These principles would also seem to apply to SDA. That is, it would be easier for children to acquire literacy in their D1 than in the D2, especially when there are some significant linguistic differences between the two. But once acquired, literacy skills can easily be transferred to the D2. In the case of the instrumental programs described in Section 8.3 above, the higher scores on tests of reading were most probably a consequence of these principles being put into practice.

In cases where the linguistic distance between the D1 and D2 is not so significant, there are also benefits from the practice in accommodation and awareness approaches of letting students read aloud in the D2 as they would speak in the D1. This practice avoids the constant correction that discourages students and makes them lose interest in reading.

Furthermore, according to the "interdependency principle" or "common underlying proficiency generalization" proposed by Cummins (1988, 2001), the combination of linguistic knowledge and literacy skills necessary for academic work, which he originally called "cognitive/academic language proficiency" (CALP), is common across languages and once acquired in one language or dialect, it can be transferred to another. Since CALP is easier to acquire in the D1 than in the D2, it appears that students in programs where the D1 was used in the classroom had a better opportunity to acquire these skills and then transfer them to general academic work in the standard dialect.

9.2.3   Greater awareness and more positive attitudes among teachers

As we saw in Sections 7.1 and 7.2.1, teachers of speakers of unstandardised dialects are often unaware of the problems their students face with regard to SDA. As a result, they may interpret "errors" students make in the standard dialect of education as carelessness or laziness, rather than a reflection of their D1, and develop negative attitudes towards these students. Teachers may also equate the lack of knowledge of the standard dialect as a lack of intelligence, and this can lead to lower expectations and the self-fulfilling prophecy of poorer student performance. Even if teachers recognise that their students come to school speaking another dialect, a lack of awareness of the legitimacy of this form of speech can result in teachers' denigrating or rejecting it, and as Au (2008: 66) pointed out, "rejecting students' home language is tantamount to rejecting the students themselves". As already mentioned, such negative attitudes may be internalised by the students, affecting their own self-image, or rejected by them, causing them to withdraw from participation in the education system. In both cases, the consequence is poor school performance.

But because of the fundamental nature of instrumental, accommodation and awareness approaches, and the knowledge and training needed to implement them, teachers involved will know that language variation and diversity are "normal". They will also be aware of the legitimacy and complex rule-governed nature of their students' D1s and how they differ from the standard. Therefore, as they understand the reasons for some of their students' "errors", they develop more positive attitudes and higher expectations, which are reflected in student performance. These factors, as well as more tolerance of the use of the D1 in the classroom, have other flow-on effects, described in the following sections.

9.2.4   Greater cognitive development among students

It is obvious that children's self-expression is facilitated if they are allowed to speak in a familiar language, especially without fear of correction (e.g. UNESCO 1968: 690). Thus, children are clearly disadvantaged when they are not free to express themselves in their own variety of language (Thomas and Collier 2002) – the situation for many speakers of unstandardised dialects, as described in Section 7.1 above. One important factor is that self-expression may be a prerequisite for cognitive development (Feldman *et al.* 1977). For example, in a study of cognitive development and school achievement in a Hawai'i Creole-speaking community, Feldman, Stone and Renderer (1990) found that students who did not perform well in high school had not developed "transfer ability". Here transfer refers to the discovery or recognition by a learner that abstract reasoning processes learned with regard to materials in one context can be applied to different materials in a new context. For this to occur, new materials must be talked about, described, and encoded propositionally. The problem in Hawai'i was that some students did not feel comfortable expressing themselves in the language of formal education, SAE, and their own D1, Hawai'i Creole, is conventionally not used in formal education.

Thus, one possible reason for the overall positive results in all three kinds of approaches using the D1 is that students were allowed to express themselves in their own varieties, thus better facilitating cognitive development.

9.2.5   Increased motivation and self-esteem among students

Most theories of SLA agree that the individual factors of learner motivation, attitudes, self-confidence and anxiety have some effect on L2 attainment. And in Section 5.1.5, we saw that an instrumental orientation and positive attitudes towards the D2 may lead to greater attainment in naturalistic SDA. These factors also appear to be important with regard to classroom SDA, and evidence suggests that the use of the D1 in formal education results in positive values for these factors with regard to learning the standard D2.

For example, Skutnabb-Kangas (1988: 29) observed that when the child's home language is valued in the educational setting, it leads to low anxiety, high motivation and high self-confidence, three factors which are closely related to successful educational programs. Wolfram and Schilling-Estes (1998: 290) also pointed out that "there is now some indication that students who feel more positive and confident about their own vernacular dialect are more successful in learning the standard one". With regard to AAE, Smitherman (2002: 172) referred to unpublished research done in the 1980s which demonstrated "that Blacks who were conscious of their own language as a legitimate system were more receptive to learning the language of wider communication [i.e. SAE]". In a discussion of awareness activities in the classroom, Baker (2002: 59) observed:

As young people become less fearful of being manipulated or disrespected, I think they can become engaged in the study of their own language competence. They can weigh their options, choose how they want to speak and write in each new setting. In this atmosphere, the mechanics and usage of vocabulary of formal English no longer threaten to demean them.

Many of the evaluations of instrumental, accommodation and awareness approaches referred to in Chapter 8 above describe increased participation and enthusiasm in the educational process. These positive attitudes are most probably a factor in accounting for the successful academic results reported for the use of these approaches.

9.3   Further steps

Despite the benefits of the three recent classroom approaches, it is clear that they would not be suitable or acceptable for all contexts. For example, as noted in Section 8.3, the instrumental approach is most suitable in situations where the D1 is clearly distinguished from the D2 and where all students in the classroom are speakers of the D1. The negative reactions to dialect readers for AAE speakers (Section 8.2.2), and more recently the furore over the Oakland Ebonics initiative (Section 7.4), demonstrate that much would need to change before such an approach would be accepted by the wider community in ethnic dialect settings. It is the awareness approach that appears to be the most feasible in the majority of settings.

However, while the awareness approach goes a long way to deal with problems faced by speakers of unstandardised dialects in formal education, it does not go far enough in some aspects. For example, it does not deal adequately with the problems of rejection of the formal education system, and peer pressure and identity, discussed in Sections 7.2.1 and 7.2.2. Such problems are especially prevalent in marginalised and disadvantaged communities who speak ethnic and regional dialects such as AAE, Australian Aboriginal

English, Appalachian English and Chicano Spanish. To deal with these problems, we have to get into issues of language and power. In the remainder of this section, I argue for an approach that takes further steps by confronting these issues and the existing ideologies and practices that currently lead to speakers of unstandardised dialects being disadvantaged in formal education.

9.3.1   Ideologies and reactions to them

The standard language ideology and the monoglot ideology were discussed in Section 7.4.3. Both these ideologies perpetuate the belief that the standard dialect is intrinsically superior and that other dialects are not appropriate for formal education. What was not emphasised was that in some situations these language ideologies serve to perpetuate and reinforce inequality and the dominance of the social groups who speak varieties close to the standard – i.e. the upper middle classes. As Fairclough (1989: 3) pointed out, "language has become perhaps the primary medium of social control and power", and it can be used to advantage some social groups and disadvantage others. This occurs in the formal education system, where, as we have seen, current practices favour students who speak dialects close to the standard and present many obstacles to unstandardised dialect-speaking students.

However, most educators are not aware of such practices and their consequences because of another ideology that is the basis for current educational policies – what can be referred to as the "egalitarian ideology".[2] This is the belief that despite differences in race, ethnicity, language, values and lifestyles, there is a basic equality among different ethnic and cultural groups, and with mutual respect and understanding, they can live happily together. Note that this ideology is not that there should be such equality, but that it already exists. Part of this view is that, in contrast to the strong version of the standard language ideology, all language varieties, including unstandardised dialects, are legitimate linguistic systems. Knowledge of the standard dialect, however, is seen as a kind of cultural capital (Bourdieu 1991), and it is believed that access to and attainment of this knowledge will lead to the skills, resources and influence that go along with it. Thus, according to this view, a major role of the schools is to give all students access to the cultural capital of the standard.

However, this ideology blinds people to the differentials in advantage and privilege that do exist between various social groups – that some groups are clearly dominant over others in terms of the skills, resources and influence they possess, and that subordinate groups may suffer from injustices (see Giroux 1988, 2001). Thus, as mentioned above, some groups have advantage and privilege while others are disadvantaged or marginalised. Again, one area of privilege has to do with language. While the varieties of language spoken by different social groups may be equal in linguistic terms, it is obvious that they are not equal in social or practical terms. The varieties spoken by the upper middle classes, upon which the standard is based, are the target of education; the unstandardised varieties of generally disadvantaged groups generally have no role in the curriculum. The standard variety is praised as being pure and logical; unstandardised varieties, as we have seen, are often denigrated as being incorrect or sloppy. Varieties close to the standard are shown to be appropriate for education, high-level employment and formal occasions; unstandardised dialects, if recognised at all, are shown to be appropriate only for casual conversation, joking and informal occasions (see Fairclough 1992b). As Sledd (1969: 1310) put it many years ago: "No dialect, they keep repeating, is better than any other – yet poor and ignorant children must change theirs unless they want to stay poor and ignorant." So, despite the egalitarian ideology, the message is clearly that varieties of language spoken by some social groups are inferior to those spoken by others.

This lack of equality of language clearly contributes to the lack of equality in the schools, as we have seen. Children from dominant social groups who come to school speaking varieties close to the standard can use their own language without restriction. Children from marginalised groups are often not allowed to express themselves in their D1, especially in writing, or at least discouraged from doing so. Children from dominant groups learn in and about a language and culture that are familiar to them; children from disadvantaged groups do not. Knowledge possessed by children from dominant social groups is valued and used in the educational process; knowledge possessed by children from disadvantaged groups is not.

As Corson (1991: 239) pointed out: "[W]hile the cultural or linguistic capital that is valued in schools is not equally available to children from different backgrounds, schools still operate as if all children had equal access to it." In other words, because of the egalitarian ideology, people ignore the disadvantage faced by some students and believe that everyone has an equal chance of success if they only work hard. Like the standard language ideology, the egalitarian ideology is hegemonic in that those who are disadvantaged also accept it, rather than striving for equality to reduce their disadvantage.

In some cases, the poor academic performance of students from marginalised groups described in Section 7.1 above might have less to do with teaching approaches than with the ideologies perpetuated by the education system itself, and reactions to them by some students from marginalised groups. Many students do not want to participate in an educational system that not only ignores their language and culture but also privileges students from upper middle-class social groups. Thus, reluctance to learn the standard variety and the dominant culture promoted in the schools may be an act of resistance (Giroux 1988: 157).

Also, as we have seen in Chapter 7, because of the monoglot ideology in particular, many students feel they have to choose between their own language and culture and that of the dominant community, and they choose the former. Furthermore, for similar reasons, as well as oppositional identity, many students from marginalised groups seem to avoid not only acquisition of the standard dialect but also academic achievement in general. They feel that since school is an institution of the dominant White upper middle class, success in this system is a characteristic of those from that particular social group. To be academically successful, then, is to turn your back on your own social group – what is often referred to as "the burden of 'acting White'" (Fordham and Ogbu 1986). The African American sociolinguist Lanehart (1998: 132) wrote:

We have come to associate being educated and literate with being white. We have come to view speaking SE [standard English] as speaking correctly, speaking white. At the same time, we have come to view being uneducated and illiterate as being cool and more "Black" or less white.

Fordham (1988) submitted that African American students who opt for academic success often develop a strategy of "racelessness" – that is, avoiding being identified with any particular racial group. (See below for alternative views.)

9.3.2   Critical examination of the awareness approach

It is clear that the awareness approach has had some success in increasing acquisition of the standard D2 and improvement in academic performance. But does it succeed in challenging the ideologies described above which serve to perpetuate the power and privilege of some social groups while disadvantaging others? And does it deal with students' reactions to the status quo that results from these ideologies?

According to Pennycook (1999) and other scholars, the only way to change things to be more equitable is to transform the social order. And many people believe change needs to begin in the education system, as exemplified in the "critical pedagogy" perspective (e.g. Freire 1985; Giroux 1988, 2001). According to this perspective, there are two important initiatives that bring about change. The first is to give disadvantaged students their "voice", so that they are no longer silenced in the educational process. This involves bringing their histories, experiences, languages and cultures into the classroom, and working with the knowledge they already have. The second initiative is to emphasise teaching not only academic skills but also critical analysis – that is, the ability to analyse current policies, practices and beliefs, including those of one's own culture, in order to identify ideologies and see how they may lead to privilege for some groups or subjugation for others. Students should gain the critical skills to become aware of the ideologies that support the current power structure, and thus have the potential to reject them.

These kinds of initiatives – giving students their voice and teaching them critical analytic skills – do not usually occur through the awareness approach. For instance, while the use of literature and music lyrics from unstandardised dialects in the accommodation component may increase students' interest or motivation, it does not really give students their own voice. In fact, the purpose of such accommodation may be only to get students interested in participating in the existing inequitable system, and thus perpetuating it (Giroux 1988: 127). Some students may see this as either tokenism, or an appropriation of their language and culture by outsiders. The sociolinguistic component may make students aware of the history that led to one particular variety becoming accepted as the standard, but it usually does not emphasise the politics or subjugation involved, or give students the critical skills they need, for example, to deconstruct the standard language and monoglot ideologies.

Thus, the awareness approach, as is currently stands, does not necessarily aim for change, or challenge existing ideologies. However, it does have the potential to do so if it adopts a more critical orientation. Such an orientation was foreshadowed in the ground-breaking work of the Language Curriculum Research Group, described in Section 8.2.3, and was more recently proposed by Murrell (1997) for teaching speakers of AAE and by Martínez (2003) for heritage learners of Spanish.

9.3.3   The critical awareness approach for SDA

A critical orientation that is relevant to the education of speakers of unstandardised dialects is "critical language awareness" (Fairclough 1989, 1992a) or "critical language study" (Clark et al. 1990, 1991). This orientation recognises the value of teaching the standard dialect, but only when it is done while critically analysing existing practices and ideologies that legitimise the stigmatisation and exclusion of particular language varieties in the educational process (Fairclough 1992a, 1992b). I refer to an approach to SDA with such an orientation as the "critical awareness approach".

The critical awareness approach could promote change leading to more equity for speakers of unstandardised dialects in at least three different ways. First, it could help both students and teachers understand and see through existing current practices and ideologies. For example, we have seen that the practice of denigrating unstandardised dialects is still common and accepted, as with AAE in the media during the Ebonics debate (Section 7.4.3).

The denigration was even worse in parodies of AAE that appeared on the internet during the debate and still can be found there (Ronkin and Karn 1999). We have also seen that students may internalise such derogatory characterisations of their D1, leading to a negative self-image. But the sociolinguistic component of a critical awareness program could be used to help students deconstruct these practices before they are internalised, and expose them for what they really are – racist caricatures that serve to put the blame for the "achievement gap" (Section 7.1.3 above) on African Americans rather than on the inequities in the education system (see Murrell 1997; Ronkin and Karn 1999).

With regard to ideologies, Fairclough (1989: 85) noted: "Ideology is most effective when its workings are least visible." The critical awareness approach could help students evaluate the workings of the language ideologies that disadvantage marginalised groups. For example, the sociolinguistic component could be an opportunity for students to examine the system of beliefs of the standard language ideology and how it has affected them personally and benefited certain segments of society. This component could also provide an opportunity to study the contradictions of the monoglot ideology – for instance, by looking at successful businessmen and world leaders who were or are bilingual or bidialectal – such as two past governors of Hawai'i who were fluent in both Hawai'i Creole and standard English.

Second, as Murrell (1997: 40–1) pointed out, the ideology that portrays AAE as inferior and inappropriate for use in education "promotes powerlessness, as people become voiceless when denied the tools with which they make meaning, communicate, think, and act reflectively". Thus by implication, speakers of AAE and other unstandardised dialects would be empowered by having their voice in the education system. Following a critical examination of the standard language ideology, including the doctrine of appropriateness, students may be more ready to make use of their own varieties of language in the educational process (and teachers more willing to encourage them to do so). In the critical awareness approach, the accommodation component would allow students to speak and write in the classroom using their D1 and cultural experience. This use of an unstandardised dialect in a context in which it is not normally used is an example of what Fairclough (1989: 243) calls "emancipatory discourse" – that is, "discourse which goes outside currently dominant conventions in some way". In other words, having their own voice in the educational process would help to free unstandardised dialect speakers from domination by other groups and bring about change to a more equitable power structure in the classroom. Although some would label this as permissiveness and an abandonment of the goal of acquiring the standard dialect, this is not the case, as we will see below in studies evaluating this approach.

The third way that the critical awareness approach may promote equitable change in the classroom is in making use of the knowledge, language capabilities and experience of the students (Fairclough 1989, 1992a). Thus, for example, in the contrastive component, the language data would be presented not by the teacher, but by the students, and the analysis would rely on their knowledge of the implicit morphosyntactic and pragmatic rules of their own dialects. This would help to shift the power relations in the classroom, as the teacher would not be the source of knowledge in this area, but rather a facilitator along with the students in making this knowledge explicit. This knowledge, as well as the students' experience, could also be important in the sociolinguistic component which examines different language varieties and attitudes and practices towards them (see Section 8.2.3 above).

Like the awareness approach described earlier, the critical awareness approach can be used with all social groups in the classroom – dominant as well as marginalised – thus avoiding any fears of ghettoisation. Students from privileged social groups could also learn to examine critically the hidden ideologies and contradictions of their own culture, and the limits and political consequences of their own culture's world view (Giroux 1988: 151). Thus Wynne (2002: 208–9) advocated the critical study of Ebonics (AAE) for White children as well as Black:

[B]y not recognizing Ebonics, we keep White children trapped in myopic visions of world realities. We give them one more reason to bolster their mistaken notions of supremacy and privilege…. [B]y discounting Ebonics, we keep White children oblivious to significant slices of their own country's history. We deny them the opportunity to look at their own ancestors and history in a way that might help them recognize their collective responsibility for injustices, as well as their collective potential for redemption.

Now we turn to a more specific discussion of how the critical awareness approach may be able to deal with the residual problems of rejection of the formal education system, and peer pressure and identity, mentioned in the introduction to this section. First, the inclusion of marginalised groups' D1, culture and knowledge in the educational system in more than a tokenistic way could diminish the perception that the system is an institution promoting only the language and culture of dominant groups. This has the potential to reduce marginalised students' resistance to the institution of education.

The affirmation and significant use of the students' own language and culture in the formal education system could also lead to increased ethnic pride, which may have a positive effect on academic performance. For example, research by Smith, Atkins and Connell (2003) showed that for African American fourth graders, higher levels of "racial-ethnic" pride correlated with higher academic achievement, as measured by both scores on standardised tests of reading and mathematics, and grades in school. This and other studies (e.g. Spencer *et al.* 2001; Horvat and Lewis 2003) appear to contradict Fordham's (1988) notion of "racelessness" as a necessary strategy for school success, at least among some students.

Furthermore, the use of the D1 in the classroom, along with the deconstruction of the monoglot ideology, may go some way towards alleviating the fear described in Section 7.2.2 that learning the D2 would mean giving up the D1 and thus abandoning one's peer group. In Hawai'i, for example, Reynolds (1999: 310) observed:

My own experience has revealed that when I am not trying to snatch away the language of my students, they do not feel that they have to hang onto it so tightly. Instead, the more we talk and plan and practice with both HCE [Hawai'i Creole English] and ASE [American standard English], the more interested we all become in both languages.

Related to this is the potential of the critical awareness approach to encourage students to examine critically hidden contradictions and ideologies in their own culture and world view, not just those in the dominant culture. Thus, for example, African American students may come to question the uncritical acceptance of having an oppositional identity, as described by Fordham and Ogbu (1986), Ogbu (1991) and Lanehart (1998), mentioned above, which leads to the rejection of not only standard English but also academic achievement in general. This questioning has already occurred to some extent. Carter (2003) gave an account of African American students who do not reject academic achievement in opposition to dominant White culture; rather they "resist the cultural default" – i.e. that academically successful students are those with "white middle-class standards of speech, dress, musical tastes, and interactional styles" (p. 137). With regard to the language aspect, this is reminiscent of Rampton's work in England (e.g. 1995, 2001) which revealed young people's rejection of essentialist categories of ethnicity and language use.

The critical awareness approach could also encourage students to examine the folk views on the true self that also underlie the monoglot ideology – among the most significant obstacles to SDA in both classroom and naturalistic contexts. Students would come to realise that they can (and do) have multiple social identities in different contexts, and therefore they can still maintain the identity associated with their D1 if they acquire and use another dialect.

9.3.4   Studies of the effectiveness of the critical awareness approach for SDA

As the critical awareness approach for SDA is rare, so are studies looking at its effectiveness. Here I describe three that evaluate methodologies that use some aspects of the approach.

Van Sickle, Aina and Blake (2002) investigated the use of students' own general knowledge and experience with regard to teaching science and mathematics. The authors conducted an in-depth qualitative study over three years on Johns Island (South Carolina). The subjects were twelve high school students who spoke an often stigmatised creole language, Gullah. The study involved working with the students, listening to their stories and discovering their own knowledge and world views. Later the researchers did content-specific language development with the students to enable them "to communicate their knowledge to the outside world" (p. 81). The authors noted (pp. 81–2):

Because our goal was definitely not to eradicate their native language and culture, we focused on code switching as a means of preserving their heritage while giving them two ways to communicate about the same topics. In addition, the alternative terminology that we used with the students was designed to stretch both their thinking and their precise use of words.

They described the results as follows (p. 82): "While maintaining their ability to describe a 'right' answer in a holistic manner (as is typical in the Gullah language), they have become more precise and detailed in their writing (more typical of Standard English)." The authors reported that all students seemed to have benefited from the project, and those in the final year of high school passed the South Carolina Exit Exam and graduated with a diploma.

The "culturally relevant pedagogy" advocated by Ladson-Billings (e.g. 1992, 1995) has also implemented aspects of the critical awareness approach. Teachers using this approach with students from marginalised social groups aim "to prepare students to effect change in society, not merely fit into it" (1992: 382). Culturally relevant pedagogy rests on three propositions (1995: 160): "(a) Students must experience academic success; (b) students must develop and/or maintain cultural competence; and (c) students must develop a critical consciousness through which they challenge the status quo of the current social order." In the classroom, this translates to finding ways to value the students' skills and life experiences, affirming and using the cultural knowledge of their community, encouraging students to express themselves in their own ways of speaking, and teaching them "to critique the cultural norms, values, mores, and institutions that produce and maintain social inequities" (1995: 162). Ladson-Billings' detailed observations of successful teachers who use this pedagogy with speakers of AAE have provided evidence of its effectiveness.

Richardson (2003) did a detailed evaluation of her African American-centred approach to teaching rhetoric, composition and literary studies to AAE-speaking university students. In this approach students examine African

American writing traditions from the early days of slavery to the modern hip hop era, and explore the values, beliefs and history expressed in this writing and in the media. They also study the discourse modes and rhetorical styles of AAE – what Richardson refers to as "Black discourse" – for example: "rhythmic dramatic evocative language, references to color–race–ethnicity, use of proverbs ... verbal inventiveness, cultural values/community consciousness ... signifying, structural call-response and testifying" (p. 100). These areas of study are in addition to learning about academic writing, doing activities that contrast AAE and SAE, and participating in writing workshops. In their writing, students are free to use morphosyntactic features of AAE and features of Black discourse. Richardson noted (p. 117): "Students' own culture and literary experiences are recognized as valuable tools which inform ways in which they explore and help shape society."

The evaluation was primarily on the basis of impromptu essays that fifty-two African American students wrote on the first and last day of class on topics concerning African American language and literacy traditions. The uses of AAE morphosyntactic features and Black discourse features in each essay were separately quantified, and each essay was scored on the basis of how well it addressed the assigned topic and how well ideas were developed. The scores were given by independent raters who were all professional teachers of writing at the tertiary level. The length of the essay (i.e. number of words) was also considered as a separate measure of achievement.

The study found that there was actually very little use of D1 morphosyntactic features in students' writing, but what there was decreased in the final essay. Thus, one conclusion was that allowing the use of morphosyntactic features of AAE in writing is not an impediment to acquiring SAE. Furthermore, for each student, the more Black discourse features used, the fewer D1 morphosyntactic features (p. 103). There was also a strong correlation between the amount of use of Black discourse, the length of the essay and the score received. Therefore, another conclusion was that the use of Black discourse accelerated rather than arrested the development of academic writing. The main research question was (Richardson 2003: 100): "Is written fluency enhanced by African American methodology?" The answer then appeared to be "yes". Students' evaluations of the curriculum were also very positive, with comments about how it improved their writing, enabled them to find and write in their own voice and gave them more control over different writing styles.

While these three studies do not describe the use of all aspects of the critical awareness approach for SDA, they do give some indication of its effectiveness in changing the social order in the classroom by reaffirming students' right to their own dialect and culture, while at the same time promoting the acquisition of the second dialect needed for academic work.

9.4   Conclusion

It is probably clear from the title and content of this book that I envisage SDA as a subfield of linguistics, informed by sociolinguistics but under the umbrella of applied linguistics or SLA. However, as we have seen, there is very little research specifically on SDA. What there is has been done mainly by sociolinguists and dialectologists, and concerns SDA in naturalistic contexts, as described in Chapters 2 to 6. This has provided answers to some of the questions outlined in Chapter 1 about the difficulties of learning a second dialect, the individual and linguistic factors affecting SDA, and the differences between SDA and SLA. But hardly any research has been done on SDA in educational contexts where it is more important to modern society and where it occurs (or is supposed to occur) much more frequently.

Sociolinguists and dialectologists have also done their part in conducting extensive research to demonstrate that unstandardised regional and ethnic dialects, as well as pidgins and creoles, are legitimate rule-governed varieties of languages. Unfortunately, as we have seen, these findings have not trickled down to many educators who teach speakers of these varieties. These educators, however, would be more interested in issues concerning the acquisition of the standard dialect used in the schools, but this is precisely where research is lacking. Rather than focusing on general achievement (as most of the studies described in Chapter 8 do), research on SDA in educational contexts needs to examine processes of acquisition and attainment in particular linguistic areas, as in the exceptional studies by Fairclough (2005) and Calchar (2004, 2005), described in Section 7.3 above. Also needed are longitudinal studies of D2 learners and fine-grained ethnographic studies of classroom SDA.

I hope that as a first attempt to define a field of SDA, this book may inspire educators, applied linguists and researchers in SLA to conduct some of this much-needed research, or encourage others to do so.

Notes

1 INTRODUCTION

1 And so has my writing, as indicated by the Australian spelling used in this book.

2 However, some American linguists do not follow IPA and use the symbol /y/ instead of /j/ for the 'y' sound (and /ü/ for the rounded high front vowel, as in French *rue*).

3 The off-glides [ɪ] and [ʊ] are sometimes shown as [j] (or [y] in the US) and [w], as in /fejs/ (or /feys/) for *face* and /haws/ for *house*. Also, the glide is sometimes super-scripted or marked with a diacritic to show it is non-syllabic – for example, /feˈs/ and /haᵘs/ or /feɪs/ and /haʊs/.

4 When the split occurred in southern British English in the eighteenth century, /æ/ became /ɑ/ in words where it preceded /f/, /s/, /θ/, /ns/, /nt/, /ntʃ/, /nd/ or /mpl/. So one could argue that D2 learners could use phonological conditioning rules. However, there are many exceptions in which /æ/ remained in words where /ɑ/ would be predicted by the rules, such as in *baffle, ant, classic, mathematics* and *cancer*. The complexity of the phonological rules plus the great number of exceptions would mean that learners would have to memorise the set of words in which /ɑ/ occurs instead of /æ/.

5 The chapters in the second part of the book include materials from some of my earlier publications (Siegel 1999a, 1999b, 2003, 2006a, 2006b, 2007).

2 ATTAINMENT IN NATURALISTIC SDA

1 There are several other studies written in Norwegian, Dutch and German that I was unfortunately unable to read.

2 [ɐ] is a low central unrounded vowel.

3 Payne (1976) was not very explicit about the ages of the "children", but from her Figure 3.2 on p. 112, it is clear they ranged from eight to twenty at the time of the interviews.

4 Based on Payne (1976: 92; 1980: 151).

5 The results for (ohr) were somewhat skewed by that fact that 60 per cent acquired the merger for the pair *more/moor* as opposed to only 20 per cent for *sure/shore* and *lure/lore*.

6 Note that in the word *atomic*, flapping does not occur because the syllable *-tom-* is stressed whereas in the word *atom*, the first syllable *a-* is stressed. Flapping can also occur when the preceding or following sound is /r/, /n/ or /l/, as in the following words: *forty, bitten, alter, turtle*.

7 Since the youngest child was only nineteen months old when she arrived in England, it might be argued that she should not be included in a study of second

dialect acquisition. However, Tagliamonte and Molfenter (2007: 657) noted that at the time of arrival, all the children were using expressive language and with entirely Canadian English variants.

8 Note that Tagliamonte used an alternative symbol for the flap: [ɒ].

9 Based on Tagliamonte and Molfenter's (2007) Figures 2 and 3, p. 663.

10 There are many different descriptions of Australian English vowels, and they do not always agree with each other. Here I am using Foreman's descriptions.

11 Based on Foreman's (2003) Table 9, p. 131.

12 Starks and Bayard (2002) also describe the acquisition of NZE by three other children. However, two started day-care at the age of six weeks and one at eleven months (p. 190), and it was then that they began to acquire NZE. Therefore NZE was not actually their D2 since they had not already acquired a different D1.

13 Trudgill (1986: 28–30) said that the recordings were done every month for six months, rather than over eight and a half months, as reported by Rogers (1981).

14 Based on Kobayashi's (1981) Table 1, p. 15.

15 Based on the figures given in Kerswill's (1994) Figure 5.1, p. 109.

16 The diacritic under the vowel indicates that it is higher than usual.

17 Based on Omdal's (1994) Table 1, p. 125.

18 Some of the single phonological variables actually concerned several separate variables; for example, one concerning four different long vowels, written as *e, å, ä* and *ö*.

19 For example, the Närpes dialect index was calculated by examining each of the seventeen variables that are exclusive to that dialect. For each one, the number of occurrences of the Närpes variant was divided by the total number of occurrences of all variants and multiplied by 100 to get the percentage of Närpes dialect use. The index was the mean of the percentages for all of these variables.

20 Based on Ivars' (1994) Table 2, p. 216.

21 These subjects were selected from a larger group of students on the basis of a questionnaire in which they reported that they could speak the Limburg dialect fluently and that they used it more or less regularly (Vousten and Bongaerts 1995: 330).

22 [œ] is a rounded [ɛ] as in French *sœur* 'sister', and [y] is a rounded [i] as in French *rue* 'street'.

23 Note that these average percentages are my own calculations based on figures provided by Vousten and Bongaerts (1995: 302).

24 Rys and Bonte (2006) reported on a portion of the larger study, considering only the phonological variables and linguistic factors.

25 Based on Rys's (2007) Table 7.1, pp. 228–33.

26 These figures do not include two apparently aberrant cases of only 3 per cent.

27 Based on Berthele's (2002) Table 2, p. 334.

28 Stanford also examined the first language acquisition of children to see which dialect features they acquired (see Stanford 2008b).

29 Based on Auer *et al.*'s (1998) Tables 3a and 3b, p. 178.

30 Based on Nuolijärvi's (1994) Table 7, p. 160.

3   ACQUIRING A SECOND DIALECT

1 For examples of overgeneralisation with standard English as D1 and Hawai'i Creole as D2, see Siegel (2008: 258–63).

2 A study by Evans (2002) aimed to demonstrate that a 29-year-old speaker's imitation of another dialect (South Midlands American English, as spoken in West Virginia) was accepted as pure and natural by native speakers of that dialect. However, as the speaker was born in that dialect area and lived there until the age of 23, one cannot rule out the possibility that he had acquired that dialect as a child and was merely switching to it.

3 The same is true for singers, and that is why the survey in Chapter 2 did not include Trudgill's (1983) analysis of British pop singers' use of American English.

4 http://en.wikipedia.org/wiki/Brassed_Off.

5 In Meryl Streep's defence, she was reportedly trying to imitate the actual accent of the character she was playing, Lindy Chamberlain, whose speech was influenced by New Zealand English.

6 However, this may not be a typical case because the girl spent every summer with her grandmother in Tokyo and maintained regular contact with her throughout the rest of the year (Kobayashi 1981: 6).

7 Dyer's son also showed remarkable metalinguistic awareness of different dialects and languages, perhaps as the result of growing up multilingual (with a Spanish-speaking father and Mandarin Chinese-speaking day-care), as well as bidialectal.

8 Exceptions include Pardo (2006), who found some evidence of phonetic convergence.

9 According to Chambers (1992: 693), this pattern is consistent with the Lexical Diffusion theory of language change (Chambers and Trudgill 1980: 174–80).

10 Stern (1988: 156) noted that once they are in school, children are taught standard German "in a Swiss context with a Swiss accent", and they soon lose their standard northern German pronunciations.

4   DIFFERENTIAL ATTAINMENT: AGE EFFECTS AND LINGUISTIC FACTORS

1 Psychological factors, such as aptitude, cognitive style and personality type, are discussed in the SLA literature but have not been considered in studies of SDA.

2 Based on Payne's (1976) Figure 3.1, p. 112, and Table 3.7, p. 121.

3 It is not clear why Payne (1976) labelled the last age group 10–14, when the oldest age of arrival, according to Figure 3.2 (p. 112), was 13.

4 Based on Omdal's (1994) Tables 1 and 2, pp. 125, 129.

5 However, on the basis of his analysis of research on age and SLA, Long (2007: 71) concluded: "Whereas late starters with native-like abilities in a foreign language may exist, current published claims to have found them do not appear to be sustainable."

5   ADDITIONAL INDIVIDUAL AND LINGUISTIC FACTORS

1 Based on Kerswill's (1994) Table 5.5, p. 116.

2 On the basis of Omdal's (1994) Tables 1 and 2, pp. 125, 129.

3 On the basis of Wells' (1973) Table 1, p. 48.

4 Based on Foreman's (2003) Table 16, p. 193.

5 Based on Foreman's (2003) Table 17, p. 194. On p. 126, Foreman described factors that may have affected the results somewhat – e.g. different recording contexts and interviewers.

6 Based on Starks and Bayard's (2002) Table 3, p. 190.

7 See Johnstone (1999) for a more recent, and more complex, analysis of Texan identity.

8 For a good overview of social network analysis and its origins, see Bortoni-Ricardo (1985: 69–122).

9 Rys (2007: 118) reported that Vousten's (1995) study in the Netherlands did not find any significant relationship between attitude/motivation and the degree of acquisition of the D2 (the Venray dialect). However, she attributed this to the fact that Vousten only examined the effect of attitudinal factors on the dialect proficiency of children who had been selected precisely because they spoke the D2 to some extent and had positive attitudes towards it.

10 See Auer *et al.* (1998: 169–70) for the forms of the variants for these variables and the others, and examples.

11 Based on Foreman's (2003) Table 14, p. 173.

6 THE DIFFICULTY OF SDA

1 And this was only among the twelve out of thirty-four subjects who acquired some AusE features.

2 Positive transfer can also occur when L1 and L2 structures are identical, but here we will consider only negative transfer.

3 Of course, this model and the validity of its predictions have more complications than I can go into here. See Markham (1997: 107–11) and Major (2001: 39–41) for further analysis and criticism.

4 http://en.wikipedia.org/wiki/List_of_words_having_different_meanings_in_British_ and_American_English. (Note that there has been some disagreement about various words on the list and their meanings.)

5 It was actually our friend and colleague Janet Holmes who enlightened us.

6 For American readers who don't know the expression "taking the piss", here it means 'mocking' or 'making fun of (something)'.

7 Thanks for to Matthew Prior for leading me to these references.

8 Accessed on 21 March 2009 from www.drphil.com/articles/article/73.

9 Accessed on 17 September 2008 from http://en.wikipedia.org/wiki/Wikipedia: Reference_desk_archive/Language/2006_July_17.

10 The term "koine" comes from the Greek word meaning 'common', which was used to refer to the mixed dialect of Greek that became the lingua franca, or common language, of the eastern Mediterranean around 300 BC.

11 These are referred to as "colonial dialects" by Trudgill (1986; 2004).

7 SDA IN CLASSROOM CONTEXTS

1 Extended pidgins and creoles are also included here under the label of unstandardised dialects, because that is the view of most of their speakers, as referred to in Chapter 1. However, as I have noted before, they are really separate languages, and many (such as Haitian Creole) have been standardised to some extent.

2 There were some methodological problems with this research, as noted by Ammon himself (1989a: 136). (See Barbour 1987 for criticism of earlier work that correlates dialect use with social class.)

3 Based on Lee, Grigg and Donohue (2007); Salahu-Din, Persky and Miller (2008); Lee, Grigg and Dion (2007); and figures on the National Center for Education Statistics website: http://nces.ed.gov/nationsreportcard/.
4 Of course, Hispanics and American Indians have similar low scores, most probably for similar reasons, as described below.
5 See Rickford, Sweetland and Rickford (2004) for a comprehensive review and bibliography of literature on AAE and education.
6 Based on Tables 6.4.5 and 6.4.6 in SCRGSP (2009: 6.23 and 6.24).
7 Singapore Ministry of Education, Performance on Primary School Leaving Exam by Subject, accessed on 21 July 2009 from www.moe.gov.sg/media/press/files/ 2008/12/performance-ethnic-groups-chart-a2.pdf.
8 Based on Geiger and Greenberg's (1976) Figure 1, p. 30.
9 An additional and very important work came to my attention only after this book was completed. Lacoste (2009) studied the learning of some phonological features of standard Jamaican English by twenty-four 7-year-old Jamaican Creole-speaking children in three rural schools. (See also Lacoste 2007.)
10 The differences between grades 3 and 5 and between grades 3 and 7 were statistically significant, but not between grades 5 and 7 (Isaacs 1996: 437).
11 Based on Fairclough's (2005) Tables 18 and 28, pp. 91, 108.
12 Fairclough (2005: 104) also gave the example of *feura* being overgeneralised to contexts where *hubiera* is required. It is not clear, however, whether this is a result of classroom learning or the use of a conventional feature of the D1.
13 Tense indicates time reference, such as past, present and future. Aspect indicates internal features of an activity or event, such as whether it is continuing or completed. The sentences *They worked* and *They were working* are both past tense, but the second differs from the first in that it has progressive aspect.
14 The percentages of accurate use of past tense marking ranged from 24.3 to 85.3 per cent, with eighteen ranging from 24.3 to 46.9, eleven ranging from 52.6 to 68.1, twelve from 71.3 to 79.4 and seven from 81.4 to 85.3 (Calchar 2005: 300–1).
15 Calchar (2005) also investigates the "narrative discourse hypothesis" (Bardovi-Harlig 1999), but this is not discussed here.
16 Memorandum Opinion and Order, Civil Action No. 7–71861, U.S. District Court, East District, Detroit, MI, p. 42. (See Smitherman 1981; Smitherman and Baugh 2002.)
17 But see Siegel (1999a) for references to conflicting reports on the extent of interference in SDA in both reading and writing.

8   EDUCATIONAL APPROACHES FOR SDA

1 For earlier overviews of teaching approaches, see Siegel (1999a) and Simmons-McDonald (2004).
2 IDEA can be found on the web at http://web.ku.edu/idea/.
3 Accessed on 8 August 2005 from www.earandspeak.com.au/esesl.html#acc.
4 www.callcentersindia.com/call_center_directory.php?id=9_callcenter.
5 Accessed on 19 February 2009 from www.paulmeier.com/testimonials.html.
6 An extensive literature on SESD and the promotion of bidialectalism in the USA appeared in the 1960s and 1970s – for example, in the volumes edited by Shuy, Davis and Hogan (1964), Baratz and Shuy (1969) and Fox (1973). For further references, see Siegel (2003).

 7 However, some methodological problems with Leaverton's study were pointed out by Baratz (1973: 107).
 8 It is noteworthy, however, that in a 2000 survey of members of CCCC and NTCE approximately two thirds of the respondents were not familiar with the resolution (Wible 2006: 443).
 9 In this article, Morren talks about the program being on all three islands of the archipelago: San Andrés, Providencia and Santa Catalina, but in later work (Morren 2004), he mentions only San Andrés.
10 The curriculum materials and teacher manual are available on the web at www.ncsu.edu/linguistics/research_dialecteducation.php.
11 Ammon (1989b) referred to materials published for teachers of dialect speakers in Germany as far back as 1908. He also described a series of booklets produced in the 1970s and early 1980s, each contrasting linguistic features of a particular dialect with standard German and presenting some of the difficulties faced by speakers of that dialect. However, these were not widely used by teachers, partly because of the high cost of the booklets (which teachers had to buy on their own).
12 The only differences were that improvement was not statistically significant between the third and fourth tests in language essay writing, and after the second test in geography essay writing. However, overall improvement was significant in both.
13 Whether the TOEFL test is appropriate for measuring SDA is another question.

9   EXPLAINING THE RESULTS AND TAKING FURTHER STEPS

 1 This should not be confused with focus on forms.
 2 For other labels and a further description of this ideology, see Giroux (1988: 123) and Pennycook (2001: 29).

References

9News. 2006. Aussie actors can sound American. Accessed on 13 November 2008, from http://news.ninemsn.com.au/ article.aspx?id=125491.

Abdul-Jabbar, Kareem and Peter Knobles. 1983. *Giant Steps: The Autobiography of Kareem Abdul-Jabbar*. New York: Bantam Books.

Aboriginal Curriculum Unit, New South Wales Board of Studies. 1995. *Aboriginal Literacy Resource Kit*. North Sydney: New South Wales Board of Studies.

Actouka, Melody and Morris K. Lai. 1989. *Project Holopono, Evaluation Report, 1987–1988*. Honolulu: Curriculum Research and Development Group, College of Education, University of Hawai'i.

Adger, Carol Temple. 1994. *Enhancing the Delivery of Services to Black Special Education Students from Non-Standard English Backgrounds: Final Report*. University of Maryland, Institute for the Study of Exceptional Children and Youth (ERIC Document no. ED 370 377).

Adger, Carol Temple, Donna Christian and Orlando Taylor (eds.). 1999. *Making the Connection: Language and Academic Achievement among African American Students: Proceedings of a Conference of the Coalition on Diversity in Education*. Washington, DC/McHenry, IL: Center for Applied Linguistics/Delta Systems.

Afaga, Lorna B. and Morris K. Lai. 1994. *Project Akamai, Evaluation Report, 1992–93, Year Four*. Honolulu: Curriculum Research and Development Group, College of Education, University of Hawai'i.

Alatis, James E. 1973. Teaching standard English as a second dialect: The unanswered questions, the successes, and the promise. In Fox (ed.), pp. 43–56.

Alleyne, Mervyn C. 1980. *Comparative Afro-American: An Historical-Comparative Study of English-Based Afro-American Dialects of the New World*. Ann Arbor: Karoma.

Alrabaa, Sami. 1986. Diglossia in the classroom: The Arabic case. *Anthropological Linguistics* 28: 73–9.

Ammon, Ulrich. 1977. School problems of regional dialect speakers: Ideology and reality. Results and methods of empirical investigations in southern Germany. *Journal of Pragmatics* 1: 47–68.

1989a. Aspects of dialect and school in the Federal Republic of Germany. In Cheshire, Edwards, Münstermann and Weltens (eds.), pp. 113–38.

1989b. Teaching materials for dialect speakers in the Federal Republic of Germany: The contrastive booklets. In Cheshire, Edwards, Münstermann and Weltens (eds.), pp. 234–41.

Andersen, Roger W. and Yasuhiro Shirai. 1994. Discourse motivations for some cognitive acquisition principles. *Studies in Second Language Acquisition* 16: 133–56.

Arthur, J. M. 1996. *Aboriginal English: A Cultural Study*. Oxford: Oxford University Press.

ASHA Multicultural Issues Board. 2002. American English dialects (technical report). Accessed on 19 February 2009, from www.asha.org/docs/html/TR2003–00044.html.

Au, Kathryn H. 2008. If can, can: Hawai'i Creole and reading achievement. *Educational Perspectives* 41: 66–76.

Auer, Peter. 1993. Zweidimensionale Modelle für die Analyse von Standard/Dialekt-Variation und ihre Vorläufer in der deutschen Dialecktologie. In Wolfgang Viereck (ed.), *Verhandlungen des Internationalen Dialektologenkongresses, Bamberg 1990*, 3–22. Stuttgart: Franz Steiner.

Auer, Peter and Frans Hinskens. 2005. The role of interpersonal accommodation in a theory of language change. In Auer, Hinskens and Kerswill (eds.), pp. 335–57.

Auer, Peter, Birgit Barden and Beate Grosskopf. 1998. Subjective and objective parameters determining "salience" in long-term dialect accommodation. *Journal of Sociolinguistics* 2: 163–87.

Auer, Peter, Frans Hinskens and Paul Kerswill (eds.). 2005. *Dialect Change: Convergence and Divergence in European Languages*. Cambridge: Cambridge University Press.

Auerbach, E. R. 1995. The politics of the ESL classroom: Issues of power in pedagogical choices. In James W. Tollefson (ed.), *Power and Inequality in Language Education*, 9–33. Cambridge: Cambridge University Press.

Baker, Judith. 2002. Trilingualism. In Delpit and Dowdy (eds.), pp. 49–61.

Baratz, Joan C. 1973. The relationship of Black English to reading: A review of research. In Laffey and Shuy (eds.), pp. 101–13.

Baratz, Joan C. and Roger W. Shuy (eds.). 1969. *Teaching Black Children to Read*. Washington, DC: Center for Applied Linguistics.

Barbour, Stephen. 1987. Dialects and the teaching of Standard Language: Some West German work. *Language in Society* 16: 227–44.

Bardovi-Harlig, Kathleen. 1999. From morpheme studies to temporal semantics: Tense-aspect research in SLA. *Studies in Second Language Acquisition* 21: 341–82.

Baugh, John. 1992. Hypocorrection: Mistakes in production of vernacular African American English as a second dialect. *Language and Communication* 12: 317–26.

2000. *Beyond Ebonics: Linguistic Pride and Racial Prejudice*. New York: Oxford University Press.

Bayard, Donn. 1995. Peers versus parents: A longitudinal study of rhotic–non-rhotic accommodation in an NZE-speaking child. *New Zealand English Newsletter* 9: 15–22.

BBC News. 2003. Sean Connery "has worst film accent". Accessed on 23 January 2009, from http://news.bbc.co.uk/2/hi/entertainment/3032052.stm.

Beebe, Leslie M. 1980. Sociolinguistic variation and style shifting in second language acquisition. *Language Learning* 30: 433–45.

Benson, Carol. 1994. Teaching beginning literacy in the "mother tongue": A study of the experimental Crioulo/Portuguese Primary project in Guinea-Bissau. PhD dissertation. University of California at Los Angeles.

2004. Trilingualism in Guinea-Bissau and the question of instructional language. In Charlotte Hoffmann and Jehannes Ytsma (eds.), *Trilingualism in Family, School and Community*, 166–84. Clevedon: Multilingual Matters.

Berry, Rosalind and Joyce Hudson. 1997. *Making the Jump: A Resource Book for Teachers of Aboriginal Students*. Broome: Catholic Education Office, Kimberley Region.

Berthele, Raphael. 2002. Learning a second dialect: A model of idiolectal dissonance. *Multilingua* 21: 327–44.

Best, Catherine T. 1995. A direct realist perspective on cross-language speech perception. In Strange (ed.), pp. 13–34.

Best, Catherine T. and Michael D. Tyler. 2007. Nonnative and second-language speech perception: Commonalities and complementarities. In Murry J. Munro and Ocke-Schwen Bohn (eds.), *Second Language Speech Learning: The Role of Language Experience in Speech Perception and Production*, 13–34. Amsterdam/Philadelphia: Benjamins.

Bialystok, Ellen. 1994. Representation and ways of knowing: Three issues in second language acquisition. In N. C. Ellis (ed.), pp. 549–69.

Bixler-Márquez, Dennis J. 1988. Dialects and initial reading options in bilingual education. In Dennis J. Bixler-Márquez and Jacob Ornstein-Galicia (eds.), *Chicano Speech in the Bilingual Classroom*, 135–41. New York: Peter Lang.

Bley-Vroman, Robert. 1989. What is the logical problem of foreign language learning? In Susan M. Gass and Jacquelyn Schachter (eds.), *Linguistic Perspectives on Second Language Acquisition*, 41–68. Cambridge: Cambridge University Press.

Block, David. 2007. *Second Language Identities*. London/New York: Continuum.

Blom, Jan-Petter and John J. Gumperz. 1972. Social meaning in linguistic structures: Code switching in northern Norway. In John J. Gumperz and Dell Hymes (eds.), *Directions in Sociolinguistics: The Ethnography of Communication*, 407–34. New York: Holt, Rinehart and Winston.

Blommaert, Jan. 2005. *Discourse: A Critical Introduction*. Cambridge: Cambridge University Press.

Blumenfeld, Robert. 2002. *Accents: A Manual for Actors* (revised and expanded edition). New York: Limelight.

Boggs, Stephen T. 1985. *Speaking, Relating, and Learning: A Study of Hawaiian Children at Home and at School*. Norwood, NJ: Ablex.

Bohn, Anita Perna. 2003. Familiar voices: Using Ebonics communication techniques in the primary classroom. *Urban Education* 38: 688–707.

Bongaerts, Theo, Susan Mennen and Frans van der Slik. 2000. Authenticity of pronunciation in naturalistic second language acquisition: The case of very advanced late learners of Dutch as a second language. *Studia Linguistica* 54: 298–308.

Bortoni-Ricardo, Stella Maris. 1985. *The Urbanization of Rural Dialect Speakers: A Sociolinguistic Study in Brazil*. Cambridge: Cambridge University Press.

Bourdieu, Pierre. 1991. *Language and Symbolic Power*. Cambridge: Polity.

Bowie, David. 2000. The effect of geographic mobility on the retention of a local dialect. PhD dissertation. University of Pennsylvania.

Brinton, Donna M., Olga Kagan and Susan Baukus (eds.). 2008. *Heritage Language Education: A New Field Emerging*. New York/London: Routledge.

Bull, Tove. 1990. Teaching school beginners to read and write in the vernacular. In Ernst H. Jahr and O. Lorentz (eds.), *Tromsø Linguistics in the Eighties*, 69–84. Oslo: Novus Press.

Bybee, Joan. 2001. *Phonology and Language Use*. Cambridge: Cambridge University Press.

Cahill, Rosemary. 2000. *Deadly Ways to Learn*. East Perth: Education Department of Western Australia, Catholic Education Office of Western Australia, and Association of Independent Schools of Western Australia.

Calchar, Arlene. 2004. The construction of Creole-speaking students' linguistic profile and contradictions in ESL literacy programs. *TESOL Quarterly* 38: 153–65.

2005. Creole-English speakers' treatment of tense-aspect morphology in interlanguage written discourse. *Language Learning* 55: 275–334.

Campbell, Elizabeth Dianne. 1994. *Empowerment through Bidialectalism: Encouraging Standard English in a Black English Environment*. MSc practicum report. Nova University (ERIC document no. ED 386 034).

Caribbean Examinations Council. 2007. *Annual Report 2007*. St Michael, Barbados.

Carter, Prudence L. 2003. Black cultural capital, status positioning, and schooling conflicts for low-income African American youth. *Social Problems* 50: 136–55.

Catholic Education Office (Kimberley Region). 1994. *FELIKS: Fostering English Language in Kimberley Schools*. Broome: Catholic Education Commission of Western Australia.

Cecil, Nancy Lee. 1988. Black dialect and academic success: A study of teacher expectations. *Reading Improvement* 25: 34–8.

Chambers, J. K. 1988. Acquisition of phonological variants. In Thomas (ed.), pp. 650–65.

1992. Dialect acquisition. *Language* 68: 673–705.

1995. Acquisition of lexical and pronunciation variants. In Viereck (ed.), pp. 3–19.

Chambers, J. K. and Peter Trudgill. 1980. *Dialectology*. Cambridge: Cambridge University Press.

Charity, Anne H., Hollis S. Scarborough and Darion M. Griffin. 2004. Familiarity with School English in African American children and its relation to early reading achievement. *Child Development* 75: 1340–56.

Charpentier, Jean-Michel. 1997. Literacy in a pidgin vernacular. In Andrée Tabouret-Keller, Robert B. Le Page, Penelope Gardner-Chloros and Gabrielle Varro (eds.), *Vernacular Literacy: A Re-evaluation*, 222–45. Oxford: Clarendon Press.

Cheshire, Jenny. 1982. Dialect features and linguistic conflict in schools. *Educational Review* 14: 53–67.

Cheshire, Jenny and Viv Edwards. 1998. Knowledge about language in British classrooms: Children as researchers. In Ann Egan-Robertson and David Bloome (eds.), *Students as Researchers of Culture and Language in Their Own Communities*, 191–214. Cresskill, NJ: Hampton Press.

Cheshire, Jenny and Peter Trudgill. 1989. Dialect and education in the United Kingdom. In Cheshire, Edwards, Münstermann and Weltens (eds.), pp. 94–109.

Cheshire, Jenny, Viv Edwards, Henk Münstermann and Bert Weltens (eds.). 1989. *Dialect and Education: Some European Perspectives*. Clevedon: Multilingual Matters.

Ching, Doris C. 1963. Effects of a six month remedial English program on oral, writing, and reading skills of third grade Hawaiian bilingual children. *Journal of Experimental Education* 32: 133–45.

Christie, Pauline (ed.). 2001. *Due Respect: Papers on English and English-Related Creoles in the Caribbean in Honour of Professor Robert Le Page.* Kingston: University of the West Indies Press.

2003. *Language in Jamaica.* Kingston: Arawak.

Clark, Romy, Norman Fairclough, Roz Ivanic and Marilyn Martin-Jones. 1990. Critical Language Awareness. Part I: A critical review of three current approaches to Language Awareness. *Language and Education* 4: 249–60.

1991. Critical Language Awareness. Part II: Towards critical alternatives. *Language and Education* 5: 41–54.

Clopper, Cynthia G. and David B. Pisoni. 2006. Effects of region of origin and geographic mobility on perceptual dialect categorization. *Language Variation and Change* 18: 193–221.

Clyne, Michael. 1992. Australian English in contact with other Englishes in Australia. In Rüdiger Ahrens and Heinz Antor (eds.), *Text – Culture – Reception: Cross-Cultural Aspects of English Studies*, 305–15. Heidelberg: Carl Winter.

Coelho, Elizabeth. 1988. *Caribbean Students in Canadian Schools, Book 1.* Toronto: Carib-Can.

1991. *Caribbean Students in Canadian Schools, Book 2.* Toronto: Pippin.

Conn, Jeff and Uri Horesh. 2002. Assessing the acquisition of dialect variables by migrant adults in Philadelphia: A case study. *University of Pennsylvania Working Papers in Linguistics* 8: 47–57.

Corson, David. 1991. Language, power and minority schooling. *Language and Education* 5: 231–53.

2001. *Language Diversity and Education.* Mahwah, NJ: Erlbaum.

Craig, Dennis R. 1966. Teaching English to Jamaican Creole speakers: A model of a multi-dialect situation. *Language Learning* 16: 49–61.

1967. Some early indications of learning a second dialect. *Language Learning* 17: 133–40.

1971. Education and Creole English in the West Indies: Some sociolinguistic factors. In Dell Hymes (ed.), *Pidginization and Creolization of Language*, 371–91. Cambridge: Cambridge University Press.

1977. Creole languages and primary education. In Albert Valdman (ed.), *Pidgin and Creole Linguistics*, 313–32. Bloomington: Indiana University Press.

1983. Teaching standard English to nonstandard speakers: Some methodological issues. *Journal of Negro Education* 52: 65–74.

1988. Creole English and education in Jamaica. In Christina Bratt Paulston (ed.), *International Handbook of Bilingualism and Bilingual Education*, 297–312. New York: Greenwood Press.

1999. *Teaching Language and Literacy: Policies and Procedures for Vernacular Situations.* Georgetown, Guyana: Education and Development Services.

2001. Language education revisited in the Commonwealth Caribbean. In Christie (ed.), pp. 61–76.

Craig, Holly K. and Julie A. Washington. 2004. Grade-related changes in production of African American English. *Journal of Speech, Language, and Hearing Research* 47: 450–63.

2006. *Malik Goes to School: Examining the Language Skills of African American Students from Preschool–5th Grade*. New York/London: Psychology Press.

Cross, John B., Thomas DeVaney and Gerald Jones. 2001. Pre-service teacher attitudes toward differing dialects. *Linguistics and Education* 12: 211–27.

Crowley, Dale P. 1968. The Keaukaha model for mainstream dialect instruction. *Language Learning* 18: 125–38.

Cukor-Avila, Patricia. 2000. Lingusitic diversity in the workplace: How regional accent affects employment decisions. Paper presented at the 29th Annual Conference on New Ways of Analyzing Variation (NWAV), Michigan State University.

Cullinan, Bernice E., Angela. M. Jagger and Dorothy S. Strickland. 1974. Language expansion for Black children in the primary grades: A research report. *Young Children* 24: 98–112.

Cummins, Jim. 1981. The role of primary language development in promoting educational success for language minority students. In California State Department of Education (ed.), *Schooling and Language Minority Students: A Theoretical Framework*, 3–49. Los Angeles: National Evaluation, Dissemination and Assessment Center.

1988. Second language acquisition within bilingual education programs. In L. M. Beebe (ed.), *Issues in Second Language Acquisition: Multiple Perspectives*, 145–66. New York: Newbury House.

1993. Bilingualism and second language learning. *Annual Review of Applied Linguistics* 13: 51–70.

2001. *Language, Power and Pedagogy: Bilingual Children in the Crossfire*. Clevedon: Multilingual Matters.

Cutler, Cecilia A. 1999. Yorkville crossing: White teens, hip hop and African American English. *Journal of Sociolinguistics* 3: 428–42.

Da Pidgin Coup. 1999. Pidgin and education: A position paper: University of Hawai'i (available on the web at www.hawaii.edu/sls/pidgin.html).

Davenport, Dawn Meade. 2008. The watercooler: How do they lose those accents? Accessed on 13 November 2008, from www.johnsoncitypress.com/Detail.php?Cat=ENTERTAINMENT&ID=65328.

Davidson, Cecilia and Richard G. Schwartz. 1995. Semantic boundaries in the lexicon: Examples from Jamaican patois. *Linguistics and Education* 7: 47–64.

Davies, Winifred. 2000. Language awareness amongst teachers in a central German dialect area. *Language Awareness* 9: 119–34.

Day, Richard R. 1989. The acquisition and maintenance of language by minority children. *Language Learning* 29: 295–303.

de Bot, Kees. 1992. A bilingual production model: Levelt's "Speaking" Model adapted. *Applied Linguistics* 13: 1–24.

2002. Cognitive processing in bilinguals: Language choice and code-switching. In Robert B. Kaplan (ed.), *The Oxford Handbook of Applied Linguistics*, 287–300. Oxford/New York: Oxford University Press.

de Bot, Kees and Robert Schreuder. 1993. Word production and the bilingual lexicon. In Robert Schreuder and Bert Weltens (eds.), *The Bilingual Lexicon*, 191–214. Amsterdam: Benjamins.

de Groot, Annette M. B. and Judith F. Kroll (eds.). 1997. *Tutorials in Bilingualism: Psycholinguistic Perspectives*. Mahwah, NJ: Erlbaum.

de Kleine, Christa. 2006. West African World English speakers in US classrooms: The role of West African Pidgin English. In Nero (ed.), pp. 205–32.

2009. Sierra Leonean and Liberian students in ESL programs in the US: The role of Creole English. In Kleifgen and Bond (eds.), pp. 178–98.

Decker, Ken. 2000. The use of Belize Kriol to improve English proficiency. Paper presented at the 5th International Creole Workshop, Florida International University.

Delpit, Lisa D. 1990. Language diversity and learning. In Susan Hynds and Donald L. Rubin (eds.), *Perspectives on Talk and Learning*, 247–66. Urbana, IL: National Council of Teachers of English.

Delpit, Lisa D. and Joanne Kilgour Dowdy (eds.). 2002. *The Skin That We Speak: Thoughts on Language and Culture in the Classroom*. New York: New Press.

Devonish, Hubert S. and Karen Carpenter. 2007. *Full Bilingual Education in a Creole Language Situation: The Jamaican Bilingual Primary Education Project*. St Augustine, Trinidad & Tobago: Society for Caribbean Linguistics (Occasional Paper No. 35).

Di Pietro, Robert J. 1973. Bilingualism and bidialectalism. In Fox (ed.), pp. 35–42.

Dörnyei, Zoltán. 2005. *The Psychology of the Language Learner: Individual Differences in Second Language Learning*. Mahwah, NJ: Erlbaum.

2009. The L2 Motivational Self System. In Zoltán Dörnyei (ed.), *Motivation, Language Identity and the L2 Self*, 9–42. Bristol: Multilingual Matters.

Dörnyei, Zoltán and Peter Skehan. 2003. Individual differences in second language learning. In Doughty and Long (eds.), pp. 589–630.

Doughty, Catherine J. 2001. Cognitive underpinnings of focus on form. In Peter Robinson (ed.), *Cognition and SLA*, 206–57. Cambridge: Cambridge University Press.

Doughty, Catherine J. and Michael H. Long (eds.). 2003. *The Handbook of Second Language Acquisition*. Oxford: Blackwell.

Doughty, Catherine J. and Jessica Williams (eds.). 1998. *Focus on Form in Classroom Second Language Acquisition*. Cambridge: Cambridge University Press.

Dulay, Heidi and Marina Burt. 1973. Should we teach children syntax? *Language Learning* 23: 245–58.

Dyer, Judith. 2004. Using metalinguistic comments to investigate a bilingual 6-year-old's acquisition of a second English dialect. Paper presented at the 33rd Conference on New Ways of Analyzing Variation (NWAV), University of Michigan.

Eades, Diana. 2007. Recontextualisation and the inconsistency of inconsistency in the legal process. Paper presented at the Annual Conference of the Australian Linguistics Society, University of Adelaide.

Eades, Diana, Suzie Jacobs, Ermile Hargrove and Terri Menacker. 2006. Pidgin, local identity, and schooling in Hawai'i. In Nero (ed.), pp. 149–63.

Edwards, John and Howard Giles. 1984. Applications of the social psychology of language: Sociolinguistics and education. In Peter Trudgill (ed.), *Applied Sociolinguistics*, 119–58. London: Academic Press.

Edwards, Viv. 1979. *The West Indian Language Issue in British Schools: Challenges and Responses*. London: Routledge and Kegan Paul.

Ellis, Nick C. (ed.). 1994. *Implicit and Explicit Learning of Languages*. London: Academic Press.

Ellis, Rod. 1994. A theory of instructed second language acquisition. In N. C. Ellis (ed.), pp. 79–114.

   2008. *The Study of Second Language Acquisition* (2nd edition). Oxford: Oxford University Press.

Elsasser, Nan and Patricia Irvine. 1987. English and Creole: The dialectics of choice in a college writing program. In Ira Shor (ed.), *Freire for the Classroom: A Sourcebook for Literacy Teaching*, 129–49. Portsmouth, MA: Boynton/Cook.

Epstein, Ruth I. and Lily X. J. Xu. 2003. Roots and wings: Teaching English as a second dialect to Aboriginal students. Accessed on 23 October 2004, from www. extension.usask.ca/ExtensionDivision/about/Staff/e-h/epsteinvitea.htm.

Epstein, Seymour. 1981. The Unity Principle versus the Reality and Pleasure Principles, *Or* The tale of the scorpion and the frog. In Mervin D. Lynch, Ardyth A. Norem-Hebeisen and Kenneth J. Gergen (eds.), *Self-Concept: Advances in Theory and Research*, 27–37. Cambridge, MA: Ballinger.

Erickson, Rebecca. 1995. The importance of authenticity for self and society. *Symbolic Interaction* 18: 121–44.

Escure, Genevieve. 1997. *Creole and Dialect Continua: Standard Acquisition Processes in Belize and China*. Amsterdam: Benjamins.

Evans, Betsy E. 2002. An acoustic and perceptual analysis of imitation. In Long and Preston (eds.), pp. 95–112.

Fairchild, Halford H. and Stephanie Edwards-Evans. 1990. African American dialects and schooling: A review. In Amado M. Padilla, Halford H. Fairchild and Concepcion M. Valadez (eds.), *Bilingual Education: Issues and Strategies*, 75–86. New York: Sage.

Fairclough, Marta. 2005. *Spanish and Heritage Language Education in the United States: Struggling with Hypotheticals*. Madrid/Frankfurt: Iberoamericana/Vervuert.

Fairclough, Norman. 1989. *Language and Power*. London: Longman.

   1992a. Introduction. In Fairclough (ed.), pp. 1–29.

   1992b. The appropriacy of "appropriateness". In Fairclough (ed.), pp. 33–56.

   (ed.). 1992c. *Critical Language Awareness*. London/New York: Longman.

Feldman, Carol Fleisher, C. Addison Stone and Bobbi Renderer. 1990. Stage, transfer, and academic achievement in dialect-speaking Hawaiian adolescents. *Child Development* 61: 472–84.

Feldman, Carol Fleisher, C. Addison Stone, James V. Wertsch and Michael Strizich. 1977. Standard and nonstandard dialect competencies of Hawaiian Creole English speakers. *TESOL Quarterly* 11: 41–50.

Ferguson, Charles A. 1959. Diglossia. *Word* 15: 325–40.

Fischer, Katherine. 1992a. Educating speakers of Caribbean English in the United States. In Siegel (ed.), pp. 99–123.

   1992b. Report. *Pidgins and Creoles in Education (PACE) Newsletter* 3: 1.

Fishman, Joshua A. and E. Lueders-Salmon. 1972. What has the sociology of language to say to the teacher? On teaching the standard variety to speakers of dialectal or sociolectal varieties. In Courtney B. Cazden, Vera P. John and Dell Hymes (eds.), *Functions of Language in the Classroom*, 67–83. New York: Teachers College, Colombia University.

Flege, James Emil. 1987. The production of "new" and "similar" phones in a foreign language: Evidence for the effect of equivalence classification. *Journal of Phonetics* 15: 47–65.

    1995. Second language speech learning: Theory, findings, and problems. In Strange (ed.), pp. 233–77.

    2003. Assessing constraints on second-language segmental production and perception. In Niels Olaf Schiller and Antje S. Meyer (eds.), *Phonetics and Phonology in Language Comprehension and Production: Differences and Similarities*, 319–55. Berlin: Mouton de Gruyter.

Fogel, Howard and Linnea C. Ehri. 2000. Teaching elementary students who speak Black English Vernacular to write in Standard English: Effects of dialect transformation practice. *Contemporary Educational Psychology* 25: 212–35.

Fordham, Signithia. 1988. Racelessness as a factor in Black students' school success: Pragmatic strategy or Pyrrhic victory? *Harvard Educational Review* 58: 54–84.

    1998. Speaking standard English from nine to three: Language as guerrilla warfare at Capital High. In Susan Hoyle and Carol Temple Adger (eds.), *Kids Talk: Strategic Language Use in Later Childhood*, 205–16. New York: Oxford University Press.

    1999. Dissin "the standard": Ebonics as guerrilla warfare at Capital High. *Anthropology and Education Quarterly* 30: 272–93.

Fordham, Signithia and John U. Ogbu. 1986. Black students' school success: Coping with the "burden of 'acting white'". *Urban Review* 18: 176–206.

Foreman, Annik. 2000. A longitudinal study of Americans in Australia. In Keith Allen and John Henderson (eds.), *Proceedings of ALS2K, the 2000 Conference of the Australian Linguistics Society*, www.als.asn.au/proceedings/als2000/foreman.pdf.

    2003. Pretending to be someone you're not: A study of second dialect acquisition in Australia. PhD thesis. Monash University.

Fox, Robert P. (ed.). 1973. *Essays on Teaching English as a Second Language and as a Second Dialect*. Urbana, IL: National Council of Teachers of English.

Freire, Paulo. 1985. *The Politics of Education: Culture, Power, and Liberation*. South Hadley, MA: Bergin and Garvey.

García, Ofilia. 1997. Bilingual education. In Florian Coulmas (ed.), *The Handbook of Sociolinguistics*, 405–20. Oxford: Blackwell.

Gardner, Robert C. 1985. *Social Psychology and Second Language Learning: The Role of Attitudes and Motivation*. London: Edward Arnold.

Gardner, Robert C. and P.C. Smythe. 1981. On the development of the Attitude/Motivation Test Battery. *Canadian Modern Language Review* 37: 510–25.

Gass, Susan M. and Larry Selinker. 2008. *Second Language Acquisition: An Introductory Course* (3rd edition). New York/London: Routledge.

Gecas, Viktor and Peter Burke. 1995. Self and identity. In Karen S. Cook, Gary Alan Fine and James S. House (eds.), *Sociological Perspectives on Social Psychology*, 41–67. Boston: Allyn and Bacon.

Geiger, Susan Lee and Bonita Renée Greenberg. 1976. The Black child's ability to discriminate dialect differences: Implications for dialect language programs. *Language, Speech, and Hearing Services in Schools* 7: 28–32.

Giacalone-Ramat, Anna. 1995. Code-switching in the context of dialect/standard relations. In Leslie Milroy and Pieter Muysken (eds.), *One Speaker, Two Languages: Cross-Disciplinary Perspectives on Code-Switching*, 45–67. Cambridge: Cambridge University Press.

Giesbers, Herman. 1989. *Code-switching tussen Dialect en Standaardtaal*. Amsterdam: P. J. Meertens-Instituut voor Dialectologie, Volkskunde en Naamkunde.

Gilbert, Matthew. 2008. Grading American accents. Accessed on 13 November 2008, from www.boston.com/ae/tv/blog/2008/11/_television_is.html.

Giles, Howard and Philip M. Smith. 1979. Accommodation theory: Optimal levels of convergence. In Howard Giles and Robert St Clair (eds.), *Language and Social Psychology*, 45–65. Oxford: Blackwell.

Giles, Howard, Nicholas Coupland and Justine Coupland. 1991. Accommodation theory: Communication, context, and consequence. In Howard Giles, Justine Coupland and Nicholas Coupland (eds.), *Contexts of Accommodation: Developments in Applied Sociolinguistics*, 1–68. Cambridge: Cambridge University Press.

Giles, Howard, D. Taylor and R. Bourhis. 1973. Towards a theory of interpersonal accommodation through speech: Some Canadian data. *Language in Society* 2: 177–92.

Gilles, Peter. 1999. *Dialektausgleich im Lëtzebuergeschen: Zur phonetisch-phonologischen Fokussierung einer Nationalsprache*. Tübingen: Niemeyer.

Giroux, Henry A. 1988. *Schooling and the Struggle for Public Life: Critical Pedagogy in the Modern Age*. Minneapolis: University of Minnesota Press.

2001. *Theory and Resistance in Education: Toward a Pedagogy for the Opposition*. Westport, CN: Bergin and Garvey.

Goodman, Kenneth. S. 1969. Dialect barriers to reading comprehension. In Baratz and Shuy (eds.), pp. 14–28.

Govardhan, Anam K. 2006. Indian versus American students' writing in English. In Nero (ed.), pp. 235–59.

Gramsci, Antonio. (1971[1948]). *Selections from the Prison Notebooks of Antonio Gramsci* (ed. and trans. Quentin Hoare and Geoffrey N. Smith). London: Lawrence and Wishart.

Granger, Robert C., Marilyn Mathews, Lorene C. Quay and Rochelle Verner. 1977. Teacher judgements of the communication effectiveness of children using different speech patterns. *Journal of Educational Psychology* 69: 793–6.

Green, Lisa J. 2002. *African American English: A Linguistic Introduction*. Cambridge: Cambridge University Press.

Grosjean, Francois. 1997. Processing mixed languages: Issues, findings, and models. In de Groot and Kroll (eds.), pp. 225–54.

Gupta, Anthea Fraser. 1991. Acquisition of diglossia in Singapore English. In Anna Kwan-Terry (ed.), *Child Language Development in Singapore and Malaysia*, 119–45. Singapore: Singapore University Press.

1994. *The Step-Tongue: Children's English in Singapore.* Clevedon: Multilingual Matters.

Haeri, Niloofar. 2003. *Sacred Language, Ordinary People: Dilemmas of Culture and Politics in Egypt.* New York: Palgrave Macmillan.

Hagerman, Barbara P. 1970. *Teaching Standard English as a Second Dialect to Speakers of Nonstandard English in High School Business Education: Final Report.* Washington, DC: Department of Health, Education and Welfare, Office of Education, Bureau of Research.

Hakuta, Kenji, Ellen Bialystok and Edward Wiley. 2003. Critical evidence: A test of the Critical-Period Hypothesis for second-language acquisition. *Psychological Science* 14: 31–8.

Han, ZhaoHong and Larry Selinker. 2005. Fossilization in L2 learners. In Hinkel (ed.), pp. 455–83.

Hargrove, Ermile and Kent Sakoda. 1999. The hegemony of English or Hau kam yu wen kawl wat ai spik ingglish wen yu no no waz. *Bamboo Ridge* 75: 48–70.

Harris-Wright, Kelli. 1987. The challenge of educational coalescence: Teaching nonmainstream English-speaking students. *Journal of Childhood Communication Disorders* 11: 209–15.

1999. Enhancing bidialectalism in urban African American students. In Adger, Christian and Taylor (eds.), pp. 53–60.

Haugen, E. 1964. Bilingualism and bidialectalism. In Shuy, Davis and Hogan (eds.), pp. 123–6.

Hawkins, Eric. 1984. *Awareness of Language: An Introduction.* Cambridge: Cambridge University Press.

Heit, Mary and Heather Blair. 1993. Language needs and characteristics of Saskatchewan Indian and Metis students: Implications for educators. In Sonia Morris, Keith McLeod and Marcel Danesi (eds.), *Aboriginal Languages and Education: The Canadian Experience*, 103–28. Oakville, ONT: Mosaic Press.

Hill, Jane H. 1999. Styling locally, styling globally: What does it mean? *Journal of Sociolinguistics* 3: 542–56.

Hinkel, Eli (ed.). 2005. *Handbook of Research in Second Language Teaching and Learning.* Mahwah, NJ: Erlbaum.

Hinskens, Frans. 1996. *Dialect Levelling in Limburg: Structural and Sociolinguistic Aspects.* Tübingen: Niemeyer.

Hinskens, Frans, Peter Auer and Paul Kerswill. 2005. The study of dialect convergence and divergence: Conceptual and methodological considerations. In Auer, Hinskens and Kerswill (eds.), pp. 1–48.

Hiramoto, Mie. In press. Dialect contact and change in the northern Japanese plantation immigrants in Hawai'i. *Journal of Pidgin and Creole Languages* 25.

Hollie, Sharroky. 2001. Acknowledging the language of African American students: Instructional strategies. *English Journal* 90: 54–9.

Holmes, Janet. 1995. A quite interesting article about linguistics. *Campus Review* 5, 49: 13.

Hoover, Mary Rhodes. 1991. Using the ethnography of African-American communication in teaching composition to bidialectal students. In Mary E. McGroarty and Christian J. Faltis (eds.), *Languages in School and Society: Policy and Pedagogy*, 465–85. Berlin: Mouton de Gruyter.

Horvat, Erin McNamara and Kristine S. Lewis. 2003. Reassessing the "burden of 'acting white' ": The importance of peer groups in managing academic success. *Sociology of Education* 76: 265–80.

Howe, Kate. 1993. Haitian Creole as the official language in education and the media. In Francis Byrne and John Holm (eds.), *Atlantic Meets Pacific: A Global View of Pidginization and Creolization*, 291–8. Amsterdam: Benjamins.

Hudson, Joyce. 1983. *Grammatical and Semantic Aspects of Fitzroy Valley Kriol.* Darwin: Work Papers of SIL-AAB A/8.

    1984. Kriol or English: An unanswered question in the Kimberleys. Paper presented at the 54th ANZAAS Conference, Canberra.

Hunter, Melanie. 2005. Black conservative group blast Ebonics plan for California schools. CNSNews.com. Accessed on 20 July 2005, from www.cnsnews.com/news/viewstory.asp?Page=%5CCulture%5Carchive%5C200507%5CCUL20050 720b.html.

Hutaff, Matt. 2005. Ebonics as education? Fo' shizzle! *Simon*, 19 July.

Hyltenstam, Kenneth and Niclas Abrahamsson. 2003. Maturational constraints in SLA. In Doughty and Long (eds.), pp. 539–88.

Ibrahim, Muhammad H. 1983. Linguistic distance and literacy in Arabic. *Journal of Pragmatics* 7: 507–15.

ILEA Afro-Caribbean Language and Literacy Project in Further and Adult Education. 1990. *Language and Power*. London: Harcourt Brace Jovanovich.

Ioup, Georgette. 2005. Age in second language development. In Hinkel (ed.), pp. 419–54.

Ioup, Georgette, Elizabeth Boustagui, Manal El Tigi and Martha Moselle. 1994. Reexamining the Critical Period Hypothesis. *Studies in Second Language Acquisition* 16: 73–98.

Irvine, Alison. 2008. Contrast and convergence in Standard Jamaican English: The phonological architecture of the standard in an ideologically bidialectal community. *World Englishes* 27: 9–25.

Irvine, Jacqueline Jordan. 1990. *Black Students and School Failure: Policies, Practices and Prescriptions*. New York: Greenwood Press.

Isaacs, Gale J. 1996. Persistence of non-standard dialect in school-age children. *Journal of Speech and Hearing Research* 39: 434–41.

Ivars, Ann-Marie. 1994. Bidialectalism and identity. In Nordberg (ed.), pp. 203–22.

Jacobs-Huey, Lanita. 1997. Is there an authentic African American speech community? Carla revisited. *University of Pennsylvania Working Papers in Linguistics* 4: 331–70.

James, Carl. 1992. Awareness, consciousness and language contrast. In Christian Mair and Manfred Markus (eds.), *New Departures in Contrastive Linguistics. Volume 2*, 183–98. Innsbruck: Institüt für Anglistik, Universität Innsbruck.

    1996. Mother tongue use in bilingual/bidialectal education: Implications for Bruneian Dwibahasa. *Journal of Multilingual and Multicultural Development* 17: 248–57.

James, Carl and Peter Garrett (eds.). 1991. *Language Awareness in the Classroom*. London: Longman.

Johnson, Jacqueline S. and Elissa L. Newport. 1989. Critical period effects in second language learning: The influence of maturational state on the acquisition of English as a second language. *Cognitive Psychology* 21: 60–99.

Johnson, Kenneth R. 1974. Teacher's attitude toward the nonstandard Negro dialect – Let's change it. In Johanna S. DeStefano and Sharon E. Fox (eds.), *Language and the Language Arts*, 148–58. Boston: Little, Brown.

Johnstone, Barbara. 1999. Use of Southern-sounding speech by contemporary Texas women. *Journal of Sociolinguistics* 3: 505–22.

Jones, Ken. 2001. A disfigurement of speech. *Jamaica Gleaner*, 25 September.

Kaldor, Susan and Ian G. Malcolm. 1991. Aboriginal English: An overview. In Suzanne Romaine (ed.), *Language in Australia*, 67–83. Cambridge: Cambridge University Press.

Kaldor, Susan, Richard D. Eagleson and Ian G. Malcolm. 1982. The teacher's task. In Richard D. Eagleson, Susan Kaldor and Ian G. Malcolm (eds.), *English and the Aboriginal Child*, 193–217. Canberra: Curriculum Development Centre.

Kellerman, Eric. 1977. Towards a characterization of the strategies of transfer in second language learning. *Interlanguage Studies Bulletin* 2: 58–145.

Kephart, Ronald F. 1992. Reading creole English does not destroy your brain cells! In Siegel (ed.), pp. 67–86.

Kerswill, Paul. 1994. *Dialects Converging: Rural Speech in Urban Norway*. Oxford: Clarendon Press.

2002. Koineization and accommodation. In J.K. Chambers, Peter Trudgill and Natalie Schilling-Estes (eds.), *The Handbook of Language Variation and Change*, 669–702. Oxford: Blackwell.

Kerswill, Paul and Peter Trudgill. 2005. The birth of new dialects. In Auer, Hinskens and Kerswill (eds.), pp. 196–220.

Kerswill, Paul and Ann Williams. 2002. "Salience" as an explanatory factor in language change: Evidence from dialect levelling in urban England. In Mari C. Jones and Edith Esch (eds.), *Language Change: The Interplay of Internal, External and Extra-Linguistic Factors*, 81–110. Berlin/New York: Mouton de Gruyter.

Kinginger, Celeste. 2004. Alice doesn't live here any more: Foreign language learning and identity construction. In Pavlenko and Blackledge (eds.), pp. 219–42.

Kirkpatrick, Andy. 2007. *World Englishes: Implications for International Communication and English Language Teaching*. Cambridge: Cambridge University Press.

Kleifgen, Jo Anne and George C. Bond (eds.). 2009. *The Languages of Africa and Diaspora: Educating for Language Awareness*. Bristol: Multilingual Matters.

Kobayashi, Chieko. 1981. Dialectal variation in child language. In Philip S. Dale and David Ingram (eds.), *Child Language: An International Perspective*. Baltimore: University Park Press.

Labov, William. 1966. *Social Stratification of English in New York City*. Washington, DC: Center for Applied Linguistics.

1972. *Sociolinguistic Patterns*. Philadelphia: University of Pennsylvania Press.

1995. Can reading failure be reversed? A linguistic approach to the question. In V.L. Gadsden and Daniel A. Wagner (eds.), *Literacy among African-American Youth*, 39–68. Cresskill, NJ: Hampton Press.

2001. *Principles of Linguistic Change. Volume 2: Social Factors*. Oxford: Blackwell.

2006. *Spotlight on Reading*. Accessed on 19 March 2009, from www.ling.upenn.edu/~wlabov/Spotlight.html.

2007. Transmission and diffusion. *Language* 83: 344–87.

Labov, William and Bettina Baker. 2006. *The Penn Reading Initiative on the Reading Road*. Accessed on 19 March 2009, from www.ling.upenn.edu/~wlabov/PRI/index.html.

Lacoste, Véronique. 2007. Modelling the sounds of Standard Jamaican English in a Grade 2 classroom. *Caribbean Journal of Education* 29: 290–326.

2009. Learning the sounds of Standard Jamaican English: Variationist, phonological and pedagogical perspectives on 7-year-old children's classroom speech. PhD dissertation (completed 2008). University of Essex and Université Paul Valery, France. UMI/ProQuest Dissertations Database.

Lado, Robert. 1957. *Linguistics Across Cultures: Applied Linguistics for Language Teachers*. Ann Arbor: University of Michigan.

Ladson-Billings, Gloria. 1992. Liberatory consequences of literacy: A case of culturally relevant instruction for African American students. *Journal of Negro Education* 61: 378–91.

1995. But that's just good teaching! The case for culturally relevant pedagogy. *Theory into Practice* 14: 159–65.

Laffey, James L. and Roger W. Shuy (eds.). 1973. *Language Differences: Do They Interfere?* Newark, DE: International Reading Association.

Lakoff, George and Mark Johnson. 1999. *Philosophy in the Flesh: The Embodied Mind and Its Challenge to Western Thought*. New York: Basic Books.

Lanehart, Sonia L. 1998. African American Vernacular English and education. *Journal of English Linguistics* 26: 122–36.

Larsen-Freeman, Dianne and Michael H. Long. 1991. *An Introduction to Second Language Acquisition Research*. London: Longman.

Lawton, David. 1964. Some problems of teaching a creolized language to Peace Corps volunteers. *Language Learning* 14: 11–19.

Le Page, Robert B. 1968. Problems to be faced in the use of English as the medium of education in four West Indian territories. In Joshua Fishman, Charles Ferguson and Jyotirendra Das Gupta (eds.), *Language Problems of Developing Nations*, 431–42. New York: John Wiley.

Le Page, Robert B. and Andrée Tabouret-Keller. 1985. *Acts of Identity: Creole-Based Approaches to Language and Identity*. Cambridge: Cambridge University Press.

Leap, William L. 1993. *American Indian English*. Salt Lake City: University of Utah Press.

Leaverton, Lloyd. 1973. Dialectal readers: Rationale, use and value. In Laffey and Shuy (eds.), pp. 114–26.

Lecky, Prescott. 1961. *Self-Consistency, A Theory of Personality* (ed. and interpreted Frederick C. Thorne). Hamden, CN: Shoe String Press.

Lee, Jihyun, Wendy S. Grigg and Gloria S. Dion. 2007. *The Nation's Report Card: Mathematics 2007* (NCES 2007–494). Washington, DC: Institute of Education Sciences, US Department of Education.

Lee, Jihyun, Wendy S. Grigg and Patricia L. Donahue. 2007. *The Nation's Report Card: Reading 2007* (NCES 2007–496). Washington, DC: Institute of Education Sciences, US Department of Education.

LeMoine, Noma. 2001. Language variation and literacy acquisition in African American students. In Joyce L. Harris, Alan G. Kamhi and Karen E. Pollock (eds.), *Literacy in African American Communities*, 169–94. Mahwah, NJ: Erlbaum.

Lemus, Irma. 2005. Ebonics suggested for district. *San Bernardino County Sun*, 17 July.

Lenneberg, Eric. 1967. *Biological Foundations of Language*. New York: John Wiley.

Leong, Susan. 2000. Attitudes toward Hawai'i Creole English: An interpretive qualitative study. Scholarly paper. Department of Second Language Studies, University of Hawai'i.

Levelt, Willem J. M. 1989. *Speaking: From Intention to Articulation*. Cambridge, MA: MIT Press.

2001. Spoken word production: A theory of lexical access. *Proceedings of the National Academy of Sciences* 98: 13464–71.

Lightbown, Patsy M. and Nina Spada. 2006. *How Languages are Learned* (3rd edition). Oxford: Oxford University Press.

Lin, San-su Chen. 1965. *Pattern Practice in the Teaching of Standard English to Students with a Non-Standard Dialect*. New York: Teachers College (Columbia University).

Lippi-Green, Rosina. 1994. Accent, standard language ideology, and discriminatory pretext in the courts. *Language in Society* 23: 163–98.

1997. *English with an Accent: Language, Ideology, and Discrimination in the United States*. London: Routledge.

Lo Bianco, Joseph. 1987. *National Policy on Languages*. Canberra: Australian Government.

Long, Daniel and Dennis R. Preston (eds.). 2002. *Handbook of Perceptual Dialectology*. Volume 2. Amsterdam/Philadelphia: Benjamins.

Long, Michael H. 1990. Maturational constraints on language development. *Studies in Second Language Acquisition* 12: 251–85.

2003. Stabilization and fossilization in interlanguage development. In Doughty and Long (eds.), pp. 487–535.

2007. *Problems in SLA*. New York/London: Erlbaum.

Los Angeles Unified School District and Noma LeMoine. 1999. *English for Your Success: Handbook of Successful Strategies for Educators*. Maywood, NJ: Peoples Publishing.

Maamouri, Mohamed. 1998. Language education and human development: Arabic diglossia and its impact on the quality of education in the Arab region. Discussion paper prepared for the World Bank. Philadelphia: International Literacy Institute, University of Pennsylvania.

Mackey, William F. 1978. The importation of bilingual education models. In James E. Alatis (ed.), *International Dimensions of Bilingual Education*, 1–18. Washington, DC: Georgetown University Press.

Maddahian, Ebrahim and Ambition Padi Sandamela. 2000. Academic English Mastery Program: 1998 Report. Program Evaluation and Research Branch, Research and Evaluation Unit, Los Angeles Unified School District.

Major, Roy C. 2001. *Foreign Accent: The Ontogeny and Phylogeny of Second Language Phonology*. Mahwah, NJ: Erlbaum.

Malcolm, Ian G. 1982. Verbal interaction in the classroom. In Robert D. Eagleson, Susan Kaldor and Ian G. Malcolm (eds.), *English and the Aboriginal Child*, 165–92. Canberra: Curriculum Development Centre.

1992. English in the education of speakers of Aboriginal English. In Siegel (ed.), pp. 14–41.

1995. *Language and Communication Enhancement for Two-Way Education: Report*. Perth: Edith Cowan University.

2007. Cultural linguistics and bidialectal education. In Farzad Sharifian and Gary B. Palmer (eds.), *Applied Cultural Linguistics*, 53–63. Amsterdam/Philadelphia: Benjamins.

Malcolm, Ian G. and Patricia Königsberg. 2007. Bridging the language gap in education. In Gerhard Leitner and Ian G. Malcolm (eds.), *The Habitat of Australia's Aboriginal Languages: Past, Present and Future*, 267–97. Berlin/New York: Mouton de Gruyter.

Malcolm, Ian G. and Farzad Sharifian. 2005. Something old, something new, something borrowed, something blue: Australian Aboriginal students' schematic repertoire. *Journal of Multilingual and Multicultural Development* 26: 512–32.

Malcolm, Ian G., Yvonne Haig, Patricia Königsberg, Judith Rochecouste, Glenys Collard, Allison Hill and Rosemary Cahill. 1999. *Two-Way English: Towards More User-Friendly Education for Speakers of Aboriginal English*. Perth: Centre for Applied Language and Literacy Research, Edith Cowan University and Education Department of Western Australia.

Markham, Duncan. 1997. *Phonetic Imitation, Accent, and the Learner*. Lund: Lund University Press (Traveaux de l'Institut de Linguistique de Lund 33).

Markley, Dianne. 2000. Regional accent discrimination in the hiring process. MA dissertation. University of North Texas.

Martínez, Glenn A. 2003. Classroom based dialect-awareness in heritage language instruction: A critical applied linguistic approach. *Heritage Language Journal* 1. www.heritagelanguages.org.

Masgoret, Anne-Marie and R. C. Gardner. 2003. Attitudes, motivation and second language learning: A meta-analysis of studies conducted by Gardner and associates. *Language Learning* 53: 123–63.

Mason-Schrock, Douglas. 1996. Transsexuals' narrative construction of the "true self". *Social Psychology Quarterly* 59: 176–92.

Matras, Yaron. 1998. Utterance modifiers and universals of grammatical borrowing. *Linguistics* 36: 281–331.

McCourtie, Lena. 1998. The politics of Creole language education in Jamaica: 1891–1921 and the 1990s. *Journal of Multilingual and Multicultural Development* 19: 108–27.

McKenry, Rosemary. 1996. *Deadly Eh, Cuz! Teaching Speakers of Koorie English*. Melbourne: Language Australia.

McWhorter, John H. 1998. *The Word on the Street: Fact and Fable about American English*. London: Plenum Press.

Meier, Paul. 1999. IDEA: An online database of accent and dialect resources. *VASTA Newsletter* 13/2. Accessed on 8 August 2005, from www.vasta.org/newsletter/99/summer06.html.

2004. *The Standard British English Dialect (Received Pronunciation)* (4th edition). McLouth, KS: Paul Meier Dialect Services.

Menacker, Terri. 1998. A visit to CAP. *Pidgins and Creoles in Education (PACE) Newsletter* 9: 3–4.

Mesthrie, Rajend and Rakesh M. Bhatt. 2008. *World Englishes: The Study of New Linguistic Varieties*. Cambridge: Cambridge University Press.

Meyerhoff, Miriam. 1998. Accommodating your data: The use and misuse of accommodation theory in sociolinguistics. *Language and Communication* 18: 205–25.

Milroy, Lesley. 1987. *Language and Social Networks* (2nd edition). Oxford: Blackwell.

Mitchell, A. G. and Arthur Delbridge. 1965. *The Pronunciation of English in Australia* (revised edition). Sydney: Angus and Robertson.

Molin, Donald H. 1984. *Actor's Encyclopedia of Dialects*. New York: Sterling.

Moore, Bruce. 2008. *Speaking Our Language: The Story of Australian English*. South Melbourne: Oxford University Press.

Morren, Ronald C. 2001. Creole-based trilingual education in the Caribbean archipelago of San Andres, Providence and Santa Catalina. *Journal of Multilingual and Multicultural Development* 22: 227–41.

2004. Linguistic results of a Creole reading inventory. Paper presented at the Conference of the Society for Caribbean Linguistics and the Society for Pidgin and Creole Linguistics, Curaçao.

Munro, Murray J., Tracey M. Derwing and James E. Flege. 1999. Canadians in Alabama: A perceptual study of dialect acquisition in adults. *Journal of Phonetics* 27: 385–403.

Murrell, Peter C., Jr. 1997. Digging again the family wells: A Freirian literacy framework as emancipatory pedagogy for African-American children. In Paulo Freire (ed.), *Mentoring the Mentor: A Critical Dialogue with Paulo Freire*, 19–58. New York: Peter Lang.

Murtagh, Edward J. 1982. Creole and English as languages of instruction in bilingual education with Aboriginal Australians: Some research findings. *International Journal of the Sociology of Language* 36: 15–33.

Nelson, Sean. 2007. Accent-uate the negative: With a nod to Russell Crowe, the 10 all time worst movie accents. Accessed on 23 January 2009, from http://movies.msm.com/movies/2007/fallmoviewguide/badaccents.

Nero, Shondel J. 1997. English is my native language ... or so I believe. *TESOL Quarterly* 31: 585–92.

2001. *Englishes in Contact: Anglophone Caribbean Students in an Urban College*. Cresskill, NJ: Hampton Press.

(ed.). 2006. *Dialects, Englishes, Creoles, and Education*. Mahwah, NJ: Erlbaum.

Nordberg, Bengt (ed.). 1994. *The Sociolinguistics of Urbanization: The Case of the Nordic Countries*. Berlin/New York: Walter de Gruyter.

Nuolijärvi, Pirkko. 1994. On the interlinkage of sociolinguistic background variables. In Nordberg (ed.), pp. 149–70.

Ogbu, John U. 1978. *Minority Education and Caste: The American System in Cross-cultural Perspective*. New York: Academic Press.

1991. Minority coping responses and school experience. *Journal of Psychohistory* 18: 433–56.

Omdal, Helge. 1994. From the valley to the city: Language modification and language attitudes. In Nordberg (ed.), pp. 116–48.

Österberg, Tore. 1961. *Bilingualism and the First School Language: An Educational Problem Illustrated by Results from a Swedish Language Area*. Umeå: Västernbottens Tryckeri.

Palacas, Arthur L. 2001. Liberating American Ebonics from Euro-English. *College English* 63: 326–52.

Pandey, Anita. 2000. TOEFL to the test: Are monodialectal AAL-speakers similar to ESL students? *World Englishes* 19: 89–106.

Papapavlou, Andreas. 2007. Language policy and planning: The role of language attitudes in decision making. In Papapavlou and Pavlou (eds.), pp. 194–215.

Papapavlou, Andreas and Pavlos Pavlou. 2007a. The interplay of bidialectalism, literacy and educational policy. In Papapavlou and Pavlou (eds.), pp. 101–21.

(eds.). 2007b. *Sociolinguistic and Pedgogical Dimensions of Dialects and Education*. Newcastle: Cambridge Scholars.

Paradis, Michel. 1994. Neurolinguistic aspects of implicit and explicit memory: Implications for bilingualism and SLA. In N. C. Ellis (ed.), pp. 393–419.

1997. The cognitive neuropsychology of bilingualism. In de Groot and Kroll (eds.), pp. 331–54.

2004. *A Neurolinguistic Theory of Bilingualism*. Amsterdam/Philadelphia: Benjamins.

Pardo, Jennifer S. 2006. On phonetic convergence during conversational interaction. *Journal of the Acoustical Society of America* 119: 2382–93.

Parodi, Claudia. 2008. Stigmatized Spanish inside the classroom and out. In Brinton, Kagan and Baukus (eds.), pp. 199–214.

Partington, Gary and Ann Galloway. 2007. Issues and policies in school education. In Gerhard Leitner and Ian G. Malcolm (eds.), *The Habitat of Australia's Aboriginal Languages: Past, Present and Future*, 237–66. Berlin/New York: Mouton de Gruyter.

Pavlenko, Aneta and Adrian Blackledge. 2004a. Introduction: New theoretical approaches to the study of negotiation of identities in multilingual contexts. In Pavlenko and Blackledge (eds.), pp. 1–33.

(ed.). 2004b. *Negotiation of Identities in Multilingual Contexts*. Clevedon: Multilingual Matters.

Pavlou, Pavlos and Andreas Papapavlou. 2004. Issues of dialect use in education from the Greek Cypriot perspective. *International Journal of Applied Linguistics* 14: 243–58.

Payne, Arvilla C. 1976. The acquisition of the phonological system of a second dialect. PhD dissertation. University of Pennsylvania.

1980. Factors controlling the acquisition of the Philadelphia dialect by out-of-state children. In William Labov (ed.), *Locating Language in Time and Space*, 143–78. New York: Academic Press.

Pennycook, Alastair. 1999. Introduction: Critical approaches to TESOL. *TESOL Quarterly* 33: 329–48.

2001. *Critical Applied Linguistics: A Critical Introduction*. Mahwah, NJ: Erlbaum.

Peterson, Robert O., Harry C. Chuck and Arthur P. Coladarci. 1969. *Teaching Standard English as a Second Dialect to Primary School Children in Hilo, Hawaii*. Final Report, Volume 1. Washington, DC: US Department of Health, Education, and Welfare, Office of Education, Bureau of Research.

Pierrehumbert, Janet B. 2003. Phonetic diversity, statistical learning, and acquisition of phonology. *Language and Speech* 46: 115–54.

Piestrup, Ann McCormick. 1973. *Black Dialect Interference and Accommodation of Reading Instruction in First Grade*. Berkeley: University of California (Monographs of the Language-Behavior Research Laboratory no. 4).

Politzer, Robert Louis. 1973. Problems in applying foreign language teaching methods to the teaching of standard English as a second dialect. In Johanna S. DeStefano (ed.), *Language, Society, and Education: A Profile of Black English*, 238–50. Worthington, OH: Charles A. Jones.

1993. A researcher's reflections on bridging dialect and second language learning: Discussion of problems and solutions. In B. J. Merino, Henry T. Trueba and F. A. Samaniego (eds.), *Language Culture and Learning: Teaching Spanish to Native Speakers of Spanish*, 45–57. London: Falmer Press.

Poulisse, Nanda. 1997. Language production in bilinguals. In de Groot and Kroll (eds.), pp. 201–24.

Pratt-Johnson, Yvonne. 1993. Curriculum for Jamaican Creole-speaking students in New York City. *World Englishes* 12: 257–64.

Preston, Dennis R. 1996. Where the worst English is spoken. In Edgar W. Schneider (ed.), *Focus on the USA*, 297–360. Amsterdam/Philadelphia: Benjamins.

Price, Ronald. 1993. Case studies of the acquisition of standard American English by speakers of Black English Vernacular. PhD dissertation. Ohio State University.

Prince, Ellen F. 1987. Sarah Gorby, Yiddish folksinger: A case study of dialect shift. *International Journal of the Sociology of Language* 67: 83–116.

1988. Accommodation theory and dialect shift: A case study from Yiddish. *Language and Communication* 8: 307–20.

Pulvermüller, Friedemann and John H. Schumann. 1994. Neurological mechanisms of language acquisition. *Language Learning* 44: 681–734.

Ramirez, J. David. 1992. Executive summary of the final report: Longitudinal study of structured English immersion strategy, early-exit and late-exit transitional bilingual education programs for language-minority children. *Bilingual Research Journal* 16: 1–62.

Rampton, Ben. 1995. *Crossing: Language and Ethnicity among Adolescents*. London: Longman.

2001. Language crossing, cross-talk, and cross-disciplinarity in sociolinguistics. In Nikolas Coupland, Srikant Sarangi and Christopher N. Candlin (eds.), *Sociolinguistics and Social Theory*, 261–96. Harlow: Longman.

Ravin, Judy. 2004. *Lose Your Accent in 28 Days: A Complete System, with Audio CD and CD-ROM*. Ann Arbor: Language Success.

Ray, Chelsey. 1996. Report: Papua New Guinea. *Pidgins and Creoles in Education (PACE) Newsletter* 7: 3.

Raynor, Kate. 2007. *The Sounds of Aus: The Story of the Aussie Accent: A Study Guide*. St Kilda West, VIC: Australian Teachers of Media (ATOM).

Reaser, Jeffrey L. and Walt Wolfram. 2007. *Voices of North Carolina: Language and Life from the Atlantic to the Appalachians. Instructor's Manual/Student Workbook*. Raleigh, NC: North Carolina Language and Life Project.

Reed, Carroll E. 1973. Adapting TESL approaches to the teaching of written standard English as a second dialect to speakers of American Black English Vernacular. *TESOL Quarterly* 3: 289–307.

Reynolds, Susan Bauder. 1999. Mutual intelligibility? Comprehension problems between American Standard English and Hawai'i Creole English in Hawai'i's public schools. In John R. Rickford and Suzanne Romaine (eds.), *Creole Genesis,*

Attitudes and Discourse: Studies Celebrating Charlene J. Sato, 303–19. Amsterdam/Philadelphia: Benjamins.

Richardson, Elaine. 2003. *African American Literacies*. London/New York: Routledge.

Richmond, John. 1986. The language of Black children and the language debate in the schools. In D. Sutcliffe and Ansel Wong (eds.), *The Language of Black Experience*, 123–35. Oxford: Blackwell.

Rickford, John R. 1999. *African American Vernacular English: Features, Evolution, Educational Implications*. Oxford: Blackwell.

2002. Linguistics, education, and the Ebonics firestorm. In James E. Alatis, Heidi E. Hamilton and Ah-Hui Tan (eds.), *Linguistics, Language and the Professions (Georgetown University Round Table on Languages and Linguistics, 2000)*, 25–45. Washington, DC: Georgetown University Press.

Rickford, John R. and Angela E. Rickford. 1995. Dialect readers revisited. *Linguistics and Education* 7: 107–28.

Rickford, John R. and Russell J. Rickford. 2000. *Spoken Soul: The Story of Black English*. New York: John Wiley.

Rickford, John R., Julie Sweetland and Angela E. Rickford. 2004. African American English and other vernaculars in education: A topic-coded bibliography. *Journal of English Linguistics* 32: 230–320.

Ringbom, Håkan. 1978. The influence of the mother tongue on the translation of lexical items. *Interlanguage Studies Bulletin* 3: 80–101.

Rist, Ray C. 1970. Student social class and teacher expectations: The self-fulfilling prophecy in ghetto education. *Harvard Educational Review* 40: 411–51.

Roberts, Peter A. 1994. Integrating Creole into Caribbean classrooms. *Journal of Multilingual and Multicultural Development* 15: 47–62.

Roberts, Sarah J. 2004. The role of style and identity in the development of Hawaiian Creole. In Genevieve Escure and Armin Schwegler (eds.), *Creoles, Contact and Language Change: Linguistic and Social Implications*, 333–52. Amsterdam/Philadelphia: Benjamins.

Rogers, Inge. 1981. The influence of Australian English intonation on the speech of two British children. *Working Papers of the Speech and Language Research Centre, Macquarie University* 3: 25–42.

Rogers, Theodore S. 1996. Poisoning pidgins in the park: The study and status of Hawaiian Creole. In James E. Alatis, Carolyn A. Straehle, Maggre Ronkin and Brent Gallenberger (eds.), *Georgetown University Roundtable on Languages and Linguistics, 1996: Linguistics, Language Acquisition and Language Variation: Current Trends and Future Prospects*, 221–35. Washington, DC: Georgetown University Press.

Ronkin, Maggie and Helen E. Karn. 1999. Mock Ebonics: Linguistic racism in parodies of Ebonics on the internet. *Journal of Sociolinguistics* 3: 360–80.

Rosenberg, Peter. 1989. Dialect and education in West Germany. In Cheshire, Edwards, Münstermann and Weltens (eds.), pp. 62–93.

Rosenthal, Robert and Lenore F. Jacobson. 1968. Teacher expectations for the disadvantaged. *Scientific American* 218: 19–23.

Rynkofs, J. Timothy. 1993. Culturally responsive talk between a second grade teacher and Hawaiian children during writing workshop. PhD dissertation. University of New Hampshire.

2008. Culturally responsive talk between a second grade teacher and native Hawaiian children during "writing workshop". *Educational Perspectives* 41: 44–54.

Rys, Kathy. 2007. Dialect as second language: Linguistic and non-linguistic factors in secondary dialect acquisition by children and adolescents. PhD dissertation. Ghent University.

Rys, Kathy and Dries Bonte. 2006. The role of linguistic factors in the process of second dialect acquisition. In Frans Hinskens (ed.), *Langauge Variation – European Perspectives: Selected Papers from the Third International Conference on Language Variation in Europe (ICLaVE3), Amsterdam, June 2005*, 201–15. Amsterdam/Philadelphia: Benjamins.

Saiegh-Haddad, Elinor. 2003. Linguistic distance and initial reading acquisition: The case of Arabic diglossia. *Applied Psycholinguistics* 24: 431–51.

Salahu-Din, Deborah, Hilary Persky and Jessica Miller. 2008. *The Nation's Report Card: Writing 2007 (NCES 2008–468)*. Washington, DC: Institute of Education Sciences, US Department of Education.

Sato, Charlene J. 1989. A nonstandard approach to Standard English. *TESOL Quarterly* 23: 259–82.

Schierloh, Jane McCabe. 1991. Teaching standard English usage: A dialect-based approach. *Adult Learning* 2: 20–2.

Schirmunski, Victor. 1928/1929. Die schwäbischen Mundarten in Transkaukasien und Südukraine. *Teuthonista* 5: 38–60, 157–71.

1930. Sprachgeschichte und Siedlungsmundarten. *Germanistisch Romanistische Monatsschrift* 18: 113–22, 171–88.

Schmidt, Richard. 1990. The role of consciousness in second language learning. *Applied Linguistics* 11: 129–58.

1993. Awareness and second language acquisition. *Annual Review of Applied Linguistics* 13: 206–26.

2001. Attention. In Peter Robinson (ed.), *Cognition and Second Language Instruction*, 3–32. Cambridge: Cambridge University Press.

Schneider, Edgar W. 2007. *Postcolonial Englishes*. Cambridge/New York: Cambridge University Press.

Schnepel, Ellen M. 2005. *In Search of a National Identity: Creole and Politics in Guadeloupe*. Hamburg: Helmut Buske.

Schumann, John H. 1978. The acculturation model for second language acquisition. In R. Gingras (ed.), *Second Language Acquisition and Foreign Language Teaching*, 27–50. Arlington, VA: Center for Applied Linguistics.

1986. Research in the acculturation model for second language acquisition. *Journal of Multilingual and Multicultural Development* 7: 379–92.

SCRGSP (Steering Committee for the Review of Government Service Provision). 2009. *Overcoming Indigenous Disadvantage: Key Indicators 2009*. Canberra: Productivity Commission.

Sebba, Mark. 1993. *London Jamaican*. London: Longman.

Segalowitz, Norman. 2003. Automaticity and second languages. In Doughty and Long (eds.), pp. 382–408.

Selinker, Larry. 1972. Interlanguage. *International Review of Applied Linguistics* 10: 209–31.

Shapiro, Bruce G. 2000. *The Australian Actor's Guide to an American Accent*. Sydney: Currency.

Sharifian, Farzad. 2005. Cultural conceptualisations in English words: A study of Aboriginal children in Perth. *Language and Education* 19: 74–88.

Sharwood Smith, Michael. 1991. Speaking to many minds: On the relevance of different types of language information for the L2 learner. *Second Language Research* 7: 118–32.

1993. Input enhancement in instructed SLA: Theoretical bases. *Studies in Second Language Acquisition* 15: 165–79.

Shnukal, Anna. 1992. The case against a transfer bilingual program of Torres Strait Creole to English in Torres Strait schools. In Siegel (ed.), pp. 1–12.

Shockey, Linda. 1984. All in a flap: Long-term accommodation in phonology. *International Journal of the Sociology of Language* 46: 87–95.

Shuy, Roger W. 1969. Bonnie and Clyde tactics in English teaching. *Florida FL Reporter* 9: 81–3, 160–1.

Shuy, Roger W., Alva L. Davis and Robert F. Hogan (eds.). 1964. *Social Dialects and Language Learning*. Champaign, IL: National Council of Teachers of English.

Sibata, Takesi. 1958. Conditions controlling standardization. In *Nihonño hōgen [The Dialects of Japan]*. Tokyo: Iwanami Shotēn (trans. Motoei Sawaki, 1990).

Siegel, Jeff. 1985. Koines and koineization. *Language in Society* 14: 357–78.

1992a. Teaching initial literacy in a pidgin language: A preliminary evaluation. In Siegel (ed.), pp. 53–65.

(ed.). 1992b. *Pidgins, Creoles and Nonstandard Dialects in Education*. Melbourne: Applied Linguistics Association of Australia (Occasional Paper no. 12).

1993. Pidgins and creoles in education in Australia and the Southwest Pacific. In Francis Byrne and John Holm (eds.), *Atlantic Meets Pacific: A Global View of Pidginization and Creolization*, 299–308. Amsterdam: Benjamins.

1997. Using a pidgin language in formal education: Help or hindrance? *Applied Linguistics* 18: 86–100.

1999a. Stigmatized and standardized varieties in the classroom: Interference or separation? *TESOL Quarterly* 33: 701–28.

1999b. Creoles and minority dialects in education: An overview. *Journal of Multilingual and Multicultural Development* 20: 508–31.

2001. Koine formation and creole genesis. In Norval Smith and Tonjes Veenstra (eds.), *Creolization and Contact*, 175–97. Amsterdam/Philadelphia: Benjamins.

2003. Social context. In Doughty and Long (eds.), pp. 178–223.

2006a. Keeping creoles and dialects out of the classroom: Is it justified? In Nero (ed.), pp. 39–67.

2006b. Language ideologies and the education of speakers of marginalized language varieties: Adopting a critical awareness approach. *Linguistics and Education* 17: 157–74.

2007. Creoles and minority dialects in education: An update. *Language and Education* 21: 66–86.

2008. *The Emergence of Pidgin and Creole Languages*. Oxford/New York: Oxford University Press.

Silverstein, Michael. 1996. Monoglot "Standard" in America: Standardization and metaphors of linguistic hegemony. In D. Brenneis and R. Macaulay (eds.),

The Matrix of Language: Contemporary Linguistic Anthropology, 284–306. Boulder, CO: Westview Press.

Simmons-McDonald, Hazel. 2001. Competence, proficiency and language acquisition in Caribbean contexts. In Christie (ed.), pp. 37–60.

2004. Trends in teaching standard varieties to creole and vernacular speakers. *Annual Review of Applied Linguistics* 24: 187–208.

Simpkins, Gary. 2002. *The Throwaway Kids.* Brookline, MA: Brookline Books.

Simpkins, Gary and Charlesetta Simpkins. 1981. Cross-cultural approach to curriculum development. In Geneva Smitherman (ed.), *Black English and the Education of Black Children and Youth*, 221–40. Detroit: Center for Black Studies, Wayne State University.

Simpkins, Gary, G. Holt and Charlesetta Simpkins. 1977. *Bridge: A Cross-Cultural Reading Program.* Boston: Houghton Mifflin.

Skutnabb-Kangas, Tove. 1988. Multilingualism and the education of minority children. In Tove Skutnabb-Kangas and Jim Cummins (eds.), *Minority Education: From Shame to Struggle*, 9–44. Clevedon: Multilingual Matters.

Sledd, James. 1969. Bi-dialectalism: The linguistics of white supremacy. *English Journal* 58: 1307–29.

1972. Doublespeak: Dialectology in the service of Big Brother. *College English* 33: 439–56.

Smith, Emillie Phillips, Jacqueline Atkins and Christian M. Connell. 2003. Family, school, and community factors and relationships to racial-ethnic attitudes and academic success. *American Journal of Community Psychology* 32: 159–73.

Smith, Winston. 2001. The southern heart [review of Caroline Miller's *Lamb in His Bosom*]. Accessed on 10 February 2009, from www.amazon.com/review/R1FN8806SVSYE3.

Smith, Zadie. 2009. Speaking in tongues. *New York Review of Books* 56: 41–4.

Smitherman, Geneva. 1977. *Talkin and Testifyin: The Language of Black America.* Detroit: Wayne State University Press.

1981. "What go round come round": *King* in perspective. *Harvard Educational Review* 51: 40–56 [republished in Smitherman 2000].

2000. *Talkin that Talk: Language, Culture, and Education in African America.* London/New York: Routledge.

2002. Toward a national public policy on language. In Delpit and Dowdy (eds.), pp. 163–78.

Smitherman, Geneva and John Baugh. 2002. The shot heard from Ann Arbor: Language research and public policy in African America. *Howard Journal of Communications* 13: 5–24.

Snow, Catherine E. 1990. Rationales for native language instruction: Evidence from research. In Amado M. Padilla, Halford H. Fairchild and Concepcion M. Valadez (eds.), *Bilingual Education: Issues and Strategies*, 60–74. Newbury Park: Sage.

Spears, Arthur K. 1982. The Black English semi-auxiliary *come. Language* 58: 850–72.

Speidel, Gisela E. 1987. Conversation and language learning in the classroom. In Keith E. Nelson and Ann van Kleek (eds.), *Children's Language. Volume 6*, 99–135. Hillsdale, NJ: Erlbaum.

Spencer, Margaret Beale, Elizabeth Noll, Jill Stolzfus and Vinay Harpalani. 2001. Identity and school adjustment: Revisiting the "acting white" assumption. *Educational Psychology* 36: 21–30.

Stanford, James N. 2007. Dialect contact and identity: A case study of exogamous Sui clans. PhD dissertation. Michigan State University.

2008a. A sociotonetic analysis of Sui dialect contact. *Language Variation and Change* 20: 1–42.

2008b. Child dialect acquisition: New perspectives on parent/peer influence. *Journal of Sociolinguistics* 12: 567–96.

Starks, Donna and Donn Bayard. 2002. Individual variation in the acquisition of postvocalic /r/: Day care and sibling order as potential variables. *American Speech* 77: 184–94.

Stern, Otto. 1988. Divergence and convergence of dialects and standard from the perspective of the language learner. In Peter Auer and Aldo di Luzio (eds.), *Variation and Convergence: Studies in Social Dialectology*, 134–56. Berlin: Walter de Gruyter.

Stevens, Gillian. 1999. Age at immigration and second language proficiency among foreign-born adults. *Language in Society* 28: 555–78.

Stewart, William A. 1964. Foreign language teaching methods in quasi-foreign language situations. In William A. Stewart (ed.), *Non-Standard Speech and the Teaching of English*, 1–15. Washington, DC: Center for Applied Linguistics.

1969. On the use of Negro dialect in the teaching of reading. In Baratz and Shuy (eds.), pp. 156–219.

Stijnen, Sjef and Ton Vallen. 1989. The Kerkrade Project: Background, main findings and an explanation. In Cheshire, Edwards, Münstermann and Weltens (eds.), pp. 139–53.

Strange, Winifred (ed.). 1995. *Speech Perception and Linguistic Experience: Issues in Cross-Language Research*. Timonium, MD: York Press.

Swain, Merrill. 1998. Focus on form through conscious reflection. In Doughty and Williams (eds.), pp. 64–81.

Sweetland, Julie. 2002. Unexpected but authentic use of an ethnically-marked dialect. *Journal of Sociolinguistics* 6: 514–36.

Tagliamonte, Sali A. 2006. *Analysing Sociolinguistic Variation*. Cambridge: Cambridge University Press.

Tagliamonte, Sali A. and Sonja Molfenter. 2007. How'd you get that accent? Acquiring a second dialect of the same language. *Language in Society* 36: 649–75.

Tamura, Eileen H. 1996. Power, status, and Hawaii Creole English: An example of linguistic intolerance in American history. *Pacific Historical Review* 65: 431–54.

Tauber, Robert T. 1997. *Self-Fulfilling Prophecy: A Practical Guide to Its Use in Education*. Westport, CN: Praeger.

Tayao, Ma. Lourdes G. 2006. A transplant takes root: Philippine English and education. In Nero (ed.), pp. 261–82.

Taylor, Hanni. 1989. *Standard English, Black English, and Bidialectalism: A Controversy*. New York: Peter Lang.

Terry, J. Michael, R. Hendrick, E. Evangelou and R. L. Smith. forthcoming. Dialect switching and African American English: Implications for early educational achievement. *Topics in Language Disorders*.

Thomas, Alan R. (ed.). 1988. *Methods in Dialectology: Proceedings of the Sixth International Conference Held at the University College of North Wales, 3rd–7th August 1987.* Clevedon/Philadelphia: Multilingual Matters.

Thomas, Andrew. 1990. Language planning in Vanuatu. In Richard B. Baldauf and Allan Luke (eds.), *Language Planning and Education in Australia and the South Pacific*, 234–58. Clevedon: Multilingual Matters.

Thomas, Wayne P. and Virginia P. Collier. 2002. *A National Study of School Effectiveness for Language Minority Students' Long-term Academic Achievement.* Santa Cruz: Center for Research on Education, Diversity and Excellence.

Torrey, Jane W. 1972. *The Language of Black Children in the Early Grades.* New London: Connecticut College.

Trudgill, Peter. 1981. Linguistic accommodation: Sociolinguistic observations on a sociopsychological theory. In Carrie S. Masek, Roberta A. Hendrick and Mary F. Miller (eds.), *Papers from the Parasession on Language and Behavior*, 218–37. Chicago: Chicago Linguistic Society.

1983. *On Dialect.* Oxford: Blackwell.

1986. *Dialects in Contact.* Oxford: Blackwell.

2004. *New-Dialect Formation: The Inevitability of Colonial Englishes.* Oxford/ New York: Oxford University Press.

Turner, Christine. 1997. The Injinoo Home Language Program: A positive community response to marginalisation and institutional racism. *Australian Journal of Indigenous Education* 25: 1–9.

Turner, Ralph H. and Steven Gordon. 1981. The boundaries of the self: The relationship of authenticity and self-conception. In Mervin D. Lynch, Ardyth A. Norem-Hebeisen and Kenneth J. Gergen (eds.), *Self-Concept: Advances in Theory and Research*, 39–73. Cambridge, MA: Ballinger.

TV Tropes Wiki. 2008. Ooh me accents slipping. Accessed on 13 November 2008, from tvtropes.org/pmwiki/pmwiki.php/Main/OohMeAccentsSlipping.

Underwood, Gary Neal. 1988. Accent and identity. In Thomas (ed.), pp. 406–27.

UNESCO. 1968. The use of vernacular languages in education: The report of the UNESCO meeting of specialists, 1951. In Joshua A. Fishman (ed.), *Readings in the Sociology of Language*, 688–716. The Hague: Mouton.

Valdés, Guadalupe. 1981. Pedagogical implications of teaching Spanish to Spanish-speakers in the United States. In Guadalupe Valdés, Anthony G. Lozano and Rodolfo García-Moya (eds.), *Teaching Spanish to the Hispanic Bilingual: Issues, Aims, and Methods*, 3–20. New York: Teachers College Press (Columbia University).

1995. The teaching of minority languages as academic subjects: Pedagogical and theoretical challenges. *Modern Language Journal* 79: 299–328.

1997. The teaching of Spanish to bilingual Spanish-speaking students. In M. Cecilia Colombi and Francisco X. Alarcón (eds.), *La Ensenanza del Español a Hispanohablantes: Praxis y Teoría*, 8–44. Boston: Houghton Mifflin.

Valdés, Guadalupe, Sonia V. González, Dania López García and Patricio Márquez. 2008. Heritage languages and ideologies of language: Unexamined challenges. In Brinton, Kagan and Baukus (eds.), pp. 107–30.

Van den Hoogen, Jos and Henk Kuijper. 1989. The development phase of the Kerkrade Project. In Cheshire, Edwards, Münstermannand Weltens (eds.), pp. 219–33.

Van Keulen, Jean E., Gloria Toliver Weddington and Charles E. DeBose. 1998. *Speech, Language, Learning and the African American Child*. Boston: Allyn and Bacon.

Van Sickle, Meta, Olaiya Aina and Mary E. Blake. 2002. A case study of the sociopolitical dilemmas of Gullah-speaking students: Educational policies and practices. *Language, Culture and Curriculum* 15: 75–88.

Vandekerckhove, Reinhild. 1998. Code-switching between dialect and standard language as a graduator of dialect loss and dialect vitality. *Zeitschrift für Dialektologie und Linguistik* 65: 280–92.

Venezky, Richard L. and Robin S. Chapman. 1973. Is learning to read dialect bound? In Laffey and Shuy (eds.), pp. 62–9.

Viereck, Wolfgang (ed.). 1995. *Verhandlungen des Internationalen Dialektolo-genkongresses Bamberg 1990. Band 4*. Stuttgart: Franz Steiner.

Vousten, Rob. 1995. Dialect als tweede taal: Linguïstische en extra-linguïstische aspecten van de verwerving van een Noordlimburgs dialect door Standaardtalige Jongeren. PhD dissertation. University of Nijmegen.

Vousten, Rob and Theo Bongaerts. 1995. Acquiring a dialect as L2: The case of the dialect of Venray in the Dutch province of Limburg. In Viereck (ed.), pp. 299–313.

Weedon, Chris. 1987. *Feminist Practice and Poststructuralist Theory*. Oxford: Blackwell.

Wegera, Klaus-Peter. 1983. Probleme des Dialektsprechers beim Erwerb der deutschen Standardsprache. In Werner Besch, Ulrich Knoop, Wolfgang Putschke and Herbert Ernst Wiegand (eds.), *Ein Handbuch zur deutschen und allgemeinen Dialektforschun*, 1474–92. Berlin/New York: Walter de Gruyter.

Weil, Karen S., James L. Fitch and Virginia I. Wolfe. 2000. Diphthong changes in style shifting from Southern English to Standard American English. *Journal of Communication Disorders* 33: 151–63.

Weinreich, Uriel. 1953. *Languages in Contact: Findings and Problems*. New York: Linguistic Circle.

Wellborn, Jane. 2003. *Accent Reduction Made Easy* (Audio CD). Carlsbad, CA: Penton Overseas.

Wells, John C. 1973. *Jamaican Pronunciation in London*. Oxford: Blackwell.

1982. *Accents of English*. Cambridge: Cambridge University Press.

Western Australia Department of Education. 2002. *Ways of Being, Ways of Talk*. Perth: Department of Education, Western Australia.

Wible, Scott. 2006. Pedagogies of "students' right" era: The Language Curriculum Research Group's project for linguistic diversity. *College Composition and Communication* 57: 442–77.

Wiener, Florence D., L. Elaine Lewnau and Ella Erway. 1983. Measuring language competency in speakers of Black American English. *Journal of Speech and Hearing Disorders* 48: 76–84.

Wiley, Terrence G. 1996. *Literacy and Language Diversity in the United States*. Washington, DC/McHenry, IL: Center for Applied Linguistics/Delta Systems.

Wiley, Terrence G. and Marguerite Lukes. 1996. English-Only and Standard English ideologies in the US. *TESOL Quarterly* 30: 511–35.

Williams, Ann. 1989. Dialect in school written work. In Cheshire, Edwards, Münstermann and Weltens (eds.), pp. 182–99.

Winer, Lise. 1985. Trini talk: Learning an English-Creole as a second language. In Ian F. Hancock (ed.), *Diversity and Development in English-Related Creoles*, 44–67. Ann Arbor: Karoma.

1989. Variation and transfer in English Creole–Standard English language learning. In Miriam R. Eisenstein (ed.), *The Dynamic Interlanguage: Empirical Studies in Second Language Variation*, 155–73. New York: Plenum Press.

1990. Orthographic standardization for Trinidad and Tobago: Linguistic and sociopolitical considerations. *Language Problems and Language Planning* 14: 237–68.

1993. Teaching speakers of Caribbean English Creoles in North American classrooms. In Arthur Wayne Glowka and Donald M. Lance (eds.), *Language Variation in North American English: Research and Teaching*, 191–8. New York: Modern Language Association of America.

2006. Teaching English to Caribbean English Creole-speaking students in the Caribbean and North America. In Nero (ed.), pp. 105–36.

Winford, Donald. 2003. Ideologies of language and socially realistic linguistics. In Sinfree Makoni, Geneva Smitherman, Arnetha Ball and Arthur K. Spears (eds.), *Black Linguistics: Language, Society, and Politics in Africa and the Americas*, 1–39. London: Routledge.

Wiruk, Edward. 1996. Report. *Pidgins and Creoles in Education (PACE) Newsletter* 7: 3.

2000. Report: Papua New Guinea. *Pidgins and Creoles in Education (PACE) Newsletter* 11: 1.

Wode, Henning. 1978. The L1 vs L2 acquisition of English negation. *Working Papers in Bilingualism* 15: 37–57.

1981. *Learning a Second Language: An Integrated View of Language Acquisition.* Tübingen: Gunter Narr.

Wolfram, Walt. 1998a. Language ideology and dialect. *Journal of English Linguistics* 26: 108–21.

1998b. Dialect awareness and the study of language. In Ann Egan-Robertson and David Bloome (eds.), *Students as Researchers of Culture and Language in Their Own Communities*, 167–90. Cresskill, NJ: Hampton Press.

1999. Repercussion for the Oakland Ebonics controversy: The critical role of dialect awareness programs. In Adger, Christian and Taylor (eds.), pp. 61–80.

2009. African American English and the public interest. In Kleifgen and Bond (eds.), pp. 249–69.

Wolfram, Walt and Donna Christian. 1989. *Dialects and Education: Issues and Answers.* Englewood Cliffs, NJ: Prentice Hall Regents.

Wolfram, Walt and Ralph W. Fasold. 1969. Toward reading materials for speakers of Black English: Three linguistically appropriate passages. In Baratz and Shuy (eds.), pp. 138–55.

Wolfram, Walt and Natalie Schilling-Estes. 1998. *American English: Dialects and Variation.* Malden, MA: Blackwell.

Woutersen, Mirjam, Albert Cox, Bert Weltens and Kees de Bot. 1994. Lexical aspects of standard dialect bilingualism. *Applied Psycholinguistics* 15: 447–73.

Wynne, Joan. 2002. "We don't talk right. You ask him". In Delpit and Dowdy (eds.), pp. 203–19.

Yiakoumetti, Androula. 2006. A bidialectal program for the learning of Standard Modern Greek in Cyprus. *Applied Linguistics* 27: 295–317.

Young-Scholten, Martha. 1985. Interference reconsidered: The role of similarity in second language acquisition. *Selecta* 6: 6–12.

Index

Lightning Source UK Ltd.
Milton Keynes UK
UKOW032058170313

207773UK00003B/124/P